DATE

DATE	STUDENT'S NAME	DIVISION
MY 29 '96	RAMONA STOEAN	804
	Xavier Kimble	004

ReF
920
Bro

3148000007714

CONTEMPORARY

Heroes and Heroines

CONTEMPORARY
Heroes and Heroines

RAY B. BROWNE
EDITOR

in association with
Glenn J. Browne
and
Kevin O. Browne

 *Gale Research Inc.*

DETROIT • NEW YORK • FORT LAUDERDALE • LONDON

Published by Gale Research Inc.

Production Manager: Mary Beth Trimper
Assistant Production Manager: Evi Seoud
Art Director: Arthur Chartow
Graphic Designer: Kathleen A. Mouzakis
Keyliner: C.J. Jonik
Production Supervisor: Laura Bryant
Internal Production Associate: Louise Gagné
Internal Production Assistants: Kelly L. Krust and Sharana M. Wier

Permissions Manager: Jeanne A. Gough
Permissions Supervisor (Pictures): Patricia A. Seefelt
Permissions Associate: Margaret A. Chamberlain
Permissions Assistants: Pamela A. Hayes and Lillian Quickly

While every effort has been made to ensure the reliability of the information presented in this publication, Gale Research Inc. does not guarantee the accuracy of the data contained herein. Gale accepts no payment for listing; and inclusion in the publication of any organization, agency, institution, publication, service, or individual does not imply endorsement of the publisher. Errors brought to the attention of the publisher and verified to the satisfaction of the publisher will be corrected in future editions.

The paper used in this publication meets the minimum requirements of American National Standard for Information Sciences—Permanence Paper for Printed Library Materials, ANSI Z39.48-1984. ∞™

Printed in the United States of America

Published simultaneously in the United Kingdom
by Gale Research International Limited
(An affiliated company of Gale Research Inc.)

Contents

Heroes and Heroines Listed by Area of Endeavor

ART AND ARCHITECTURE
O'Keeffe, Georgia
Wright, Frank Lloyd
AVIATION AND SPACE
Armstrong, Neil
Challenger Crew
Earhart, Amelia
Glenn, John
Lindbergh, Charles A.
Ride, Sally
Shepard, Alan
Yeager, Chuck
Yeager, Jeanna and Dick Rutan
BUSINESS
Iacocca, Lee
Jobs, Steven
Russell, Bill
CONSERVATION
Adamson, Joy
Carson, Rachel
Fossey, Dian
Goodall, Jane
EDUCATION
Collins, Marva
Escalante, Jaime
Jordan, Barbara
Wiesel, Elie
ENTERTAINMENT AND PERFORMING ARTS
Cosby, Bill
Disney, Walt
Geldof, Bob
Gregory, Dick
Hope, Bob
Hepburn, Katharine
Jillian, Ann
Neal, Patricia
Perlman, Itzhak
Spielberg, Steven

JOURNALISM
Bourke-White, Margaret
Cronkite, Walter
LAW
Deloria, Vine, Jr.
Kennedy, John F.
Nader, Ralph
O'Connor, Sandra Day
MEDICINE
Cousins, Norman
Koop, C. Everett
Salk, Jonas
Spock, Benjamin
NOBEL PEACE PRIZE RECIPIENTS
Arias Sanchez, Oscar
Bunche, Ralph
Corrigan, Mairead and Betty Williams
Hammerskjold, Day
King, Martin Luther, Jr.
Kissinger, Henry
MacBride, Sean
Mother Teresa
Pauling, Linus
Sadat, Anwar
Sakharov, Andrei
Tutu, Desmond
Walesa, Lech
Wiesel, Elie
POLITICS AND DIPLOMACY
Aquino, Corazon
Arias Sanchez, Oscar
Bradley, Bill
Bunche, Ralph
Chisholm, Shirley
Ford, Betty
Gandhi, Indira
Gandhi, Mohandas K.

Preface

Your guide to more than 100 twentieth century figures and their achievements, *Contemporary Heroes and Heroines* presents biographical portraits of people whose activities reflect a variety of heroic traits. You'll find inspiring profiles of prominent figures in many fields of endeavor, from art to technology, from aviation to social activism, all in one volume. It's the only reference source that brings together in one place lively sketches of contemporary figures collected around the theme of heroism.

Variety of Figures Profiled Helps You Define Contemporary Heroism

The more than 100 heroines and heroes profiled in this volume were chosen after 900 public and school librarians were surveyed for their help in defining heroic traits and figures in the latter half of the twentieth century. The survey yielded a wide range of individuals for inclusion. From pioneering geneticist Francis Crick to Mitch Snyder, spokesperson for the homeless, this collection represents many fields of endeavor. International in scope, *Contemporary Heroes and Heroines* includes essays on Philippine president Corazon Aquino, Soviet dissident Andrei Sakharov, and South African archbishop Desmond Tutu. The survey's results also demonstrate the spectrum of qualities that are considered heroic. Of course, no individual embodies every heroic ideal, but each listee was selected on the basis of a heroic aspect evident in her or his accomplishments.

Like test pilot Chuck Yeager, some listees face an element of risk in contributing to modern life, while others, such as comedian Bob Hope, combine talent and charitable work to garner both prominence and wide admiration. Some listees, like humanitarian Mother Teresa, illustrate an altruistic type of heroism, joining those—Costa Rican president Oscar Arias Sanchez, for example—who make a significant contribution to contemporary society. Conservationist Rachel Carson is among the heroines and heroes profiled in this volume who were selected for the lasting nature of their accomplishments, and like Mohandas K. Gandhi others were chosen for the example they provide of achieving goals without violating another's rights to freedom, life, and dignity.

Graceful determination in the face of overwhelming obstacles characterizes the activities of listees such as teacher Jaime Escalante, cancer-research fund raiser Terry Fox, and baseball great Jackie Robinson, who broke the "color barrier" in the major leagues. While some twentieth-century figures profiled—like Amelia Earhart, Dag Hammarskjold, and Frank Lloyd Wright—

enjoy enduring status, other listees—like Bob Geldof, Lee Iacocca, and Sally Ride—are active entering the 1990s.

Entry Format Sets Your Stage for World-Class Research

- A vivid photograph, a telling quote, and a "vital statistics" box open each entry in *Contemporary Heroes and Heroines*, giving you an immediate sense of the person whose profile you're about to read.

- You'll look forward to reading the appealing essays, which provide an overview of the heroines' and heroes' lives and spotlight their remarkable achievements.

- Source citations at the end of each entry lead you to more information about the heroine or hero you're interested in.

Features Put the Information You Need in the Limelight

- With its unique focus, *Contemporary Heroes and Heroines* brings you essays selected and collected on the basis of heroic criteria, eliminating your search for information scattered in a variety of sources.

- The Introduction, written by the volume's editor, popular culture expert Ray B. Browne, discusses a variety of heroic traits and helps you understand the concept of heroism—how it has changed over time and how it is currently viewed.

- The primary table of contents in *Contemporary Heroes and Heroines* includes a one-line descriptor that lets you match a name with its claim to fame.

- A second table of contents grouping biographees by category is headed Heroes and Heroines Listed by Area of Endeavor; it allows you to scan names in a desired field and learn more about who has made a lasting contribution in a given arena.

- The volume's General Index lists key words, places, events, awards, institutions, and people cited in the essays, giving you the tools to trace a common thread through several profiles.

Put Contemporary Heroes and Heroines on Your Team

- If you're a student researching contemporary heroic figures, no other source will present you with short, readable essays collected according to a heroism theme.

- Working as a researcher in current events, history, or popular culture, you'll turn to *Contemporary Heroes and Heroines* for the biographical material that personalizes the topic you're investigating.

- As an educator, member of the media, or interested general reader, when a "local hero" makes the news, you'll appreciate the backdrop provided by *Contemporary Heroes and Heroines* that puts it all in perspective.

Make Your Contribution—Send Suggestions

Just as we looked for your input before compiling *Contemporary Heroes and Heroines*, the editors welcome your comments and suggestions for future editions, so that we can best meet the needs of the greatest number of users. Send comments or suggestions to:

The Editors
Contemporary Heroes and Heroines
Gale Research Inc.
835 Penobscot Building
Detroit, MI 48226-4094

Or, call toll-free at 1-800-347-GALE.

Introduction

"On God and Godlike men we build our trust."
—Alfred Lord Tennyson

"The heroes whom we see everyday through the TV screen may be the gods of our age."
—Hidetoshi Kato

Heroes and heroines serve as models and leaders of people and nations because they reflect the feelings, dreams, fantasies, and needs of individuals and of society itself. There is in society, writes Ernest Becker in *Denial of Death*, a constant hunger for heroes, a need for the power they give us, because we realize our own limitations and know that we all must die with our aspirations and hopes largely unfulfilled. To Becker, modern life is not full enough "to absorb and quicken man's hunger for self-perpetuation and heroism." So we continue to create heroes and heroines because they can concentrate the power of a people—of a nation—and serve as the driving force for the movement and development of individuals and society.

Heroes Perpetuate Society's Goals

In a simple society such as the Greeks' of three thousand years ago, the heroes' world was straightforward and uncomplicated. It was, in the words of Joseph Campbell, a world of "monomyths": it had single goals, definite and clear purposes. The heroes and heroines of that society spoke for and perpetuated mankind's goals and purposes. In more complicated societies, such as our own, heroes and heroines wear many faces because of their numerous responses to the varied needs of individuals, groups of people, and national purposes.

As a society's needs become more complicated, so too do the heroes and heroines; as people become more sophisticated the heroes and heroines become less modeled on the conventional demi-gods of the past, less clear-cut and obvious. In a swiftly moving society like America today, heroes and heroines undergo rapid transformation. They frequently develop in ways and for purposes that are not immediately apparent. Twentieth-century American heroes and heroines, existing in a highly technological society and driven by the electronics of mass communication, change quickly. They often are hailed as heroic today and forgotten tomorrow. But though they may disappear rapidly, they serve useful and needed purposes while they endure.

Today's Heroes Help Define Our World

Earlier societies did not demand much information about the reality of the heroes and heroines and their heroic actions because they accepted the stature of the hero or heroine on faith; they were less critical and analytical about the real accomplishments of those individuals. Our current civilization has little patience for the misty semi-divine heroes and heroines who were popular in the past. The kind of hero or heroine needed and created today—the down-to-earth, realistic role-model that demonstrates how a person can develop all of his or her potential—serves present-day society well. Yet they are no less genuine heroes and heroines and serve no less important purposes than did their counterparts of old. In fact, in their capacity as role models, modern-day heroes and heroines share the conventional body and soul of their predecessors. They still serve the mythological purpose of helping to explain ourselves to ourselves, of clarifying the meaning of life and eternity, of illustrating some of the purposes of our world. In doing so they help us maintain a personal stability and a social purpose. They assist us in making sense of the world and ourselves. Our sophisticated population likes its heroes and heroines more its own size, more believable. The heroes and heroines of contemporary life serve more as role models, less as spiritual leaders.

Heroic Diversity Reflects Our Culture

Heroes and heroines are also more numerous in kind now than they were in the past. In old societies the hero developed in several predictable roles, as explained by Joseph Campbell in his book *The Hero With a Thousand Faces*. That is, the similar kinds of heroes and heroines developed in similar kinds of societies to fulfill similar functions. In twentieth-century America, a richly diverse society of two hundred and fifty million people, the various heroic faces have grown into the many thousands, and the number is expanding all the time as the needs for heroes and heroines multiply and change. Thus the diversity of the more than one hundred heroes and heroines discussed in this book, and of the thousands of others known locally, regionally, nationally, and globally. They are *our* heroes and heroines, created to serve our world and ourselves. They continue to work with and for us.

Communication Fosters Fame

Since heroes and heroines live in the minds and hearts of people other than themselves, their existence as heroic figures depends on the communication that makes them known. In historical times, the medium that carried their fame was oral tradition. Later it was print—newspapers, books, and magazines. Now, of course, the medium is primarily television, the most widespread and effective creator and popularizer of heroes and heroines ever known. What we see in the television hero and heroine represents the changed tastes and needs of the receiving public, and consequently the changed heroic role. In newscasts, game shows, soap operas—in all the many faces worn by television—we see people who may illustrate the qualities that we think our society needs.

To many observers, the contemporary media create not heroes and heroines but celebrities, and therefore we live in a world in which there are no real heroes. "The hero," as Daniel Boorstin, ex-Librarian of Congress, phrases it, "was a big man, the celebrity is a big name." The celebrity, Boorstin feels, is *a person who is known for his well-knownness*. As such he or she cannot be a true hero or heroine. Yet even these heroes-for-a-day, if that is all they are, serve a purpose, or else they would not be elevated to the status. They incorporate the qualities that we wish we had or that many of us do in fact possess to some degree, qualities that we think society needs.

Take, for example, Lenny Skutnik. Not many of us today remember Skutnik. He was forced into being a hero by circumstances over which he had no control. On an afternoon in early 1982, Skutnik, a minor Federal Government employee, happened to be on a bridge outside Washington, D.C., when an Air Florida jetliner on take-off hit the bridge and crashed into the Potomac River. Skutnik dove into the freezing waters and rescued an injured and drowning crash survivor. His deed was recorded by television cameras and he was, for a couple of days, a national hero. Skutnik was lionized because the public saw themselves in his face and actions. We wanted to think that Skutnik was only one among the thousands of us who would have done the same—and possibly greater—deed under the circumstances. We somehow need to feel that, like Skutnik, we are prepared to risk life and limb in an unselfish willingness to aid, or even to die for, other people.

Heroes Can Embody Our Ideal Selves

We like to see in ourselves the qualities of Dag Hammarskjold, the one-time Secretary-General of the United Nations whose profile appears in this volume; he believed that "no life was more satisfactory than one of selfless service to your community—or humanity." Or, as another heroine whose career is outlined in this volume, Eleanor Roosevelt, demonstrated, "Our own success, to be real, must contribute to the successes of others." The ultimate and final unselfish act is, of course, death in the service of others. And many still feel the noble willingness to give their lives for others. Heroism probably provides no better example of such willingness than that of Martin Luther King, Jr., whose life is also traced in this book; he often said, "Certainly I don't want to die. But if anyone has to die, let it be me."

Many products of television heroism last much longer than Lenny Skutnik's fame. King's influences, for example will never fade. More to the point, thousands of other heroes and heroines in our midst today are in their individual and usually unheralded ways, willingly or unwillingly, achieving heroic status and providing us with models of philosophy, behavior and actions that we want to emulate. The hundred-plus examples in this collection, a handful among thousands that could have been chosen, provide excellent examples of the qualities that make good modern-day world citizens and show us what we can do in order to become as great as our heroes and heroines. In their totality they help profile the wishes and accomplishments of the ideal contemporary citizen.

Our Ideals—Illustrated By Heroes

What is this ideal illustrated by our present-day heroes and heroines? For some, it is the belief in the merit of the individual as opposed to the collective, belief that it is the individual who counts. This is the lesson taught by educator Marva Collins, who feels it is important to tell her students, "You are unique—there is no one else like you." As revealed in this collection, unique individuals, she feels, can become heroes and heroines. For others, the ideal that the hero or heroine illustrates is the realization that an individual can be whatever he or she wants to be, can accomplish whatever goal is desired. Margaret Bourke-White, one of the world's leading photographers, is quoted in her entry for this book: "Life is beating against the school windows. You must quickly open the doors and go out to learn that no door must be locked against you." In the words of Lee Iacocca, whose profile in this volume recounts a compelling success story, "Get all the education you can, but then, by God, *do* something."

Another heroic ideal of contemporary society is well stated by Terry Fox, a long-distance runner and cancer-research fund-raiser also profiled in this volume who said: "Life doesn't mean money. It doesn't mean success. It just means doing things as well as you can without worrying about anything else." Values other than material gain were also important to Charles A. Lindbergh, another hero covered in this volume, who stated, "As our civilization advances...I feel sure we will realize that progress can be measured only by the quality of life—all life, not human life alone. The accumulation of knowledge, the discoveries of science, the products of technology, our ideas, our art, our social structures, all the achievements of mankind have value only to the extent that they preserve and improve the quality of life."

Leisure Pursuits, Democratic Choice Demonstrated In Heroes

Another prominent aspect of contemporary life illustrated in the examples gathered in this collection is the love of leisure and sports. Twenty-one of the individuals elevated to heroic stature in this collection are sports figures, from all kinds of sports. Sports have always yielded a certain number of figures viewed as role models. Some critics have noted that taking sports figures as role models might reduce the public to a position of passive observer, instead of participant. But many of the sports figures profiled here merge ideals of thought and action, and as such are honored for their achievements.

There are, of course, many other forms of leisure and recreation activities available to the public as arenas for the creation of heroes and heroines. Bob Hope, a stand-up comedian well into his eighties, is an example of how a humorist can accomplish humanitarian ends. One of the most widespread contributions to the world of leisure and recreational activities came from Walt Disney, who, through his theme parks, movies, and television programs became synonymous with the imaginative arts. So great has been his influence that it is little wonder that, despite his critics, Disney has become one of the country's outstanding heroes.

An additional aspect of contemporary life found in the era's heroes and heroines is the burgeoning democracy revealed in society's choice of our honorees. Men and women of all races, ethnicities, and nations have a place in today's pantheon.

Heroes Inspire With Faith Or Action

Two final aspects of contemporary culture are revealed in our heroes and heroines. One is the constant presence of religion in our lives. In a world where God—in any of His/Her manifestations—is so much a part of political and popular culture, there is no wonder that some of the spokespeople for religion are viewed as heroes and heroines. This phenomenon is reflected in the present collection of essays.

Lastly, an examination of the pantheon of contemporary society's heroes and heroines reveals that many of these personages have changed the world. Some rose from humble beginnings, providing real-life role models for today, and as such continue to serve as catalysts for further change. These hundred-plus examples of contemporary heroes and heroines demonstrate sharply the influence of these kinds of people in a society like ours. They provide a framework on which ordinary people can develop their goals and reshape their world. They are excellent examples of what boys and girls, men and women, can become and how they can work to accomplish the highest of aspirations. The world will be altered accordingly.

— *Ray B. Browne*

Hank Aaron

"The only thing I ever thought about was to be as good as I could. I never thought about being the greatest baseball player or anything, just to be as good as I could."

Born February 5, 1934, in Mobile, Alabama, Hank Aaron is a former major league baseball player and current baseball executive.

H ank Aaron began playing major league baseball with the Milwaukee Braves in 1954, a time when most ballplayers were white and racial bigotry was still open and accepted. Aaron was one of the early black players in the sport, and throughout his career had to endure verbal abuse and threats from the less enlightened elements of American society. His career began innocently enough; he was a young man of superb talent, like countless other ballplayers. Unlike other players, however, he began to string together many consecutive seasons of excellent play, both in the field and at the plate. He consistently batted over .300 and hit over 30 home runs. Through the 1950s and 1960s, consistency was the hallmark of his play. By the time the early 1970s rolled around, Aaron was still the right fielder for the Braves, and his career home run and runs batted in (RBIs) numbers were creeping toward the all-time records in the sport. The all-time home run record was the much-hallowed 714 by the legendary Babe Ruth. In 1974, Aaron surpassed Ruth's record, the most revered record in baseball and the one followers of the sport had believed would never be broken. Aaron also ended his career holding the career mark for RBIs. "Hammerin' Hank," as he was called, left baseball with some of the most significant achievements in the sport.

Henry (Hank) Aaron was born in Mobile, Alabama, in 1934, to a relatively poor family. His father was a boilermaker's assistant at the Alabama Dry Dock and Shipbuilding Company, and Hank had two brothers and two sisters. The Aarons lived a block from Carver Recreation Park, where the boys played several different sports. Hank attended Central High School in Mobile, excelling in football and basketball. He also played sand-lot baseball. One day Hank's father took him to watch Jackie Robinson and the Brooklyn Dodgers play an exhibition game in Mobile. His father later recalled: "Hank told me he would be up in the major leagues with Robinson before Jackie was through. He was too." Hank's mother once commented on her son's love for the sport: "He didn't have many friends when he was young. He was so interested in baseball, he didn't have time for friends." When Hank was just eighteen, a scout from the Indianapolis Clowns Negro League baseball team signed him to a contract for a handsome salary of $200 per month. Hank made his first trip away from home to attend the Clowns' training camp in Winston-Salem, North Carolina.

While Hank was playing for the Clowns, he was scouted by several major league teams. In 1952, he was signed to a minor league contract by the National League's Milwaukee Braves, and was sent to their minor league team in Eau Claire, Wisconsin. As a shortstop, he batted .336 and was named the league's "Rookie of the Year." The next season he moved to a team in Jacksonville, Florida, and was named the league's

"Most Valuable Player." During Aaron's year with the Jacksonville team, he encountered considerable prejudice from white fans. He was verbally abused at the ballpark, and when the team was travelling he could not stay with the white players at hotels, and so was accommodated by black families in their homes. Although he was hurt by the taunts and threats, he never showed any emotion, and never wavered from his determination to make the major leagues.

In 1954, he finally got his chance in the major leagues with the Braves. Although he had played shortstop in the minors, the Braves wanted him to play outfield. He got his chance to play when right fielder Bobby Thomson broke his ankle during the exhibition season. Although Aaron broke his own ankle late that same season, he still ended up with a .280 batting average, 13 home runs, and 69 RBIs for the year. The following season, Aaron began to achieve stardom when he hit .314 and drove in 106 runs. In 1956, he won the National League batting title with an average of .328.

The 1957 season was a very special one for Aaron and the Braves. Aaron had another outstanding season, leading the league in home runs and RBIs, and the Braves won the National League pennant. In the World Series they faced the mighty New York Yankees, a team filled with the likes of Mickey Mantle, Whitey Ford, Yogi Berra, and Tony Kubek. The Braves defeated the Yankees, however, and brought the city of Milwaukee its only World Series triumph.

The Braves won the pennant again in 1958, but this time were defeated in the World Series by the Yankees. Aaron's road to stardom was already well on its way to being paved, however. In 1959, Aaron again led the National League in batting with a .355 average. The manager of the Braves, Fred Haney, said, "A manager would be crazy to tell [Aaron] anything about hitting." Through the 1960s, Aaron played an excellent right field and was a terror at the plate. He led the league in home runs in 1963, 1966, and 1967, and was the RBI leader in 1960, 1963, and 1966.

Because of his consistently strong statistics, Aaron began to gradually close in on some of baseball's most cherished records. Babe Ruth's home run and RBI records, long thought to be out of reach, suddenly did not seem so unreachable. In 1972, Aaron hit home run number 650; a few more good seasons and Ruth's record could be within his grasp. Suddenly, Aaron became a celebrity; he was a shy man thrust into the spotlight. The Braves had moved from Milwaukee to Atlanta in the mid-1960s, but there had been no more pennants or World Series for the Braves. The focus of fan and media attention was thus almost exclusively on Aaron. In 1973, Hank came close to breaking Ruth's home run record. He ended the 1973 season with 713 lifetime home runs, just one shy of Ruth's record.

The pressure on Aaron toward the end of 1973 had been almost unbearable. Aaron was a private man, but suddenly his entire life was open to public scrutiny. And again the ugly specter of racism reared its head. At many ballparks Aaron was subject to verbal abuse, and he received death threats from lunatic white supremists. Fortunately, he also received many thousands of letters of encouragement and praise from adoring fans. The 1973-74 off-season was not an easy one for Aaron. Despite the media attention and the threats to his life, he was determined to open the 1974 season successfully.

The Atlanta Braves opened the 1974 campaign in Cincinnati's Riverfront Stadium. The Reds' pitcher that day was Jack Billingham. Aaron strode to the plate in the first inning with two men on base and one out. The count ran to 3 balls and 1 strike on Aaron. Billingham fired in a pitch over the plate, and Aaron sent it into the left field seats in front of more than 52,000 cheering fans. He had tied "the Babe," with number 714. He trotted around the bases to a standing ovation from the Cincinnati fans.

Several days later, the Braves returned to Atlanta for their home opener against the Los Angeles Dodgers. The Dodger pitcher that Monday evening in April was Al Downing. In the second inning of the game, Aaron came to the plate for the first time. Downing was careful with Aaron, and walked him. Braves' fans booed Downing lustily. Aaron later scored on a Dodger error, and broke Willie Mays' all-time record for runs scored with 2063. In the fourth inning Aaron came to bat for a second time. Darrell Evans had just reached base on a Dodger error. The first pitch to Aaron was in the dirt for Ball 1. The second pitch was a high fastball that Downing and the national television audience watched sail over the left field fence. Aaron had broken Babe Ruth's record, the record that many baseball fans thought would never be broken. The game was stopped, and Aaron was honored by the Braves, the National League, and representatives from the office of the commissioner of baseball. It was estimated by Western Union that Aaron received 20,000 telegrams after his historic homer.

Even as he broke Ruth's record, Aaron's career was winding down. The 1974 season was his 21st in baseball, and following the season he was traded to the Milwaukee Brewers of the American League. Thus he returned to the place of his baseball roots, and he was happy to do so. At a civic luncheon before the home opener, he told the audience, "I always thought you people were responsible for my career. When I made mistakes on the field, you stuck with me. Young players are blessed to be in a city like this."

Aaron retired in the mid-1970s with career records in many of the most significant baseball statistics. His all-time home run total was 755, a record that no one has approached since. He also holds major league records for RBIs and runs scored, as well as many others. He was elected to the Baseball Hall of Fame in his first year of eligibility, a feat shared by few other players.

Aaron is now an executive in the front office of the Atlanta Braves. He is a regular speaker at civic meetings, and has called for increased hirings of blacks and other minorities in baseball manager and executive positions. Regardless of what he does in the future, Hank Aaron will always be remembered by sports fans as a man who triumphed over poverty and racism to break baseball's greatest records.

Sources

▶ Books

Aaron, Henry, and Furman Bisher, *Aaron*, Crowell, 1974.

Hirshberg, Al, *Henry Aaron: Quiet Superstar*, Putnam, 1969.

Money, Don, and Herb Anastor, *Man Who Made Milwaukee Famous: A Salute to Henry Aaron*, Agape Pub., 1976.

Plimpton, George, *One for the Record: The Inside Story of Hank Aaron's Chase for the Home-Run Record*, Harper, 1974.

▶ Periodicals

Newsweek, "It Comes Naturally," June 15, 1959, p. 94, "Hank Aaron Wastes No Time," April 15, 1974, p. 72.

Saturday Evening Post, "Born to Play Ball," August 25, 1956, p. 30.

Sports Illustrated, "End of the Glorious Ordeal," April 15, 1974, pp. 20-23, "Back Where He Belongs," April 21, 1975, pp. 71-72.

Time, "Henry Aaron's Golden Autumn," September 24, 1973, pp. 73-77.

Ralph D. Abernathy

*"*M*y granddaddy was born a slave and lived a slave till he was 12 years of age, and he said to me, one day the bottom rail is coming to the top. He said, 'The black people will rise to the top and I beg of you to be a part of the movement to bring that about.'"*

Born March 11, 1926, Ralph D. Abernathy is a clergyman and civil rights activist.

I n 1955, Ralph D. Abernathy and Martin Luther King, Jr., organized a bus boycott in Montgomery, Alabama, to protest segregated public transit. After a year, the boycott finally paid off; the U.S. Supreme Court ruled that bus segregation was illegal. The success of the action led the two ministers to found the Southern Christian Leadership Conference in 1957. The organization was meant to promote civil rights for black Americans. King was elected president of the SCLC, while Abernathy served as secretary-treasurer. During the civil rights turbulence of the early 1960s, in which marches, demonstrations, and boycotts were the norm, Abernathy played a prominent role in the movement. "My home has been bombed," he once remarked, "my church has been dynamited, my body has been beaten, I have been jailed 36 times for my participation in demonstrations, I have been harassed." In 1968, with the assassination of King in Memphis, Tenn., Abernathy became president of the SCLC.

Abernathy was born in Linden, Alabama, where his family had been farmers for many years. After a stint in the U.S. Army during the Second World War, Abernathy was ordained a Baptist minister in 1948 and went on to earn a B.S. in mathematics at Alabama College and an M.A. in sociology at Atlanta University. It was in Atlanta while a new pastor at the West Hunter Baptist Church that Abernathy met King, another young minister at a local black church. The two men shared a mutual interest in the budding civil rights movement. By 1955, with a bus segregation dispute in Montgomery capturing headlines, they had organized a successful boycott of the city's buses. In 1958, they founded the Southern Christian Leadership Conference, a group which quickly grew into a national force for civil rights. King and Abernathy were among the most prominent leaders of the national civil rights movement.

By the mid-1960s, the civil rights movement had won most of the government legislation they had set out to create. But conditions for blacks had not improved as they had hoped they would. King decided that poverty must be the next area to be addressed by the government, and so he began to organize what he labeled a Poor People's Campaign in 1968. This campaign was to gather together people of all races for demonstrations on behalf of increased aid for the poor. King's dream of such a campaign was cut down in Memphis on April 4, 1968, when he was killed by an assassin's bullet. Abernathy assumed the leadership of both the SCLC and the Poor People's Campaign.

That summer the Poor People's Campaign held a demonstration in Washington, D.C., and set up a "Resurrection City" in a city park. For over a month the "city," consisting of makeshift shanties and tents, was occupied by Abernathy and several hundred followers as they attempted to pressure Congress to agree to their demands. Eventually, Abernathy and others were arrested after their permits to stay on the land expired and they refused to leave.

Since the Poor People's Campaign, Abernathy has served as pastor at his church, headed the SCLC, and worked on behalf of black political candidates. His own bid for a congressional seat in 1977 was a failure, garnering only 5 percent of the vote. "So many people thought that my being elected to the Congress would have taken me from the civil rights movement," Abernathy explained. "This is where they wanted me to stay, with the movement, because the struggle is not over. . . . My role really is to tell the Pharoah, 'Let my people go.'"

Sources

▶ Books

Ploski, Harry A., editor, *Negro Almanac*, Bellwether, 1971.

Who's Who Among Black Americans, 1988, Educational Communications, 1988.

▶ Periodicals

Biography News, "Struggle More Difficult, Civil Rights Leader Says," October, 1974, p. 1093.

Ebony, "What Happens to Stars After the Cheering Stops?", December, 1982, p. 122.

Jet, "Dr. Ralph Abernathy Feted During Atlanta Celebration," December 2, 1985, p. 10.

Newsweek, April 9, 1979.

Time, "Abernathy Steps Down," July 23, 1973, p. 31.

Joy Adamson

"**W**ildlife is something which man cannot construct.
Once it is gone, it is gone forever. Man can
rebuild a pyramid, but he can't rebuild ecology, or a
giraffe."

Born January 20, 1910, in Troppau, Silesia (now Opava, Czechoslovakia), Joy Adamson was a conservationist, illustrator, and renowned author of *Born Free*—an account of her work in returning
Elsa the lioness to the African wilds. Adamson died January 3,
1980, in Shaba Game Preserve, Kenya.

J oy Adamson was born Joy-Friedericke Victoria Gessner in what is now Czechoslovakia. Her father Victor was an architect and town planner, and her mother Traute the daughter of a wealthy family who owned a paper manufacturing business. Joy's early years were happy ones, playing in the forests with her cousins, and attending the big family parties held on the large estates owned by her maternal grandparents. It was at this time that Joy acquired her enduring love of wildlife, for she would often accompany the Gessners' resident game-keeper on his rounds through the family estate.

When Joy was twelve her parents separated, and although she went to live with her maternal grandmother, with whom she was very close, the shock and unhappiness caused by this experience left her psychologically vulnerable for the rest of her life.

She was educated in Vienna, Austria, where she studied dressmaking, metal work, sculpture, and photography. She also studied piano and was a very promising student, although her husband would later recall that "all through her life, Joy's mind seemed to zig-zag from one subject to another." While Joy Adamson was in Vienna her father died, and she was devastated. Shortly thereafter she was involved in a traffic accident in which a man was killed, and the added stress proved too much for her. She suffered a nervous breakdown which, she admitted later, caused her to contemplate suicide.

Joy Adamson's unhappiness led her into the study of psychology and biology, and while she was still a student she met and married Victor von Klarvill, an Austrian businessman. For a short time they enjoyed an exhilirating life of skiing trips and socializing before the imminent threat of invasion by Nazi Germany prompted them to reconsider their future.

After Joy had a miscarriage, it was agreed that she should take a vacation in Kenya, both to recuperate and to see if she would like to live permanently in that country. While traveling to Mombasa by sea, she met a Swiss botanist named Peter Bally. Their shipboard romance spelled the end of her first marriage, and her first encounter with Africa foretold the end of her life in Europe. She immediately "fell in love" with Kenya and vowed to return.

She and Bally did return the following year. "For ten years," said Joy Adamson of the period following their arrival, "I did nothing but paint flowers." She accompanied Bally on his flower-collecting safaris, and, with his encouragement, discovered she had a great gift for painting the blooms he brought back. Her illustrations would ultimately be included in five books depicting the varied flora of East Africa, among them Arthur Jex-Blake's *Gardening in East Africa* (1939) and his wife's *Some Wild Flowers of Kenya* (1948).

In 1942 Joy met George Adamson, a senior game warden in the Kenyan park service, and they were married a year later. From that time onward, most of her time would be spent accompanying her husband on his extensive rounds in northern Kenya and the Serengeti National Park, painting the plants, animals, and people they encountered. She enjoyed life in the bush, although George Adamson would later observe that she was "haunted by doubts" about living so far from the urban world she had known in her youth. In 1947 the Royal Horticultural Society exhibited some of her seven hundred flower illustrations in London and awarded her the Grenfell Gold Medal for her work, and two years later she was commissioned by the Kenyan government to paint twenty of the country's tribes.

Speaking of her commitment to record the vanishing peoples and wildlife of Kenya, Joy Adamson told the *New York Post* in 1966 that she sometimes felt overwhelmed by the size of the undertaking. "There is so much that needs to be done. . . . There's no end to it. . . . the tribes that are disappearing, the insects, the reptiles. I need another lifetime."

Her awareness of the importance of conservation and a sense of ecological responsibility on the part of humanity came early, at a time when such ideas were unfashionable. It was not until 1960, however, that she would receive the opportunity she needed to spread her message far and wide. In 1956 George Adamson had shot a lioness in self-defense and taken home her three orphaned cubs. Joy responded to their plight with energy and devotion, and though they kept only one cub, which they christened Elsa, they set about rearing her and training her for an unprecedented reintroduction into the wild.

They did so in the belief that, as George Adamson asserted, "the mentality that condones wild animals in life-long captivity is little removed from the mentality that condoned the slave trade." Together, George and Joy taught Elsa how to hunt and kill other animals, and when she was two years old, they released her into the bush.

Despite some difficulties Elsa survived to raise cubs of her own, and Joy Adamson's book about her story and the tender relationship she and the lioness maintained was published as *Born Free*. It was an immediate success and eventually sold over thirteen million copies worldwide. The author followed with *Living Free* and *Forever Free*, which received critical acclaim. Poet Ted Hughes declared *Born Free* to have "genuine educational virtues: clear, firm, vivid prose, sensitive observation, courage and patience, intense sympathy for life." The *New York Herald Tribune* wrote that "her book reads like a letter from Eden to homesick humanity." The story of Elsa was portrayed in a faithful and popular screen adaptation starring Virginia McKenna and Bill Travers, and the remaining two books in the Elsa trilogy were also adapted for movies. Joy Adamson also wrote *Elsa: The True Story of a Lioness* and *Elsa and her Cubs* for younger readers.

Despite initial successes, the Adamsons' wildlife repatriation program encountered some problems. Elsa's cubs had to be removed to an isolated game park after they began killing domestic animals, and the Adamsons' were criticized for their interference in the laws of nature.

In 1967, the Kenyan government published 132 of Joy Adamson's commissioned portraits of the country's tribes in *The Peoples of Kenya*. Between 1964 and 1967, she rehabilitated a young cheetah named Pippa, the story of which was told in *The Spotted Sphinx*. The cheetah's subsequent experiences as a mother were recounted in *Pippa's Challenge*. In the last three years of her life Joy Adamson cared for a leopard named Penny, and *Queen of Shaba*, the story of that experience, was published posthumously. In January of 1980 the conservationist was found dead in the bush, having apparently been mauled by a lion. Subsequent investigations, however, showed that she had been murdered by a disaffected former employee.

Joy devoted the majority of her life to the care and restitution to the wild of Africa's endangered big cats, and the success of her books allowed her to address conservation problems on a wider basis through the Elsa Wild Animal Appeal. Her principal achievement was in raising the public awareness of the need for wildlife conservation at a time when such issues were little known. "People don't realize the terrible depletion of animals in the last few years . . . how it destroys the balance of nature," she once said.

Although separated from George Adamson and plagued by the numerous small disabilities she had suffered during her life in the bush, Joy never lost faith in her life's work. "I am after something important. I not only want to breed animals under natural conditions so that they will survive after they have become endangered by man's influence, but also I want to learn from them where man can play a more constructive part in the balance of nature—and thus survive himself."

Sources

▶ **Books**

Adamson, Joy, *Born Free: A Lioness of Two Worlds*, Pantheon, 1960.

Adamson, Joy, *Living Free*, Harcourt, 1961.

Adamson, Joy, *Forever Free*, Harcourt, 1962.

Adamson, Joy, *The Story of Elsa*, Harcourt, 1966.

Adamson, Joy, *The Peoples of Kenya*, Harcourt, 1967.

Adamson, Joy, *The Spotted Sphinx*, Harcourt, 1969.
Adamson, Joy, *Pippa's Challenge*, Harcourt, 1972.
Adamson, Joy, *Joy Adamson's Africa*, Harcourt, 1972.
Adamson, Joy, *The Searching Spirit: An Autobiography*, Collins & Harvill, 1978.
Adamson, Joy, *Queen of Shaba: The Story of an African Leopard*, Harcourt, 1980.
Adamson, Joy, *Friends From the Forest*, Harcourt, 1981.
▶ **Periodicals**
Atlantic Monthly, November 1961.
Christian Science Monitor, July 15, 1969, p. 15.
Newsweek, "The Lady and the Lion," January 14, 1980, p. 52.
New York Post, May 29, 1966, p. 39, October 11, 1969, p. 29.
People, October 4, 1976.
Saturday Review, "Brave Record of a Vanishing Culture," December 23, 1967, p.28, August 1981.
Time, "The Woman Who Loved Lions," January 14, 1980, p. 49.

Maya Angelou

"Courage is the most important virtue, because without courage you can't have the other virtues."

Born Marguerite Johnson on April 4, 1928, in St. Louis, Missouri, Maya Angelou is an author, poet, playwright, director, actress, and singer.

T hrough her autobiographies, poems, plays, films, and songs, Maya Angelou has recounted her experience as a black American woman in the twentieth century and established herself as a significant literary figure and remarkable Renaissance woman. "The fact that the adult American Negro female emerges as a formidable character is often met with amazement, distaste and even belligerence," she writes in her first autobiography, *I Know Why the Caged Bird Sings.* "It is seldom accepted as an inevitable outcome of the struggle won by survivors and deserves respect if not enthusiastic acceptance."

After her parents divorced when she was three years old, Angelou and her older brother were sent to live with their maternal grandmother, a country grocer in Stamps, Arkansas, who taught the children the importance of religion, work, and courage in the face of bigotry. Her emerging confidence in herself was destroyed, however, when, during a visit to her mother's home in St. Louis, the eight-year-old Angelou was raped by her mother's boyfriend. Added to the rape, she was forced to endure first a trial and then feelings of guilt when the man was murdered by her uncles. In response to these traumatic events, she remained silent for the next five years.

The next twenty years of Angelou's life were characterized by many ups and downs. By the time she was in her early twenties, she had been a Creole cook, San Francisco's first black woman streetcar conductor, a dancer, a madam, and a single parent. Her late twenties and early thirties saw her emerge as a successful singer and actress, performing in a 1954 production of "Porgy and Bess" that toured Canada, Europe, and Israel, and in Off-Broadway productions such as "Calypso Heatwave," Jean Genet's "The Blacks," and "Cabaret for Freedom," which was also produced.

In the early 1960s, Angelou turned to the civil rights movement with its emerging sense of Afro-American identity. She spent one year working for Martin Luther King, Jr., and then went to Africa. There, she worked as a journalist first in Cairo at the English-language weekly *Arab Observer* and then in Accra, Ghana, at the *African Review.* While in Ghana, Angelou also taught dance and music at the University of Ghana. Upon her return to the United States in 1966, Angelou resumed work in theater and wrote ten one-hour programs on African influences to American life for National Educational Television.

Angelou began writing her autobiography after some notable friends, including the author James Baldwin, heard her telling stories of her childhood in Arkansas, Missouri, and California. *I Know Why the Caged Bird Sings,* the chronicle of her life up to age sixteen and ending with the birth of her son, Guy, was published in 1970 and achieved great critical and commercial success. Along with the traumas of her early years, the book recounts the self-awakening of the young Angelou. "Her genius as a writer is her ability to recapture the texture of the way of life in the texture of its idioms, its idiosyncratic vocabulary and especially in its process of image-making," comments a *Southern Humanities Review* contributor. To date, Angelou has published four other volumes of her autobiography.

Since the 1970s, Angelou has brought her experience to the academic arena. She has served as a visiting professor at a number of universities across the United States, including the University of California at Los Angeles, California State University at Sacramento, Kansas State University, and Wichita State University. In 1981, Angelou moved back to the South, accepting a lifetime appointment as a professor at Wake Forest University in North Carolina. Her career has earned her nominations for the National Book Award, the Pulitzer Prize, the Tony Award, and several honorary degrees.

Despite these successes, Angelou believes: "I have nothing to rest upon. Every time I write I still have to face an empty page." For her, writing is still a painful process of "dragging my pencil across old scars to sharpen it." Yet, despite this pain, or perhaps because of it, Maya Angelou is capable of asserting: "I will go anywhere at any time. No one frightens me."

Sources

▶ **Books**

Angelou, Maya, *I Know Why the Caged Bird Sings*, Random House, 1970.

Angelou, Maya, *Gather Together in My Name*, Random House, 1974.

Angelou, Maya, *Singin' and Swingin' and Gettin' Merry Like Christmas*, Random House, 1976.

Angelou, Maya, *The Heart of a Woman*, Random House, 1981.

Angelou, Maya, *All God's Children Need Traveling Shoes*, Random House, 1986.

Thomas, Arthur, *Like It Is*, Dutton, 1981, pp. 1-15.

▶ **Periodicals**

Ms., "No Longer Out of Africa . . . ," August 1986, pp. 36-38.

People, "Maya Angelou," March 8, 1982, pp. 92-99.

Southern Humanities Review, fall, 1973.

Corazon Aquino

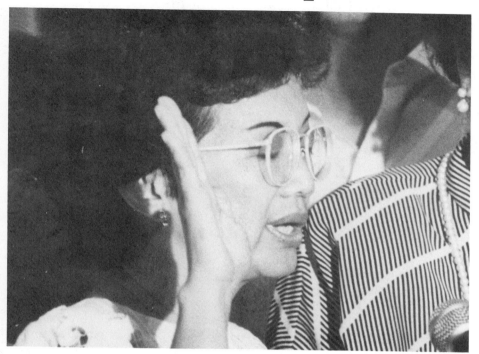

"The Filipino is worth dying for . . . twenty years of corruption, greed, waste and near-despair have finally ended. They were ended by a revolution of peace, prayers, rosaries, radios and, above all, human courage."

Corazon Aquino, who was born January 25, 1933, was elected President of the Phillipines in February of 1986.

W hen Filipino politician Benigno Aquino was gunned down at Manila's airport as he descended the steps of the airplane returning him from exile in the United States, the pent-up reaction against twenty years of dictatorial rule in the Philippines by Ferdinand Marcos erupted in mass demonstrations. Returning to preside over her husband's funeral, Corazon Aquino found herself the symbolic head of the growing anti-Marcos movement. Theretofore a traditional wife and mother, Aquino was catapulted into the middle of Philippine politics. When Marcos called for elections in November, 1985, Corazon Aquino (nicknamed Cory by her supporters) was pressured to run for president in opposition. Originally given little chance of winning, she became a rallying point for the opposition. When Aquino won the election in February, 1986, Marcos tried to deny the victory, but a military insurrection and mass public demonstrations finally forced him to flee the country, and Aquino was declared president. Her "people power" revolution had toppled the entrenched dictatorship. Solving the Philippines' massive political and economic problems, however, has proven to be extremely difficult for Aquino.

Born Maria Corazon Cojuangco on January 25, 1933, in Tarlac Province north of Manila, she was the sixth of eight children. She is of the wealthy lineage of Chinese, Malay, and Spanish mix who have ruled the Philippines for centuries. Her family was the wealthiest in the province, growing sugar cane as well as having banking and commercial interests. The Cojuangcos also had good political connections, with her grandfather, father, and brother all serving in national office. Corazon attended an elite girls' school in Manila and at thirteen was sent to the United States where she attended Catholic schools in Philadelphia and New York. She graduated from Mount St. Vincent College in the Bronx in 1953, majoring in French.

Corazon met Benigno (nickname Ninoy) Aquino on a summer vacation. He was a journalist from a wealthy family in the same province. Initially rebuking him after returning to the Philippines and entering law school, Cory eventually became more receptive and dropped out of school in 1954 to marry him. Ninoy's political career skyrocketed—he became the youngest major, governor, and senator in Philippine history. Corazon was "the classic Oriental wife" for twenty years, serving as hostess and bearing five children. As one observer put it, "He was the warrior. She polished his sword and took care of his horse."

Corazon Aquino's political awareness became aroused in 1972 when Marcos declared martial law in the Philippines to extend his rule beyond the constitutional limit of two terms. The first person jailed was Benigno, Marcos' likely successor, on fabricated charges of murder, subversion, and firearms possession. He was to spend the next seven and one-half years in prison. Corazon acted as Benigno's liason to the outside world. She memorized his messages and speeches and delivered them to the press. She was subjected to routine strip searches and other indignities, and was in constant fear for her husband's life. She "got lessons from the jailhouse in politics," according to *Newsweek* magazine, and learned that those in privileged positions quickly forget those who have fallen from privilege. In 1980 U.S. president Jimmy Carter pressured Marcos to release Benigno to come to the United States for heart surgery, and the Aquinos moved to the Boston area, where Benigno taught at the Massachusetts Institute of Technology and Harvard University.

When Benigno was assassinated on arrival at the Manila airport after deciding to return to help with parliamentary elections, the opposition held Marcos responsible for the murder, and the public erupted in rage. Corazon returned to preside over her husband's funeral, and she led over one million mourners in a ten–hour procession. Vowing to continue her husband's work, Corazon Aquino demonstrated her political skill in leading the opposition to one-third of the parliamentary seats the following year.

With the Communist New People's Army (NPA) insurgency gaining in strength in the southern islands and an economy rapidly deteriorating, Marcos was being pressured to make major reforms. He called for elections in November, 1985, to be held the following February, to show he still had popular support. Pressured to run against him, Aquino responded, "What do I know about being President?" Her mind changed, however, after the Philippine courts overturned the convictions of those responsible for Benigno's murder. Early in the campaign her lack of experience became evident, but as she began abandoning her prepared speeches to speak from her heart, she presented her lack of political experience as a moral alternative to Marcos' corruption.

On voting day, February 7, 1986, the government stole ballot boxes and intimidated voters. Despite this, it was clear Aquino was winning, but Marcos sought to steal the election. Both parties claimed victory. The stalemate was broken when Defense Minister Juan Ponce Enrile and Deputy Chief of Staff Fidel Ramos defected to Aquino and barricaded themselves in the Defense Ministry Building. When advancing government troops were surrounded by thousands of Aquino supporters who gave them flowers, they retreated, and a few days later Marcos fled. "People power" had won for the day. As one commentator put it, Aquino "had proved to her countrymen and to an astonished world that a political neophyte with little besides courage, tenacity and innate good sense could embark on a moral crusade and defeat a dictator who had controlled the country through brutality and bribes for twenty years."

19

Quickly inaugurated, Aquino's political honeymoon was brief. She had to deal with the insurgency, economic problems, and an entrenched Marcos bureaucracy. One of her first moves was to release over 500 political prisoners, and she even freed four Communist leaders as an offer of reconciliation. Aquino refused to use the Marcos' opulent Malacanang Palace, preferring to set up office in a guest house. She promised free enterprise, social justice, land reform, and the dismantling of the cronyism of the Marcos era, in an effort to revive the faltering economy. In July, 1986, an attempted coup was crushed, and Aquino declared, "While moderation will remain the yardstick of our responses, let it be understood that any incident like this will not be allowed to happen again." In September, 1986, Aquino traveled to the United States, impressing Congress and receiving $200 million in aid. That same month she made truce agreements with Moslem separatists on the island of Jolo, and with tribal rebels in the Cordillera mountains.

Aquino has experienced other major problems during her tenure as well. The NPA insurgency has continued to grow, and Aquino has adopted a harder line militarily against the rebels during the last few years. Commenting on the NPA and the nation's economy, she said, "I believe you can't solve the one without the other." She has also been slow to redistribute land, halt corruption, and deal forcefully with growing violence in the cities and countryside, and she has not completely come to terms with a restless military. In August, 1987, a fifth coup attempt—a nearly successful one—occurred. A mutiny of rebel troops left fifty-three dead and 300 wounded amid a battle in Manila's streets. For Aquino this may have been a loss of innocence. She took a tougher stance toward the rebels: "They gunned down innocent civilians who cheered for our government. We shall defeat and punish these traitors."

For Corazon Aquino the long-term problems of the Philippines remain acute. She remains in power but arguably relatively little has changed. Certainly the threat of chaos remains strong. She is idealistic, taking as a model "(Mohandas) Gandhi's work—that gives me so much inspiration, and I really feel that this is what I was cut out to be." Whether or not she can usher in a period as peaceful as Gandhi envisioned, in a country wracked by poverty and violence, remains to be seen.

Sources

▶ **Books**

Komisar, Lucy, *Corazon Aquino: The Story of a Revolution*, Braziller, 1987.

▶ **Periodicals**

Newsweek, "Mutiny in Manila," September 7, 1987, pp. 26-29.

New York Times Magazine, "The Embattled Mrs. Aquino," November 15, 1987, pp. 42-43.

People, "A Matter of Family Honor," March 17, 1986, pp. 34-39.

Time, "An Interview With Corazon Aquino," September 22, 1986, p. 55.

Oscar Arias Sanchez

"That's the test here in Central America—whether we can demonstrate to the world that rationality should prevail over war."

Oscar Arias Sanchez, president of Costa Rica since 1986, author and peace advocate, was born September 13, 1941 in Heredia, Costa Rica.

I n February, 1987 President Oscar Arias Sanchez of Costa Rica met
with the presidents of Guatemala, Honduras, and El Salvador to
put forth his broad peace plan, which called for immediate cease-
fires in the guerilla wars in Nicaragua, El Salvador, and Guatemala, plus
the suspension of all outside military aid to rebel groups, a general
amnesty, and negotiations between conflicting parties. These were to
be followed by free elections and an eventual reduction in military
forces. "If we arrive at an agreement," Arias said, "and Nicaragua does
not fulfill the obligations, then it will put an end to this ambiguity which
has permitted the Sandinistas to receive the support of both democratic
and totalitarian governments." This plan was endorsed a month later
by both the United States Senate and Nicaraguan President Daniel
Ortega and, in August 1987, a similar plan was signed by all five Central
American presidents. For his efforts to end the nine year old Contra war
in Nicaragua and the guerilla wars in El Salvador and Guatemala,
perhaps the most comprehensive and successful effort in recent years,
Oscar Arias Sanchez was awarded the Nobel Peace Prize in 1987.

Arias Sanchez was born near the capital, San Jose. His parents were
Juan Rafael Arias Trejos and the former Lilian Sanchez, and were one of
the country's most prosperous coffee-growing families. They also had
good political connections. Oscar received his early education in Costa
Rica, then came to the United States, originally to study medicine.
When he watched the Kennedy-Nixon debates on television in 1959,
Arias Sanchez decided to make John Kennedy his role model, and even
met him once in Massachusetts. Returning to Costa Rica, Arias Sanchez
studied law and economics in San Jose. During the mid-1960s he was
active in politics with the Partido de Liberacion Nacional party, helping
to organize for the unsuccessful presidential campaign of Daniel Oduber.
He then went to England to study economics and political science at the
London School of Economics, and received his Ph.D from the University of Essex in 1969 for his study of the socioeconomic origins of Costa
Rican political leadership.

Arias Sanchez returned to Costa Rica and took a professorship in
political science at the University of Costa Rica from 1969-72. From
1970-77 he served on the board of directors of the Banco Central de
Costa Rica. He also served from 1972 to 1977 as planning minister for
Costa Rica, and is considered one of the finest such in that country's
history, designing and implementing programs to stimulate economic
growth and technological development, as well as the building of a
cultural park in downtown San Jose. In February, 1978, Arias Sanchez
was elected to the national Assembly, a position he resigned three years
later to help with presidential campaign of Luis Monge.

In 1984 Arias Sanchez decided to seek the presidential nomination. It was a time of severe economic problems in Costa Rica, coupled with the pressure of having the Contras operating out of Costa Rican territory and having to provide for the 250,000 Nicaraguan refugees in the country. He ran on the slogan "roofs, jobs and peace," emphasizing himself as the "peace" candidate. In February, 1986 Arias Sanchez was elected. He said the people had "chosen bread" over guns. In his inaugural address he said: "We will keep Costa Rica out of the armed conflicts and political means to prevent Central American brothers from killing each other." As president Arias Sanchez has worked for more equal income distribution, for raising taxes on middle and upper income groups, for increasing health care, education, and housing. "What Costa Rica needs as much as anything", he said, "is improvement of its education. . . . We have to have technical vocational schools. . . . Perhaps most of all we need a substantial improvement in the quality of teachers."

Arias Sanchez has consistently worked for a negotiated settlement to the conflicts in Central America. Though Costa Rica is relatively stable, has no army, and is by Central American standards prosperous, despite its recent double digit inflation, there has been right-wing pressure from within Sanchez's own country to adopt a militant anti-Sandinista stance. He has resisted this pressure and has strongly opposed U.S. funding of the Contras. "The more you give to the Contras," he said, "the more Ortega gets from the Soviets." He has also been decisive in working against Contra activities inside Costa Rica. "We're going to throw them out no matter who they are if we catch them helping the Contras," he said.

In May 1986 Arias Sanchez met with the other four Central American presidents to discuss the then existing peace plan for the region, the Contadora plan. After that he began working on a plan to resolve key differences that still existed, and presented his own plan in February, 1987. "I told them [the Central American presidents]," he said, "that twenty-four million people in Central America want and deserve peace." He also believes in the region's ability to come to terms with its own problems. "I saw no reason why other nations should tell Central Americans how to solve their problems," he said. Arias Sanchez has also been outspoken in his opposition to the Reagan Administration's policy of supporting the Contras. "As long as Washington is convinced," he says, "that the only way to achieve democracy in Nicaragua is by military aid to the Contras, [it] will remain isolated [throughout] all Latin America." Though Costa Rica receives a large amount of economic aid from the United States, he has not let that sway his views. "I value nothing more than friendship . . . [which] implies loyalty, but loyalty is not synonymous with servitude or unconditionality," he says. At a

24

meeting at the White House with Reagan in which the U.S. President was trying to pressure him into supporting U.S. policy, Arias Sanchez told Reagan: "You think the Contras are part of the solution. I think they are part of the problem." At the same time Arias Sanchez is not a supporter of the Sandinistas. He told Nicaraguan President Daniel Ortega: "What you call democracy isn't democracy here or in any other part of the world."

When the Nobel Peace Prize was awarded to Arias Sanchez in October, 1987 it was seen as a blow to Reagan's Contra policy. The Costa Rican president said, "The prize is a catalyst. It's a stimulus so that we don't lapse in our efforts." Sensing new opportunities for peace in the region, he added: "There's a new mood in Central America now. I hope President Ortega will revise his position and accept dialogue."

Arias Sanchez married Margarita Peñon Góngora, a biochemist, in 1973, and the couple has two children. A highly erudite man, he has written several books and numerous articles. He has sought to find a peaceful solution, through dialogue and understanding, to the region's conflicts. Of his approach he says: "I learned to look at things from a different perspective than that of a superpower." Lasting peace, however, remains elusive. In February, 1989 an agreement between the five Central American presidents made plans for the final Contra removal from foreign territory. One signed August 7, 1989 sets plans to end the war in Nicaragua within 120 days, with the Contras to lay down their arms in exchange for free elections, scheduled for February, 1990. Whether or not this plan works as a final solution to the conflict, Arias Sanchez says he will work, as long as he is able, for a peaceful solution to the problems of Central America.

Sources

▶ **Periodicals**

Commonweal, "What Can Arias Deliver?", May 9, 1986, p. 272-274.

Newsweek "The Nobel Difference," October 26, 1987, pp. 44-46, "Arias: Is Costa Rica Big Enough?", October 26, 1987, p. 46.

People, "Nobel Winner Oscar Arias Makes Costa Rica the Mouse That Roars for Peace in Central America," November 9, 1987, pp. 57-61.

Omni, "Oscar Arias Sanchez," July, 1988, pp. 76-78.

Time, "We Have to be Realistic," June 29, 1987, p. 34, "Golden Opportunity for Don Oscar," October 26, 1987, pp. 44-49.

Wisconsin State Journal, August 8, 1989.

Neil Armstrong

''O ne small step for man, one giant leap for mankind.''

Born August 5, 1930 in Wapakoneta, Ohio, Neil Armstrong was a military pilot, astronaut, and the first man to walk on the moon.

T he late 1960s was an exciting time in space exploration. Rapid advances in technology made scientists optimistic about travel to other celestial bodies. Up to that point, astronauts had not strayed far from the earth's orbit. The United States and the Soviet Union were locked in a struggle for supremacy in space, with both attempting to develop the capabilities to extend space travel out into the solar system. Among the American astronauts ready to lead the way was Neil Armstrong.

The oldest of three children, Neil Armstrong was born in Wapakoneta, Ohio, a small town in northwestern Ohio. As a small child, he became irresistibly attracted to flight following a plane ride he took with his father. When he was fourteen years old, he worked after school at a pharmacy to earn money to fly light airplanes at a nearby air field. He earned his pilot's license on his sixteenth birthday, before he even had an automobile driver's license.

Although Armstrong's family was not poor, they did not have the means to send their children to college. Neil overcame that problem, however, by earning a Navy college scholarship and enrolling at Purdue University in 1947 to study aeronautical engineering for two years. Armstrong then left for a naval flight training base in Florida, after which he went to Korea to fight in the Korean conflict. He flew a total of 78 combat missions, and was awarded the Air Medal three times. He had several near-fatal disasters during the war, including several times when he was forced to fly crippled planes to safety after being hit by enemy gunfire.

After the war, Armstrong returned to Purdue and finished his Bachelor of Science degree. It was there that he met Janet Shearon, whom he married in 1956. He had joined NASA in 1955, and soon thereafter transferred to Edwards Air Force base in southern California. While at Edwards, Armstrong served as a research test pilot with men such as Chuck Yeager, and flew experimental aircraft, including the X-15 and X-1 rocket airplanes.

Following John Glenn's successful circumnavigation of the earth in 1962, Armstrong was chosen to join NASA's team of astronauts. In 1966, he was selected as the Commander Pilot for the Gemini 8 flight into space. He was accompanied by astronaut David Scott, and their mission was to dock their command vehicle to a burned-out rocket stage, the first docking attempted in space. However, while the docking was in progress, one of Gemini 8's rocket thrusters short-circuited, and Armstrong was forced to undock and stabilize the command capsule so the astronauts could return safely to earth. It was the first flight ever to have to return to earth early because of a malfunction.

Another narrow escape for Armstrong occurred in 1968. While training in a lunar module at Ellington Air Force Base near Houston, Texas, the module suddenly went out of control. Armstrong, however, was able to parachute to safety seconds before the module crashed and exploded. His numerous brushes with death did not make him afraid of further travel in space. He once said, "I have been in relatively high-risk businesses all of my adult life. . . . I have confidence in the equipment, the planning, the training."

Early in 1969, Armstrong was chosen to command Apollo 11, which was scheduled to land on the moon in July of that year. His fellow astronauts on the voyage would be Edwin "Buzz" Aldrin and Michael Collins. On July 16, 1969, the astronauts lifted off without incident from Cape Kennedy. After several orbits of the earth, a Saturn rocket booster pushed them toward the moon. Three days later, the command module reached lunar orbit. At this stage, Armstrong and Aldrin climbed into the lunar module, named "Eagle," and prepared to head down to the surface of the moon. Collins would stay behind and pilot the command module in its lunar orbit. As the lunar module set down gently on the moon's surface, Armstrong uttered his first immortal words to mission control in Houston: "The Eagle has landed." Soon thereafter, Armstrong and Aldrin stepped out onto the surface, the first human beings ever to walk on the moon. As Armstrong put his first foot out of the Eagle, he uttered his second immortal line: "That's one small step for man, one giant leap for mankind." Much of the world was able to watch this event live on television, experiencing first-hand through miraculous technology what the two astronauts were seeing. Armstrong and Aldrin collected specimens from the moon's surface, and frolicked about almost playfully at times. A tense exit from the moon followed, in which the lunar module left the surface and rendezvoused with the command module still orbiting the moon. This was accomplished, and the astronauts returned safely to earth to a hero's welcome.

Following his historic trip in Apollo 11, Armstrong returned to graduate school, receiving a master's degree in aerospace engineering from the University of Southern California in 1970. In 1971, he resigned from NASA to become a professor of aeronautical engineering at the University of Cincinnati. He remained at the university until 1981, when he left to become the chairman of Computing Technologies for Aviation, Inc., in Charlottesville, Virginia.

A quiet and private man, Armstrong and his family have successfully avoided the limelight which usually accompanies fame and fortune. However, in 1986, he was appointed to assist in the government investigation into the crash of the *Challenger* spacecraft, in which all the crew members were killed. Although he has largely avoided the public eye, people will not forget Neil Armstrong. His courage and skill allowed him to fulfill a dream of scientists and poets, philosophers and kings: to walk on the moon.

Sources

▶ Books

Collins, Michael, *Carrying the Fire: An Astronaut's Journey*, Farrar, Straus, 1974.

Fifty Who Made the Difference, Villard, 1984, pp. 62-69.

Leipold, L. Edmond, *Heroes of Today—The Astronauts*, Denison, 1973, pp. 53-64.

Mailer, Norman, *Of a Fire on the Moon*, Little, Brown, 1969.

Segel, Thomas D., *Men in Space*, Paladin, 1976, p. 38.

Westman, Paul, *Neil Armstrong, Space Pioneer*, Lerner Publications, 1980.

Wolfe, Tom, *The Right Stuff*, Farrar, Straus, 1979.

▶ Periodicals

Life, "Three Men Bound For the Moon," July 4, 1969, p. 16D-21.

National Geographic, "Man Walks On Another World: Historic Words and Photographs," December, 1969, p. 738-49.

U.S. News and World Report, "Apollo II's Team: The Three Who Will Carry the Flag," July 21, 1969, p. 33.

Daniel and Philip Berrigan

"To stop this war [Vietnam] I would give my life tomorrow, and I can't be blamed if I have little time for those who want to run ads in the New York Times. . . . In a word, I believe in revolution, and I hope to continue a non-violent contribution to it. In my view, we are not going to save this country or mankind without it."—Philip Berrigan

The brothers Daniel and Philip Berrigan, who are Roman Catholic priests and social activists, were born in Minnesota, Daniel on May 9, 1921, in Virginia, Minnesota, and Philip on October 5, 1923, in Two Harbors.

I n 1967, widespread protest against American involvement in Vietnam began in full earnest. In October of that year Philip Berrigan and three others entered the Selective Service office in Baltimore, Maryland, "anointed" draft records with duck blood and waited to be arrested. According to Berrigan, this protest against the pitiful waste of American and Vietnamese blood marked the first time a Roman Catholic clergyman was jailed in the United States for political crimes. The following year, Philip, his brother Daniel, also a Roman Catholic priest, and seven others burned draft records in nearby Catonsville, Maryland. The subsequent trial of the "Catonsville Nine," which was highly publicized, pushed these two brothers into the forefront of the anti-Vietnam War movement. Both became committed to non-violent revolutionary action in an attempt to force the U.S. Government into taking a less militaristic stance around the world.

Daniel and Philip Berrigan were both born in northern Minnesota, Daniel on May 9, 1921, in Virginia, Minnesota, and Philip on October 5, 1923, in Two Harbors, the youngest sons of Thomas and Frida Berrigan. In those days northern Minnesota was still frontier country, and though Thomas had a job with the railroad, the family was poor. In a recent autobiography, *To Dwell in Peace,* Daniel described his mother as compassionate, protective, and stoic, while Philip called his father a "tyrannical" man. Although Philip maintains that his father caused him to rebel against authority, Daniel claims it was an obsession with poverty "which made revolutionaries of us."

After losing his job with the railroad, Thomas Berrigan moved his family to Syracuse, New York, where the children attended Catholic school and worked on the family farm. At eighteen Daniel applied to the Society of Jesus (Jesuits), and began a rigorous thirteen-year course of intellectual and spiritual training. After high school Philip cleaned trains, played semi-professional baseball, and spent one semester in college in Toronto before being drafted in 1943. He participated in some of the fiercest battles of World War II in France. After the war Philip received his B.A. from Holy Cross College and then followed his brother Jerome into the Society of St. Joseph (Josephite Order).

Daniel was ordained in 1952, then spent a year in France, where he became involved in social causes. He taught French and theology in Brooklyn, New York, for three years followed by six years at LeMoyne College in Syracuse, where he also worked on civil rights and radical social work. Philip was ordained in 1955 and was assigned to New Orleans, where he worked with such organizations as the Student Non-Violent Coordinating Committee and the Urban League, took civil rights Freedom Rides, and begged money to give it away to the poor. "From the beginning he stood with the urban poor," Daniel commented on Philip's philosophy. "He rejected the traditional, isolated stance of the Church in black communities. He was also incurably secular." Philip could not understand how the poverty and injustice from which black people suffered could be allowed to continue.

Philip was transferred to Newburgh, New York, where he continued to organize protests on behalf of the poor and to speak out against the war. He saw the growing U.S. involvement in Southeast Asia as a direct counterpart to the problems of racial and economic oppression at home. He asked if it were "possible for us to be vicious, brutal, immoral and violent at home and be fair, judicious, beneficent and idealistic abroad?" Because of this speech, Philip was transferred, this time to inner-city Baltimore. Daniel, meanwhile, spent time abroad, and "returned to the United States in the autumn of 1964 convinced . . . of one simple thing. . . . I began . . . as loudly as I could, to say 'no' to the war." He participated in sit-ins and teach-ins, picketed, and fasted in protest.

When Philip and three others caused a furor by pouring blood on Selective Service records on October 27, 1967, it also marked a turning point for Daniel. While out of jail awaiting trial, Philip convinced his brother to join him in such tactics, and the two brothers and seven others entered, on May 17, 1968, the Catonsville Selective Service office, piled 1-A draft records in trash cans, and burned them in the parking lot. Daniel later offered this justification of the act: "Our apologies, good friends, for the fracture of good order. The burning of paper, instead of children . . . when will you say no to this war? . . . This war stops here." Daniel also wrote a play about the events surrounding the incident, *The Trial of the Catonsville Nine.*

Philip received a six year prison sentence for the Baltimore incident, and a three and one-half year one for Catonsville to be served concurrently. On April 9, 1970, the date they were to begin serving, he and Daniel went into hiding. Philip was captured by the FBI twelve days later and sent to the federal penitentiary in Pennsylvania. Secret correspondence between Philip and Elizabeth McAlister, a nun he had secretly married in 1969, was copied by an FBI informant and led to Daniel's arrest and subsequent indictments. The convictions were later overturned on appeal.

Philip who was excommunicated from the Church when he revealed he was married, has continued social protests. In 1976 he and twenty-one others were arrested for throwing red liquid on military aircraft; the charges were later dropped. In 1980 he and others also attacked nuclear missiles with hammers. Of him biographer Francine Gray has written: "Philip wants them to transform society totally."

Daniel continues his work as a Jesuit priest, in recent years has worked in New York City with a peace group, and has counseled AIDS and cancer victims at a hospice center. In addition, Daniel has authored numerous books of essays, plays, and an autobiography, lectures around the country, and visits such places as El Salvador and Nicaragua. Of the U.S. policy around the world he says: "we have been willing to lose a great deal to win wars but we haven't been willing to lose anything to make peace."

That the Berrigan brothers' tactics are controversial is obvious. They do, however, bring attention to injustices and short-sighted and inhumane policies and follow in a long line of respected practitioners of civil disobedience. Of the Berrigans, a fellow Jesuit priest said "We will be dead, long dead, before history comes up with some kind of impartial verdict on the Berrigans . . . they will be in history as another chapter in that oldest story, the collision of conscience with the state."

Sources

▶ **Books**

Berrigan, Daniel, *To Dwell in Peace*, Harper, 1987.

Casey, William Van Etten and Phillip Nobile, editors, *The Berrigans*, Praeger, 1971.

Curtis, Richard, *The Berrigan Brothers*, Hawthorn Books, 1974.

Gray, Francine du Plessix, *Divine Disobedience: Profiles in Catholic Radicalism*, Knopf, 1969.

▶ **Periodicals**

Time, "New Roles for an Old Cast," April 15, 1985, pp. 52-57.

Dietrich Bonhoeffer

"Thinking and acting for the sake of the coming generation, but being ready to go any day without fear or anxiety—that, in practice, is the spirit in which we are forced to live. It is not easy to be brave and keep that spirit alive, but it is imperative."

Born February 4, 1906, in Breslau, Prussia (now Wroclaw, Poland), Dietrich Bonhoeffer was a Lutheran minister and author whose anti-Nazi activism during World War II resulted in his imprisonment and death.

I n Nazi Germany of the 1930s an official belief in the triumph and ultimate supremacy of one small portion of humanity firmly took root. Even the official Christian church was dedicated to this basic principle. In those early days of Nazi power few people were farsighted or courageous enough to consider the ultimate effects of such a belief, which, according to Adolf Hitler's plan, included the complete annihilation of all those considered "inferior" to the Aryan ideal. But Christian theologian Dietrich Bonhoeffer, a man with a passionate concern for the oneness of humanity, understood fully the destructive power of Nazism and dedicated himself to an active, open opposition to Hitler's reign of hatred. For Bonhoeffer, a belief in Christianity meant nothing unless it resulted in a fervent involvement in the events of this world. He wrote that, like Christ, "the Christian must involve himself in the alleviation of hunger, injustice and all the other worldly miseries." In the end Bonhoeffer's beliefs cost him his life.

Dietrich Bonhoeffer was born in Breslau, Prussia, on February 4, 1906, just minutes before a twin sister, making him the sixth of eight children. The son of an eminent psychiatrist, and the great-grandson of a famous church historian, Bonhoeffer grew up in a bustling, happy household, where singing, books, joking, and games were enjoyed by all, but always with a strong emphasis on what it meant to live a Christian life. His genuine warmheartedness touched all who knew him, and even as a child he was preoccupied with his own relationship with God. His sister Sabine wrote that, when still quite young, he already possessed "the gift of perfect assurance of manners; he listened attentively and attached a great value to dealing politely with other people and keeping a certain distance—not from haughtiness, but from respect of the other's personality on which he did not want to impinge." He was a perfectionist in everything he undertook, excelling in athletics as well as academics.

An extremely talented student, Bonhoeffer received his doctorate in theology from Berlin University in 1927 at the age of twenty-one. In his dissertation, *Act and Being*, he demonstrates his lifelong concern with the Christian church as a union of people who must act together to face the concrete realities of life. After completing his doctorate, Bonhoeffer spent a year in Spain as pastor for a German-speaking congregation and a year in New York pursuing further studies at Union Theological Seminary. There an American friend, Paul Lehman, was impressed by his "contagious humanity." In 1931 Bonhoeffer returned to Berlin as a lecturer in theology at the University.

When the Nazis rose to power in 1933, Bonhoeffer helped to organize the Pastor's Emergency League, which eventually grew into the Confessing Church of Germany, an organization opposed to the Nazi-sponsored "German Christian" church movement. In the same year, utterly opposed to Hitler's regime, Bonhoeffer left Germany in protest. While working as a pastor for two German congregations in London, he sought to forge links between the churches of Germany and the rest of the world in opposition to German power. In 1935 he returned to his homeland to train ministers for the Confessing Church. Though the seminary in Finkenwalde was harassed by the Gestapo, and officially suppressed in 1937, Bonhoeffer persisted in teaching there. In retaliation the government stripped him of his right to teach at a university, the right to speak in public, and the right to publish. While at the seminary he formed strong bonds with his students, regarding life at the school as a study in Christian community. Also while there, he completed some of his most important writing, including *The Cost of Discipleship,* a work discussing the obedience owed by every Christian to Christ, and *Life Together,* a study of life in a Christian community.

With war appearing all but inevitable, friends of Dietrich Bonhoeffer arranged a lecture tour for him in the United States in hopes he would remain there safely for a time. He arrive in June, 1939, but decided to return to Germany only six weeks later. If indeed there was to be a war, then he chose to return and be one with his people. He wrote in his diary while still in the United States: "I do not understand why I am here. . . . The short prayer in which we thought of our German brothers almost overwhelmed me. . . . If war comes, I shall not stay in America." During the voyage home he wrote, "Since I came on board ship, my mental turmoil about the future has gone."

As events in Germany worsened, Bonhoeffer was forced to rethink his personal belief in total pacifism. As he later explained to a fellow prisoner, "If a drunken driver is at the wheel, it is not just the minister's job to comfort the relations of those he has killed, but if possible to seize the steering wheel." By 1940 he had fully committed himself to subversive activities aimed at the overthrow of the Nazi regime, including, if possible, the assassination of Hitler. As a courier for the Counter-Espionage Service he made use of his contacts with church officials around the world in support of the German resistance movement. In 1942 he risked his life to help seven Jews escape to Switzerland.

In what should have been a promise of happier times, Bonhoeffer was engaged to his longtime friend Maria von Wedemeyer in January of 1943. But only three months later, on April 5, he was arrested and taken to Tegel Prison for his part in an unsuccessful attempt on Hitler's life. Bonhoeffer's biographer, Eberhard Bethge, describes the scene: "We made the room as ready as we could for the expected visit—documents were placed in safety, and others, which might provide misleading and unimportant information, were left on the table. Things took their expected course and Bonhoeffer was arrested."

Throughout his imprisonment, Bonhoeffer's warm personality and concern for others made him well liked and respected by his wardens, and he was allowed to write a great deal, corresponding with friends and relatives, writing sermons and essays. The result, *Prisoner for God: Letters and Papers From Prison*, is among Bonhoeffer's most accessible works. In one moving piece, "After Ten Years," he discusses the plight of Germans suffering under Nazi oppression. "Are we still of any use? What we shall need is not geniuses, or cynics, or misanthropes, or clever tacticians, but plain, honest, straightforward men. Will our inward power of resistance be strong enough, and our honesty with ourselves remorseless enough, for us to find our way back to simplicity and straightforwardness?"

Virtually all of Bonhoeffer's fellow prisoners testified to his dignity and compassion for others, as did his jailers. He served as pastor for the other inmates and did much to lift their spirits under all-but-impossible circumstances. Payne Best, an English officer imprisoned with Bonhoeffer, wrote of him: "Bonhoeffer . . . was all humility and sweetness; he always seemed to diffuse an atmosphere of happiness, of joy in every smallest event in life, and a deep gratitude for the mere fact that he was alive." On Sunday, April 8, 1945, in the second year of his imprisonment, Pastor Bonhoeffer celebrated a service with his fellow prisoners. The next day, he was hanged at Flossenberg by officers of the Third Reich.

While still suffering in prison Bonhoeffer had written in a letter: "To renounce a full life and all its joys in order to escape pain is neither Christian nor human." Life, for him, was a gift to be happily accepted, shared, and used to help others. And when it was over, he wrote, "Death is the last great festival on the road to freedom."

Sources

▶ **Books**

Bethge, Eberhard, *Dietrich Bonhoeffer*, Harper, 1977.

Bethge, Eberhard, and others, *Dietrich Bonhoeffer: A Life in Pictures*, Fortress, 1987.

Bonhoeffer, Dietrich, *Prisoner for God: Letters and Papers from Prison*, Macmillan, 1953.

Zimmerman, Wolf Dieter and Ronald Gregor Smith, editors, *I Knew Dietrich Bonhoeffer*, Harper, 1966.

Margaret Bourke-White

"Life is beating against the school windows. You must quickly open the doors and go out to learn that no door must be locked against you."

Born June 14, 1904, in New York, New York, Margaret Bourke-White died in 1971. She was a prize-winning photographer and journalist.

Bourke-White was born to fight against the everyday and hum-drum in life. Her parents encouraged her independence. In life, they taught, "The only real handicap is fear. Be unafraid. . . . Go right up and look your fears in the face—and then *do* something." Her mother told her: "Margaret, you can always be proud that you were invited into the world." Bourke-White always acted like an honored guest: self-confident, perhaps arrogant, and surely indifferent to opinion and criticism.

In her autobiography, *Portrait of Myself,* she voiced her credo about art and photography this way: "I believe any important art coming of this industrial age will draw inspiration from industry because industry [is] alive, vital. Art must have flesh and blood. Industrial subjects [are] close to heart of life today. Photography [is] suitable [to] portray industry because [it is] an honest kind of medium. Beauty of industry lies in its truth and simplicity."

Growing up in New Jersey, Bourke-White at first wanted to become a scientist. She was taught by her father the ethic of work and was introduced to the magic and power of machines. Thus she came naturally to her love of industrial photography and all its potential and power. She was trained in photography at the University of Michigan by Clarence T. White, one of the nation's most influential teachers of photography, and at Cornell University. In 1927, Bourke-White left Cornell and went to Cleveland, Ohio, where she was determined to be a "good photographer," she said, and to tell the truth about Cleveland. She saw Cleveland mainly near Terminal Tower, photographing that landmark so much and so well that it launched her career as an excellent photographer.

With access to the right people, Bourke-White's career soon began a meteoric rise. In 1929 she was invited by Henry Luce to come to New York City to work on the forthcoming magazine *Fortune,* and it was later said that her photographs made *Fortune* successful. By 1930, aged twenty-six, Bourke-White was making $50,000 a year, but she was unable to control the money which fame brought her.

In 1931, the Soviet government invited Bourke-White to come to Russia. Armed with many cameras and a great supply of film, she began the first of three trips to the Soviet Union during which she photo-graphed everything. In 1934, Hollywood brought out two of her trave-logues—*Eyes on Russia* and *Red Republic*—and, later in the year, *Our Daily Bread.* But Bourke-White was not satisfied with these works and she never did any more movies.

By the mid-Thirties, Bourke-White's politics leaned to the left. Perhaps she had seen what she thought was freedom and opportunity in the

USSR. In the early 1950s, Bourke-White fell victim to McCarthy and McCarthyism because of this interest in the Soviet Union. Actually, she was politically naive and indifferent. In the 1950s, she wrote: "I am not politically minded. Toward the late Thirties I decided not to allow my name to be used on any letterheads or committees because I felt that being in an absolutely important position was very important to my work as a photographer."

At work, Bourke-White dealt well with her male co-workers. While in Cleveland, she had said, "I can do anything I want to with these men, and through it all I like them." But she was not successful in marriage. When she was just one day short of being twenty years of age, Bourke-White had married another photographer named Everett Chapman in an act of defiance. In 1939, she married Erskine Caldwell, with whom she had worked and produced the social document, *You Have Seen Their Faces*, in 1937. In 1941, again loaded down with photography equipment and supplies, Bourke-White returned to the Soviet Union; and, by the next year, she and Caldwell had begun to drift apart.

It was in 1936 that Bourke-White began her long and famous association with *Life* magazine, entering her position two months before publication of the first issue. With this fame came Bourke-White's opportunity to photograph people like Franklin Roosevelt, Eleanor Roosevelt, Winston Churchill, Haile Selassie, and the humble Gandhi. During World War II, she went to Algeria, flew on a bombing mission, and photographed the allied advance into Germany. About the war she said: "There is no use fighting a war unless we leave behind a better world, and to do that we must get the youth of Europe on our side." After World War II, Bourke-White became a role model. She was given honorary degrees by universities, and Canada named a lake after her. In 1947, *Real Fact Comics* devoted an issue to her life. She had always shown unbounded energy and drive in her obsession with her work and the freedom to do it. "It is my whole life," she said, "this freedom to take trips. . . . It's a way of life I've invented for myself."

By 1951, Bourke-White had shown symptoms of Parkinson's disease. Her strong and reliable body was becoming undependable, but she refused to give in to the disease. In 1955, she forced Luce, who was owner and editor of *Life* Magazine, to give her an assignment on the first rocket trip to the moon. Luce said of Bourke-White: "Maggie won't take no for an answer." In her notes she rhetorically asked: "What is life for but not to give up and die? You're part of a great pool complex from which you can draw and to which you can also give." In *Portrait of Myself*, she wrote: "Nothing attracts me like a closed door. I cannot let my camera rest till I have pried it open, and I wanted to be first." And elsewhere she also noted: "You are responsible for what you have done and the people whom you have influenced. IN THE END IT IS ONLY THE WORK THAT COUNTS."

For Bourke-White, work meant a great deal. She had taken photos of thirty-four countries and the Arctic, had served as war correspondent for *Life* from 1942-45, and had worked as a United Nations correspondent in Korea in 1952. For her work Bourke-White was awarded First Prize by the Cleveland Museum of Art in 1928, the American Woman of Achievement Award in 1951, and received numerous other recognitions. Throughout her life, Bourke-White was a pioneer in the field of photography and led the way for women to enter the professional world. She wrote a dozen books, and, in 1936, was named one of America's top ten living American women. As a result of her personality and the quality of her work, Bourke-White has achieved a level of respect that will stand unsurpassed for years to come.

Sources

▶ Books

Bourke-White, Margaret, *Eyes on Russia,* Simon & Schuster, 1931.

Bourke-White, Margaret, *U.S.S.R., A Portfolio of Photographs,* Argus, 1934.

Bourke-White, Margaret, and Erskine Caldwell, *You Have Seen Their Faces,* Viking, 1937.

Bourke-White, Margaret, and Erskine Caldwell, *North of the Danube,* Viking, 1939.

Bourke-White, Margaret, and Erskine Caldwell, *Say, Is This the U.S.A.?,* Duell, Sloan, Pearce, 1941.

Bourke-White, Margaret, *Shooting the Russian War,* Simon & Schuster, 1942.

Bourke-White, Margaret, *They Called It "Purple Heart Valley,"* Simon & Schuster, 1944.

Bourke-White, Margaret, *Dear Fatherland, Rest Quietly,* Simon & Schuster, 1946.

Bourke-White, Margaret, *Halfway to Freedom: A Study of the New India,* Simon & Schuster, 1949.

Bourke-White, Margaret, and John Lefarge, *A Report of the American Jesuits,* Farrar, Straus, 1956.

Bourke-White, Margaret, *Portrait of Myself,* Simon & Schuster, 1963.

Goldberg, Vicki, *Margaret Bourke-White,* Harper & Row, 1986.

▶ Periodicals

Atlantic, "Green Days and Photojournalism, and the Old Man in the Room," August, 1972, pp. 62-6.

Life, "Gallery: Photographs," January 29, 1971, pp. 6-9, "Scenes from Our First Issue: Photographs, "November 24, 1972, pp. 34-5.

Popular Photography, "She Held a Mirror to the World," January, 1972, pp. 104-7.

Readers Digest, "Unforgettable Margaret Bourke-White," August, 1972, pp. 69-74.

Bill Bradley

"[A]n athlete] approaches the end of his playing days the way old people approach death. He puts his finances in order. He reminisces easily. He offers advice to the young. But an athlete differs from the old person in that he must continue living."

Born July 28, 1943, in Crystal City Missouri, Bradley is a U.S. Senator from New Jersey and a former professional basketball player.

A s a child Bill Bradley had only one goal: to become a profession-al basketball player. After leading the Princeton University basketball team to the national tournament semifinals one season, Bradley studied as a Rhodes Scholar at Oxford University before joining the National Basketball Association's New York Knicker-bockers in 1967. Despite his love for the game, Bradley soon showed political aspirations. On road trips, rather than lounging in hotel rooms with his teammates, Bradley would talk to the average people in the cities he visited, asking them about their concerns and eliciting their opinions on the major problems facing the nation. He also contacted local politicians to learn about campaign strategies. After helping the Knicks win two world championships during his ten-year career, Bradley retired from basketball in 1977 and ran for the U.S. Senate the following year. Despite his lack of political experience, he was elected, and reelected in 1984. A very popular senator, Bradley has been mentioned as a possible Democratic presidential candidate for the 1992 election.

William Warren Bradley was born in a small town on the Mississippi River about thirty miles south of St. Louis. He was the only child of Warren, a banker, and Susan, a junior high school teacher, both of whom instilled in their son the values of hard work, discipline, and self-determination. "Programmed to become a gentleman," he later admit-ted, Bradley actively pursued his interests, taking extracurricular les-sons in French horn, dance, typing, and boxing, while maintaining a straight-A average in school. But Bradley's first love was basketball. He began playing the sport at the age of nine and soon refused to winter with his parents in Florida so that he could stay in Missouri and practice. "By the time I was 14, I was self-motivated," he remarked. "Whatever raced inside me was more demanding than any pressures from parents or teachers."

Bradley entered Crystal City High School in 1959 and immediately became the star of its basketball team. By the time he graduated he was twice named All-American; he was also elected president of the Missouri Association of Student Councils. After graduation, although he was offered athletic scholarships to more than seventy-five schools, Bradley enrolled at Princeton, because, he later said, it offered a good mix of academics and basketball.

The Ivy League had not been noted for its athletic teams for some years, but with the help of Bradley, Princeton was finally able to hold its own against larger and more powerful teams. In 1965, he led the Tigers to the semifinals of the National Collegiate Athletic Association (NCAA) tournament, where they were defeated by the University of Michigan. As in high school, Bradley was twice named to the All-America team. In addition, he was a starter on the U.S. Olympic basketball team that won the gold medal in Tokyo in 1964.

Deeply interested in politics, one of the primary reasons Bradley enrolled at Princeton was to attend its Woodrow Wilson School of Public and International Affairs. During college Bradley worked for politicians and he graduated in 1965 with honors in American history. Offered a Rhodes Scholarship, Bradley attended Oxford University, where he studied European literature and history and was especially intrigued by Joseph Conrad and Albert Camus. These authors, as well as Leo Tolstoy and Fedor Dostoevsky, "became personal agents for me," Bradley later said. "Through them I started defining my own values and their directions."

After returning from England in 1967, Bradley joined the New York Knicks. The Knicks had been a strong team in the NBA for some years in the 1950s, but had not done well during the 1960s and had never won a world championship. When Bradley entered the league he was one of the most highly publicized and highly paid rookies in sports history. Unfortunately, his first season was disappointment, as he did not live up to the lofty expectations of the press and the fans. Pretty much a "one man team" in college, Bradley now had to become a team player, one who melded with the other professionals, most of whom were more talented physically than he was.

By the late 1960s, however, the Knicks began to develop into an outstanding team. Bradley had adjusted to his role on the Knicks as the starting shooting forward, and the team had acquired forward Dave DeBusschere from the Detroit Pistons. With Willis Reed at center, Bradley and DeBusschere at forward, Walt Frazier and Dick Barnett at guard, and talented reserves such as Jerry Lucas and Phil Jackson, the Knicks appeared ready to challenge for the league championship. During the 1969-70 season, the team ended the regular season in first place in the Eastern Division. They won their playoff series and advanced to the NBA championship series against the powerful Los Angeles Lakers, who were led by Elgin Baylor, Wilt Chamberlain, and Jerry West. Despite the might of their opponents, the Knicks won the series and their first world championship.

The Knicks continued to play well in the early 1970s. In 1971 they ended the season in first place in the Atlantic Division, but lost in the playoffs. They soon acquired flashy guard Earl "The Pearl" Monroe from the Baltimore Bullets, and appeared ready to again challenge. In 1973, although the Boston Celtics won the Atlantic Division, the Knicks made the playoffs. They advanced to the championship series, again facing the Los Angeles Lakers. In a dramatic series, the Knicks again defeated the defending champion Lakers. Commenting later on his basketball career, Bradley remarked that "certainly winning is important. If you didn't win, you wouldn't have proved anything by the way you played." Yet he also discussed the importance of losing, stating, "Part of personal growth is being able to deal with [losing]. Losing has a flavor, a taste all its own. And in some sense it is as much responsible for the personal growth component in sport as winning."

The Knicks began to fade as championship contenders in the mid-1970s, and Bradley retired from basketball in 1977. He had prepared himself for his retirement by reading and discussing politics as much as possible during his basketball career. In the off-seasons, he and his wife Ernestine worked to promote prison reform and environmental protection, and Bradley worked for the Office of Economic Opportunity in Washington, D.C. After he retired, he immediately considered running for office.

Friends urged Bradley to run for a county or a small state office, but Bradley had loftier ambitions. He decided to run for the U.S. Senate in the 1978 election for the seat of New Jersey Republican incumbent Clifford Case. Case was a four-term Senator who was defeated in the Republican primary election by Jeffrey Bell. Despite not receiving the support of the New Jersey Democratic Party and Governor Brendan Byrne, Bradley still won the Democratic primary with 61 percent of the vote. In the months prior to the election, Bell campaigned on what seemed to be his lone concern, cutting taxes, while Bradley campaigned on a liberal ticket. Although he did favor reducing taxes and maintaining a strong defense, Bradley campaigned for free choice in abortion matters, for the Equal Rights Amendment, against capital punishment, and for increased investment in solar power. When the returns were in, Bradley had won election to the Senate with 56 percent of the vote. At age thirty-five he came the youngest member of the Senate.

In the Senate, Bradley gradually became well respected among his colleagues as a leading advocate of environmental protection and tax reform. He advocated lowering tax rates for most people by eliminating tax breaks for the wealthy and privileged, and a version of the bill proposed by Bradley was eventually implemented in Congress. Bradley was elected to a second term in the Senate in 1984, was prominent at the Democratic National Convention in 1988, and has been mentioned as a possible Democratic candidate for president in 1992.

Bradley lives with his wife and daughter in Washington, D.C., and in Denville, New Jersey. Throughout his life, he has been persistent in achieving his goals. A colleague said recently, "Bill has always had a sense of where he wants to go, and he is very patient about getting there." That patience has paid off for Bradley in two outstanding careers. He left his mark in professional basketball and he was elected to the basketball Hall of Fame in 1983. As a U.S. Senator, he has become a nationally-respected politician. If there were a Hall of Fame for politicians, Bradley would probably end up there as well.

Sources

▶ **Books**

Bradley, Bill, *Life on the Run*, Quadrangle, 1976.

Halter, Jon C., *Bill Bradley: One to Remember*, Putnam, 1975.

McPhee, John, *A Sense of Where You Are: A Profile of William Warren Bradley*, Farrar, Straus, 1978.

▶ **Periodicals**

Life, "He's a Stubborn Idealist with a Romantic Streak," January 19, 1968, pp. 57-68, "Interview: Bill Bradley," December, 1987, pp. 17-20.

New Republic, "Run, Bill, Run," August 11, 1986, pp. 7-9.

Newsweek, "Dollar Bill," May 10, 1976, pp. 115-117.

Sports Illustrated, "Answer to the Bradley Riddle," March 16, 1968, pp. 38-41.

Time, "New Faces in the Senate," November 20, 1978, p. 30, "A Sense of Where He Is," June 20, 1986, pp. 37-38.

Ralph Bunche

"Let me say a word or two against brotherhood. A lot of people I know I wouldn't want for cousins, let alone brothers. In human relations the concept of tolerance and mutual respect is far more important."

Born August 7, 1904, in Detroit, Michigan, Ralph Bunche was a U.N. official and negotiator who received the Nobel Peace Prize. He died on December 9, 1971, in New York, New York.

I n the Middle East, shortly after World War II, age-old hostilities between Palestinian Jews and Arabs broke out in frightening force. A specially appointed United Nations commission recommended a partitioning of the territory into separate Arab and Jewish states. But Arab factions, unwilling to give up power and land to what they felt were a relatively small number of Jews, refused to agree; thus, late in 1947, the area erupted into civil war. On May 14 of the following year, however, the new Jewish state of Israel was proclaimed, heightening the conflict, and the brutal war dragged on as neighboring Arab states joined in the fight against Israel's Zionist forces. It seemed a hopeless situation, but behind the scenes U.N. negotiators were at work, trying to forge a solution. Chief among these negotiators was Count Folke Bernadotte of Sweden, but when he was assassinated in September of 1948, American mediator Ralph Bunche was directed to take charge. Demonstrating consummate diplomacy and tireless optimism, Bunche was able to work out an armistice agreement between the warring factions. This peace, albeit temporary, was considered an extraordinary achievement; in recognition of his efforts, Bunche was awarded the 1950 Nobel Peace Prize, making him the first black ever to receive that honor.

One of two children, Ralph Bunche was born in Detroit on August 7, 1904, to Olive Agnes Johnson, a musician, and Fred Bunche, a barber. When he was ten, his family moved to New Mexico in order to provide a more comfortable climate for his mother, who was ill. Three years later, however, both of Bunche's parents died within a three-month span, leaving him an orphan. Lucy Johnson, the boy's maternal grandmother, took both children to live with her in Los Angeles. During his youth in California, Bunche was influenced by his strong-willed grandmother, who was determined that her obviously brilliant grandson should succeed in the world. Later he would remember her as "the strongest woman I ever knew, even though she stood less than five feet high." Bunche attended Jefferson High School in Los Angeles, graduating as the class valedictorian in 1922.

Demonstrating an early interest in global conflicts and resolutions, Bunche studied international relations at the University of California at Los Angeles. While attending school, Bunche financed his education by working a variety of jobs, including positions as a janitor, a part-time carpet layer, and a petty-officer's messman. He received numerous scholarships for both academics and sports, starred on baseball, football, and basketball teams, and participated in oratorical and debating contests. Elected a member of Phi Beta Kappa, Bunche graduated summa cum laude in 1927 and went on to Harvard University to earn his masters degree in government.

While teaching at the all-black Howard University in Washington, D.C., Bunche married on of his students, Ruth Harris, in 1930. After four years in Washington, Bunche returned to Harvard to begin his doctorate. Years later, President Truman would ask Bunche to return to Washington as Assistant Secretary of State, which would have made him the highest-ranking black ever in the U.S. government; Bunche would refuse, however, objecting to the oppressive discrimination practiced against blacks in the city.

Working on his thesis on African colonialism, Bunche traveled around the interior of the continent by truck to meet with people first-hand. He later did post-doctoral work at Northwestern University, the London School of Economics, and Cape Town University in South Africa. From 1938 to 1940 Bunche worked with Swedish sociologist Gunnar Myrdal on his monumental work on U.S. race relations, *An American Dilemma.* Research took the pair far into the deep South, where they narrowly escaped lynching on two occasions. Deeply influenced by the prejudices and discrimination experienced in his own life, Bunche developed his own set of biases. "I have a deep-seated bias against hate and intolerance," he once said. "I have a bias against racial and religious bigotry. I have a bias against war, a bias for peace. I have a bias which leads me to believe that no problem of human relations is ever insoluble."

During World War II, Bunche worked for the U.S. government as an expert on colonial affairs in the Office of Strategic Services. In 1944 he moved to the State Department, where he became one of the authors of the United Nations Charter. Then, in 1946, he went to work for the U.N. and established himself as one of the organization's most effective negotiators. Brian Urquhart remembered him as "a marvelous mixture of intellect, diplomatic skill, down-to-earth humor, responsibility, and sheer kindness." Always a perfectionist, but never taking himself too seriously, he hated pretentious notions and was known for being cool under overwhelming circumstances.

Bunche was in constant danger during the Palestinian negotiations, and just barely avoided being assassinated along with Count Bernadotte. Still, his wry sense of humor was always apparent. When negotiations bogged down during the Arab-Israeli armistice talks, Bunche pulled out a set of Rhodes pottery he had purchased as gifts for the negotiators and remarked: "I was going to give you these when we finished today, but now it looks as if I shall have to break them over your heads."

Though he received the Nobel Prize for his efforts in the Arab-Israeli war, Bunche considered his greatest achievement to be his work as the architect of United Nations peacekeeping techniques. In 1956, he helped organize a 6,000-man peace-keeping force in Egypt's Sinai Peninsula and Gaza Strip, thus successfully maintaining peace in the region for eleven years. "For the first time," he said, "we have found a way to use military men for peace instead of war."

While concentrating primarily on international matters, Bunche was also known for his stand in the Civil Rights movement at home. A member of the board of directors of the NAACP, he took part in Martin Luther King's huge 1963 demonstration at the Washington Lincoln Memorial, in 1965 protest marches in Selma and Montgomery, Alabama, and was present, in 1968, at King's funeral. When not involved in negotiations around the world, Bunche lived quietly with his wife and three children in New York City.

In his time, Bunche was the highest ranking American in the United Nations. Nevertheless, wrote Urquhart, "despite the extraordinary demands placed upon him, Bunche was never too worried or too tired to think about the feelings—if not the inconvenience—of others. . . . Although he often ridiculed pretension or pomposity, I never heard him utter a malicious word. After bringing people down to earth, he was kindness itself. But he hated to see anyone humiliated or treated unjustly, and here his anger was formidable. . . . His personal integrity was matched by a demanding intellectual integrity. He did not let himself, or anyone else, get away with sloppy, self-serving work."

Suffering from failing health, Bunche was forced to resign from the U.N. in 1971; six months later, he died. "Bunche had achieved a unique status," commented one writer, "a black without color and an American who belonged to all the nations." Truly an internationalist, he worked to the end to forge peaceful bonds between all nations. "I have come to believe," he once said, "that what is good for the world is good for my country."

Sources

▶ **Books**

Haskins, Jim, *Ralph Bunche: A Most Reluctant Hero*, Hawthorn, 1974.

Linton, Howard P., ed., *Ralph Johnson Bunche: Writings by and about Him from 1928 to 1966.*

Mann, Peggy, *Ralph Bunche: U.N. Peacemaker*, Coward, McCann & Geoghegan, 1975.

▶ **Periodicals**

Look, "Ralph Bunche and His Golden Key," February 27, 1962, p. 115.

Newsweek, "Never Did He Despair," October 11, 1971, p. 44.

New Yorker, "Crisis," July 29, 1967, pp. 20-23.

Time, "Man Without Color," December 20, 1971, p. 34.

Yale Review, "Remembering Ralph Bunche," spring, 1987, pp. 448-451.

Helen Caldicott

"I find that less than 1 percent of American audiences even know what a strategic weapon is. The level of ignorance about the arms race is frightening."

Born August 8, 1938, in Melbourne, Australia, physician Helen Caldicott is an internationally known antinuclear activist.

D isturbed by the proliferation of nuclear weapons and the operating hazards and waste-management problems of nuclear power plants, Helen Caldicott has actively opposed nuclear technology since the early 1970s. Regarded as the antinuclear movement's most effective public speaker, she has used her knowledge and compassion as a physician and parent to convince her audiences of the consequences of radiation and to persuade them, in turn, to take action. Although her critics have called her a radical, Caldicott counters that she is actually a conservative: "I'm for conserving lives."

The third child of a factory manager and an interior designer, Helen Broinowski became sharply aware of nuclear technology at the age of fourteen, when she read Nevil Shute's novel *On the Beach*, about the end of humanity due to nuclear holocaust. She remained haunted by the book even after graduating from medical school and marrying William Caldicott in 1962; while pregnant for the first time, she began to have nightmares about such a catastrophe occurring and killing her children. As a pediatrician with experience in genetic diseases such as cystic fibrosis, Caldicott knew that radiation damages cells and makes such diseases and cancers more likely, especially in children, in whom damaged cells reproduce rapidly. Reading about the radioactive substances released during nuclear weapons tests and routine reactor operation strengthened her resolve to oppose the technology and practice "real preventive medicine," as she told *Ms.* magazine. In 1971, when Caldicott became aware of French atomic bomb testing in the atmosphere over the southern Pacific Ocean, she began her assault on the nuclear age.

Caldicott's letters to newspapers and appearances on Australian radio and television news programs alerted the public to the existence of the tests and the dangers they posed, sparking a widespread protest. As a writer for *Ms.* noted, Caldicott "has a gift for making the hard scientific facts meaningful to the public." Her revelation of government documents that admitted to high levels of radiation in Australian drinking water, paired with medical discussions of the effects of such radiation, helped convince a majority of the Australian population to join her. In 1973 France was persuaded to end the aboveground tests. When in 1974 her country bowed to the international energy crisis caused by an oil embargo by Arab nations, promoting Australian uranium as an energy source for nuclear power plants, Caldicott turned to the uranium miners for support. Her accounts of the harm uranium radiation would do to the miners and their children proved potent: in 1975 the country's trade unions won a ban on mining and selling uranium that lasted until 1982.

After taking a post at a cystic fibrosis clinic in Boston, Massachusetts, in

1975, Caldicott became involved in the American antinuclear campaign. Watching the country exporting nuclear reactors to other countries and increasing its nuclear arsenal in competition with the Soviet Union, she considered it "imperative that the American public understand that nuclear power generation is neither safe, nor clean, nor cheap; that new initiatives are urgently required if we are to avoid nuclear catastrophe in a world armed to the teeth with atomic weapons; and that these initiatives must begin with awareness, concern, and action on the part of the individual citizen." A strong believer in the power of democracy, Caldicott strove to alert citizens and encourage them to voice their opinions. Her tactics included co-authoring *Nuclear Madness: What You Can Do!*, described in the *New York Times Book Review* as "a primer on the medical hazards of nuclear fission," and founding and strengthening antinuclear groups. In the United States, she revived Physicians for Social Responsibility (PSR), a sixteen-year-old organization that had become largely inactive, and founded Women's Action for Nuclear Disarmament; abroad, she helped organize activists in England, Belgium, the Netherlands, and West Germany. Under Caldicott's direction, PSR has attacked both nuclear reactor and weapons issues, and in 1981 it produced the documentary film "Eight Seconds to Midnight," which was nominated for an Academy Award. Caldicott also took part in a Canadian film, "If You Love This Planet," that won an Oscar the following year, but she laments that neither film enjoyed much American exposure: "It's obscene that the commercial [television] stations don't play this stuff." In fact, Caldicott notes, "If You Love This Planet" was "banned by the U.S. Justice Department as foreign propaganda." U.S. President Ronald Reagan himself, long a target of Caldicott's, proved "not receptive at all to what I had to say" when she managed to arrange a private meeting with him in 1982. She has, however, been warmly received in Canada, Sweden, and other Western nations and was nominated for the Nobel Peace Prize in 1985.

Throughout her antinuclear campaign Caldicott has used lectures and speeches extensively to raise awareness and garner support, focusing on a personal approach bolstered by medical facts. She addresses churches—Methodist, Presbyterian, Mormon, Mennonite, Catholic—and students and medical professionals as well as labor unions. Often she uses blackboard drawings to explain technological and medical details, and though she includes many statistics, "she doesn't hesitate to raise moral questions or display intense emotions about these matters that are life-threatening in the extreme," observed a *Ms.* writer. As Caldicott remarked in the *Los Angeles Times*, "To be unemotional about the end of the world is sick."

Caldicott's passion for her cause led her to leave medicine in 1980, and despite the toll of her subsequent heavy lecturing schedule, she remains convinced of the urgency of her mission. "Nuclear war is the final medical epidemic for which there is no cure," she has said. Despite the weight of all her grim statistics and political opposition, she retains a sense of hope. "There is now a vast movement in this country which is more politically sophisticated and knowledgeable than it's ever been before," notes Caldicott, as well as a burgeoning of literature on nuclear issues that she finds "exciting." Newfound spirituality has given her further strength. Formerly an atheist, Caldicott skeptically experimented with meditation and prayer and "found that it worked, that there is a higher force that I can tap into." Finding such a force has helped her cope with the magnitude of the issues and "release the outcome. . . . I'll do the best I can and be guided rather than feeling total responsibility."

Sources

▶ **Books**

Caldicott, Helen, Nancy Herrington, and Nahum Stiskin, *Nuclear Madness: What You Can Do!*, Autumn Press, 1978.

Caldicott, *Missile Envy: The Arms Race and Nuclear War*, Morrow, 1984.

▶ **Periodicals**

Humanist, "Commitment to Life," September-October, 1982, pp. 5-11.

Los Angeles Times, June 27, 1984.

Ms., "Helen Caldicott: The Voice the Nuclear Industry Fears," July, 1979, pp. 50-52 and 92-93.

New York Times Book Review, "Knocking the Nukes," August 26, 1979, pp. 12 and 25.

People, "Pediatrician Helen Caldicott Rallies Her Fellow Doctors Against the Bomb," November 30, 1981, pp. 89-93.

Ernesto Cardenal

"*Manrique said our lives were rivers/going down to the sea which is death/but the death they flow down to is life.*"

Born January 20, 1925, in Granada, Nicaragua, Ernesto Cardenal is a priest and a poet of revolutionary literature.

E rnesto Cardenal, a Nicaraguan poet and priest, is a major figure in Latin-American revolutionary literature. Reacting against the repressive regime of Nicaraguan leader Anastazio Samoza in the early 1950s, Cardenal wrote revolutionary poems recognizing the need for violence to overthrow repressive governments but, in 1956, at the age of 31, Cardenal had a spiritual conversion and enrolled in the Monastery of Our Lady Gethsemani to study under the Order of the Trappist Monks in Kentucky. His perspective on violence changed and he began to write poems with the message that love should be the prime force in life. In 1966, Cardenal founded a Christian commune in Nicaragua called Solentiname, where he developed his ideas and served the poor.

Ernesto Cardenal was born to Rodolpho and Esmeralda (Martinez) Cardenal on January 20, 1925, in Granada, Nicaragua, where he attended high school at the Colegio Centroamerica. In 1943, he left Nicaragua to study for a degree in Philosophy and Letters at the National University in Mexico. In 1949 he obtained a Doctorate of Philosophy from Columbia University in New York City.

Cardenal's poetry is influenced by the works of poet Ezra Pound. As in Pound's poetry, Cardenal uses concrete images, sometimes including sections of news clippings or historical documents in his poetry. His early poems were love poems, but as Cardenal became more deeply involved in revolutionary plotting, the poems turned political. In response to the repression and killings of Anastazio Samoza and the mercenary "Death Squads," as they were called, Cardenal joined Unidad Nacional de Accion Popular (UNAP), an illegal revolutionary group. The group planned an April 3, 1954 assault on the presidential palace, but someone betrayed the plot to the Guard Nacional. Cardenal was one of few in the group who escaped capture and death. It was while in hiding that Cardenal composed his most well-known poem, "La Hora O" ("Zero Hour"). It was published in 1980 in *Zero Hour and Other Documentary Poems,* a book which relates events that led to the 1979 revolution in Nicaragua.

In 1956, two episodes affected Cardenal; Samoza was assassinated and Cardenal had a spiritual crisis which led him to denounce all violence. The assassination did not end the Samoza rule, as Samoza's son, Anastazio Samoza De Bayle, took power in Nicaragua. Cardenal applied for and was granted admission to the Trappist Monastery of Gethsemani, in Kentucky, where he came under the guidance of the Catholic priest and scholar Thomas Merton. Merton became the dominant influence on Cardenal's spiritual life and on his way of viewing social problems. In connection with social non-violence, Cardenal always names Merton and Gandhi as his role models.

In 1957 ill health forced Cardenal to leave the monastery for a short time, and in 1959, he moved to the Benedictine community at Guernavaca, in Mexico. He had not been allowed to write poetry while at the Trappist monastery, but he kept a journal. In 1960, from notes in the journal, Cardenal wrote a book of short, tight poems titled *Gethsemani, Kentucky.* In the book's introduction, Merton likened them to Chinese poetry in which a whole effect is achieved with just a few phrases. These poems espoused a lyrical version of a universe formed by the outpouring of God's love. It was a dramatic change from the revolutionary theme of his earlier poetry.

While at Guernavaca, Cardenal wrote an epic dealing with the history of Central America from its discovery by Spaniards to the destruction of Leon Viejo, the first capital in Nicaragua. Also at the Benedictine community, Cardenal began his extensive research on pre-Columbian South and Central American cultures. The work led to the poem "Lost Cities" in which an evocation of a distant way of life becomes by implication a critique of the values and actions of modern capitalist societies. Most of these poems were brought together in 1969 in *Homage to the American Indians.* At Guernavaca, Cardenal also wrote poems that were meditations on contemporary life. Each poem criticized the values underlying affluent societies (such as the United States) which are reflected in national magazine advertisements. The most popular of these poems is "Prayer for Marilyn Monroe."

Already well-advanced at this time were his plans to start a community of simple Christian living. In 1961, he moved to the seminary of La Ceja in Columbia, where his interest in the past and contemporary culture of native Indian peoples increased. He traveled the Upper Amazon and worked on several anthropological library collections. In 1965 he returned to Managua, Nicaragua, and was ordained a priest on August 15th of that year. In early 1966, he began clearing land near Managua for his Christian commune, Solentiname. Here Cardenal began a life in which hard manual labor, contemplation, charity, scholarship, and the writing of his poetry could be combined, according to an ideal plan he had worked out with Merton. In his research on Indians, he became interested in the moneyless culture of the Incan empire, which contrasted greatly with profit-oriented modern society. This contrast fueled many poems that attacked the modern socio-economic system of the West.

In 1970 Cardenal spent three months in Cuba. He was aware of the shortcomings of Fidel Castro's revolution, but at the same time he was inspired that many improvements could be implemented in his country if the social order could be radically changed. All that the Cuban system seemed to lack, Cardenal thought, was Christian basis of beliefs and compassion. He said his Cuban visit was a "second conversion" and returned convinced that the form of simple Christian society he was practicing in miniature at Solentiname could be "writ large" if the people of Nicaragua could be convinced to support it. Recognizing that society might not restructure without violence, his poetry after the visit to Cuba became somewhat more militant.

In 1972 Nicaragua was devastated by an earthquake, and when it became known that Samoza was pilfering the relief coffers, the country turned against him. The culmination of the people's anger was the June, 1979 overthrow of Samoza by the Marxist Sandinistas. Cardenal was Minister of Culture for the new regime, but when the human rights atrocities of the Sandinista regime came to light in the early 1980s, Cardenal and the Church distanced themselves from the Sandinistas. In the role of a poet and priest, Cardenal sees himself as an initiator of social change, and he views his poetry as a message of warning to all tyrants.

Sources

▶ Books

Borgeson, Paul Walter, Jr., *The Poetry of Ernesto Cardenal*, Dissertation Abstracts International, 38, 1977, 1429A.

Smith, Janet L., *An Annotated Bibliography of and About Ernesto Cardenal*, Arizona State University, 1979.

▶ Periodicals

Chicago Review, "The Painter-Peasants of Solentiname, Nicaragua," 1984, pp. 94-124.

Christianity and Crisis, "Who is Ernesto Cardenal," 1983, pp. 108-109.

Rachel Carson

"**E**ventually it dawned on me, that by becoming a biologist I had given myself something to write about."

Born May 27, 1907, in Springdale, Pennsylvania, Rachel Carson died on April 14, 1964. Carson was a biologist known for her influential book on pesticides, *Silent Spring*.

During the late 1940s and throughout the 1950s the use of chemical pesticides in the United States and around the world grew enormously, spread on crops and in pest control programs. Chief among this new generation of pesticides was DDT, billed as the "savior of mankind" for smothering typhus epidemics in Italy and for its remarkable effectiveness, initially, in killing pests. The widespread use of these toxic chemicals went largely unquestioned during these years, a time when people believed in the infallibility of science and the need to conquer Nature. It was rare for a dissenting voice to be heard, especially one challenging both scientific progress as well as the big business of the petrochemical and agricultural business industries. One such voice, however, belonged to Rachel Carson. A biologist and author, she began to notice that within a few generations after being sprayed with DDT, mosquitos developed a resistance to the chemical. She also discovered that DDT worked its way through the food chain in increasing toxicity, culminating in the reduction of bird populations due to the thinning of their eggshells. A meticulous scientist, Carson spent four years researching the problem and published her results in her controversial and enormously influential book, *Silent Spring*, which did much to change the course of pesticide use and led to the banning of certain chemicals, including DDT.

The third child of Maria and Robert Carson, Rachel spent much of her early life outdoors on her family's sixty-five acres of land. "As a child I spent long days out-of-doors in fields and woods, happiest with wild birds and creatures as companions." The dominant influence in her life was her mother, who introduced her to the wonders of nature. Rachel also showed an early affinity for writing. At age eleven, her story called "A Battle in the Clouds" was published in *St. Nicholas* magazine's section for young authors, and a year later two more of her stories appeared in the same magazine.

Rachel attended the Pennsylvania College for Women in Pittsburgh. Though her school and classmates tried to discourage her from pursuing biology, she persisted in her interest, and in 1929 she received her B.A. in Science *magna cum laude*. Rachel received a summer fellowship at Woods Hole Marine Biological Laboratory, and a graduate scholarship in zoology to Johns Hopkins University. After receiving her master's degree Carson worked as a teaching assistant, then got a job writing radio scripts for the U.S. Bureau of Fisheries. The next year she was hired as an aquatic biologist with the same agency. Not only a marine biologist, Rachel Carson was also a talented writer with a great ability to impart facts while telling a wonderful story. Not surprisingly, her stories are about the sea. "Ever since childhood I've been fascinated by the sea, and my mind has stored up everything I have ever learned about it." In 1937 she had her first major story, "Undersea", published in *Atlantic Monthly*, to considerable acclaim.

Over the next few years Carson continued to write, publishing articles in various magazines. "Eventually it dawned on me, that by becoming a biologist I had given myself something to write about." In 1941 Carson published her first book, *Under the Sea Wind*. Due to America's entering World War II the book was largely overlooked. Carson herself became caught up in her government work. In 1949 she was appointed editor in chief for the U.S. Fish and Wildlife Service. But she was not completely satisfied with her work. "The old desire to write began to reassert itself." At this time she began researching a book about the sea. "I like nothing better than to be within sight and sound of the sea." Her research led her to take a ten-day sea voyage to Georges Bank off the coast of Nova Scotia, Canada. In 1951, after two years of research, she published *The Sea Around Us*. This book was on the bestseller list for eighty weeks, and was translated into thirty-two languages. It was voted "Outstanding Book of the Year" by the *New York Times* poll, and won the National Book Award in 1952. Referring to *The Sea Around Us*, the *New York Times* said "once or twice a generation does the world get a physical scientist with literary genius."

In 1952 Carson quit her government job to pursue her writing and to care for her mother. Her books were all carefully researched. "I am a slow writer, enjoying the stimulating pursuit of research far more than the drudgery of turning out manuscript," Carson said. Her next book, *The Edge of the Sea* (1955), was on the bestseller list for twenty weeks and was voted "Outstanding Book of the Year" by the National Council of Women. One of her most satisfying honors was her election to the American Academy of Arts and Letters, a group with only fifty members.

Carson was a very private person, shy and reserved. She devoted her time to her research and writing. "A writer's occupation is one of the loneliest in the world, even if the loneliness is only an inner solitude and isolation, for that he must have at times if he is to be truly creative," Carson said. Her method of writing might be summed up in this statement: "The discipline of the writer is to learn to be still and listen to what his subject has to tell him."

During the 1950s Carson became increasingly alarmed by the wide-spread use of toxic pesticides, chemicals which had never been tested for their environmental effects. The correspondence between the rise in use of DDT and other pesticides and the resistance of mosquitoes and other pests, and the disturbing reduction in many bird populations led her to question the safety of the chemicals. After four years of exhaustive research on DDT, *Silent Spring* was ready for publication in 1962.

Public response to the condensed version of the book, published in the *New Yorker,* was very positive. After the publication of *Silent Spring,* in which Carson strongly criticized the careless and uncontrolled use of pesticides and fertilizers, both the book and Carson came under the attack of the chemical industries. Despite this the book became a bestseller, selling over 500,000 copies in hardcover, and was selected by the Book of the Month Club. All of the facts and interpretations in *Silent Spring* were substantiated by President Kennedy's Science Advisory Committee in 1963. By the end of the year there were over forty bills in state legislatures to regulate pesticides.

Throughout her work on *Silent Spring* Carson suffered from arthritis and an ulcer. In 1960 she was diagnosed as having cancer. Carson died on April 14, 1964, of cancer and heart disease.

Silent Spring provided the first clear public statement of what pesticides were doing to our environment, and started a world-wide environmental revolution, including a ban on the use of DDT in the U.S. Said one government official: "There is no question that *Silent Spring* prompted the federal government to take action against water and air pollution—as well as against persistent pesticides—several years before it otherwise would have moved." In honor of her literary and scientific contributions, in 1980 President Jimmy Carter awarded a posthumous Presidential Medal of Freedom, the highest civilian award, to Rachel Carson.

Sources
▶ **Books**

Brooks, Paul, *The House of Life: Rachel Carson at Work,* Houghton, 1972.
Gartner, Carol B., *Rachel Carson,* Ungar, 1983.
Graham, Frank, Jr., *Since Silent Spring,* Houghton, 1970.

The Crew of the *Challenger*

"They had a hunger to explore the universe and discover its truths. They wished to serve, and they did—they served all of us."

The seven astronauts of the space shuttle *Challenger*—Gregory Jarvis, Christa McAuliffe, Ronald McNair, Ellison S. Onizuka, Judith A. Resnik, Francis R. Scobee, and Michael J. Smith—perished in the worst accident in the history of the United States space program.

On January 28, 1986, at 11:38 a.m., the space shuttle *Challenger* lifted off from Cape Canaveral, Florida, on what was to be a routine flight of the shuttle. It was a cold day, with ice on and around the launch pad, but the decision had been made to launch. Seventy-three seconds after lift-off, *Challenger* exploded, vanishing from the sky in full view of millions of television viewers throughout the world. Although the seven astronauts aboard apparently survived the initial explosion, they did not survive the fall to earth, and all perished.

In the aftermath of the catastrophe, many questions were asked, and some horrifying answers discovered. The cause of the explosion was faulty O-rings in the solid rocket boosters manufactured by Morton Thiokol Co. Engineers at Morton Thiokol had been aware of the problem with O-ring performance in cold weather for at least a year, but officials at the company and at NASA and the Marshall Space Flight Center in Alabama (who also knew of the problem) had successfully diverted attention from the danger and avoided any outside investigation into the problem. As it turned out, the questionable decision to launch in the cold weather (which was itself a product of political pressures) caused the O-rings to fail, allowing fuel to leak and explode. The result was a serious blow to the American space program and the deaths of seven astronauts.

Born 1944 in Detroit, Michigan, shuttle payload specialist Gregory Jarvis grew up in Mohawk, New York, and attended Mohawk High School. He received a bachelor's degree in electrical engineering from the State University of New York at Buffalo, and a master's degree in engineering from Northeastern University. He joined the U.S. Air Force in 1969 and became a specialist in tactical communications satellites. In 1973, he went to work for the Hughes Aircraft Corp., and continued to work on satellite design. In July 1984, he was selected by the National Aeronautics and Space Administration (NASA) to be a payload specialist on the flight of the space shuttle *Discovery* in March of 1985. However, in a bit of political maneuvering, Senator Jake Garn of Utah replaced Jarvis on the flight. Rescheduled to fly on *Columbia* late in 1985, he was again replaced by a member of Congress, this time Representative Bill Nelson of Florida. Jarvis' duties aboard *Challenger* were to test the effects of weightlessness on fluids and to collect information to aid in the design of communications satellites.

Christa McAuliffe, chosen to be the first private citizen in space, was born September 2, 1948, in Framingham, Massachusetts, the daughter of an accountant. She attended high school in Framingham and later graduated from Framingham State College in 1970. In the early 1970s, McAuliffe and her husband moved to Washington, D.C., where she earned a master's degree in education from Bowie State College while her husband earned a law degree. They later moved to Concord, New Hampshire, where she became a high school social studies teacher.

As in the case of Jarvis, the selection of McAuliffe to fly in the space shuttle was politically charged. The first private citizen to fly in space had been scheduled to be a journalist. However, President Reagan felt vulnerable in the 1984 presidential campaign on the issue of education, and he decided that a teacher on the space shuttle would help his campaign. Christa McAuliffe was selected from among 11,000 applicants to be the first "Teacher in Space." McAuliffe became an instant media celebrity, and a high-profile role model for American women. Her duties on the spacecraft would be those of a payload specialist.

Mission specialist Ronald McNair was born in 1950 in Lake City, South Carolina. McNair attended segregated schools as a youth in South Carolina. He later attended North Carolina A & T University in Greensboro, and went on to earn a Ph.D. in physics from the Massachusetts Institute of Technology. After receiving his doctorate, he went to work for the Hughes Research Laboratories in California. In the late 1970s, NASA began looking for a new breed of astronaut, a "scientist-astronaut" whose background was in science training rather than test piloting. In 1977, McNair applied for admission to the space program as a scientist-astronaut, and was accepted to the program in 1978. In 1984, McNair became the second black man in space when he flew aboard *Challenger* and helped to launch a communications satellite into space. Remarking on the subject of courage, McNair said, "The true courage of space flight is not sitting aboard 6 million lbs. of fire and thunder as one rockets away from this planet. True courage comes in enduring . . . persevering, the preparation and believing in oneself."

Born 1946 in Kealakekua, Hawaii, mission specialist Ellison S. Onizuka grew up on the Kona Coast of Hawaii, the grandson of Japanese immigrants. He was the first Hawaiian and first person of Japanese descent to fly in space. He was an honors student in high school and an Eagle Scout. He later attended the University of Colorado and received undergraduate and graduate degrees in aerospace engineering. Following his education he spent eight years in the Air Force as a test pilot. He was selected to become an astronaut in 1978. In 1985, he rode aboard the space shuttle *Discovery*, performing various tasks including the filming of Halley's comet. Of that task, he remarked, "I'll be looking at Halley's comet. They tell me I'll have one of the best views around." Onizuka felt a strong sense of pride and heritage and a strong sense of obligation to the community to which he belonged, that of Edwards Air Force Base in California. He worked a great deal with local scouting and 4-H groups.

Judith A. Resnik, another mission specialist, was born in 1949 in Akron,

Ohio. She attended Firestone High School in Akron, and excelled in mathematics and at playing the piano. She later attended Carnegie-Mellon University in Pittsburgh, and received a Ph.D. in electrical engineering from the University of Maryland. After receiving her doctorate, Resnik went to work for Xerox Corporation. In 1978, she was selected from many thousands of applicants as one of the first six female astronauts. Because she was one of the first females selected, she was subject to a great deal of media attention, a fact which she did not appreciate. She became the second American woman in space in 1984, when she rode aboard the shuttle *Discovery*. Her duties aboard that flight included operating the *Discovery*'s remote-control arm. Commenting on space travel, she once said, "I think something is only dangerous if you are not prepared for it, or if you don't have control over it." Resnik was scheduled to perform experiments in space on the *Challenger* mission.

Francis R. Scobee, the commanding officer on the final flight of *Challenger*, was born in 1939 in Cle Elum, Washington, and grew up south of Seattle, the son of a railroad engineer. He attended Auburn High School, where he was described as an average student, and enrolled in the Air Force at age 18. While working as an Air Force mechanic, he was able to attend night school and earned a bachelor's degree in aerospace engineering from the University of Arizona. He later became an Air Force pilot, and flew thousands of hours in many different types of aircraft. He also flew missions in the Vietnam War. Scobee was selected as an astronaut in 1978, and in 1984 he piloted *Challenger* into space to retrieve and repair a damaged satellite.

Shuttle pilot Michael J. Smith was born in 1945 in Beaufort, North Carolina, and grew up on a 14-acre farm in that state. He attended Beaufort High School, where he was a quarterback on the football team and an honors student. He was also piloting an airplane while still a teenager. Smith attended the U.S. Naval Academy in Annapolis, Maryland, and became a pilot. During the Vietnam War, he flew 225 combat missions. He was selected by NASA to become an astronaut in 1980. Commenting before the launch of the *Challenger* on his career, Smith said, "Whenever I was conscious of what I wanted to do, I wanted to fly. I can never remember anything else I wanted to do but flying. To tell you the truth, it's been wonderful."

Sources
▶ **Books**

Lewis, Richard S., *Challenger: The Final Voyage*, Columbia University Press, 1988.

McConnell, Malcolm, *Challenger: A Major Malfunction*, Doubleday, 1987.

▶ **Periodicals**

Newsweek, "What Happened?" February 17, 1986, pp. 32-33.

Time, "Looking for What Went Wrong," February 10, 1986, pp. 36-38, "Seven Who Flew for All of Us," February 10, 1986, pp. 32-35.

U.S. News and World Report, "Out of Challenger's Ashes—Full Speed Ahead," February 10, 1986, pp. 16-19, "NASA Faces Wide Probe," February 17, 1986, pp. 18-19.

Wilt Chamberlain

"F or a long time, fans of mine had to put up with
people saying Wilt couldn't win the big ones.
Now maybe they'll have a chance to walk in peace, like I
do."

Born August 21, 1936, in Philadelphia, Pennsylvania, Wilt Chamberlain is considered one of the world's all-time greatest professional basketball players.

Wilt Chamberlain was born in Philadelphia and was one of nine children. His father lived in a racially-mixed middle-class neighborhood, and Chamberlain had a relatively pleasant childhood. At Shoemaker Junior High School, Wilt began to play on the basketball team, and he also played on the playgrounds against older players who taught him a lot about the game. He later said, "I still think you could pick up a team from the street corners of Philly that would give most colleges a real hard time." Wilt attended Overbrook High School in Philadelphia beginning in 1952. At that time he was already 6'11" tall, and had developed what he termed a "deep love for basketball."

Chamberlain's high school basketball career was astounding. In three seasons he scored more than 2200 points. More than two hundred universities recruited Chamberlain, but he wanted to get away from big cities and preferred to play in the midwest. After seriously considering Dayton, Michigan, Indiana, and Kansas Universities he chose Kansas because of the recruiting by Hall of Fame coach Phog Allen.

At the University of Kansas, Chamberlain continued his brilliant play on the basketball court, scoring fifty-two points in his first varsity game. During his first varsity season he led the Jayhawks to the finals of the National Collegiate Athletic Association tournament, but they lost to North Carolina in double overtime. During his college career he averaged over thirty points per game and was twice selected to All-American teams. Following his junior year, he decided to quit college and become a professional because, he said, "The game I was forced to play at [Kansas] wasn't basketball. It was hurting my chances of ever developing into a successful professional player."

Because he did not play his final season at Kansas, Chamberlain was not eligible to join an NBA team until one more year. So he joined the Harlem Globetrotters and spent the year travelling the world and entertaining adults and youngsters alike. He still claims that his year with the Globetrotters was his most enjoyable season of basketball.

In 1959, Chamberlain joined the Philadelphia Warriors of the NBA. The great centers of the day were Clyde Lovellette, Johnny Kerr, Johnny Green, and, of course, Bill Russell of the Boston Celtics. But Chamberlain made an immediate impact on the league. He could score almost at will, and opposing teams gave up trying to stop him and instead tried only to contain him. His scoring average during the 1959-60 season of 37.9 points per game was more than eight points per game higher than anyone else had ever scored in the history of the league. He was named both rookie of the year and most valuable player, the first person to receive both awards in the same season.

For the next six seasons, Chamberlain led the league in scoring. In 1961-62 he averaged 50.4 points and scored 100 in one game. In 1962-63 he averaged 44.8 points per game. Chamberlain was simply the greatest scoring machine in the history of basketball.

Despite his scoring achievements, Chamberlain and his teammates were not winning NBA championships. The late 1950s and 1960s were dominated by the Boston Celtics and their center Bill Russell. Russell had revolutionized basketball as much with his defense as Chamberlain had with his offense, and Russell always had a great group of supporting players, including Bob Cousy, Bill Sharman, John Havlicek, and Sam Jones. Chamberlain often had strong supporting players as well, but Russell always seemed to pull out the championship. Chamberlain always took a great deal of abuse from the media and fans because of his lack of success against Russell.

Finally, in 1967, Chamberlain reversed his fortunes. The Warriors had moved to San Francisco, and Wilt had gone with them, but he was later traded to the new Philadelphia team, the 76ers. In 1967, the 76ers had a great supporting cast, including Chet Walker, Luke Johnson, Hal Greer, Wally Jones, and Billy Cunningham. They finished the regular season with the best record in the history of the league. In the championship series, the 76ers polished off the San Francisco Warriors to win the first world title for Chamberlain.

Several years later Chamberlain was traded again, this time to the Los Angeles Lakers. The Lakers had featured numerous great players through the years, including Elgin Baylor and Jerry West, but had not won a championship since moving to Los Angeles from Minneapolis in 1960 (they *lost* in the championship series seven times between 1962 and 1970). For the last two losses, in 1969 and 1970, Chamberlain was on the team. The 1969 loss was particularly devastating, since it was to Russell and the Celtics again. In the final game, Chamberlain was injured and played very little. Russell later criticized Chamberlain for not playing, thus infuriating Chamberlain and removing the last remnants of friendship between the two men.

In 1972, however, the Lakers seemed poised to finally win a championship. They finished the year with the best regular season record in history, breaking the record set by Chamberlain and the 76ers in 1967. In addition to Chamberlain, the team now featured Happy Hairston, Gail Goodrich, Jim McMillan, Jerry West, and a strong set of reserves. In the playoffs, the Lakers first defeated the Milwaukee Bucks, with Chamberlain completely outplaying the Buck center, Kareem Abdul-Jabbar. In the championship series, the Lakers played the powerful New York Knickerbockers, led by Willis Reed, Dave DeBusschere, Bill

Bradley, and Walt Frazier. In the fourth game of the series, Chamberlain suffered a fractured wrist. Although the Lakers led the series three games to one the series still seemed in doubt because of Chamberlain's injury. Despite understandable pain, Chamberlain played the next game with football linemen's pads on both hands. He scored twenty-four points, grabbed twenty-nine rebounds, and blocked ten shots. The Lakers won the game and the series, four games to one and brought the first world championship to Los Angeles. After the final game Wilt said, "For a long time, fans of mine had to put up with people saying Wilt couldn't win the big ones. Now maybe they'll have a chance to walk in peace, like I do."

Following the 1973 season, Chamberlain left the Lakers to become the coach of the San Diego Conquistadors of the old American Basketball Association (ABA). Chamberlain left the NBA as the all-time leader in points scored (more than 30,000) and rebounds (over 22,000), and with four Most Valuable Player awards and more than forty league records. The ABA was a different sort of challenge, however; the athletes were not generally as good as in the NBA, and Chamberlain had never been a coach before. The Conquistadors were a poor team, even by ABA standards, and Chamberlain left the coaching ranks shortly thereafter for a well-deserved retirement.

In recent years, Chamberlain has been involved in a wide variety of activities. He has sponsored a lot of amateur athletic groups, including volleyball teams and track clubs. He has invested wisely through the years and remains a wealthy man. He has also kept in outstanding physical condition. When he walks into a room or onto a basketball court today, he is a legendary presence.

Sources

▶ **Books**

Chamberlain, Wilt, and David Shaw, *Wilt: Just Like Any Other 7-Foot Black Millionaire Who Lives Next Door*, MacMillan, 1973.

Libby, Bill, *Goliath: The Wilt Chamberlain Story*, Dodd, 1977.

Sullivan, George, *Wilt Chamberlain*, Grosset, 1971.

▶ **Periodicals**

Ebony, "Captain Wilt Leads L.A. Lakers to Best Pro Sports Record Ever," April, 1972, pp. 114-121.

Esquire, "The Dipper's Lament," May, 1988, pp. 53-56.

Life, "Long Way with West—All the Way with Wilt?" March 13, 1970, pp. 46-50.

Look, "Why I Am Quitting College," June 10, 1958, pp. 91-94, "Pro Basketball Has Ganged Up On Me," March 1, 1960, pp. 51-57.

Sports Illustrated, "High but No Longer Mighty," October 29, 1973, pp. 44-48, "Doing Just Fine, My Man," August 18, 1986, pp. 62-76.

Time, "One for the Dipper," May 22, 1972, pp. 47-50.

Cesar Chavez

*"*T*he schools treated you like you didn't exist. Their indifference was incredible."*

Born March 31, 1927, near Yuma, Arizona, the second child of Librado and Juana Chavez, Cesar (Estrada) Chavez is president of the United Farm Workers of America (UFW) and a leading spokesperson for the rights of migrant workers.

Present address: United Farm Workers of America, P.O. Box 62-LaPaz, Keene, Calif., 93531.

I n the spring of 1965, south of Delano, California, Filipino grape pickers of the Agricultural Workers Organizing Committee (AWOC) went out on strike for higher pay. When the workers and the strike came north to Delano, Cesar Chavez and his National Farm Workers Association (NFWA) voted to join the strike to protest the conditions of migrant farm workers in California. The publicity generated by this strike brought widespread attention to the plight of migrant workers and thrust soft-spoken Cesar Chavez into the national spotlight as the leading spokesperson for "La Causa"—the term which came to signify both the strike of the grape pickers and the larger struggle of migrant workers everywhere.

Cesar Chavez grew up knowing well the plight of migrant workers in the United States. Chavez spent the first ten years of his life on a ranch run by his parents; however, when the Depression came, the county sheriff served the family papers and kicked them off their land. Penniless, the family moved to California in search of work, along with thousands of other people. There, they began to experience the hardships that face migrant workers. They first worked in the Imperial Valley tying carrots for a total daily pay of one to two dollars. They then went to the vegetable fields of Oxnard, and then the grape vineyards near Fresno, where they worked for weeks on a promise of pay—only to have the contractor disappear one day, leaving the family destitute. Chavez has said that the worst work in those days was thinning crops in the fields with short-handled hoes—bent over all day—for eight to twelve cents an hour. Winters were especially difficult for the family. "[The] winter of '38," he recalls, "I had to walk to school barefoot through the mud, we were so poor." After school, Chavez would fish in the canals and cut wild mustard greens to help his family survive.

As the migrant lifestyle began to settle in for the Chavez family, so did feelings of prejudice and rejection—living, for example, in segregated areas where "White Trade Only" signs were the norm. Discrimination against migrant farm workers also carried over into schools. By the time he dropped out of school in the eighth grade, Cesar had attended thirty to forty different schools. Sometimes students had to write "I won't speak Spanish" three hundred times on the blackboard. Describing the poor treatment of migrant children, Cesar recalls: "The schools treated you like you didn't exist. Their indifference was incredible." As a teenager, he began to rebel. Chavez rejected Mexican music, medicine, styles of dress, and some aspects of the Catholic Church. In 1943, at the age of sixteen, Cesar went to a segregated movie theater in Delano and sat in the "whites only" section. When the police came they pried his hands off the seat and dragged him to the police station. The anger, humiliation, and powerlessness from this incident made a deep impression on Chavez.

Chavez began his involvement in the fight for migrant rights during the late 1940s after he returned from Navy service in World War II. In the autumn of 1947, Cesar began working for the grape harvest in Delano, where workers had gone on strike demanding recognition of their farm labor union. The local sheriff and the U.S. Immigration Service intimidated the workers by raiding their camp nineteen times looking for illegal aliens. Chavez's first real taste of farm strikes, however, came in 1949 when cotton growers tried to reduce the wages of workers. Though his participation in the strike was small, and the workers went back to the fields, Cesar sensed the lack of leadership and disorganization in the strike and decided that something needed to be done about it.

In 1951 Chavez met Fred Ross, a community labor organizer, from whom he would learn the art of organizing. Hired by Ross and the Community Services Organization (CSO), Cesar first worked as an organizer in Oakland, California, and the poor urban centers of the East San Francisco Bay area. Following that experience, he returned to the rural *barrios* to organize farm workers and the poor, registering them to vote. In 1958, Chavez became director of the CSO, but resigned in 1962 because he felt the group was not doing enough for poor farm workers. He moved his family back to Delano and, with the help of his wife Helen, began organizing the National Farm Workers Association.

By the time of the 1965 Delano grape strike, Chavez's group was well organized and prepared. Chavez and AFL-CIO organizer Larry Itliang held the striking workers together until they finally won the strike and the growers agreed to a contract. In 1966, the NFWA merged with the Agricultural Workers Organizing Committee of the AFL-CIO to become the United Farm Workers Organizing Committee (UFWOC). By 1972, UFWOC was a legitimate union within the AFL-CIO, with 147 contracts covering 50,000 workers on farms in California, Arizona, and Florida. Now under the name of the United Farm Workers of America, Chavez's group numbers more than 100,000.

The work of Cesar Chavez on behalf of migrant farm workers has continued unabated to this day. One of the dramatic tactics he has adopted, in order to bring attention to the plight of workers, is the hunger strike. In 1968, Chavez fasted for twenty-five days and, in 1972, for twenty-four days. In 1988, Chavez did a thirty-six day fast in Delano to dramatize the UFWA's four-year boycott against California grape growers, protesting the reckless use of pesticides. It was one of Chavez's most publicized actions since "La Causa" twenty-three years earlier. By the time Chavez was persuaded to end his fast, he had lost thirty-three pounds. The fast for "La Causa" was continued, however, by Jesse Jackson and others. Asked about personally harmful actions such as hunger strikes, Chavez summed up the struggle for "La Causa" by saying: "It is not a fast unless you suffer."

Sources

▶ **Books**

Dunne, John Gregory, *Delano*, Farrar, Straus, 1967.

Levy, Jacques E., *Cesar Chavez*, Norton, 1975.

Taylor, Ronald B., *Chavez and the Farm Workers*, Beacon Press, 1975.

▶ **Periodicals**

People, "Cesar Chavez Breaks His Longest Fast as His Followers Pray for an End to the Grapes of Wrath," September 5, 1988, p. 52.

Shirley Chisolm

"**I** was the first American citizen to be elected to Congress in spite of the double drawbacks of being female and having skin darkened by melanin. When you put it that way, it sounds like a foolish reason for fame. In a just and free society it would be foolish. That I am a national figure because I was the first person in 192 years to be at once a congressman, black and a woman proves, I think, that our society is not yet either just or free."

Born on November 30, 1924, in Brooklyn, New York, Shirley Chisolm became the first black female member of the United States Congress.

I n the late 1960s, the American civil rights movement had brought about significant changes in state and national laws regarding discrimination against blacks. The movement had also greatly affected the consciousness of many American citizens, both white and black, making the very idea of racial equality a national issue. In that same time the women's movement was gaining momentum, though not as quickly as did that civil rights movement. While there were already ten or so black United States congressmen, a black *female* member of Congress was still entirely unheard of. But Shirley Chisolm was not one easily daunted by the prospect of setting new precedents. Because of her outspokenness and her refusal to cooperate with the schemes of the New York political machine, she was forced to fight her way to victory the hard way, earning her the nickname "Fighting Shirley Chisolm." Labeled a maverick throughout her political career, she learned quickly that "if you decide to operate on the basis of your conscience, rather than your political advantage, you must be ready for the consequences and not complain when you suffer them. There is little place in the political scheme of things for an independent, creative personality, for a fighter. Anyone who takes that role must pay a price."

Chisolm's father, Charles St. Hill, was a British Guiana native who worked at a variety of unskilled factory jobs. With little formal education he was still "an omnivorous reader." Her mother, Ruby Seale St. Hill, was a seamstress and domestic from Barbados who "was thoroughly British in her ideas, her manners and her plans for her daughters. We were to become young ladies—poised, modest, accomplished, educated, and graceful, prepared to take our places in the world."

When only three years old, Chisolm and two of her three sisters were sent to live with their grandmother on a farm in Barbados, so their parents could save money for their college education. Remaining until age eleven, she profited by the island's school system: "Years later I would know what an important gift my parents had given me by seeing to it that I had my early education in the strict, traditional British-style schools of Barbados. If I speak and write easily now, that early education is the main reason."

Returning to Brooklyn was difficult and required many adjustments. The family was poor, and Chisolm was responsible for caring for her young sisters while her parents worked. Both parents were very strict, requiring absolute obedience at home and excellence in school. With her mother, she and her sisters attended church three times a day on Sundays and were allowed little socializing with friends. But "as we got older," she recalls, "naturally we began to rebel."

Chisolm did well in junior high and high school and went on to attend

Brooklyn College in 1942. There, she says, she "began to bump up against more of the world." She became involved with community service organizations and gradually resolved to "do something about the way whites treated my people. Political action was hardly even a fantasy for me at the time. But I decided that if I ever had a chance, somehow I would tell the world how things were as I saw them." She majored in sociology and decided to become a teacher since, at that time, "there was no other road open to a young black woman." After graduation, she went to work teaching nursery school and started on her master's degree in elementary education at Columbia University. She eventually became a recognized authority on child welfare and education and was named consultant to the New York City Division of Day Care.

Meanwhile, Chisolm was developing a reputation as a political agitator. She worked her way into the male-dominated New York political clubs and refused to submit to the long-established hierarchies and power systems which ruled politics in the city. The political clubs, she discovered, exploited women by depending on them to raise money, but refusing to allow them any real power. As she struggled against the prejudices of politically powerful men, Chisolm was to remark that throughout her career, "Of my two 'handicaps,' being female put many more obstacles in my path than being black."

Then, for a time, the activist all but dropped out of politics. Her fiance revealed that he had another family in Jamaica and was deeply involved in immigration fraud. The sudden end to their engagement, and his subsequent deportment, left Chisolm in a state of emotional strain. Family friends arranged for her to stay on a farm in the country, and there, she remembers, "In the quiet, surrounded by fresh air and affection, tempted by country cooking, I groped my way back to reality." Returning to the city she eventually married fellow Columbia student Conrad Q. Chisolm on October 8, 1949.

By 1960 Shirley Chisolm was back in politics. She and six others founded the Unity Democratic Club and managed to do what other clubs had failed to do: "take over the entire Seventeenth Assembly District political organization and boot out the failing but still potent white machine." She ran for the New York State Assembly in 1964 and won, waging an old-fashioned street corner campaign, speaking fluent Spanish in Puerto Rican neighborhoods, and winning especially the trust of women voters in the district. Reelected twice, Chisolm spent a total of four years in Albany, declining to play the role of the quiet freshman lawmaker but instead pressing for legislation that directly benefited her poor constituents.

When a redistricting of Brooklyn, designed to give minority areas an equal vote, was announced, Chisolm announced her candidacy in the 1968 congressional elections. Running against nationally known black civil rights leader James Farmer, she found herself up against a well-funded "big, black male image." Again depending on grass-roots support, and especially on the support of women voters, she campaigned under the slogan, "Fighting Shirley Chisolm: Unbought and Unbossed." Chisolm won the election by margin of 2.5 to 1, making her the first black woman member of Congress in history. Once in Washington, she made a point of hiring women for her staff, and devoted much of her time to aiding individual constituents through her influence as a representative.

Viewing herself primarily as a spokesperson for the disadvantaged, Chisolm was often criticized for her refusal to forge firm political alliances and to take part in the practical, day-to-day bargaining of political life. "I do not see myself," she has said, "as a lawmaker, an innovator in the field of legislation. America has the laws and the material resources it takes to insure justice for all its people. What it lacks is the heart, the humanity, the Christian love that it would take. It is perhaps unrealistic to hope that I can help give this nation any of those things, but that is what I believe I have to try to do." In her first speech on the House floor she spoke out against the Vietnam War, announcing her plans to vote against any and every military appropriations bill while in Congress.

In 1972 Chisolm waged a campaign for the Democratic presidential nomination, gaining the support of many disadvantaged groups. Claiming to have triumphantly broken oppressive traditions, Chisolm nevertheless splintered the liberal vote at the Democratic National Convention. In 1982 she announced her decision to leave the Congress; exhausted by the demands of public life, she sought to spend time with her second husband, Arthur Hardwick, and to pursue a career teaching at the college level. Regarding her achievements, she has commented that, though being black and female has put her in a remarkable class, "I hope that if I am remembered it will finally be for what I have done, not for what I happen to be."

Sources
▶ **Books**

Chisolm, Shirley, *Shirley Chisolm: Unbought and Unbossed*, Houghton Mifflin, 1970.

Chisolm, Shirley, *The Good Fight*, Harper, 1973.

Stineman, Esther, *American Political Women*, Libraries Unlimited, 1980.

▶ **Periodicals**

Black Enterprise, "Chisholm to Teach," October 1982, p. 28.

Essence, "Mrs. Chisolm Calls It Quits" (interview), August, 1982, pp. 72-74.

Newsweek, "Campaign Veteran on the Trail," May 21, 1984, p. 11A.

Roberto Clemente

"Winning the World Series in 1960 was not the biggest thrill I'll ever have in my life. The biggest thrill was when I came out of the clubhouse after the last Series game and saw all those thousands of fans in the streets. It was something you cannot describe. . . . I walked the streets among them."

Major League baseball player Roberto Clemente was born August 18, 1934 in Carolina, Puerto Rico, and died December 31, 1972, off the coast of San Juan, Puerto Rico.

Roberto Clemente was born in Puerto Rico and came to the United States to play professional baseball. Although he played brilliantly with the National League's Pittsburgh Pirates for many years, he always felt he did not receive the recognition he deserved. Although he was not generally included among such baseball greats as Mickey Mantle, Willie Mays, and Hank Aaron, knowledgeable baseball fans now tend to agree that Clemente was one of the dominant players of his era. He won four batting titles and is considered the best fielding right fielder of his day. A fiercely proud man, Clemente spent many years attempting to improve the conditions for Latin American players in the major leagues. In addition to encountering racial prejudice, Hispanic players were often poorly understood since English was usually their second language. Clemente himself never really mastered the language, although he worked hard at it. Clemente's dream was to build a youth sports facility in Puerto Rico which would be open only to poor children. The children would attend free of charge and would learn the value of discipline and teamwork. Unfortunately, construction had only just begun on the facility at the time of Clemente's death in 1972.

Robert Clemente grew up in a middle class family (by local standards) in Puerto Rico. He was the youngest of seven children. His father was a foreman on a sugar cane plantation, and his mother ran a grocery store for plantation workers. As a child Roberto aspired to become an engineer, but his athletic talents were so astounding that he decided to play baseball. He played amateur softball on the sandlots of his hometown of Carolina until he was spotted by a scout from the Santurce professional hardball team in Puerto Rico. The team offered Roberto a $500 signing bonus and $40 per month to play for the team.

Clemente was a star on the Santurce team for three seasons, and drew the attention of major league scouts from the United States. Following the 1953 season, the Brooklyn Dodgers signed him to a contract which included a $10,000 bonus, a huge sum of money for Clemente and his family. The Dodgers assigned Clemente to their minor league team in Montreal; in those days, players making more than $4,000 per year could be drafted from minor league teams by other major league clubs. Montreal attempted to disguise Clemente's talents by using him sparingly, but a scout for the Pittsburgh Pirates noticed Clemente. The scout, Clyde Sukeforth, was the same man who had discovered Jackie Robinson. The Pirates drafted Clemente from the Dodgers' system following the 1954 season.

Clemente's major league career began without great fanfare as he learned how to play in the big leagues. Forbes Field in Pittsburgh was a cavernous ballpark, with a great deal of room in the outfield. This showcased Clemente's incredible fielding abilities; he was swift afoot and possessed a powerful throwing arm. From remote spots in the outfield, Clemente often threw out runners who were attempting to score. He also adjusted his hitting style to take advantage of the large gaps between opponents' outfielders. He became a "spray hitter," scattering line–drive doubles and triples into the gaps. Although his number of home runs never compared with those of Mays or Aaron, his record was excellent coming from a ballpark as large as Forbes Field.

Clemente batted over .300 only once in his first five seasons in the league. In 1960, however, he hit .314 and helped lead the Pirates to the National League pennant. In the World Series the Pirates were to face the mighty New York Yankees, who had players such as Mickey Mantle, Roger Maris, Yogi Berra, and Whitey Ford. The World Series became one of the most memorable in history. The teams played even baseball, and through six games the Series was tied at three games apiece. In the seventh and deciding game, Pirate Bill Mazeroski hit a home run in the bottom of the ninth inning to win the championship for Pittsburgh. Clemente batted .310 in the Series. The first of many disappointments for Clemente came following the season, however, when he finished only eighth in the balloting for the league's Most Valuable Player. Clemente believed that the vote was a reflection of anti-Hispanic sentiment.

Clemente used his disappointment to rise to greater heights. In 1961 he led the National League in batting for the first time with his highest batting average to date, .351. He began regularly to hit above .300. Between 1960 and 1972 he batted under .300 only once. In 1964 he won his second batting title with an average of .339. He followed with his third title the next season, hitting .329. The 1966 season was perhaps his finest overall. He batted .317, with 119 Runs Batted In (RBIs) and 29 home runs, and was named the National League's Most Valuable Player. In 1967 he won his fourth and final batting championship with an average of .357.

Throughout his career, Clemente had a large number of nagging injuries. An automobile accident in 1954 caused lower back pain that recurred for the rest of Clemente's career. He also had numerous other ailments, including wayward disks in his back, bone chips in his elbow, stomach disorders, and tension headaches. He developed the reputation for being a complainer for these and other reasons. Doctors diagnosed part of the problem as being a low threshold for pain. Another part of the problem seemed to be communication; teammate Bill Mazeroski once said, "Roberto's carefree outlook on life began to change when the press started to misunderstand him when he talked about his injuries. When he was hurt he had trouble explaining himself because of the language problem."

The Pirates as a team had not won a National League pennant since the glorious 1960 season. In the early 1970s, however, they seemed poised to win again. Although Clemente was now in his mid-thirties, he had lost little of his athletic ability. In 1971 the Pirates won another pennant and faced the Baltimore Orioles in the World Series. The Orioles had won the American League pennant for the last three seasons, and they were defending world champions. They were led by Frank Robinson, Brooks Robinson, Boog Powell, Dave McNally, Mike Cuellar, and Jim Palmer. Early in the Series Clemente said, "Nobody does anything better than me in baseball," and he then attempted to prove it. He batted an astounding .414 in the Series, and he made numerous astonishing plays in the outfield. For his efforts he was named the Series' Most Valuable Player. The Pirates upset the favored Orioles, four games to three.

Perhaps more than any other star, Clemente is remembered for his fielding wizardry as well as his batting. Throughout his career Clemente made playing the outfield an art, and he established himself as arguably the greatest right fielder in the history of the game. Many times he threw strikes to home plate from more than 400 feet in the outfield. He was fearless in his pursuit of the ball, diving into the outfield grass and crashing into the wall. He left the game holding the all-time record for assists from the outfield. He also won the Gold Glove for the outstanding fielder at his position twelve times.

Clemente's batting statistics were outstanding as well. He batted over .300 thirteen times, and he won four batting titles. He left the game with the highest active lifetime batting average, .317. He also became only the eleventh player in major league history to collect 3,000 hits in a career. For his heroics in the field and at the plate, he was selected to the National League All-Star team twelve times. Big league managers Dick Williams and Harry Walker each said that Roberto Clemente is "the greatest ballplayer I ever saw."

Clemente was always a strong promoter of Hispanic players and Hispanic pride, for he felt that Latin players did not receive the recognition or respect they deserved. Commenting on his throwing ability, he once said, "If (Mickey) Mantle have the arm I have you will put it in the headlines 'cause he is an American. You never give me credit." Following his outstanding 1971 World Series play, Clemente told the press, "Now they (writers) know they can't be sarcastic about Latins, which is something I have fought all my life."

Clemente's concern for Latin America was reflected in other ways as well. His large home in Puerto Rico was always open to admiring fans. He and his wife and three children put up with fans touring through the house at all hours of the day. Clemente's dream was to build a sports complex for poor children in Puerto Rico to provide the children opportunities to learn and grow. He said, "What we want to do is exchange kids with every city in the U.S. and show all the kids how to live and play with other kids."

Late in 1972, following massive earthquakes in Managua, Nicaragua, Clemente helped organize relief efforts in Puerto Rico. Not content to just lend his name to the project, Clemente accompanied relief supplies to Managua. On December 31, 1972, he boarded an antiquated airplane whose engines failed during and immediately after takeoff. The pilot attempted to return to San Juan, but the place crashed about a mile and a half off the coast. Everyone aboard was killed.

The baseball world and all of Latin America mourned the death of Roberto Clemente. He had symbolized achievement and courage for a generation of young people in both Latin America and the United States. The baseball Hall of Fame, suspending the rule that a man must be retired for five years before being eligible for election, immediately inducted Roberto Clemente into the Hall of Fame. The eulogies for Clemente were many, but perhaps the most eloquent came from the governor of Puerto Rico, Rafael Hernandez Colon, who said: "Roberto died in moments in which he was serving his fellow man. Our youth loses an idol and an example. Our people lose one of their glories."

Sources

▶ **Books**

Brondfield, Jerry, *Roberto Clemente, Pride of the Pirates*, Garrard, 1976.

Hano, Arnold, *Roberto Clemente, Batting King*, Putnam, 1973.

Musick, Phil, *Who Was Roberto? A Biography of Roberto Clemente*, Doubleday, 1974.

Wagenheim, Kal, *Clemente!*, Praeger, 1973.

▶ **Periodicals**

Ebony, "Viva Roberto!," September, 1967, pp. 38-41, "Roberto Clemente: Sad End for a Troubled Man," March, 1973, pp. 50-54.

Life, "The Strain of Being Roberto Clemente," May 24, 1968, pp. 70-71.

Newsweek, "Roberto the Great," January 15, 1973, p. 75.

Sports Illustrated, "Aches and Pains and Three Batting Titles," March 7, 1966, pp. 30-34, "Golden Triumphs, Tarnished Dreams," August 30, 1976, pp. 32-36.

Time, "Requiem for Roberto," January 15, 1973, pp. 42-43.

Marva Collins

"Y ou are unique—there is no one else like you."

Born August 31, 1936, in Monroeville, Alabama, the daughter of
Alex L. and Bessie Maye (Knight) Nettles, Marva Collins is a
nationally-recognized educator.

Present address: Westside Preparatory School, 4146 West Chicago
Ave., Chicago Ill. 60641.

I n the way public school teachers can be heroes to the little people they teach, Marva (Deloise Nettles) Collins is a shining example. Collins has succeeded in helping underprivileged children realize their potential, finding joy in learning, in themselves, and in the possibilities that await them.

Marva had important influences in becoming a heroic teacher. From her earliest childhood, Marva showed a special love for reading and literature. As a small child, she discovered the music of the sounded word from her grandmother, who used to read aloud to her. When she was able to read herself, she read everything she could get her hands on. Marva was especially fond of fairy tales, fables, and the Bible, in particular the Book of Proverbs. Marva also found magic in the writings of the English playwright and poet William Shakespeare. Marva's love of reading was significant to her becoming a good teacher later on.

Marva's own experience being taught by teachers was also an important influence. As a child, Marva attended grade school in her native Monroeville, Alabama, at the Bethlehem Academy. Her first teacher, who was negative, strict, critical, and uninspiring, was an example of how *not* to teach. In fourth grade, however, Marva found a positive example of *how* to teach. This teacher, who reinforced Marva's love of learning, was patient, effective, and praised hard work. Marva later attended Escambia County Training School and, after graduating, knew she must attend college. Her ambition took her to Clark College in Atlanta, Georgia, an exclusive all-black liberal arts school for girls.

Marva graduated from Clark College in 1957 and, after some time, took a teaching job in Chicago, Illinois. Once there, however, she was not happy with her fellow teachers and the books that they used in teaching. Marva found that the books were old, simple, and conservative, and that they dampened the children's imaginations and desire to learn. Furthermore, she felt the teachers were not all that interested in teaching. Marva therefore abandoned the required reader and started teaching from such books as Aesop's *Fables,* the Grimm Brothers' *Fairy Tales,* Jean de La Fontaine's *Fables,* and Leo Tolstoy's *Fables and Fairytales.* Marva did not feel restricted by the books she was using. She brought in related material to place the material in context, and then delivered it with love, respect, and enthusiasm. To Marva, learning was an adventure.

On September 8, 1975, Marva founded the Westside Preparatory School in one of the poorest neighborhoods in Chicago. Here she was allowed more leeway in teaching and selecting subject matter. Marva made the air electric with the joy of learning. She convinced underprivileged children that they were important as individuals and that they needed self-reliance and hard work to reach their goals. Marva always compiled lists of positive, motivating slogans to pass on to the children, such as "You are unique—there is no one else like you" and "The world moves aside to let you pass only if you know where you are going."

To Marva, teaching is one of the more important and challenging opportunities in the world. Therefore, she is especially concerned with teachers and how they are chosen for teaching jobs. She once said, "The one question that ought to be asked on a teaching application is: do you love children? To me that's the most important criterion for a teacher, more important than credentials or college degrees. A devotion to children was the quality I looked for in all the people who applied for teaching jobs at Westside Prep." Marva insists on establishing and maintaining high standards for teachers, knowing that time and hard work pay off in schools.

Collins has received numerous honorary awards and degrees for her accomplishments, and in 1981 was offered the position of U.S. Secretary of Education, which she later refused. Marva has also become something of a celebrity for her creative and effective teaching methods. In 1979, she appeared on ABC-TV's *Good Morning America*, and in the same year was featured on CBS-TV's *Sixty Minutes*. In 1981, the television movie based on her life, "The Marva Collins Story," touched off arguments among the teachers in the Chicago school system where she worked and, eventually, throughout the United States. Among the charges were reports that the positive results of Collins's teaching methods had been inflated and that she had misrepresented federal grant money received. In a two-hour segment of "The Phil Donahue Show" Collins successfully responded to the charges and counter-charges. Several publications also came to her defense. *The Wall Street Journal* charged that Collins's success with students bred envy in other teachers who had failed in their own work. *Newsweek* commented that reaction to Collins points to an important lesson, one of "how much trust, faith, and hope the nation will invest in a teacher who holds out the simple promise, once taken for granted, of teaching kids to read." Marva once responded to the *New York Times* on her role as a model teacher: "I've never said I'm a superteacher, a miracle worker, all those names they gave me. It's unfair to expect me to live up to it. I'm just a teacher."

Sources

▶ **Books**

Tamarkin, Civia and Marva Collins, *Marva Collins' Way*, Tarcher, 1984.

▶ **Periodicals**

Black Enterprise, "Trashing Marva Collins," June, 1982, p. 46.

Essence, "Something Good Is Happening Here," October, 1981, p. 106.
Newsweek, "The Marva Collins Story," March 8, 1982, p. 64, "Report on Marva Collins," June 27, 1983, p. 13.

Mairead Corrigan and Betty Williams

"We want for our children, as we want for ourselves, our lives at home, at work and at play, to be lives of joy and peace." ("Declaration of the Peace People")

Both born in Belfast, Northern Ireland, Mairead Corrigan (January 27, 1944) and Betty Williams (May 22, 1943) are Irish peace activists and winners of the 1976 Nobel Peace Prize.

Address: Peace House, 224 Lisburn Rd., Belfast 9, Northern Ireland.

A fter years living in a Northern Ireland racked by a conflict between the Catholic Irish Republican Army (IRA) and the Protestant Ulster Defense League, Corrigan and Williams were brought together as a result of one of the region's many acts of violence. One witnessed the tragedy, the other was related to the victims; both agreed that the killing of armed combatants and innocent women and children must cease, so they joined forces in an attempt to bring an end to the violence. Their efforts, which were credited with reducing the death toll in Northern Ireland by half, earned the two a Nobel Peace Prize.

Mairead Corrigan was the second child in a family of five girls and two boys. She attended Catholic schools but was forced to leave at age fourteen because her family was unable to pay the tuition. At this time, Corrigan's desire to help people in the community first evidenced itself when she joined the Legion of Mary, a Catholic lay organization whose purpose, as she explained, was "to better the life of each individual, to teach the basic principles of Christianity, to help one have a better knowledge and a better understanding of the faith, and to help others." Her work in this organization continued through her adult years.

In her youth, Corrigan was influenced by the traditions of Catholicism, but not by the traditions of the Republicans, those factions of Northern Ireland's Catholic minority seeking to unite the province with the Republic of Ireland. "The old Republican tradition," she said, "had disappeared. Young people like myself were not interested in that sort of thing. We didn't even want to hear about it. We wanted to live our own lives." In time, her Catholic training and being revolted against the violence that was beginning to encircle her: "You can't be much of a believer if you can imagine Christ resorting to violence in response to . . . provocation," she once said.

Betty Williams was born into a family of mixed religions. Her Jewish grandfather, Catholic mother, and Protestant father taught her to turn away from bigotry. Her adolescence required her to take responsibility for the care of others; at thirteen, when her mother was debilitated by a stroke, young Betty took on the role of raising her younger sister. After attending Catholic schools and later a trade school, Williams pursued a career as a secretary but was drawn into the public arena by an event common to the streets of Belfast.

On August 10, 1976, Anne Maguire and her three children were out for a walk when they were hit by a runaway IRA car; the three children were killed. Maguire was Mairead Corrigan's sister. Corrigan took to television with her brother-in-law Jackie Maguire to condemn the violence of the IRA. In a separate action, Williams, who witnessed the tragedy, developed a petition and went door to door quickly collecting six thousand signatures; she presented the petition on television two days after the tragedy. Corrigan and Williams joined forces at the funeral of the Maguire children and decided to work for peace. At first, they called their effort Women for Peace, but soon renamed it the Community for Peace People. By the end of the first month, thirty thousand women were walking for peace. On the third march, Catholics and Protestants joined forces as allies working for peace instead of enemies waging war.

In the fall and early winter of 1976, Corrigan and Williams led tens of thousands of Belfast women on "peace marches." The marchers, especially Corrigan and Williams, were openly suspected of collaborating with the "enemy," either Catholic or Protestant; at times, they were seriously beaten and their lives threatened. But they stuck to their purpose, spreading the word of their movement through media attention and by traveling to England, New Zealand, Australia, Canada, Mexico, Germany, and the United States. Continually, they attempted to move the mountain of hatred toward peace.

These two leaders of the Peace People represent a study in contrasts. Corrigan is small and dark, "green-eyed, straight-forward, always smiling and always ready with a retort." Williams, on the other hand, is larger, louder and more ready to have an emotional response. According to Williams, she and Corrigan were called "the Saint and the Sinner." Richard Deutsch, who wrote a book about the movement, described Mairead as emanating "a spiritual quality that tends to 'electrify' crowds she is addressing," while Betty impresses initially by her outgoing and forceful personality. But regardless of their differences, they joined in their determination to put a stop to the killing in Northern Ireland.

In her work for the peace movement, Corrigan expressed her conviction that the killing would stop only after considerable reeducation. "I think one of the most important things the peace movement has to do," she said, "is to persuade the members of the different paramilitary organizations that there is a way other than with pistols and rifles. After all, those things have been tried and obviously have not worked." But she thought that conventional education and attitudes perpetuated the old hatreds. People must learn to question. "Unfortunately, we never question our educational system," she said. "We never doubt it because we're apparently incapable of stopping to examine what we say and of asking: Is this true? Is it fair? Is it valid? . . . If we stop to evaluate a lot of our old ideas and concepts, we find that they're myths, that they're false; and that bigotry has created the fear and the hatred that divides our people." One change Corrigan believed necessary involved the

Irish character; she said: ". . . People, especially young people, need compliments and admiration. We must give them a sense of their importance and dignity, and we must encourage them to use and develop all their talents."

Betty Williams could find no sense in the violence around her and turned to the peace movement to give voice to her views. "We reach a point, I think, when we can no longer remain passive, when we feel that we must do something. What changed my outlook, what made me stop and think, was the fact that I actually saw a young soldier killed before my eyes in the city. At that moment I asked myself: Are you going to keep on doing nothing, or are you going to do something?" The goal of her activism became the unification of all of Northern Ireland: "To me, since the peace movement began, all Northern Irish are the same, regardless of whether they're Catholic or Protestant. We all have the same idiosyncracies. If you scratch any of us hard enough, you'll find a certain amount of bigotry beneath the surface." To IRA calls for peace with justice, she responded: "Where was the justice in the death of a child not yet three years old? . . . All I could see was that the young men and boys of my area were becoming violent, aggressive, almost murderers; and that they were rapidly becoming the heroes of the community. Was that justice?" This violent mind-set would destroy the region, she believed, and therefore, the organization she and Corrigan headed was vital to the future of Northern Ireland: "What we're doing is absolutely necessary to save lives. . . . [The Peace People] are a very serious organization that is going to change the structures of the province." Change the structures the organization did.

For their work the two women received world-wide recognition. They were awarded the Carl von Ossietzky Prize of the Federal Republic of Germany in December 1976. They were given honorary degrees by Yale University in June 1977. In the summer of 1977 they visited Queen Elizabeth II. They went to Oslo to receive donations of $340,000 to be used for expansion of the Peace People organization. In October 1977 they were given the Nobel Peace Prize and the $140,000 which accompanied it. On April 15, 1978, Corrigan and Williams announced their resignation from the movement and their return to other ways of life. Williams eventually left Belfast for the United States. Corrigan later returned to the Peace People, an organization whose membership and influence had dwindled, to continue her efforts toward reconciling Northern Ireland's two warring sides.

Both these women demonstrate how events and cultural settings can bring forth heroic qualities in ordinary people.

Sources

▶ **Books**

Deutsch, Richard, *Mairead Corrigan/Betty Williams*, Woodbury, 1977.

▶ **Periodicals**

Christian Century, "Good News from Norway," October 26, 1977, p. 973.

Newsweek, "Two Women of Ulster," October 24, 1977, p. 61.

Time, "Two Peace Prizes from Oslo," October 24, 1977, p. 54.

U.S. News and World Report, "Is Peace in Northern Ireland Becoming Possible at Last?" October 26, 1977, p. 84.

Bill Cosby

"*I* *'m trying to reach all the people. I want to play Joe Q. Public.*"

Born July 12, 1937 in Philadelphia, Pennsylvania, Bill Cosby is an actor and comedian.

When Bill Cosby made his television debut in 1965, he was the first black actor ever to have a lead role in an American television series. The television program was *I Spy*, in which Cosby and Robert Culp co-starred as American secret agents. The civil rights movement of the 1960s was in full force, and Cosby's role in some ways legitimized the new role for blacks in America. Although his role in "I Spy" was a dramatic one, Cosby was a comedian by trade, and following the cancellation of the series he went back to comedy. In the late 1960s and 1970s, Cosby tried several comedy and variety television series with little success, although he did host a popular Saturday morning children's program entitled "Fat Albert and the Cosby Kids" beginning in 1972. In 1984, Cosby appeared in yet another comedy series, but unlike his previous efforts, this one became highly successful. Entitled simply "The Cosby Show," the program became the television ratings leader for the season, and has remained the number one program for several years since then. The huge appeal of Bill Cosby can be traced to his de-emphasis of race. He did not tell racial jokes as a comedian, and his television program deals with real people and real problems, not racially-stereotyped situations. Rising from a childhood of poverty in a Philadelphia ghetto, Cosby has transcended the imaginary boundaries of race to entertain millions of Americans in a humane and inevitably funny way.

Bill Cosby was born in an all-black ghetto area of north Philadelphia in 1937. He was the eldest of three sons. His father was a mess steward for the U.S. Navy, and his mother was a domestic worker. Cosby's mother read to her boys often, favoring passages from Mark Twain. As a child, Cosby was an excellent athlete and a would-be comedian. He was also fascinated by salesmanship, and paid close attention to the way television advertising salesmen hawked products. In school he always did well on standardized tests which purported to measure I.Q., but his grades were poor. He was always trying to make people laugh, and neglected his studies. As a student at Germantown High School in Philadelphia, he was captain of both the track team and the football team. Unfortunately, Cosby's grades were so poor that he failed the tenth grade, and rather than repeat the grade, he dropped out of school and joined the Navy.

During his four years in the Navy, Cosby was assigned to both land and sea duty at various times, and earned a high school diploma through correspondence courses. After he left the Navy, he entered Temple University in Philadelphia on a track scholarship. While at Temple, he majored in physical education and played on the track and football teams. To earn money, Cosby substituted as a comedian at nightclubs and cafes. After his junior year at Temple he quit college to pursue a fulltime career as a comedian.

Cosby's early career as a comedian was similar to the careers of many other young comics, except in the types of jokes he told. He performed in clubs around the country, sharing the stage with the likes of Woody Allen, but his humor was a gentle middle-class America humor. He did not tell racial or sexual jokes, but rather concentrated on everyday situations in familiar family contexts. In 1965 he got his big break during an appearance on the *Tonight Show*. He was spotted by producer Sheldon Leonard, and offered a part in Leonard's new television series "I Spy," which would involve the adventures of two globetrotting American secret agents travelling under the guise of a tennis pro and his trainer. Although the program was a drama, the scripts allowed the humor of both Cosby and his co-star Robert Culp to come through. The wry humor accounted for much of the program's popularity.

Cosby's casting in "I Spy" was the first time a black person had been cast in a starring role in a television series. Although Cosby offered a positive image of a black man defending America's interests, rather than a stereotypical cartoon-like caricature, he was criticized by some of the more militant members of the black movement of the 1960s as portraying a character who was too bland and unrepresentative of American blacks. Cosby's response was that "I Spy" was not a series about the problems of blacks in America, and that his portrayal of a black as a human being without regard to race was what made the program effective. For his role, Cosby received three consecutive Emmy awards as the outstanding actor in a dramatic series.

After the cancellation of "I Spy" in 1968, Cosby tried another series beginning in 1969. Entitled "The Bill Cosby Show," the program was about a physical education teacher at a Los Angeles high school. The high school was in a lower-middle class neighborhood, and the program concerned the relationships of Cosby's character with students, family, and fellow teachers. Although it achieved high ratings during its first season, it went downhill during its second season and was cancelled.

At the same time that he was starring in television series, Cosby was performing live at Las Vegas clubs and making comedy records. *Life* magazine reported in 1969 that Cosby had sold more records than any other entertainer except Herb Alpert, and that his comedy concerts netted Cosby about $50,000 per show. By the time he was in his early 30s, Cosby was a millionaire several times over.

In 1972, Cosby began another television series, a Saturday morning a program for children. Entitled "Fat Alpert and the Cosby Kids," the cartoon show featured characters based on real-life people from Cosby's childhood. In 1984, the program was still a Saturday morning staple on NBC television. Cosby also began to make a few feature films during the 1970s. His first, in 1972, was "Hickey and Boggs," in which Cosby was reunited with his old companion from "I Spy," Robert Culp. Other films followed through the years, including "Uptown Saturday Night," "Mother, Jugs, and Speed" and "Leonard Part VI." Cosby also stayed in the public eye with a seemingly endless number of commercials for various products. Many of his commercials for products such as Jell-O pudding, Coca-Cola, and Kodak film are classics, and his long-running contracts promoting the same products attest to his mastery of salesmanship.

During this time, Cosby also became interested in pursuing further education, so he enrolled in a part-time doctoral program in education at the University of Massachusetts at Amherst. Despite the fact that he did not even have a Bachelor's degree, in 1977 he received a doctoral degree in education. He was later criticized by at least one member of his doctoral committee, however, who said that Cosby attended no classes to receive the degree and received credit for life experiences including his guest appearances on television programs such as "Sesame Street" and "The Electric Company." Another professor, however, later defended Cosby's performance.

Cosby appeared in two other television series during the 1970s, but they were unsuccessful. Both were variety programs featuring Cosby and guests, and lasted only one season. In 1984, Cosby approached the major television networks about yet another series. This one was to take place in New York City, and was to be about a family similar to Cosby's real-life family. Only NBC, the perennially third-rated network, was willing to take a chance on the new program.

Entitled "The Cosby Show," the program premiered in September of 1984. It was about the Huxtable family, and was centered in a Manhattan townhouse. Cliff Huxtable (Cosby), an obstetrician and his wife Claire (Phylicia Rashad), an attorney, had five children, four girls and one boy (just like the real-life Cosby family). The program became the television ratings surprise of the season. It not only was the number one (most watched) program among all the networks, it achieved audience levels not reached by network programming for many years. An estimated 60 million Americans tuned in for "The Cosby Show" each week. The program remained extremely popular for several years, proving that it had the substance to be more than just a passing fad. The show was the number one rated program every year through 1989.

The success of "The Cosby Show" was a reflection of the gentle, humane humor of Bill Cosby. The program avoided sexual and racial humor at all costs, and tried simply to present the trials and joys of a family in America. Some critics complained that the program was a very unrealistic model for American blacks in general, but Cosby responded with his usual reply: he was trying to reach *all* the people of the world, not just blacks. The values reflected in the program were human values, and were intended to speak to human beings without regard to race.

The huge success of "The Cosby Show" provided even greater financial rewards for Bill Cosby. Syndication rights for the program set monetary records in the initial sale to local stations (for re-runs), and may eventually reach $1 billion. Cosby owns one-third of those rights. Cosby's fees for appearances and commercials are also at all-time highs.

The success of Bill Cosby can be traced not only to hard work and dedication, but to his unique vision of the values of humor and of what is funny. Rather than play to people's insecurities and fears, Cosby has always joked about the joys of life. His emphasis on family values and everyday situations which are encountered by everyone have made Cosby unusual, if not unique, among American comedians. His grand successes in books, records, concerts, and television have shown that his humor does indeed reach *all* the people.

Sources

▶ **Books**

Cosby, Bill, *Fatherhood*, Doubleday, 1986.

Cosby, Bill, *Time Flies*, Doubleday, 1987.

Haskins, James, *Bill Cosby: American's Most Famous Father*, Walker & Co., 1988.

▶ **Periodicals**

Ebony, "Raceless Bill Cosby," May, 1964, pp. 131-132.

Life, "I Am Two People, Man," April 11, 1969, pp. 74-84.

Newsweek, "Riiight," June 17, 1963, p. 89, "Color-Blind Comic," May 20, 1968, pp. 92-97, "Cosby's Fast Track," September 2, 1985, pp. 50-56.

Saturday Evening Post, "Bill Cosby: Prime Time's Favorite Father," April, 1986, pp. 42-45.

Time, September 28, 1987, "Cosby, Inc.," pp. 56-60, "I Do Believe in Control," pp. 62-64.

Norman Cousins

*''*W*e are not perfect. We may never be perfect. But I think that the desire to become better in every respect has not just anthropological but philosophical and political implications. . . . We need not worship our limitations.''*

Born June 24, 1915, in Union Hill, New Jersey, Norman Cousins is an advocate of world peace and holistic medicine, an author, and a former magazine editor.

Address: c/o U.C.L.A. School of Medicine, Slichter Hall Room 2859, Los Angeles, California 90024.

"Cousins has led a wonderful, if strangely related, series of overlapping lives," a *Publishers Weekly* interviewer once noted. "He is a complex meshing of science and letters. He is serious and silly, intellectual and maniacal." In addition to serving as longtime editor of the *Saturday Review*, Norman Cousins has been a proponent of world peace, a diplomat under three presidential administrations, and an author. While maintaining this high level of public involvement, Cousins has also triumphed in overcoming life-threatening health problems, experiences he has tapped in pursuing his latest career as a professor of medical humanities.

After serving during the late 1930s as an education editor for the *New York Evening Post* and then as a reviewer and managing editor for *Current History*, Cousins assumed the editorship of the *Saturday Review of Literature* in 1940. In his two terms as its editor (1940 to 1971 and 1973 to 1977) Cousins made the magazine his own, changing its focus from literature to American culture and current affairs and its title to the *Saturday Review*. Cousin's ability to attract respected columnists and contributors as well as his willingness to take on the controversial issues of the day earned praise from critics and increased the magazine's circulation to 650,000 at its high point.

While at the *Saturday Review*, Cousins also pursued his convictions outside the press arena. In response to the United States' atomic bombing of Hiroshima and Nagasaki, he initiated a campaign to promote world government as the best means of turning the destructive powers of atomic energy to more practical peacetime use. During the 1950s, he joined a number of organizations devoted to world peace, world government, and nuclear arms control, serving as president of the United World Federalists and international president of the World Association of World Federalists. Cousins also published two books during these years, *Who Speaks for Man?* and *In Place of Folly,* both of which further develop his ideas and helped establish him as a powerful voice in the anti-nuclear lobby.

Cousins has in recent years devoted his time to promoting research on the healing powers of laughter and other positive emotions, an interest born from his own experience with disease. In the mid-1960s, he was diagnosed as having ankylosing spondylitis, a degenerative disease that causes the breakdown of collagen, the fibrous tissue that binds together the body's cells. Almost completely paralyzed and given only a few months to live, Cousins had himself released from the hospital where he had been undergoing a battery of tests. He was moved into a hotel room and began treating himself with megadoses of vitamin C, believing that the ascorbic acid would oxygenate his blood and counteract the effects of the disease. At the same time, intent on maintaining a positive mental outlook, Cousins exposed himself to equally high doses of humor—old "Candid Camera" tapes, Marx Brothers movies, and books by P.G. Wodehouse, Robert Benchley, and James Thurber. Soon, his self-healing regimen began to take effect. At first he regained the use of his arms and legs and then, as the months saw steady improvement, he returned to work and resumed a normal life. Cousins recounts the story of his sickness and recovery in his book *Anatomy of an Illness as Perceived by the Patient.*

In 1980, Cousins suffered a near-fatal heart attack. Again, he used a positive emotional outlook and laughter to fuel his recovery. His book *The Healing Heart* offers the insights he gained in this battle to overcome heart disease. Since returning to an active life, Cousins has joined the faculty of the medical school at the University of California at Los Angeles where he pursues his research interests and lectures students on the regenerative effects of a positive mental outlook. He once said, "We are not being called upon to rearrange the planets in the sky or to alter the composition of the sun. We are called upon to make decisions affecting our own welfare. The only price we have to pay for survival is decision."

Sources
▶ **Books**

Cousins, Norman, *Who Speaks for Man?*, Macmillan, 1953.

Cousins, Norman, *In Place of Folly*, Harper, 1961.

Cousins, Norman, *Present Tense: An American Editor's Odyssey*, McGraw-Hill, 1967.

Cousins, Norman, *Anatomy of an Illness as Perceived by the Patient*, G.K. Hall, 1979.

Cousins, Norman, *The Healing Heart*, Norton, 1983.

Katz, Milton S., *Peace Heroes in Twentieth-Century America*, Indiana University Press, 1986.

▶ **Periodicals**

Mother Earth News, "The Plowboy Interview: Norman Cousins—Spokesman for the Human Race," November-December, 1984.

Newsweek, "Last Saturday Review," August 30, 1982, p. 64.

Publishers Weekly, "PW Interviews Norman Cousins," September 23, 1983, pp. 78-79.

Saturday Review, "Personal Laboratory," September/October 1983, pp. 55-57.

Francis Crick

"I came to the conclusion, first, that the self-replication of genes was important . . . although I did not realize that the genetic material was pure DNA."

Born on June 8, 1916, in Northampton, England, Francis Crick helped to discover the double helical structure of DNA, and is considered by many to be the father of molecular biology.

F rancis Crick's father was a shoe manufacturer until after World War I, when the business failed. The Crick family subsequently moved to London, where Francis attended Mill High School, concentrating on science and mathematics courses. He entered University College, London, in 1934, and received a Bachelor of Science degree in physics four years later. He remained at University College, intending to earn a doctorate in physics, but his studies were suspended when England entered World War II.

During the war Crick worked at an Admiralty Research Laboratory, helping to develop magnetic mines. While still with the Admiralty department, Crick read physicist Erwin Schroedinger's *What is Life?*, a book concerning the application of physics and chemistry principles to biological problems. He attended a lecture given by noted chemist Linus Pauling on the same subject. Crick's interests consequently turned from physics to biology, and after leaving the Admiralty in 1947, he enrolled in Cambridge University. After two years at Cambridge, Crick joined the Medical Research Council Unit at Cavendish Laboratory in Cambridge, where he planned to earn his doctorate. Soon Crick became interested in the questions surrounding deoxyribonucleic acid (DNA), the substance that controls heredity in living cells. Scientists at that time were trying to discover DNA's structure as well as the mechanism by which genetic material is duplicated during cell reproduction.

In 1951 Crick began his long association with James Watson, an American graduate student assigned to Crick's laboratory at Cavendish. Learning of their mutual interest in the structure of DNA, the two scientists began working together; by the end of the year Crick and Watson made a first attempt at a model of DNA. That first model was based on Pauling's 1950 hypothesis that DNA had a helical structure as well as on x-ray diffraction photographs taken by Maurice Wilkins and Rosalind Franklin, a pair of researchers at King's College, London. The model's three strands of matter were arranged in a helical structure, but the representation did not correspond closely enough to the x-ray images, and Crick and Watson were forced to start again.

Crick and Watson made another attempt to discover DNA's structure. The final breakthrough came when Watson was visiting Wilkins and Franklin in London and deduced from an x-ray photograph that the structure of the DNA molecule was a double helix. Watson later said, "The instant I saw the picture, my mouth fell open and my pulse began to race. The pattern was unbelievably simpler than those obtained previously . . . the black cross of reflections which dominated the picture could arise only from a helical structure." Back in their laboratory in Cambridge, Crick and Watson constructed a three-dimensional model of the molecule with a double helical structure. In March, 1953, they succeeded in correctly modeling DNA, and within a matter of days they had prepared an outline for a paper to be sent to the prestigious British science journal *Nature*. The final paper was published on April 25, 1953. Identifying the molecular structure of DNA has been ranked in importance with Darwin's theory of natural selection, Einstein's work on relativity, and the discovery of the laws of quantum mechanics. The discovery all but created the field of molecular biology—a synthesis of biology, physics, and chemistry that carries on the study of genetic inheritance and protein synthesis.

Crick and Watson clarified more than just the structure of DNA, however. In addition, they correctly hypothesized the way in which DNA passes along its code to succeeding cells. The spiral strands in the DNA molecule unwind just before the nucleus of the cell splits, and each strand then becomes the pattern for the new half of the DNA molecule. Two strands, one old and one new, then combine in the nucleus of each new cell. This theory was in many ways as significant as the discovery of the structure of DNA.

Crick continued to work on DNA through the 1950s and 1960s, unlocking several secrets of DNA coding processes, such as the importance of RNA (ribonucleic acid) in translating genetic codes into proteins. Crick also formed the hypothesis of "sequentialization," which posited, as he explained, that "the unique feature of protein synthesis is . . . that for any particular protein the amino acids must be joined up in the right order." In 1962, in recognition for their work with the DNA molecule, Crick, Watson, and Wilkins shared the Nobel prize in medicine.

Crick worked at Cambridge until 1977, when he left to join the Salk Institute in La Jolla, California. He left his research on DNA to concentrate on problems in neurobiology, the field of biology that studies the brain. One line of research he has pursued at the Salk Institute has concerned the function of dreams during sleep. Crick has hypothesized that dreams help humans throw away unimportant information to keep from becoming overloaded with too much information.

Francis Crick has earned a place among the great scientists of the 20th century for his work in several disciplines. His joint discovery of the structure of DNA and of how DNA passes on information stands as one of the towering scientific achievements of our age. His later work on DNA and RNA is only slightly less remarkable, and his research in neurobiology has been quite significant. He remains today one of the great scientific minds of our time.

Sources
▶ **Books**

Crick, Francis, *Life Itself: Its Origins and Nature,* Simon & Schuster, 1981.

Crick, Francis, *Of Molecules and Men,* Washington University Press, 1968.

Crick, Francis, *What Mad Pursuit: A Personal View of Scientific Discovery,* Basic Books, 1988.

Gribben, John, *In Search of the Double Helix,* McGraw, 1985.

Watson, James D., *The Double Helix: A Personal Account of the Discovery of the Structure of DNA,* Norton, 1980.

▶ **Periodicals**

Newsweek, "Biology's Rosetta Stone," October 29, 1962, p. 83.

Time, "Nucleic Noblemen," October 26, 1962, pp. 46-69, "Commemorating a Revolution," October 3, 1983, p. 67.

Walter Cronkite

"*I don't consider myself an entertainer or personality. I am a reporter and I am giving the viewer a front page that I hope is interesting and informative. We're giving them the news, not telling them how to think.*"

Born November 4, 1916 in St. Joseph, Missouri, Walter Cronkite is a former reporter and television anchorman.

Address: CBS News, 524 W. 57th St., New York, NY 10019.

C ronkite joined the news staff of the Columbia Broadcasting System (CBS) television network in 1950. Initially assigned as a news anchor for the CBS affiliate in Washington, D.C., he was selected to anchor the network's coverage of the 1952 political conventions. His work was critically acclaimed, and he continued to anchor political conventions and public affairs programs through the 1950s. In 1962, Cronkite became the anchorman of the *CBS Evening News*, a position which he held until his retirement in 1981. As a television journalist, Cronkite personally covered many of the important news events of the 1960s, including the Vietnam War. During the landing of the Apollo 11 capsule on the moon in 1969, Cronkite remained on the air for 24 consecutive hours. During the Watergate scandal in 1972, in which President Nixon and other administration officials attempted to cover up a break-in at the Democratic party national headquarters, Cronkite used his influence on the CBS newscasts to help bring the details of the scandal into the homes of millions of Americans.

Throughout his career, Walter Cronkite was credited with remaining a "neutral observer" in his newscasts. He believed that journalists should be as objective and unbiased as humanly possible. In 1966, *Time* magazine called him "the single most convincing and authoritative figure in TV news." In a public opinion poll taken in 1973, Cronkite easily outdistanced everyone else in the survey as the most trusted public figure in the United States.

An only child, Cronkite was born in St. Joseph, Missouri, in 1916 and moved to Houston, Texas, when he was quite young. While attending high school, he worked on the student newspaper and decided to become a journalist. After graduating from high school, Walter began attending the University of Texas at Austin.

At the university, Walter's studies included journalism and political science, and he worked part-time for a local radio station and for the Houston *Post* newspaper. He gradually became less and less motivated by his classes, however, and dropped out of the university during his junior year to work full time for the *Post*. He continued to work for the *Post* for another year, then moved to Kansas City, Missouri to take a job with a radio station KCMO. While at KCMO, Cronkite became something of a local celebrity because of his "faked" football telecasts. In those days, football games often were not broadcast live by sportscasters at the stadium, but rather were broadcast locally by announcers using Western Union teletype reports of the game. Because the announcer did not know the actual circumstances of the game, only the scores and highlights, he had to make up the remainder of the action in the game. Cronkite became very adept at "faking" the action. He got photographs of each team's players and stadium and recordings of the college bands' music to play as background during the broadcast. He even called the wives of local sports fans attending the game to find out what the fans would be wearing that day so he could pretend to recognize them during the game. His flair for creating drama made him a star in Kansas City.

In 1939, Cronkite joined United Press International (UPI) as a correspondent. During his first several years he worked in the south central United States, including assignments in Houston, Dallas, El Paso, and Kansas City. In 1941, with the beginning of the U.S. involvement in World War II, Cronkite was sent to Europe to cover the war. He witnessed first-hand many important battles, and once even used a machine gun himself to ward off German attackers. He was at the U.S. attacks on North Africa, landed with the Allies during the invasion at Normandy, and parachuted into occupied Holland with the 101st airborne division. His eyewitness accounts of the war filled the pages of newspapers in the United States.

In covering the final stages of the war, Cronkite occasionally arrived in towns in the Netherlands, Belgium, and Luxembourg before the liberating Canadian forces. Cronkite said, "I got a lot of garlands and heard a lot of welcoming speeches. The Canadians were not amused." Immediately following the war, he continued reporting from Western Europe and served for a time in Moscow. He was also a chief correspondent at the trial of German war criminals at Nuremburg. In 1948, he returned to the U.S., left UPI, and began working as the Washington correspondent for a group of radio stations. In 1950, he joined CBS, hoping to be sent to the Far East to cover the Korean Conflict. Instead, CBS assigned him to anchor television newscasts at its new station in Washington, D.C.

In the early 1950s, television was just beginning to become a news and entertainment medium. Much of the United States still could not receive television signals, particularly in the western states (except California). A "national" network program in those days really did not reach the entire nation, only those people who could receive the signal. After proving himself to CBS executives in his Washington newscasts, Cronkite began to host a number of national network programs, including *You Are There, Eyewitness to History,* and *It's News To Me.* He also hosted the first CBS morning show, launched to compete with NBC's *Today* show. In 1952, CBS chose Cronkite to anchor its political convention coverage. His coverage drew a respectable-sized audience and critical acclaim, and Cronkite was on his way to fame.

Through the 1950s, Cronkite continued to work as a correspondent for CBS, anchoring political conventions and hosting various public affairs programs. The opportunity of his career came in 1962 when CBS selected him to take over the telecasts of the *CBS Evening News*. At first 15 minutes in length, the newscasts were soon expanded to half an hour. The most-watched newscasts at this time were those of Chet Huntley and David Brinkley on NBC. Although Cronkite's newscasts trailed the Huntley-Brinkley Report in terms of audience size for the first five years, he finally overtook the formidable NBC duo in 1967.

The 1960s were a time of tremendous social change and unrest in the United States and around the world. In many ways, it was perhaps the most exciting decade to be a news correspondent. Cronkite and his world-wide, 800-person CBS news team reported on events from around the globe. Cronkite and CBS emphasized reporting rather than witty newswriting, and utilized more field reports and interviews than rival NBC (until the 1980s, ABC was never a serious rival in the evening news). Cronkite was in the anchor's chair to report on the most exciting and horrifying events of the decade. Because he took such pains to appear objective and unbiased in his reporting of the news, when Cronkite did show emotion it often affected the entire nation. In 1964, with tears in his eyes, he reported the assassination of President John F. Kennedy: "From Dallas, Texas, the flash—apparently official—President Kennedy dies—at 1 p.m. Central Standard Time. . . ." A great enthusiast for space flight, Cronkite relished his coverage of the U.S. space program. When Apollo 11 lifted off for the moon, Cronkite exclaimed what must have been on the lips of millions of Americans: "Go, baby, go!" The 1968 Democratic National Convention in Chicago was marred by riots and police brutality. Watching CBS correspondent Dan Rather as he was knocked down by security guards on the convention floor, Cronkite was moved to exclaim, "I think we've got a bunch of thugs here, Dan—if I may be permitted to say so." Cronkite, although always attempting to be objective, was honest, a trait no doubt accounting for some of his popularity with his millions of viewers. Former CBS News president Fred Friendly once said, "When the news is bad, Walter hurts. When the news embarrasses America, Walter is embarrassed. When the news is humorous, Walter smiles with understanding."

Cronkite never lost his reporter's instinct. He occasionally went into the field himself to report on an important story. In 1968, he went to Vietnam to view the war on a more intimate basis. Having seen the conflict in all its ugliness, he returned to the U.S. convinced that the American effort was hopeless and doomed. He anchored a prime-time special on CBS, during which he called for the withdrawal of American troops from Southeast Asia. *Time* magazine reported that President Johnson, who still supported the war effort, apparently turned to an aide following Cronkite's broadcast and said, "Well, if I've lost Cronkite, I've lost Middle America."

Cronkite also played an important role in bringing news of the Watergate scandal to Americans. Reporters for the *Washington Post* newspaper had first published reports of the cover-up, and Cronkite had then ordered an investigation of the incident by his CBS News staff. On October 27, 1972, Cronkite opened his evening newscast by saying, "Watergate has escalated into charges of a high-level campaign of political sabotage and espionage apparently unparalleled in American history." Broadcast historian Marvin Barrett later said that Cronkite's initial broadcasts of the cover-up "for the first time put the Watergate story clearly and substantially before millions of Americans. In broadcast terms, it was an act of considerable courage."

Cronkite continued to report the evening news for CBS throughout the 1970s. His newscast was easily the most-watched of any of the networks, and he was becoming an American institution. CBS founder William Paley called Cronkite "the stalwart kingpin of CBS News." A columnist for the *New York Daily News* wrote that Cronkite was "as solid as a mountain, as reliable as sunrise." A 1973 public opinion poll found him to be the "most trusted man in America." In 1981, Cronkite decided that he had had enough of the daily challenge of broadcasting, and announced his retirement from the job of anchorman. "The anchor man has a tremendous load," he once said. "Memory to be called on. Knowledge to be called on. A set of events to be kept in perspective. The job of taking instructions, throwing cues, watching the monitors. . . . You've got to know what you're doing now and what you're going to do next." Although retiring as anchor, he would remain with CBS News to do special programming. The American news media generally regarded Cronkite's retirement as very significant, almost as the end of an era in American history. *Time* magazine said "The Age of Cronkite Passes," and *Newsweek* reported on "TV's War After Cronkite."

While the CBS news anchorman, Cronkite had also served as host of numerous prime-time specials, reporting on various events and interviewing many world leaders. After his retirement as anchor, he hosted a limited-run science series for CBS entitled "Universe," which won critical acclaim. He also hosted several other specials for CBS, including one on Leonardo da Vinci. He is reluctant to completely retire from newscasting; perhaps it is because, as his old boss Fred Friendly put it, "he cares so deeply for the news." Cronkite himself once said, "All my life I've lucked out. I can't think of anything more fun or more worthwhile than being a reporter."

Cronkite married Mary Elizabeth Maxwell (nicknamed Betsy) in 1940, and they have three children. Throughout his career as anchor, his other consuming passion, besides journalism, was sailing. He owns a 42-foot boat named *Wyntje*, and he and Betsy have been avid sailors for many years. Cronkite continues to stay active, and now spends most of his time sailing, writing books, and speaking to various organizations around the U.S. Although he is no longer with us at the dinner hour every evening, Walter Cronkite remains a household name in America and around the world. Cronkite's popularity is perhaps best described by David Halberstam: Cronkite is "the definitive centrist American who reflects the essential decency of American society as much as anyone can."

Sources

▶ **Books**

Aaseng, Nathan, *Walter Cronkite*, Lerner Publications, 1981.

Bassow, Whitman, *The Moscow Correspondents: Reporting on Russia from the Revolution to Glasnost*, Morrow, 1988, pp. 119-120.

Jakes, John, *Great War Correspondents*, Putnam, 1967, pp. 175-188.

Metz, Robert, *CBS*, Playboy Press, 1975, pp. 346-361.

▶ **Periodicals**

Look, "The Prime Time of Walter Cronkite," March 26, 1971, pp. 50a-57.

New Republic, "And That's the Way It Seems," February 14, 1981, pp. 19-23.

Newsweek, "TV's War After Cronkite," March 9, 1981, pp. 52-58, "Walter Cronkite Still at the Helm," December 5, 1983, pp. 24-26.

Saturday Evening Post, "The Secret Life of Walter (Mitty) Cronkite," March 16, 1963, pp. 65-67.

Time, "Most Intimate Medium," October 14, 1966, pp. 56-64, "The Age of Cronkite Passes," March 9, 1981, pp. 42-43.

Vine (Victor) Deloria, Jr.

*"*I*ndians will survive because we are a people unified by our humanity, not a pressure group united for conquest."*

Born March 26, 1933, in Martin, South Dakota, Vine Deloria, Jr., is a writer, lawyer, and social activist.
Address: c/o Macmillan Co., 866 3rd Ave., New York, N.Y. 10022.

V ine Deloria, Jr., was born on the Pine Ridge Indian Reservation to the Reverend Vine Deloria and Barbara (Eastburn) Deloria. His grandfather and father were both Episcopal priests who worked in the Indian mission field. Deloria was educated in the reservation schools, at the Kent school in Connecticut, and at Iowa State University, where he got his B.S. degree in 1958. During college he also spent two years in the U.S. Marine Corps. He then went on to earn a master's degree in theology at Augustana College in Illinois in 1963.

Deloria got a job working for the United Scholarship Service developing a placement program for Indian students. He felt that high academic standards were important, and said: "It seemed to me that this was the only way for Indians to gain the white man's respect. I didn't think we should cry our way into schools, that kind of sympathy would destroy the students we were trying to help." But certain founders of the program disagreed with his standards and he left the position.

Deloria then became the director of the National Congress of American Indians in Washington, D.C. He felt his experience there was very educational: "Every conceivable problem that could occur in an Indian society was suddenly thrust at me from 315 different tribal directions. . . . There were solutions, but few could be successfully put into effect or even tried because of those who worked night and day to destroy the unity we were seeking as a people." As head of NCAI, Deloria worked with the Interior Department's Bureau of Indian Affairs to reform government policies. The Bureau had a reputation for inefficiency, and Deloria felt that the Indians should play more of a role in managing their own affairs: "We want the right to plan and program for ourselves. We want the right to talk to people as equals. We want to be free to go to all the federal departments . . . for technical help with programs we can develop ourselves." Deloria realized that he needed more knowledge of the law if he really wanted to help his people overcome their problems, and decided to attend the University of Colorado School of Law, receiving his degree in 1970.

His first book, *Custer Died for Your Sins* (1969), was aimed at younger Native Americans, addressing issues which they seemed to be unaware of; it also dealt with reasons why Indians may harbor negative feelings toward white people. Robert Mayer of *Newsday* wrote: "Deloria lives with the knowledge that the white men who settled America systematically murdered his ancestors, burned their homes, stole their cattle, confiscated their land, and herded the survivors into rural slums called reservations. He is tired of the Indians' being polite about these indiscretions, and his book is a sharp indictment of American hypocrisy . . . which helped make Indians the true forgotten Americans."

Deloria's second book, *We Talk, You Listen* (1970), deals with the return to tribalism, which he felt was already taking place in American society among small, "off-center" groups from Chicanos to hippies. His dread of the environmental crisis gave credibility to his idea that tribal organization was necessary for society to survive. He used the American Indian as an example, citing the fact that tribes lived in harmony with the natural world.

In 1973, Deloria published *God is Red*, a comparison of Indian tribal religions and Christianity. In a discussion of the creation, Deloria explains: "In the Indian tribal religions man and the rest of creation are cooperative and respectful of the task set for them by the Great Spirit. In the Christian religion both are doomed from shortly after the creation event until the end of the world."

Deloria has been a member of the Board of Inquiry on Hunger and Malnutrition in the United States and of the National Office for the Rights of the Indigent, and has worked for the Select Senate Committee on Aging. He founded the Institute for the Development of Indian Law and is working on a political history of the Sioux nation. His fourth book, *The Indian Affair*, was published in 1974.

Vine Deloria, Jr., married Barbara Nystrom, a librarian, in 1958, and they have three children. Deloria wears his hair long, is six feet tall, and is a big man at 225 pounds.

He feels that Indian tribalism may provide a good model for a solution to the problems of individual alienation and the destruction of the environment.

Sources

▶ Books

Deloria, Vine, *The Aggressions of Civilization: Federal Indian Policy Since the 1880s*, Temple University Press, 1984.

Deloria, Vine, *American Indians, American Justice*, University of Texas Press, 1983.

Deloria, Vine, *Behind the Trail of Broken Treaties*, Delacorte Press, 1974.

Deloria, Vine, *Custer Died for Your Sins*, Macmillan, 1969.

Deloria, Vine, *God Is Red*, Dell, 1975.

Walt Disney

"[T]he California Institute of the Arts, a professional school devoted to the creative and performing arts, is] the principal thing I hope to leave when I move on to greener pastures. If I can help provide a place to develop the talent of the future, I think I will have accomplished something."

Born December 5, 1901, in Chicago, Illinois, Walt Elias Disney died December 15, 1966, in Los Angeles, California. He was an animator, producer of motion pictures and television productions, and a founder of theme parks and other family entertainment enterprises.

From his beginnings as a young commercial artist experimenting with cartoon animation during the silent film era, Walt Disney developed into a visionary pioneer of the entertainment industry. First in animated cartoons, then in feature-length films and television, and eventually in amusement and theme parks, Disney's creative output became the standard for family entertainment in modern America. He combined technical innovation with a progressive outlook and a keen sense for popular tastes, serving as the force behind some of the nation's best-loved cultural icons. "The world of Walt Disney," asserted a 1983 *Esquire* profile, "is etched in the American mind almost as if we were born with it there, it is that primeval. . . . No American child born since 1940, indeed, hardly any kid anywhere the world over, has escaped Disney's influence."

Disney, the fourth child in a family of five children, was the son of a Canadian father and a mother from Ohio. Born in Chicago, Disney grew up on his uncle's farm near Marceline, Missouri, one hundred miles northeast of Kansas City. In later years he recalled the pleasure of growing up on this farm and used many of the farm animals he knew well in his animated cartoons.

Disney moved to Hollywood, with his brother and long-time associate Roy, in 1923. His first early successful creation was Mickey Mouse, who debuted in the first fully synchronized sound cartoon, "Steamboat Willie," with Disney himself supplying the voice for the mouse. Mickey was first named "Mortimer Mouse," but Disney's wife, Lillian, said "Mickey" sounded better, and Walt agreed. As Mickey, the mouse appeared in many popular cartoons that were to stimulate America's imagination and create a vast marketing empire. Toys, dolls, games, watches, clothing, comic books, toothbrushes, T-shirts, furnishings, and even automobile decorations feature the character. For years Disney feared that he would go down in history as the man who had created Mickey Mouse. "Fancy being remembered around the world for the invention of a mouse," he once complained.

But Disney's creations included far more than the "invention" of Mickey Mouse, Minnie, Goofy, and other cartoon characters. He became one of the entertainment industry's most prominent and influential figures.

At the time of his death in 1966, Disney's output amounted to 21 full-length animated films, 493 short subjects, 47 live-action features, 7 True-Life Adventure features, 330 hours of Mickey Mouse Club television programs, 78 half-hour Zorro television adventures, and 280 other television shows. His Walt Disney Productions estimated that around the world 240,000,000 people saw a Disney movie, 10,000,000 watched a Disney television show weekly, 800,000,000 read a Disney book or magazine, 50,000,000 responded to Disney music or records, 80,000,000 bought Disney-licensed merchandise, 150,000,000 read a Disney comic strip, 80,000,000 saw Disney educational films, and 6.7 million visited Disneyland in Anaheim, California.

Disney launched his own studio in Hollywood, on borrowed money, with the "Alice in Cartoonland" series, which he peddled to local theaters. From this modest beginning his studio grew dramatically. In 1932 Disney developed the first cartoon to be made in full color, "Flowers and Trees," an installment in his "Silly Symphony" series. The world's first full-length animated film, "Snow White and the Seven Dwarfs," appeared in 1937. Other important full-length animated films included "Pinocchio," 1940, "Fantasia," 1940, "Dumbo," 1941, "Bambi," 1942, "Cinderella," 1950, "Peter Pan," 1953, "Lady and the Tramp," 1955, "Sleeping Beauty," 1959, "101 Dalmatians," 1961, "The Sword and the Stone," 1963, and "The Jungle Book," 1967. Disney combined live action with animation for the first time in "The Three Caballeros," 1945, and followed it with the successful "Song of the South," 1946, and "Mary Poppins," 1964. He also produced the successful live-action films "Davy Crockett," 1954, "Old Yeller," 1957, "Pollyana," 1960, "The Absent-Minded Professor," 1961, and "Emil and the Detectives," 1964. "Walt Disney's World" was the first entry by a major Hollywood studio into television. It debuted on October 27, 1954.

Besides his many films, Disney is also remembered for introducing the theme park, an amusement park built around a central idea. His Disneyland, the world's first theme park, opened on July 18, 1955 in Anaheim, California, and features rides based on Disney film characters and settings. The idea for the park came to him years earlier. "It all started," Disney remembered, "when my daughters were very young, and I took them to amusement parks on Sunday. I sat on a bench eating peanuts and looking all around me. I said to myself, 'dammit, why can't there be a better place to take your children, where you can have fun together?' Well it took me about fifteen years to develop the idea." Disney remarked at the park's opening: "Disneyland will never be completed, as long as there is imagination left in the world." In 1971, after Disney's death, his second planned theme park, Disney World, opened in Orlando, Florida.

Disney had also dreamed of developing a city of the future, a dream realized in 1982 with the opening of EPCOT, which stands for Experimental Prototype Community of Tomorrow. EPCOT, which cost an initial $900 million, was conceived of as a real-life community of the future with the very latest in high technology. The two principal areas at EPCOT are Future World and World Showcase, both of which appeal to adults rather than children. Like Disneyland and Disney World, EPCOT is designed to grow as imagination and demands dictate. Disney Enterprises has franchised Disneylands in Tokyo and Paris.

In addition to his several theme parks, Disney created and endowed a new university, the California Institute of the Arts, known familiarly as Cal Arts. He thought of this institute as the ultimate in education for the arts, where people in many disciplines could work together, dream and develop, and create the mixture of arts needed for the future. Of this dream, Disney remarked: "It's the principal thing I hope to leave when I move on to greener pastures. If I can help provide a place to develop the talent of the future, I think I will have accomplished something."

Disney's many accomplishments earned him numerous awards. In 1939 he received an honorary Oscar; in 1954 he was given four Academy Awards; in 1964 President Lyndon Johnson presented Disney with the Presidential Medal of Freedom; and in 1965 Disney was presented the Freedom Foundation Award. At the opening of Disney World, his brother Roy remarked in his short speech: "My brother Walt and I first went into business together almost a half-century ago. And he was really, in my opinion, truly a genius—creative, with great determination, singleness of purpose, and drive; and through his entire life he was never pushed off his course or diverted to other things." Appropriately at this gathering the services ended with the carillon playing a popular song which perhaps best exemplified Disney: "When You Wish Upon a Star."

"I've always been bored with just making money," Disney once revealed. "I've wanted to do things, I wanted to build things, get something *going*." One of Disney's associates commented on his friend's talents: "Walt Disney did things that made other people do things, too, things that didn't seem possible on paper. He had a way of bringing out the best in people, of lifting them to their highest level of performance."

Sources

▶ **Books**

Leebron, Elizabeth, *Walt Disney: A Guide to References and Resources*, G. K. Hall, 1979.

Mosley, Leonard, *Disney's World: A Biography*, Stein & Day, 1985.

Schickel, Richard, *The Disney Version: The Life, Times, Art, and Commerce of Walt Disney*, Simon & Schuster, 1968.

Thomas, Bob, *Walt Disney: An American Original*, Simon & Schuster, 1976.

▶ **Periodicals**

Esquire, "Uncle Walt: Welcome to the Wonderful World of Walt Disney: Clean, Well-Lighted, and Ultimately Empty," December, 1983, pp. 164-68.

National Review, "Walt Disney, RIP," January 10, 1967, p. 12.

Newsweek, "Walt Disney (1901-1966) Imagineer of Fun," December 26, 1966, pp. 68-69.

Time, "Magic Kingdom," April 15, 1954, p. 84, "Disney's Last Dream: Epcot Center, a Toytown to Entertain and Educate," October 4, 1982, pp. 60-61, "Creatures of a Subhuman Species: Who Framed Roger Rabbit," June 27, 1988, p. 72.

Amelia Earhart

*"*I *want to do something useful in the world."*

Born July 24, 1898, in Atchison, Kansas, Amelia Earhart disappeared between July 29 and 30, 1937 near Howland Island in the Mariannas, South Pacific. She was a leading airplane pilot and adventurer.

A melia Earhart gave evidence from early childhood that she was going to live an unusual and self-directed life. She was an irrepressible tomboy who spent much of her childhood years growing up on the farm of her uncle Otis, near Atchison, Kansas. She loved to explore river caves and engage in other tomboy activities, such as playing football, baseball, basketball and other sports that required great amounts of physical energy. She was also willful and stubborn. When asked by her parents why she persisted in doing the things she did, she responded: "Because I want to." Later she was the first to admit that she had been something of a problem as a child: "I was a horrid little girl," she often said. Earhart was inventive, original and determined. She liked house painting, metal working, disassemblying mechanical gadgets and flying airplanes. And she loved school. As she said later: "Like many horrid children I loved school, though I never qualified as teacher's pet. Perhaps the fact that I was exceedingly fond of reading made me endurable. With a large library to browse in, I spent many hours not bothering anyone after I once learned to read."

Throughout life Earhart believed firmly in the benefits of sports activities: "Exercise of all kinds gave me intense pleasure," she said, but also stated, "I might have been more skillful and graceful if I had learned the correct form in athletics. I could not get any instruction so I just played and acquired a lot of bad habits."

She first tried flying by constructing a roller coaster out of planks. It turned over and nearly injured her. But she gathered herself together and reassembled her flying machine. On July 24, 1907, her ninth birthday, she moved with her family to Des Moines and saw her first airplane. However she was not terribly impressed with the contraption.

Earhart also possessed an idealism that made her want to serve humankind. In 1917, during World War I she was in Toronto, Canada, and saw the effects of the war on Canadians and Americans. She felt that she should become a nurse's aid and contribute to the war effort. "I want to do something useful in the world," she said, and determined to leave high school in order to serve people. She never did finish high school.

While in Toronto, Earhart watched soldiers training in airplanes and her intense interest in flying rekindled. In 1920, at age twenty-two, she took her first dramatic step toward developing this passion. While in California she took a flight in a plane and told her father that she wanted to learn to fly. He reluctantly allowed her to take lessons.

As she learned she advanced slowly but thoroughly. She seemed to lack the keenness for airplanes that she had shown for other machines, but once she seized the principles of flight, she developed her knowledge. When Earhart made her first solo flight she had difficulty in landing and had an embarrassing and bumpy set-down. But more than embarrassed, she was proud of herself for not having been afraid. Pride in her own courage and a desire for accomplishment characterized her actions in the air and on the ground thereafter.

As a pilot her accomplishments were dramatic and her fame constantly growing. On June 17, 1928 she became the first woman passenger to fly across the Atlantic Ocean. On July 6, 1930 she set the woman's speed record in an airplane, 181.18 miles per hour. On May 20-21, 1932 she became the first woman to fly solo across the Atlantic, and on August 24-25 of the same year she set the woman's non-stop transcontinental speed record by flying from Los Angeles, California to Newark, New Jersey.

In 1934, when she was thirty-six, Earhart, or AE as she was generally called, was the first speaker at a conference in New York City sponsored by the *New York Herald Tribune* called "Women and the Changing World." Earhart was introduced as "evidence against a 'lost generation'," which was the term used by intellectuals of the time for the preceding generation. The man who introduced Earhart said: "I remind you that no generation which could produce Amelia Earhart can be called a lost generation. She has set a pace for those of her age and time. She has never been content to rest on her laurels. She has worked, and is working, and will continue to work hard to further the science to which she has dedicated her life."

Earhart's response to this introduction indicated that she was interested in far more than furthering science, though that was one of her major concerns: "It is true that there are no more geographical frontiers to push back, no new lands flowing with milk and honey this side of the moon to promise surcease from man-made ills. But there are economic, political, scientific, and artistic frontiers of the most exciting sort awaiting faith and the spirit of adventure to discover them."

She then broadened her approach to include economics and the younger generation: "For the economic structure we have built up is all too often a barrier between the world's work and the workers," she said. "If the younger generation finds the hurdle too absurdly high, I hope it will not hesitate to tear it down and substitute a social order in which the desire to work and learn carries with it the opportunity to do so."

After the speech Amelia was offered a professorship at Purdue University. She accepted the offer and was introduced to the faculty as one who "better than any other young woman of this generation (represents) the spirit and courageous skill of what may be called the new pioneering."

With her usual enthusiasm and thoroughness, Amelia surveyed the eight hundred female students at Purdue and learned that 92% of them wanted to be productive workers after graduation. In numerous talks with groups of students she advised: "After all, times are changing and women need the critical stimulus of competition outside the home. A girl must nowaways believe completely in herself as an individual. She must realize at the outset that a woman must do the same job better than a man to get as much credit for it. She must be aware of the various discriminations, both legal and traditional, against women in the business world." To Earhart work was fun and "fun is the indispensable part of work."

Earhart was a reluctant realist who understood the harzards of continual flying. Once after a very narrow escape from death she remarked: "Someday I will get bumped off. There's so much to do, so much fun here; I don't want to go. But when I do go, I'd like to go in my plane. Quickly." On another occasion she said: "The time to worry is three months before a flight. Decide then whether or not the goal is worth the risks involved. If it is, stop worrying. To worry is to add another hazard. It retards reactions, makes one unfit."

One of her desires was to fly around the world at the Equator from west to east because it had not been done. In commenting on this proposed flight she said to her husband, George Putnam: "I've weighed it all carefully, [and] with it behind me, life will be fuller and richer. I can be content. Afterwards it will be fun to grow old."

But growing old was not to be her fate.

On July 3, 1937 she began her unprecedented flight. She had chosen for her navigator a man named Fred Noonan, who had proven several times that his ability as a navigator was questionable. Earhart knew very well that a slight error in navigation when her goal was a continent could be a nuisance but was correctable. But when her destination was a small island in the Pacific Ocean a small error could prove fatal. Still, she believed in Noonan and in herself to correct any errors.

Sometime between July 29 and 30, her plane was headed from New Guinea to tiny Howland Island. She could not find the island, and in searching for it was lost at sea. The U.S. ship *Itasca* monitored her flight and her efforts to find the island. The ship could hear her and in return broadcast directions as to her location and where she could find land. But technical troubles plagued the communication, and she never heard the instructions. Her last words recorded by the *Itasca* were frantic but professional, as she continued to search the airwaves for directions of where and how to land.

Ships from the U.S. Navy continued for days to search the seas for her or for wreckage of the plane. Nothing was ever found. Criticism of the efforts to locate her abounded. Rumors that her loss at sea was a hoax and that she and her navigator had simply run off together were numerous, and distressed her husband.

Another story grew up which seemed to be possible. Extended inquiry unearthed that a tall blonde woman and a large blond man—which described Earhart and Noonan—had landed in a plane similar to theirs in the Marianas, near Saipan, and that the two were apprehended by Japanese soldiers and executed on the spot.

Thus, one of America's most famous aviators ended her life shrouded in mystery. She had been appreciated by the whole American community. She had received at least forty-four medals of all kinds, including the Lindbergh medal in 1928, and the American National Geographic Society Award medal, which had been presented by President Herbert Hoover in 1932.

Amelia Earhart, whose life had demanded great personal courage, once wrote a poem on the subject:

Courage is the price that Life exacts for granting peace.
The soul that knows it not
Knows no release from little things:
Knows not the livid loneliness of fear,
Nor mountain heights where bitter joy can hear
the sound of wings.

Nor can life grant us boon of living, compensate
For dull gray ugliness and pregnant hate
Unless we dare
The soul's dominion. Each time we make a choice, we pay
With courage to behold the resistless day,
And count it fair.

The poem stands as a fitting memorial to a courageous and daring woman.

Sources
▶ **Books**

Briand, Paul L., *Daughter of the Sky: The Story of Amelia Earhart*, Pyramid, 1967.

Burke, John, *Winged Legend: The Story of Amelia Earhart*, Putnam, 1970.

Earhart, Amelia, *Last Flight*, Harcourt Brace, 1965.

Earhart, Amelia, *The Fun of It: Random Records of My Own Flying and of Women in Aviation*, Gale, 1975.

Goerner, Fred G., *The Search for Amelia Earhart*, Doubleday, 1966.

▶ **Periodicals**

Commonweal, "Appreciation," July 30, 1937, P. 326.

Indiana Woman, "Memorial: Amelia Earhart Foundation," April, 1938, p.110.

Newsweek, "Warships and Planes Sweep Pacific for Lost Flyers," June 17, 1937, p. 25.

Time, "Lost Earhart", July 12, 1937, pp. 50-1, "One in a Million", July 19, 1937, pp. 45-6, "Search Abandoned," July 26, 1937, p. 36.

Jaime Escalante

"Calculus need not be made easy—it is easy already."

Born in 1931 in Bolivia, Jaime Escalante transformed the lives of thousands of disadvantaged California high school students with his inspiring, no-nonsense teaching methods.

I n May 1982, eighteen students from Garfield High School in East Los Angeles passed an advanced placement calculus exam as part of their college entrance requirements. Their achievement was exceptional as Garfield High School was then known for its gangs, drug use, and bottom-of-the-barrel academic standards. The driving force behind the students was Jaime Escalante, a teacher who would not allow the kids to languish below their potential. His gritty, understated style of teaching is motivated by his desire to inspire pride in his students, young people whose typical day generally revolves around their struggle against poverty and self-contempt. Escalante's achievements—or rather, the achievements of his students—caught the attention of the nation in 1988 when a popular movie was made about his teaching, and when President Ronald Reagan called him a hero on national television.

Escalante began teaching calculus in La Paz, Bolivia, in 1964, when political strife in that country prompted him and his wife, Fabiola, to take their son Jaime, Jr., and to flee the country. "It was my wife who insisted we leave Bolivia," Escalante said. "She said, 'In America is everything you need.'" The Escalantes were granted permission to immigrate to the United States. However, Escalante spoke no English, and his teaching credentials were of no value in Pasadena, California, where he and his family settled. While working in a coffee shop, Escalante taught himself English, and then landed a job in the parts department at the Burroughs Corporation.

But Escalante was not satisfied; teaching was his passion. For seven years he spent nights earning a math degree from California State University and in 1974 he found a job at Garfield High School. On the first day of teaching, Escalante knew the students were in trouble. "They were using their fingers adding stuff at the board," he said. "They came in without supplies, with nothing. Total chaos." In his usually intriguing way, Escalante skipped the lecturing, donned an apron and a chef's hat, set an apple on his desk, withdrew a meat cleaver from his bag, smiled, and chopped the apple in half. "Let's talk about percentages," he said. No one in the room said a word.

Escalante said he was at first frightened by the tough kids. "But then I started to get some feedback. They started to call me Kemo, short for Kemo Sabe (Tonto's nickname for the Lone Ranger), the man who knows. I knew I was going to stay." In 1979 he held his first calculus class. Only five students attended. Four of them passed the advanced placement test, "and I felt great," Escalante said. The next two years were similarly successful for Escalante and his students. But in 1982, Escalante suffered a minor heart attack, and fourteen of his eighteen calculus students were accused of cheating on the advanced placement test. Because their errors appeared suspiciously similar, they would have to take a new, more difficult test or have their scores invalidated. Escalante was angry, but his students were determined. Twelve took the test (two others began working and opted to not go to college), and all twelve passed.

The incident received much local publicity and caught the attention of film producer Tom Musca and director Ramon Mendenez. The two believed that the students' scores would never have been questioned if they were not predominantly Hispanic and from the ill-reputed Garfield High School. Mendez and Musca approached Escalante about making a movie of his triumphs. "Go ahead and write it," he told them, "but I really don't have much time to deal with you." Later, he was more cooperative, and allowed Edward James Olmos, who played Escalante in the movie, "Stand and Deliver," to spend eighteen hours a day with him for a month.

Escalante begins his classes with cheerleading to the tune of a pop song, and decorates his classroom with signs with such messages as "Ganas," which means desire, passion, and guts—one of Escalante's favorite words. "You just have to know how to motivate these kids," he says. Unwavering discipline leavened with humor is his style; if a student's attention wanders, he or she gets pelted with a little red pillow. If someone is tardy, he is relegated to a chair built for kindergarteners. "It embarrasses them," Escalante said. "They also don't come into class late anymore." He also gives his students encouragement. "I tell them, 'You are the best, you are our hope for the future; remember that.'" Escalante fought for money to provide decent breakfasts and summer scholarships to his students, and he won. His classes have been referred to as intellectual boot camps, with students eagerly volunteering to join the ranks.

The gangs and drugs are now gone from Garfield High, and the grounds are well kept. Thanks to Escalante, the school's administration—and teachers nationwide—have renewed vigor for their mission. Today, although only 2 percent of America's high school seniors attempt the grueling math test for advanced placement, all of Escalante's kids take it—and roughly 80 percent pass.

Sources

▶ **Books**

Matthews, Jay, *Escalante: The Best Teacher in America*, Holt, 1988.

▶ **Periodicals**

Mother Jones, "Reel Life," April, 1988, pp. 24-26.
People, "Beating Long Odds. . . ," April 11, 1988, pp. 57-58.

Medgar Wiley Evers

"T he things I don't like, I will try to change."

Born July 2, 1925, on a farm near Decatur, Mississippi, civil rights activist Medgar Wiley Evers died in Jackson, Mississippi, June 12, 1963.

Medgar Evers was one of six or seven children born to James and Jessie Evers on a farm outside Decatur, Mississippi. Medgar's most notable sibling was James Charles Evers (1923-), also a civil rights activist.

Medgar grew up in Senator Theodore Bilbo's Mississippi, where violence was always just one insult away. Like his father, who would not let whites intimidate him, Medgar, constantly resisted limitations based on race. After his junior year in a high school in nearby Newton, Medgar started going to Chicago in the summer to make money, and enjoyed the freedom that came with living in that city. During World War II Medgar volunteered and served in France in a segregated battalion.

After the war, Medgar and his brother Charles enrolled in Alcorn College in Mississippi. There he majored in business administration and was active in student affairs. He was a strong debater, sang in the choir, played football and ran track, and edited the campus newspaper. As a senior he was chosen for *Who's Who in American Colleges.*

After graduation, Medgar settled in Philadelphia, Mississippi, and sold insurance around Clarksdale. In this work he talked with poor black farmers, saw how they suffered under racial discrimination, and became increasingly frustrated. He heard about Jomo Kenyatta, the leader of the Mau Mau in Kenya, Africa, and wanted to start a similar political organization in Mississippi.

In 1953 Medgar volunteered to be the first Negro to attempt to enroll at the University of Mississippi. When his application was rejected, he decided to drop the application. Beginning to work quietly for civil rights, Medgar increased his tempo and by 1954 moved to Jackson, where he worked furiously to organize the blacks. As the first field secretary of the National Association for the Advancement of Colored People (NAACP), he traveled throughout the state signing up Negroes and organizing voter-registration drives and economic boycotts. Medgar raged over the way black members of the NAACP were harassed with the threat of violence and economic pressure. He was especially infuriated at the practice of sex between white men and black women. His wife said: "Medgar felt the deprivation of every Negro as though it were his own. He suffered with every Negro whose suffering he knew."

The murder of Emmett Till and the dumping of his body into the Tallahatchie River became a cause and rallying point for increased black activity in Mississippi. As secretary of the Mississippi NAACP, Medgar urged blacks to exert whatever strength they could against the prevailing social system. He insisted that if the whites cut off financial credit, the blacks should buy only from Negroes. Tension throughout the state grew during the early 1960s. Such civil rights groups as the Student Non-Violent Coordinating Committee (SNCC), Congress of Racial Equality (CORE), and the Southern Christian Leadership Conference (SCLC) were bringing pressures on every front.

Medgar knew of likely violence that might be done to him; he had talked it over with his wife. On June 12, 1963, President John F. Kennedy spoke to the nation on civil rights and his determination to enforce them.

A few hours later, Medgar was returning home and was murdered on his own front porch. The murder brought him into the national spotlight. He was buried with full military honors in Arlington National Cemetery and was awarded the 1963 Spingar Medal of the NAACP. Subsequently The Medgar Evers College of the City University of New York was named in his honor.

Like many other blacks who had grown up in the South, Medgar loved his state and wanted to improve racial conditions there so that he could live in the part of the country he loved. "This is my home. Mississippi is a part of the United States," he said, "and whether the whites like it or not, I don't plan to live here as a parasite. The things I don't like, I will try to change." Once he told an *Ebony* Magazine reporter: "I love the South. I don't choose to live anywhere else. . . . There is room here for my children to play, and grow, and become good citizens—if the white men will let them."

Though Medgar became a victim of the civil rights struggles in the South and throughout the United States, his rage over racial injustices was a part of the larger movement that eventually brought change to the Mississippi that he loved. A life-size bronze statue memorializing Evers was scheduled to be unveiled in Jackson, Mississippi, in 1990.

Sources

▶ **Books**

Evers, Mrs. Medgar, *For Us the Living*, Ace Books, 1970.

▶ **Periodicals**

Life, "Trail of Blood; A Negro Dies," June 21, 1963, pp. 28-29, "Martyr to an Immoral System," June 28, 1963, p. 4, "Negroes Walk to Freedom; Murder Lies on a Nation's Conscience," July 6, 1963, pp. 32-33.

Newsweek, "End and a Beginning," June 24, 1963, pp. 32-33.

Time, "Life and Death in Jackson," June 21, 1963, pp. 17-18.

Betty Ford

"Y ou never know what you can do until you have to do it."

Born April 8, 1918, in Chicago, Illinois, Betty Ford is a former First Lady and founder of a substance abuse clinic.
Present address: Rancho Mirage, CA 92270.

Ford was born Elizabeth Ann Bloomer, the daughter of Hortense Neahr and William Stephenson Bloomer. When she was two years old, her family moved from Chicago to Grand Rapids, Michigan, where Ford and her two older brothers, Bill and Robert, grew up. As a child Ford aspired to be a dancer. "Dance was my happiness," she recalled. In her late teens she had the "ecstasy of being able to dance eight hours a day." To her, "modern dancing was exhilirating, it was release, it was the freedom to be able to express [herself] through her body." For a time, Ford studied dance with Martha Graham in New York City.

Ford married William Warren in 1942 and, before bearing children, divorced him when she was twenty-nine years old. On October 15, 1948, she married Gerald R. Ford, with whom she bore four children, Mike, Jack, Susan, and Steve. Active in her children's affairs, Ford served as a den mother, Sunday school teacher, and neighborhood baby-sitter. When she and Gerald—then a U.S. Representative—moved to Washington, D.C., Ford became friendly with Jacqueline Kennedy and Lady Bird Johnson.

At age forty-six Ford pinched a nerve in her back, and according to her, "looked like an old woman of ninety, a crippled old woman." Ford, however, was determined to overcome her ailment. "I made up my mind I wasn't going to go that way," she declared and subsequently became active with Republican wives and other politicians.

As time passed, though, Ford began to feel abandoned by her husband, whose job required much travel, and unneeded by her children, who were growing older. Ford consequently suffered a nervous breakdown. Again conquering disability, Ford recovered, and in 1969 she and Betty Vanik, wife of Ohio Congressman Charles Vanik, talked Westinghouse into underwriting forty half-hour programs concerning the three branches of the Federal Government.

When husband Gerald was appointed Vice President of the United States under President Richard M. Nixon in 1973, Ford was dismayed. "If I had known what was coming," she said later, "I think I would have sat right down and cried." Although the wife of the Vice President did not like to talk in public about politics, Ford earned a reputation to always being candid. After Gerald became President in 1974—following the resignation of Nixon—Ford, as First Lady, continued to do things her way. "I figured, okay, I'll move to the White House," she recalled, "do the best I can, and if they don't like it, they can kick me out. But they can't make me be somebody I'm not."

When asked if she changed while responding to the challenges of the White House, Ford replied, "I still believe in God and country. I'm still against the exploitation of children—and other forms of pornography—and while I hope I never get too old to learn and grow, I think it wasn't so much that the White House altered me in any essential way as that I found the resources with which to respond to a series of challenges. You never know what you can do until you have to do it."

During her time in the White House, Ford was most concerned with the Equal Rights Amendment, mental health, child abuse, and abuse of the elderly, and she urged her husband to appoint a woman to the U.S. Supreme Court. She created a furor on the CBS television program "60 Minutes" when she admitted she was in favor of abortion and was not sure whether drugs—especially marijuana—should be outlawed, though she was sure it was a "sin" to introduce children to drugs.

Although strong in her political stances, Ford was consistently weakened by health problems. Shortly after becoming First Lady, Ford discovered that she had cancer and would lose one breast. Surmounting depression, she was out of the hospital in two weeks and resumed her duties as First Lady. Ford, however, continued to suffer from other health problems, including arthritis and muscle spasms, and had subsequently grown accustomed to taking various medications. In addition, she began to lose her tolerance for alcohol.

At the age of sixty, Ford's tolerance finally broke, and she voluntarily checked in to the Long Beach Alcohol and Drug Rehabilitation hospital for a drinking problem. She chose to make her problem known to the public, hoping to serve as an inspiration to others in similar states.

Ford was cured. In her autobiography relating her problem and its treatment, she wrote: "I've learned a lot about myself. Most of it is all right. When I add up the pluses and subtract the minuses, I still come out pretty well." About her future, she said: "As I continue to study and learn and work toward an aware future, I'm sure more will be revealed to me, and I'm looking forward to that. Stubborn Betty Bloomer Ford intends to make it." In 1982 Ford founded the Betty Ford Center, an alcohol and drug rehabilitation unit in Rancho Mirage, California.

Although out of the White House for a long time, Ford continues to be a fondly remembered First Lady, one who was always frank in her opinions and determined to be herself. Renowned for her courage, Ford has earned a reputation for helping other face adversity.

Sources
 Books

Caroli, Betty Boyd, *First Ladies*, Oxford University Press, 1987.
Ford, Betty, *The Times of My Life*, Harper, 1979.

Ford, Betty, with Chris Chase, *Betty: A Glad Awakening*, Doubleday, 1987.

Weidenfeld, Sheila Rabb, *First Lady's Lady*, Putnam, 1979.

▶ **Periodicals**

Good Housekeeping, "Betty Ford's Secret Strength," September, 1978, p. 84, "Betty Ford: A Lesson in Caring," September, 1978, p. 108.

Ladies Home Journal, "Betty Ford: Finding Courage in Pain," January, 1981, p. 42, "Betty Ford's Brave Mission," June, 1987, p. 80.

Newsweek, "Prisoners of Pills," April 11, 1978, p. 77.

People, "Frank as Ever: Former First Lady Betty Ford Describes Her Harrowing Years of Addiction," March 9, 1987, pp. 88-93.

Time, "Betty's Ordeal," April 24, 1978, p. 31, "Unveiling of a New Ford," October 23, 1978, p. 87.

Dian Fossey

"I had this great urge, this need to go to Africa. I had it the day I was born. Some may call it destiny. My parents and friends called it dismaying. I call it fortuitous."

Born January 16, 1932, in San Francisco, California, Dian Fossey was murdered December 17, 1986, in Rwanda, Africa. She was a scientist known for her passionate defense of mountain gorillas, described in her book *Gorillas in the Mist*.

A frica in the early 1960s was a place of great political upheaval, with many new nations achieving independence from European colonial powers and suffering from burgeoning populations, both of which were putting great pressure on large numbers of animal species. One of these species discovered by Europeans in the early 1900s is the mountain gorilla, an animal whose habitat had already been reduced to a few volcanic peaks in the Central African countries of Zaire, Uganda, and Rwanda. Into this precarious situation Dian Fossey, a former occupational therapist, inserted herself in 1966 when she made her second trip to Central Africa, this time to study the mountain gorillas on a long-term basis. Her first objective was to gain the acceptance of the gorillas in order to study them closely. Later, she became involved in the struggle for the gorillas' survival, fighting to protect them from poachers and bringing their plight to international attention.

Fossey received her bachelor's degree in 1954 from San Jose State College (now University), where she was a prize-winning equestrienne. She then moved to Kentucky to work as a occupational therapist at a children's hospital in Louisville. During all this time, Fossey never lost a childhood desire to see Africa.

Thinking that "dreams seldom materialize on their own", Fossey took out a three year bank loan in 1963 to travel to Tanzania to visit Dr. Louis Leakey, and to Zaire to see the mountain gorillas. At Leakey's camp she cracked her ankle running down a hill, yet two weeks after leaving their camp she was climbing the mountains in Zaire to the gorillas' habitat. She first met them on the volcanic slopes, and knew one day she would return. About her first encounter with a gorilla she said: "Sound preceded sight. Odor preceded sound in the form of an overwhelming musky-barnyard, human-like scent. The air was suddenly rent by a high-pitched series of screams followed by the rhythmic rondo of sharp *pok-pok* chestbeats from a great silverback male."

Fossey's determination to return to study the gorillas persisted. On the advice of Leakey she had her healthy appendix removed. Telling her that anyone serious about African research should do so, he later told her it was just a test of her determination. In 1966, with Leakey's help and some monetary backing from Leighton Wilkie, who also financed Jane Goodall's research on chimpanzees, Fossey was on her way back to Africa to carry on a long-term study of the mountain gorillas. It took a long time for Fossey to even be able to approach the gorillas. They are by nature very shy and defensive. Initially she had to pretend to eat foliage to gain their trust. She also made some errors. "For a number of months I imitated the gorillas' chestbeats by slapping my hands against my thighs in studious mimicry of their rhythm. The sound was an instant success in gaining the gorillas' attention. I thought I was very clever but did not realize I was conveying the wrong information. Chestbeating is the gorillas signal for excitement or alarm. . . ." At one point she was charged by five male gorillas, and had to kneel motionless on the ground for thirty minutes before the gorillas would leave.

After about a year in Zaire, Fossey was taken into custody by soldiers during a political military uprising. Using a ruse that she had to go to Uganda to get money to transfer her car registration to Zaire, she escaped from her drunken guards with two chickens, a pistol, and a Land Rover. She learned that she would be shot on sight if she returned to Zaire. After lengthy discussions with the American Embassy in Nairobi, Kenya, Fossey was finally allowed to return to the gorillas. She went to Rwanda and set up the Karisoke Research Center in the Virunga volcano range where she was scientific director from 1967 to 1980, and endured great solitude, discomfort, and hardship. The natives called her *Nyiramachabelli,* "the old lady who lives in the forest without a man."

In 1967 the Parc des Volcans in Rwanda had only a dozen guards. Fossey constantly fought against the poaching of gorillas, antelope, and other animals by cutting traplines and releasing animals. She also spent much time clearing the area of illegal cattle which were destroying gorilla habitat. Because of her efforts she was the target of black magic (*sumu*) practiced by the poachers. Pressure on the gorillas' habitat also came from the legitimate needs of the Rwandese people. The most densely populated country in Africa, and one of the world's poorest, the government reduced the park's area to allow for cattle grazing and agricultural needs. Fossey not only had to battle poachers, who would kill a dozen adult gorillas to capture one baby, but trophy hunters, government officials, and even game wardens, who once killed eighteen adults to capture two infants to sell to a German zoo.

While at Karisoke Fossey studied fifty-one gorillas in four relatively stable groups. She found them amiable and family-oriented, curious and gentle. With strong kinship bonds, they lived in units of about fifteen to twenty with one dominant male (silverback). They were generally peaceful but would fight if threatened, and especially to protect an infant. She reported that each gorilla had an individual personality and facial characteristics. Taking fifteen years to mature, the silverback could also be remarkably gentle, as in releasing other gorillas from snares. Fossey identified fifteen sounds that the gorillas made, including chuckling, grunting, and growling. She also experienced many poignant moments with the gorillas, as when the one she named Peanuts became the first ever to touch her. Another was when Coco, orphaned by poachers, climbed on the bench in Fossey's cabin, looked out the window to the forest, and began to sob.

Though the Karisoke Research Center grew from two tents to eight cabins, the gorilla population was decreasing. From 1960 to 1980 the population was cut in half to an estimated 242 animals. Fossey lamented that the gorilla "may be doomed to extinction in the same century in which it had been discovered." Poachers were partly to blame for the decrease in the gorillas population, and it was a great blow to Fossey when several of her favorite animals were killed. To publicize the plight of the gorillas Fossey worked with *National Geographic* magazine, and wrote a book called *Gorillas in the Mist*. One reviewer remarked that she "designed this book with one purpose foremost: understanding, conservation and survival of her study subjects." Another stated that Fossey had disproved the "King Kong" mythology, showing the gorillas are "a less complicated version of ourselves."

The world was shocked when Fossey was found murdered in her camp on December 27, 1987. The government of Rwanda charged Fossey's assistant, Wayne McGuire, with the crime, but many people suspected that poachers were actually responsible. Fossey was buried in the graveyard that she had established for the victimized gorillas.

In 1988, actress Sigourney Weaver portrayed Fossey in the film "Gorillas in the Mist," a dramatization of the scientist's life and work.

Sources

▶ **Books**

Fossey, Dian, *Gorillas in the Mist*, Houghton, 1983.

▶ **Periodicals**

Chicago Tribune, October 3, 1983, p. 15.

Los Angeles Times Book Review, October 16, 1983.

Newsweek, "Inside a Vanishing Kingdom," August 29, 1983, p. 61.

New York Times Book Review, "A Less Complicated Version of Ourselves," September 4, 1983, pp. 2, 15.

Science Digest, "Close Encounters with the Great Apes," August, 1983, pp. 66-71, 105-106.

Time, "Under the Volcanoes," August 15, 1983, p. 60.

Terry Fox

"Life doesn't mean money. It doesn't mean success. It just means doing things as well as you can without worrying about anything else."

Born July 28, 1958, in Winnipeg, Manitoba, Terry Fox was a long-distance runner and cancer research fund raiser who died of cancer June 28, 1981, in New Westminster, British Columbia.

T erry Fox, the second child in a family of four children, was raised in the British Columbia town of Port Coquitlam. Terry was sports-minded from an early age, playing road hockey with his father, brothers, and neighborhood kids, and he began running in high school, excelling in the longer cross-country distances. He abandoned running in his last two years of high school, however, opting instead for soccer and basketball. Upon graduating from Port Coquitlam Senior Secondary, Terry shared the school's Male Athlete of the Year Award with his best friend, Doug Alward.

Fox entered Simon Fraser University in the fall of 1976, majoring in kinesiology, the study of the mechanics of body movement. He also earned a spot on the university's junior varsity basketball team. While playing for the team, Terry developed knee problems, which he thought were due to SFU's hard playing surface. He was given pain killers, but his discomfort increased. Fox noted that one day, "I came home and all of a sudden the pain in my knee was getting worse again. The next morning, I woke up and that was it. I couldn't walk or put any weight on the leg." That morning, Terry and his father went to the Royal Columbian Hospital where it was discovered that Terry suffered from osteogenic sarcoma—primary cancer of the bone. As a result, his right leg had to be amputated above the knee.

Terry was determined to continue a normal life after the operation. After learning of the measures necessary to save his life, as Stan Shatenstein described in *Runner's World*, Terry "understood, he cried and then he prepared himself emotionally and mentally so that life after the operation would resemble, as much as humanly possible, life as it had been before." He completed his first-year university studies while recuperating in the hospital, and he was taking courses on campus the next fall. Two months after the amputation, he was playing 18 holes of golf, then 27. Despite continued chemotherapy treatments, he became manager of his old basketball team and played on a wheelchair squad himself.

While Terry was still in the hospital, his high school basketball coach had given him an article about Dick Traum, an amputee who had run the New York City Marathon. It was then that Terry had first thought of running across Canada to collect donations to combat cancer. At first it was just a fantasy, but as time wore on he took the idea more seriously. When his chemotherapy treatments ended in early 1979, he started training for the journey. The first day he tried to run a quarter-mile. "It was pouring down rain that first day, and the track was covered in mud. My back was sore and my knee was sore, and I really felt, 'How am I ever going to run even half a mile, let alone across Canada?'" But he persisted. The next day he ran half a mile, and by the end of the summer he was running 11 miles a day, six days a week.

That September Terry entered a 17-mile race in Prince George, British Columbia. Though he finished last, it took him only three hours and nine minutes to complete the race, finishing only 10 minutes behind the last two-legged runner. Now he was more determined than ever to run from one coast of Canada to the other. He approached the Canadian Cancer Society for support, and though they approved his fund-raising plans, Fox had to line up his own sponsors. While he did that, he continued to build his stamina, working up to twenty miles a day. It was no meager feat—"At times I had shin splints, bone bruises and swelling in my foot. I lost toenails, I had chafing and sometimes my stump was bleeding. I went through bad weather and snow, and every day I completed the mileage; I didn't miss a day. I knew then that if I could do it in training, I could do it when it counted."

By the beginning of 1980, Terry felt he was ready for his transcontinental marathon, which he labelled "The Marathon of Hope." On April 12 of that year he dipped his artificial right leg into the Atlantic Ocean and began his journey. The early going was not easy. On the fourth day, it snowed heavily and the roads were so icy he had to stop, but then the weather improved and he was able to make 16 miles that day. He continued through the eastern portion of Canada at an average pace of 24 miles a day. To be able to complete such distances he had to rise at 4 o'clock every morning and be on the road by five.

Then, on the Thunder Bay bypass headed for the Red River Road in Northern Ontario, the runner's quest came to a sudden halt. Terry hadn't been feeling well for the previous two or three days, but he wasn't about to quit. While running that final day, Terry recalled, "There was hardness of breath. I was coughing. I started to choke, I didn't know what was going on." Even though he experienced extreme pain, he kept on running. There were people lined up alongside the road ahead of him and he didn't want to stop until they could no longer see him. "There was no way I going to stop running, not with all those people there."

After completing one final mile, Terry was taken to the Port Arthur General Hospital in Thunder Bay, Ontario, where he was diagnosed as having tumors in both lungs; his cancer was no longer in remission. Although the Marathon of Hope had ended after four months and 3339 miles, the process Terry started continued. He received thousands of letters every day, some from children who donated every penny they had to cancer research. The Canadian Television Network broadcast a tribute to him entitled *Terry Fox: The Marathon of Hope Continues,* which raised $10 million for the Canadian Cancer Society. Terry was also honored by his alma mater, Simon Fraser University, when it created a Terry Fox Gold Medal to be given each year to the student who best exemplifies the qualities of courage in adversity and dedication to society. Finally, the Canadian government honored him by naming him a Companion of the Order of Canada, the nation's highest civilian award.

The runner's health continued to decline, however, and in June of 1981, Fox finally died of his cancer. But even in death, Terry Fox was honored for his determination. Prime Minister Pierre Trudeau paid tribute to Fox's "courage and awesome determination [which] inspired this country as no one else has ever done." Flags were ordered to be flown at half staff on all federal buildings, military bases, and government ships, the first time this honor had been bestowed on a civilian. A commemorative stamp was issued with his likeness on it. In 1983 *The Terry Fox Story* opened in Canadian theaters and was shown on American pay TV. Terry Fox might have been chagrined by all this, however. He once said, "People were calling me a hero and looking up to me and thinking so much of me, but I really feel I'm no different. I've got nothing that can't be acquired by anybody. I really feel that each person has to believe that they're of importance. If everybody felt that way, that their vote or their belief counted, then the accumulation of it all will have an effect." In his final interview, Fox stressed the importance of his work over his own personal achievement, saying: "Dreams never die, although people do."

Sources

▶ **Periodicals**

Maclean's, "The Agony and the Ecstasy of Terry Fox," September 15, 1980, pp. 26-28, "The Nature of Heroism," January 12, 1981, p. 29.

People, "In the Image and Spirit of Terry Fox," May 30, 1983, pp. 46-48.

Runner's World, "Terry Fox Attempted to Carry Hope to Cancer Victims across Canada," December, 1980, pp. 62-65, "Making a Legend Indelible," April, 1983, pp. 37-41.

Anne Frank

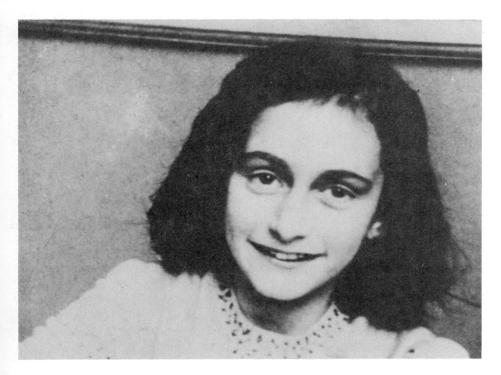

"I simply can't build up my hopes on a foundation consisting of confusion, misery, and death. I see the world gradually being turned into a wilderness, I hear the ever approaching thunder which will destroy us too, I can feel the suffering of millions and yet, if I look up into the heavens, I think that this cruelty too will end, and that peace and tranquility will return again."

Born June 12, 1929, in Frankfurt, Germany, Anne Frank was a writer and victim of the Holocaust who died in March, 1945, in the Bergen-Belsen concentration camp in Germany.

I f she had lived under different circumstances, Anne Frank could have been like any other talkative adolescent girl interested in boys and books. Unfortunately for her, she was Jewish in a time and place where that meant almost certain death. After the Dutch Green Police found her family's hiding place and they were sent to the Bergen-Belsen concentration camp under orders of the Nazi occupational government, Anne and all members of her family died, with the exception of her father, Otto Frank, who returned to Holland and published his daughter's diary. In it she had written: "I want to go on living after my death!" This has happened via her diary, which has sold eighteen million copies in fifty-two editions; it has been translated into over fifty languages and been adapted for the stage and screen. Reading his daughter's diary, Otto Frank rued the fact that he had not given her more attention during the two years they spent in hiding: "Anne developed under our eyes in that room, but we went on treating her as though she still was a giddy little girl. All of us were too wrapped up in our own troubles to give her the understanding that she needed."

Anne Frank was the second daughter of fairly wealthy German-Jewish parents of good standing. Her father had even been an officer in the German army during World War I. But when Adolf Hitler came to power in Germany in 1933, establishing an anti-Semitic atmosphere and repressive laws, the Franks decided to flee to Amsterdam, Holland, where Mr. Frank set up the Opekta firm.

The Franks led an idyllic life in Amsterdam until Germany invaded Holland in 1940. Then Hitler began instituting the same anti-Jewish laws that had been existence in Germany. Anne had been attending the elite Montessori school in Amsterdam, but when Jews were banned from attending non-Jewish schools, Anne had to go to the Jewish Lyceum. Jews were no longer allowed to own businesses, so Mr. Frank had to turn ownership of his firm over to one of his employees, Mr. Kraler, who would later help hide the Franks.

The degree of anti-Semitism in Nazi laws was severe, at least as harsh as the "Jim Crow" laws aimed against blacks in the 19th and early 20th centuries in the United States. Anne discussed these laws at length at the beginning of her diary: "After 1940 good times rapidly fled: first the war, then the capitulation, followed by the arrival of the Germans, which is when the sufferings of us Jews really began. Anti-Jewish decrees followed each other in rapid succession. Jews must wear yellow star, Jews must hand in their bicycles, Jews are banned from trams and are forbidden to drive. Jews are only allowed to do their shopping between three and five o'clock and then only in shops which bear the placard 'Jewish shop.' Jews must be indoors by eight o'clock and cannot even sit in their own gardens after that hour. Jews are forbidden to visit theaters, cinemas, and other places of entertainment, Jews may not take part in public sports. Swimming baths, tennis courts, hockey fields, and other sports grounds are all prohibited to them. Jews may not visit Christians. Jews must go to Jewish schools, and many more restrictions of a similar kind."

The Franks went into hiding on July 5, 1942, after an order came for Margot, Anne's older sister, to report to a labor camp. The Franks had been preparing for this eventuality, setting up a hiding place in a portion of Mr. Frank's office building—what Anne referred to as the "Secret Annex." When the order came for Margot, the family quickly moved in, Anne wearing "two vests, three pairs of pants, a dress, on top of that a skirt, jacket, summer coat, two pairs of stockings, lace-up shoes, woolly cap, scarf, and still more; I was nearly stifled before we started, but no one inquired about that."

From her hiding place Anne could see the daily deportation of Jews to concentration camps; and the effects of being holed up with another family she didn't particularly care for, the Van Daans, as well as a dentist named Mr. Dussel, took their toll. The fugitives had to be absolutely silent during business hours and had to be to bed early in the evening so as not to arouse suspicion. Anne occupied herself by reading, performing household chores, and writing in her diary. The entries were addressed to an imaginary friend named "Kitty," "in order to enhance in my mind's eye the picture of the friend for whom I have waited for so long. I don't want to set down a series of bald facts in a diary like most people do, but I want this diary itself to be my friend." Anne's entries, or letters to Kitty, were thoroughly candid and detailed her growing into adolescence, her disputes with her roommates, and her bitterness toward those who were making it so difficult for Jews to live, if they allowed them to live at all.

The Franks managed to live in their hiding place undetected for twenty-five months. Then on August 4, 1944, someone tipped off the police and the Franks, the Van Daans, and Mr. Dussel were sent to the Bergen-Belsen concentration camp in Germany. Mrs. Frank died on January 6, 1945; Margot died at the end of February or the beginning of March. Although Anne was not informed of her sister's death, as Ernst Schnabel wrote in his book on Anne Frank: "She sensed it, and soon afterward she died, peacefully, feeling that nothing bad was happening to her." The three members of the Van Daan family and Mr. Dussel also died.

When Otto Frank, the lone survivor of the Secret Annex, returned to Amsterdam, he was handed his daughter's diary by Miep Gies and Elli Vossen, two of Mr. Frank's former employees who had helped the family while they were hiding. A Dutch university professor urged Mr.

Frank to publish Anne's diary, and the first edition came out in June of 1947. Since that time the diary has become immensely popular, due to its strength as both a document of the enormous oppression that Jews suffered during Hitler's reign and as an exceedingly cogent testimony of a girl becoming a young woman.

To honor the effect that a simple teenager's diary has had on the world and to remember the murder of six million other Jews, the Montessori school Anne once attended has been renamed the Anne Frank School, and an Anne Frank Foundation has been set up in Amsterdam. An exhibit of photographs of Anne and her family toured the world in 1985. As dark and depressing as her situation was, Anne never gave up hope, as she wrote in her diary: "Go outside, go to the fields, enjoy nature and the sunshine, go out and try to recapture happiness in yourself and in God."

Sources

▶ **Books**

Frank, Anne, *The Diary of a Young Girl*, Doubleday, 1952.

Frank, Anne, *The Works of Anne Frank*, Doubleday, 1959.

Schnabel, Ernst, *Anne Frank, A Portrait in Courage*, Harcourt, 1958.

▶ **Periodicals**

History Today, "Anne Frank: Forty Years On," March, 1985, pp. 48-50.

Maclean's, "Anne Frank's Diary: The Epilogue," September 29, 1980, pp. 8-10.

People, "Anne Frank," September 16, 1985, pp. 95-98, "Miep Gies, Who Hid Anne Frank, Adds a Coda to the Famous Diary," April 18, 1988, pp. 123-24.

Betty Friedan

"*S*ome people thought I said, 'Women of the world unite—you have nothing to lose but your men.' It's not true. Your have nothing to lose but your vacuum cleaners."

Betty Friedan, who was born February 4, 1921, in Peoria, Illinois, is credited with inspiring the modern feminist movement with her 1963 book *The Feminine Mystique*.

I n the late 1940s and 1950s in the United States the image of the ideal feminine woman was one who did not want a career, political rights, or higher education. Independence and opportunities were not seen as important. What was accepted was the image of the "housewife," the wife and mother who is happy serving others in her ideal home in the suburbs. In the mid-1950s sixty percent of the women who did attend college dropped out either to marry or because they thought education would be a barrier to marriage. Women were no longer going to work in careers. The forces that were supposed to be the "chief enemies of prejudice"—education, sociology, psychology, and the media—were actually supporting traditional roles and pushing women into believing they should be perfectly happy being only wives and mothers. But a sense of emptiness and unease was growing for many women, a problem which at first no one could name, a sense of "never being myself." This dissatisfaction was shrugged off by men as an inability of women to adjust to their proper roles, but nevertheless their "have everything" role as suburban housewives was coming up desperately bankrupt. Betty Friedan, herself a suburban housewife and mother who had given up a promising professional career, was strongly feeling this emptiness in her life. "Eight schizophrenic years of trying to be a kind of woman I wasn't, of too many lonesome, boring, wasted hours" led Friedan to question the role prescribed for women by society, and when she learned that large numbers of other women were afflicted with the same malady she decided to write about it. The result was *The Feminine Mystique,* a book which instantly put a name on the unease and galvanized women into action, effectively launching the women's movement.

As the child of Harry and Miriam Goldstein, Betty was not encouraged to challenge traditional roles. She later attributed her awareness of oppression partly to being Jewish. "When you're a Jewish girl who grows up on the right side of the tracks in the Midwest, you're marginal. You're in, but you're not, and you grow up an observer." While in high school Betty founded a literary magazine, and she graduated as class valedictorian. She attended Smith College, where she graduated *summa cum laude* in 1942. She describes her experience at Smith as "a great marvelous thing for me, an unfolding of the mind, and I wasn't a freak for it." She was offered a fellowship to pursue a doctorate in psychology, and she remembers the pressures involved in her decision making. "We walked in the Berkeley hills and a boy said: 'Nothing can come of this, between us. I'll never win a fellowship like yours.'" Friedan gave up the fellowship, a loss of which she felt the pain for years, to the pressure of the "feminine mystique" to take a non-professional job, marry, and have children. She married Carl Friedan in 1947, and they settled in Queens, New York, and soon had three children.

By the mid-1950s Friedan was quite dissatisfied with her life. She prepared an extensive questionnaire for her Smith classmates, many of whom were feeling the same way. Friedan sees the feminine mystique as largely born of Freudian notions of femininity. The Freudian views of "penis envy," and the sexual nature of women, in particular, were the arguments men used to assert that American women should be happy to love and serve men. In the 1950s new neuroses were developing among American women, along with widespread anxiety and depression. Women were visiting Freudian psychiatrists in large numbers and "taking tranquilizers like cough drops" in order to try to continue living the mystique. They were finding themselves at middle age with a "mysterious ailment," their days deadened with the meaningless details of "creative housekeeping."

Friedan was soon to learn that the malaise affecting American women was more widespread than she had previously suspected, and that it was not confined to highly educated women. Through responses to a 1960 article in *Good Housekeeping,* titled "Women Are People Too," she learned how pervasive was the discontent and decided to write about it. She "holed up in that house and wrote a book I couldn't have written had I not lived those years as a suburban housewife." *The Feminine Mystique* became an immediate bestseller and has been translated into thirteen languages. One reviewer wrote of the book and its results: "Friedan began to analyze the fantasy; she interviewed housewives about the reality of their lives; she thought about the reasons for the promotion of such a false notion. She gave the image a name: the Feminine Mystique."

The publication of *The Feminine Mystique* is regularly credited with starting the women's movement. "Some people thought I said, 'Women of the world unite—you have nothing to lose but your men.' It's not true. You have nothing to lose but your vacuum cleaners." Believing the need for women's civil rights had reached an explosive level, Friedan founded the National Organization for Women (NOW) in 1966. Largely working to end job discrimination, NOW has been criticized by some feminists as too conservative. It has, however, remained the largest and most visible feminist organization in the United States. Friedan remained president of NOW until 1970. She then helped organize a nationwide Women's Strike for Equality, which occurred on August 26, 1970.

From 1970 to 1973 Friedan wrote a column for *McCall's,* titled "Betty Friedan's Notebook," that regularly reached more than eight million American women. Saying there are no blueprints for revolutions, Friedan wrote that she did not like the "folly of pseudo-radical smugness" she saw growing in the movement, and she retreated from active participation in movement organizations. She expressed dissatisfaction with some of the more radical women in the movement, feeling that "an overfocus on sexual issues, on sexual politics, as opposed to the condition of women in society in general, may have been accentuated by those who wish to immobilize the movement politically." Friedan felt the movement had to be more inclusive, saying "you don't have to hate men and renounce motherhood to be a liberated woman," and maintaining that the movement must transcend polarization to become "human liberation." The key for women, according to Friedan, was education that would allow women to work with men as equals rather than as inferiors.

Friedan has continued to write and be active in the struggle for equality. Commenting on the lethargy and ennui which often seems to pervade American society, she says: "As for me, I'm very unbored. . . . I get mad. But, by God, I'm absorbed in what I'm doing." Friedan has been absorbed in charting the next stage in the struggle, which she describes in her 1981 book, *The Second Stage*, about the necessity for women and men to strive together for equality. She is "still awed by the revolution that book [*The Feminine Mystique*] helped spark,"but she is far from content. "The second stage cannot be seen in terms of women alone. . . . [It] may not even be a women's movement. Men may be at the cutting edge of the second stage."

Sources

▶ **Books**

Friedan, Betty, *The Feminine Mystique*, Norton, 1963.

Friedan, Betty, *It Changed My Life: Writings on the Women's Movement*, Random House, 1976.

Friedan, Betty, *The Second Stage*, Summit Books, 1981.

▶ **Periodicals**

Esquire, "Emancipation of Betty Friedan," December, 1983, pp. 10-14.

New York Post, November 26, 1966, p. 25.

Indira Gandhi

"I f I die a violent death as some fear and a few are plotting, I know the violence will be in the thought and the action of the assassin, not in my dying . . ."

Born November 19, 1917, in Allahabad, India, politician and author Indira Gandhi died on October 31, 1984.

W hen the first prime minister of India after independence, Jawaharlal Nehru, died of a stroke in 1964, his daughter Indira was not seriously considered as a successor. However, when two years later the new prime minister Lal Shastri also died suddenly, Indira was chosen to fill the leadership void in India, and overnight became the leader of the world's largest democracy and perhaps the most powerful woman in the world.

India had been ruled by England for over a century prior to its independence in 1947. While the British had built many roads, schools, and hospitals, they had also acted as a superior colonial power, whom the majority of Indians greatly resented. The organized struggle for freedom began early in this century and grew until after World War II when the British finally realized they could no longer hold India. The ascension of a woman to the highest position in the world's most populous democracy was a symbol of strength, hope, and self-determination both for Indian women, traditionally considered subservient to men, and for the people of other Third World nations.

The life of the two-year-old daughter of Jawaharlal and Kamala Nehru was drastically changed in 1919 when her wealthy and prominent family was visited by Mohandas Gandhi, then recently returned from exile in South Africa. Gandhi converted the Nehrus to the cause of Indian independence, and the family gave up all of their Western possessions and values and joined in the struggle. Her family's house became a hub of the independence movement, and the constant series of meetings and parental absences denied Indira a normal childhood. Though spoiled by her grandfather Motilal, Indira later described her childhood as "insecure." She was four when her father and grandfather were first jailed. The jailings of these two, along with her mother, were frequent after that.

Because of the insecurities of her childhood Indira hardened herself and became resolved not to be hurt, as her mother Kamala had been, by the rigidity of India's social customs. She grew up as a solemn and precocious child. Her games were related to the independence struggle against the British. For example, at age eleven she organized the Monkey Brigade. Imitating the Monkey Army in the epic *Ramayana* story, this group of children took part in the struggle by writing and delivering notices, making flags, cooking food and spying on police moves. Indira often visited Gandhi while he was in prison and she was in school in Poona in the early 1930s. Later, she recalled that Gandhi "was always present in my life; he played an enormous role in my development." At sixteen Indira spent a peaceful year at a university in Bengal, followed by a trip to Switzerland to be with her mother, who was dying of tuberculosis. When Kamala died a few months later,

Indira was devastated, and spent the next five years seemingly without direction, studying sporadically in Europe and India.

Though she earlier vowed never to marry, thinking it might interfere with her politics and India's need, while in Europe Indira decided to marry Feroze Gandhi, who had been a friend of the family back in Allahabad. Feroze was a Pharsee, a member of a small but cohesive cultural group who had fled Persia centuries earlier to escape Muslim persecution. The Nehrus, on the other hand, were of the Brahmin or priestly class of India. Indira suffered criticism on her marriage choice not only from her father but also from the public, because of the status of her family in society. Despite the criticism, Indira married Feroze in 1942.

A few months after her marriage to Feroze, Indira was jailed for nine months, in what she describes as one of the most important events of her life. After her release Indira gave birth to two sons, Rajiv and Sanjay, and became increasingly involved in politics. After India's independence in 1947 Jawaharlal Nehru became the first prime minister, and needed his daughter to act as an official hostess. Indira and Feroze drifted apart, and though they never divorced, they lived separately until his death in 1960.

Indira lived in her father's shadow for years, but gradually began to speak out on her own campaigns and at functions which he could not attend. In 1955, at age 38, Indira became a member of the Working Committee of the Congress Party. In 1959 she became president of the India National Congress. Nehru, who had socialist leanings, greatly influenced Indira's views. She brought a fresh approach to the Party, and sought to increase women's participation in politics. Viewing politics as essentially a power game, she demonstrated her political skill by maneuvering the Communist Party out of power in the southern state of Kerala in 1957.

Indira's ascension to power as prime minister in 1966 is all the more impressive because India's culture is traditionally dominated by men. Indira paid a high personal price to achieve what she did, however. She was a very private person who seemed nervous with those around her. Her austere life and experience of political machinations engendered an attitude of mistrust, some would say paranoia, which would cost her dearly in the 1970s.

While Indira was prime minister India made great strides in the areas of food production and the development of an industrial base. However, it was also a tumultuous time politically. In 1971 Indira successfully engineered a fifteen day war with Pakistan that led to the creation of Bangladesh from East Pakistan. In 1975 she proclaimed a state of emergency and suspended civil liberties. Over the next several years her political fortunes rose and fell dramatically. In 1977 her party was swept out of power. In 1978 she won her parliamentary seat back and in 1980 was voted back in as prime minister to serve her fourth term. By then, Indira Gandhi had become the symbol of India. Her face was recognized even in the remotest villages. Often warm and charming, dominant, politically shrewd and at times ruthless, she was a private and complicated woman.

It was perhaps her ruthlessness which lead to her death. In June, 1984, Indira sent the Indian Army to the Punjab to flush Sikh guerrillas out of the Golden Temple, an event in which 600 people died. The Sikh community of India held Indira responsible and vowed revenge. In a letter written to a friend not long before her death and published in Dorothy Norman's *Indira Gandhi: Letters to an American Friend*, Indira seems to have both summed up her commitment to India and presaged what was to follow: "If I die a violent death as some fear and a few are plotting, I know the violence will be in the thought and the action of the assassin, not in my dying—for no hate is dark enough to overshadow the extent of my live for my people and my country; no force is strong enough to divert me from my purpose and my endeavor to take this country forward."

In 1984 Indira Gandhi was assassinated by two of her Sikh security guards while walking to her office for an interview. In death as in life she was in the public eye, surrounded by controversy, yet remaining a powerful force and symbol of an emerging nation.

Sources
▶ Books

Bhatia, Krishan, *Indira: A Biography of Prime Minister Gandhi*, Praeger, 1974.

Currimbhoy, Nayana, *Indira Gandhi*, F. Watts, 1985.

Gandhi, Indira, *My Truth*, Grove Press, 1980.

Mohan, Anand, *Indira Gandhi*, Van Rees Press, 1967.

Moraes, Dom, *Indira Gandhi*, Little, Brown, 1980.

Norman, Dorothy, *Indira Gandhi: Letters to an American Friend*, Harcourt, 1985.

Mohandas Gandhi

"I have nothing new to teach the world. Truth and nonviolence are as old as the hills. All I have done is to try new experiments in both on as vast a scale as I could do. . . . Those who believe in the simple truths I have laid down can propagate them only by living them."

Born October 2, 1869, in Porbandar, India, Mohandas "Mahatma" Gandhi was an Indian activist who advocated nonviolence, peace, and unity in creating an independent Indian nation. He was assassinated on January 30, 1948, and died five days later in New Delhi, India.

I n July, 1914, Mohandas K. Gandhi and his family left South Africa to return to their native India. This small, frail-looking man had one determined goal: to achieve, through nonviolent civil disobedience, freedom for India from oppressive British rule. Gandhi had given up a successful law practice and Western ideals in South Africa, and for seven years had tested his spiritual principles of *satyagraha* ("holding on to truth", or "soul force") and *ahimsa* (nonviolence) in a struggle to repeal laws discriminating against Indians. He returned to India with the dedication to apply these beliefs on an immense scale: to inspire millions of both poverty-stricken and wealthy Indians, Brahmins and "untouchables," to resist the British, not with arms, but with love and active non-cooperation. For over thirty years he led innumerable *satyagraha* actions and, despite imprisonment and violence from the English, never bore his oppressors any malice. Finally, following World War II, it became an untenable proposition for the British to maintain their domination over India; they granted independence in 1947. Gandhi's principles of *satyagraha* and *ahimsa* have inspired many other leaders in liberation struggles around the world as well, such as Martin Luther King, Jr.'s direction of the American civil rights movement. Gandhi has been called by Lewis Mumford "the most important religious figure of our time." When Gandhi was once asked his secret, he responded simply: "renounce and enjoy."

The certainty and determination with which Gandhi lived the second half of his life was vastly different than his early years. Mohandas Karamchand Gandhi was born October 2, 1869, in Porbandar, India, the son of a statesman and his fourth wife. As a young man he had a violent temper, was very shy and self-conscious, and was a less than average student. At age thirteen, while still in high school, Gandhi married a young girl named Kasturbai. Passionate and jealous, Gandhi thought he was her superior and teacher; it was only much later that he realized that it was Kasturbai, through her patience and enduring love and forgiveness, who had taught him much. Gandhi went to college and, after failing at every subject, withdrew after only five months. An uncle persuaded him to go to England to study law, and after his family raised the money by selling many personal possessions, including Kasturbai's jewelry, Gandhi left his wife and child to pursue his studies.

In London Gandhi maintained the vows he had given his mother to abstain from meat, alcohol, and women; but while he found his law studies easy, he remained lonely and socially inept. After he returned to India, Gandhi proved totally inadequate as a lawyer. He was so self-conscious and awkward that no one would give him a case—the one time he did appear in court, he could not utter a single word. Feeling like a failure, Gandhi was a offered a minor clerical position with a firm in South Africa and jumped at the chance. While there he decided to work on improving his demeanor, and approached the task with his customary dedication. He learned some self-confidence in helping to resolve an out of court settlement for a bitter legal dispute involving his firm. Commenting on the joy of that moment, Gandhi said: "I had learnt to find out the better side of human nature and to enter men's hearts."

Gandhi began trying to approach all situations as a way of rendering service rather than gaining personal profit. Within a few years he was a successful lawyer with a good income. He brought his wife and children to live with him, and urged them to adopt his newly acquired Western lifestyle. But at the same time he was embracing these new values, Gandhi began to notice the suffering of the Indian community in South Africa, and he was moved to help them. One time, he recounted, "a leper came to my door. I had not the heart to dismiss him with a meal. So I offered him shelter, dressed his wounds and began to look after him." A transformation was occurring within Gandhi. He was reading the world's scriptures and beginning to simplify his life, discarding the materialist values he had espoused only a few years before. Outside the city of Durban a small community was growing around him, based on service to others. He was still authoritative in his marriage, however, refusing gifts of jewelry for his wife as well as himself—though he later said "I have never regretted the step. It has saved us from many temptations." Because his relationship with Kasturbai had been stormy, Gandhi gradually learned that rather than demand his "rights" he needed to try to fulfill his responsibilities to the relationship.

An incident occurred in Gandhi's first year in South Africa from which his later methods of nonviolent resistance were born. While traveling in a first-class train compartment he was asked to go to the third-class compartment; when he refused, he was forced to leave the train. During that long night in the cold train station, Gandhi resolved never to yield to force nor use force to win a cause. "I object to violence," Gandhi said, "because when it appears to do good, the good is only temporary; the evil it does is permanent." He began applying his methods to protest South Africa's new racial laws oppressing Indians, most of which were eventually repealed. "Civil disobedience," he said, "is the inherent right of a citizen. . . . Above all, [it] must have no ill will or hatred behind it."

After twenty years in South Africa, Gandhi felt compelled to return to India and apply *ahimsa* and *satyagraha* to the struggle against British rule. "We are constantly being astonished these days at the amazing discoveries in the field of violence," Gandhi said. "But I maintain that far more undreamt of and seemingly impossible discoveries will be made in the field of nonviolence." He traveled from the Himalayas to Ceylon with his message of selflessness and love. One of the first to listen was Jawaharlal Nehru, who later became the first prime minister of independent India; Nehru gave up all of his Western values and possessions to work for independence. Disturbed by the inequities of India's caste system, Gandhi also gave the lowest caste "untouchables" a new name, *Harijans*—the children of God. He refused to enter temples that were closed to low caste Indians, saying: "There is no God here. If God were here, everyone would have access. He is in every one of us." Temple doors began to open to all. Gandhi was given the honorific title of *Mahatma,* meaning "Great Soul."

During World War I, Gandhi began urging Indians to participate in a program of civil disobedience against the British. These protests for independence continued for many years, during which thousands were arrested for noncooperation. Gandhi himself was tried for sedition, and he turned the trial into a condemnation of imperialism. Gandhi's protests, spontaneous, unpredictable and guided by intuition, confounded the British, as did the protestors' courage in the face of superior arms. "A *satyagrahi* bids goodbye to fear. He is therefore never afraid of trusting the opponent," Gandhi stated. ". . . . It is never the numbers that count; it is always the quality, more so when the forces of violence are uppermost."

A turning point in the independence struggle came in 1930, when Gandhi's Salt *Satyagraha* brought India's situation to world attention. After ten years of limited compromise and continued repression by the British, Gandhi decided to lead a twenty-four day march to the sea to protest the British monopoly on salt. At dawn he picked up a pinch of salt from the sand, and millions around the country began to ignore the law banning home-made salt. Despite brutal police reprisals, the country celebrated. Gandhi was soon arrested, as he would be many times over the next years, and he approached prison with the same joy he did everything else. Many British were won over to the cause and joined him in the struggle. All people were the same to Gandhi. "I believe that if one man gains spiritually," Gandhi said, "the whole world gains with him and, if one man falls, the whole world falls to that extent."

From prison Gandhi was invited to London for a conference to decide India's fate. He had asked all Indians to wear homespun cloth—*Khadi*—and boycott all foreign cloth, to break the British monopoly on clothing production, and *khadi* became a symbol of independence, linking rich and poor Indians together. While in London Gandhi wore only *khadi,* even when visiting Buckingham Palace. He also spoke to British textile workers in Lancashire who were put out of work by the boycott, and won many of them over to the cause. Gandhi felt the love and truth he spoke touched people's hearts: "[*Satyagraha*] is a force that works silently and apparently slowly. In reality, there is no force in the world that is so direct or so swift in working."

By 1945 the British realized they could no longer hold India, and conceded independence to the country. In September, 1946, Jawaharlal Nehru became Prime Minister. On the eve of independence, however, Muslims and Hindus began killing each other, each fearing the others would seize power after the English left. Thousands died in Calcutta alone. Gandhi, disheartened at the killing, went with followers into the afflicted villages to live peacefully; they transformed the areas where they went. Eventually, however, the country was to split into India and Pakistan. In the midst of this chaos, Gandhi was aware that his love and tolerance infuriated some people. He said: "If someone killed me and I died with a prayer for the assassin on my lips and God's remembrance and consciousness of His living presence in the sanctuary in my heart, then alone would I be said to have had the non-violence of the brave." These words proved prophetic, for on January 25, 1948, Nathuram Godse, a thirty-five year old high caste Brahmin and publisher of a weekly Hindu magazine shot Gandhi point-blank as the Mahatma rose to address a crowd at a New Delhi prayer meeting. Gandhi's last words as he fell were "Oh, God"; he died five days later.

Tributes from around the world poured in after Gandhi's death. U.S. Secretary of State George Marshall said that "Mahatma Gandhi was the spokesman for the conscience of all mankind." Albert Einstein commented: "Generations to come, it may be, will scarce believe that such a one as this ever in flesh and blood walked upon this earth." One of the most fitting statements came from Prime Minister Nehru, who in telling India of Mahatma Gandhi's death, said: "The light that has illumined this country for these many years will illumine this country for many more years, and a thousand years later that light will still be seen in this country, and the world will see it and it will give solace to innumerable hearts."

Sources

▶ **Books**

Ashe, Geoffrey, *Gandhi*, Stein & Day, 1968.

Easwaran, Eknath, *Gandhi the Man*, Nilgiri Press, 1978.

Fischer, Louis, editor, *The Essential Gandhi*, Vintage Books, 1962.

Gandhi, Mohandas K., *Gandhi: An Autobiography*, Beacon Press, 1957.

Gandhi, Mohandas K., *The Words of Gandhi*, Newmarket Press, 1982.

Bob Geldof

"I *can't sit in front of the TV and watch people die and not do anything about it."*

Bob Geldof was born in Dublin, Ireland, around 1954. He is a singer, actor, and famine relief activist.

Present address: c/o Columbia Records, 51 W. 42nd St., New York, NY 10019.

G eldof is an example of how entertainment people can become deeply involved in affairs outside their immediate concern. A prominent rock star, Geldof became more widely known when he organized benefit concerts in behalf of Ethiopian famine victims. His efforts raised some $100 million for the cause.

Geldof was born to parents of modest means, and worked as a butcher, a bulldozer operator, a photographer, and a writer before landing a job at *Melody Maker* magazine. The British music magazine offered him the opportunity to learn about the rock music business, and working as a correspondent kept him abreast of the local rock scene.

In 1975, Geldof formed the band Nightlife Thugs with several friends, including guitarist Garry Roberts, keyboardist Johnny Fingers, bassist Pete Briquette, drummer Simon Crowe, and guitarist Gerry Cott. The band became a popular attraction in Ireland's music scene. In 1977, the Thugs became The Boomtown Rats and Mercury Records in America signed them up, giving the band an entry to the American "punk rock" movement. But while the American punk bands rejected wealth and fame, Geldof's Boomtown Rats openly desired commercial success. Although the band enjoyed a small following in the U.S., they never achieved the status Geldof desired.

In 1980 their biggest single, "I Don't Like Mondays," peaked at number seventy-three in the United States. The song was considered controversial because it told the story of a tragic incident that had occurred in 1979. Brenda Spencer was a seventeen-year-old San Diego high school student who went on a shooting spree, killing one person and injuring several others because, as she put it, "I guess I just don't like Mondays." Many people felt that a murder was not a suitable topic for a rock song, and the record was pulled from the play list of a number of radio stations. Spencer's family threatened to file a lawsuit. But Geldof did not regret writing the song: "To me it was a song about not needing a reason to do anything, not even the most extreme human act of all . . . I regret the barks that followed it. I regret that it wasn't a hit because I'd love to have a hit in America, for financial reasons if not for anything else."

The Boomtown Rats were more successful in England. Their first single, "Looking After No. 1," climbed to number eleven on the British charts, and by 1981 the group had scored nine consecutive top fifteen singles in England. When his friends from the rock group Pink Floyd gave him the starring role in their movie "Pink Floyd—The Wall, "Geldof seemed to be at the pinnacle of success. He played the part of Pink, a moody, introspective character. His acting debut was a success in England as well as in America, and reviewers praised him for his ability to play the role to "perfection."

Geldof is most famous, however, for his role in organizing the benefit concert "Live Aid," created to raise relief money for famine victims in Ethiopia. He got the idea after seeing a news report on the horrors of famine in Africa. "I felt disgusted and ashamed by what was going on in Africa, and I felt that if I didn't do something, I was taking part in some crime. It wasn't enough to simply put my hand in my pocket and give money," Geldof recalled. He got on the phone, asking various famous friends in the music business to participate in a charity recording session, which lasted twenty-four hours and produced the huge-selling single, "Do They Know It's Christmas?." Musicians who helped out included Boy George, Paul McCartney, Phil Collins, Sting, and Duran Duran. "I just phoned everybody up, and they said, 'Absolutely.' There were a million efforts made because they felt the same way I did," Geldof said.

Then in 1985, Geldof expanded his idea and did a simultaneous double "Live Aid" concert for African relief, one at London's Wembley stadium, and one at JFK stadium in Philadelphia. The show reached an estimated 1.5 billion people worldwide via radio and television. Geldof received a Nobel Peace Prize nomination for his charitable efforts. As one publicist said, "He's a saint in my eyes." Fellow band member Crowe remarked, "A lot of Doubting Thomases feel Bob might have done it to further his own career . . . He definitely did it for all the right reasons."

Not trusting the Marxist military regime of Ethiopia, Geldof set up a private foundation to oversee distribution of relief funds. He also traveled to Africa to make sure that the supplies were received by the needy. All in all, he helped to raise well over $100 million. The "Live Aid" concerts were, Geldof explained, "the ultimate expression the pop industry can make."

Sources

▶ **Periodicals**

Newsweek, "The Deadly Politics of African Aid Efforts," June 3, 1985, p. 22, "African Aid Concert," July 15, 1985, p. 3.

Time, "Rock's Grandest Extravaganza. . . . ," July 22, 1985, p. 3.

John Glenn

''[I decided] to reassess my views as to my responsibilities and where we were going in this country. I decided I would run for the Senate. I didn't want to do it as an ego trip. . . . The challenge is to make a better place for the people still to come.''

Born July 18, 1921, in Cambridge, Ohio, John Glenn has been a military pilot, an astronaut—he was the first American to orbit the earth—and a U.S. Senator from Ohio.

Address: 503 Hart Senate Bldg., Washington, DC 20510

J ohn Glenn, now a U.S. Senator from Ohio, is perhaps unique among American heroes because he has enjoyed three careers of considerable merit. He was a much-decorated Marine Corps pilot during World War II and the Korean War, and in the early 1950s became a military test pilot. While serving as a test pilot, he made the first supersonic flight across the North American continent. Chosen in 1959 as an one of the first seven American astronauts by the National Aeronautics and Space Administration (NASA), in 1962 Glenn became the third American in space and the first person to orbit the earth. In 1964, seeking a new way to serve his country, Glenn resigned from NASA to begin a career in politics. After two unsuccessful attempts at gaining a seat in the U.S. Senate, Glenn was elected in 1974, and is now serving his third term as a Senator from Ohio.

John Glenn was born in Cambridge, Ohio, a small city in the southeastern portion of the state. When he was still a little boy, his family moved to New Concord, a small town about twenty-five miles west of Cambridge. His father was a plumber, and, according to Glenn, taught him the value of hard work. As a teenager, Glenn began attending New Concord High School (since renamed John Glenn High School), and proved to be both an excellent student and athlete. He served as the president of his junior class, earned academic honors, and lettered in three varsity sports.

Shortly after the Glenns moved to New Concord, they became friends with Dr. and Mrs. Homer Castor and their two daughters. One night at a potluck dinner, three-year-old John Glenn met four-year-old Annie Castor. The two became inseparable almost immediately. They were good friends as children and began to date as teenagers. Glenn and Annie Castor entered nearby Muskingam College in 1939. For two years they enjoyed the relative shelter of college life, but that came to a halt in 1941, when Japanese bombers attacked the U.S. Navy installation in Hawaii's Pearl Harbor. Glenn immediately dropped out of college and enlisted in the Naval Air Corps. He was stationed in Corpus Christi, Texas, to begin training as a pilot.

After a year of training, Glenn joined the Marine Corps. Before he was shipped overseas, however, Glenn and Annie Castor were married. Annie remained in New Concord while Glenn was shuffled around the country, waiting for a fighter plane to become available. Eventually Glenn was sent to Hawaii to begin flying fighter missions. Glenn flew a total of fifty-nine missions in the Pacific in the Marshall Islands campaign. He was a fearless and extraordinarily successful pilot, and won numerous air medals and Distinguished Flying Crosses "for heroism while participating in aerial flights." He later recalled, however, the horror of his efforts: "I can remember walking around on the beach . . . and seeing what looked like pieces of petrified flesh. Starting up my engines once, I saw the exhaust stir up skulls and bones out of the sand."

In 1952, Glenn, by then a major in the Marine Corps, returned to the Far East as a fighter pilot in the Korean conflict. He once again distinguished himself as a pilot during ninety combat missions, and added more awards to his already long list. Following the war, he became a military test pilot, and in 1957 made the first transcontinental supersonic flight, from Los Angeles to New York. In recognition of this feat, he was awarded his fifth Distinguished Flying Cross. Following his promotion to lieutenant colonel in 1959, Glenn along with six other test pilots were selected to become astronauts by NASA. At that time the United States was locked in an intense struggle with the Soviet Union over the exploration of space, and Glenn played a part in the struggle.

The initial U.S. manned space ventures were in the *Mercury* series spacecraft, and there was tremendous competition among the seven original astronauts to be chosen as the *Mercury* astronaut who would be the first American in space. After much deliberation, NASA chose Alan Shepard. Glenn was extremely upset that he had not been chosen, and because the announcement was not made public for some months, Glenn had to keep his rage to himself. The press had been assuming that Glenn would be the choice, because he was the eldest and most militarily-decorated of the group; this only heightened Glenn's feelings of humiliation. His disappointment lasted for months, but with the help of his wife and friends, he gradually overcame his anger and reestablished his goals in the space program.

In 1961, John Glenn was chosen to make the first American orbital flight in space. The historic launch was delayed ten times because of weather conditions or equipment failures. The spacecraft was finally launched successfully on February 20, 1962, and was scheduled to make three orbits of the earth. Following the first orbit, however, an automatic control mechanism failed, and Glenn was forced to take over manual control of the spaceship for the remaining two orbits. As the craft reentered the earth's atmosphere, a potentially fatal problem developed with its heat shield, but Glenn landed safely in the Atlantic Ocean. Some years later, Glenn described his feelings on that voyage: "I was fully aware of the danger. . . . No matter what preparation you make, there comes the moment of truth. You're playing with big stakes—your life. But the important thing to me wasn't fear, but what [I could] do to control it."

In 1964 Glenn resigned from NASA to pursue a political career. This idea had first surfaced when Glenn and his wife had been invited to

Attorney-General Robert Kennedy's house for dinner in December, 1962. Kennedy suggested that Glenn run for a U.S. Senate seat in Ohio in 1964. Glenn took Kennedy's advice and ran in the Democratic primary against the long-time Ohio Senator Stephen Young, but was defeated. He then began a career in business, serving as president of Royal Crown Cola International, and hosting a television series that focused on historic expeditions.

In 1970 Ohio's Senator Young retired from the Senate, and Glenn again decided to run for his seat. This time his opponent in the primary was Howard Metzenbaum. Metzenbaum ran a well-financed, well-organized campaign, and again Glenn was defeated, but this time by only about thirteen thousand votes. Glenn later said he learned a great deal about politics during that campaign, and in 1973, he launched his campaign for the Senate seat opening the following year. Metzenbaum, who had lost the 1970 election to the Republican nominee, was again his opponent in the primary. This time Glenn defeated Metzenbaum, and went on to win the Senate seat with a landslide victory over the Republican candidate. Despite their early confrontations, Glenn and Metzenbaum are today the two U.S. Senators from Ohio, and Glenn appeared in numerous influential advertisements for Metzenbaum during the 1988 Senate campaign, in which Metzenbaum won re-election.

In the Senate, Glenn has campaigned his colleagues for political financing reform, and has been a strong supporter of liberal domestic programs aimed at improving education and health care. He has taken more moderate positions in foreign affairs, demanding verifiable evidence of promises made by the Soviet Union, but also sponsoring legislation requiring that executive agreements made between the president and other nations be subjected to a Senate review process. Glenn's demeanor in the Senate is perhaps best described by fellow Senator Sam Nunn, who has said, "I've seen him in several situations where he was frank and candid at his own peril. He had an option of remaining silent in a couple of places and not making anybody mad, when he came forth pretty strongly." Glenn ran an unsuccessful campaign for the Democratic presidential nomination in 1984, losing to nominee Walter Mondale. However, he was easily re-elected to a third term in the Senate in 1986.

Sources

▶ **Books**

Carpenter, Malcolm S., et al, *We Seven, by the Astronauts Themselves*, Simon & Schuster, 1962.

Carroll, Peter N., *Famous in America*, Dutton, 1985, pp. 67-86.

Douth, George, *Leaders in Profile*, Sperr & Douth, 1975, pp. 526-35.

Fellowes-Gordon, Ian, *Heroes of the Twentieth Century*, Hawthorne, 1966, pp. 277-83.

Pierce, Philip, and Karl Schuon, *John H. Glenn, Astronaut*, F. Watts, 1962.

Shelton, William Ray, *Flights of the Astronauts*, Little, Brown, 1963, pp. 101-71.

Thomas, Shirley, *Men of Space*, Chilton, 1962, v. 5, pp. 1-47.

Van Riper, Frank, *Glenn: The Astronaut Who Would Be President*, Empire Books, 1983.

Wolfe, Tom, *The Right Stuff*, Farrar, Straus, 1979.

▶ **Periodicals**

Newsweek, "John Glenn: One Machine The Worked without a Flaw," March 5, 1962, pp. 19-24.

Time, "Space," March 2, 1962, pp. 11-18.

Jane Goodall

*"*B*ecause of our work with the chimps, we understand more about humans than we did before. We know we are not as different from the rest of the animal kingdom as we once thought we were."*

Born April 3, 1934, in London, England, Jane Goodall is one of the premiere animal behavior scientists and naturalists working in Africa, and has done more to detail the life and perilous existence of the chimpanzee than any other person.

J ane Goodall was born in London in 1934, one of two daughters of an engineer and his wife. When Jane was five her family moved to France, but they were forced to return to England only a few months later when Hitler's armies began World War II. Jane's father soon enlisted to fight in the war, and Jane and her mother and sister settled in Bournemouth, a large city in the county of Dorset on the English Channel. Jane attended school in Bournemouth, but did not care much for the confinement it required. She much preferred being in the garden or the woods, watching birds or climbing trees.

A turning point in Jane's childhood came one day when her mother brought her a book from the library: Hugh Lofting's *The Story of Doctor Dolittle*, a fantasy about a doctor who learns to talk to animals and travels to Africa to help them. Seven year-old Jane decided then that she must go to Africa someday. She began reading all the books about animals and Africa she could find. She and a friend made up stories about animals that lived in the garden, and Jane opened a small "conservatory" in her mother's house which included flowers, shells, and even a human skeleton. She also began the "Alligator Club" magazine, which she said "was filled with nature notes, drawings of insect anatomy, and other such things."

After she graduated from high school, Jane entered secretarial school in London, because her mother "said secretaries could get jobs anywhere in the world." After she graduated, Jane went to work for a physio-therapist in Bournemouth, and later for a documentary film company in London, a job she loved. She still longed to go to Africa, but lacked both the funds and an excuse. Her chance came when an old school friend invited Jane to come visit the friend's family in Nairobi, Kenya. Jane made enough money to go, and sailed by ship all the way from London, around the Cape of Good Hope, to Mombasa, Kenya. She then took a train to Nairobi.

In Kenya, Jane used her secretarial skills to land a job with a large corporation, but she soon found a much better situation. A friend told her about a man named Louis Leakey, a paleontologist and anthropolo-gist who was searching for evidence of early man in Kenya. Jane arranged an interview with Leakey. Impressed by her knowledge of animals, and desperately in need of a secretary, he hired Jane. She soon began accompanying Leakey and his wife Mary to sites such as Olduvai Gorge in Tanganyika. A few years later, the Leakeys would find there the remains of *Homo Habilis*, the earliest ancestor of man known to make and use tools.

After working with the Leakeys for some time, Jane was able to save enough money to bring her mother to Africa for a visit. She said, "All my life, up to that time, [my mother] had been doing things for me. Now, at last, I could do something for her." Mrs. Goodall loved Africa, as it turned out, and the two spent several happy months together. Meanwhile, Jane contemplated her future. Louis Leakey had suggested that she study a group of chimpanzees living near a lake in Tanganyika, believing that such a study would shed light on the behavior of man's ancestors. But studying the chimps would require money, and that would mean securing funding from somewhere. Although Jane had a good working knowledge of many species of animals, she had no formal scientific training and no university degree, so it would be difficult for her to receive any funding. Louis Leakey offered to try to raise the money, and Jane returned to England.

Back in England, Goodall took a job at the London Zoo, and read everything she could find about chimpanzees. Less than two years later, she received a letter from Louis Leakey saying that he had been able to arrange funding for a chimpanzee project in Tanganyika. The money and governmental permission had been difficult to obtain, Leakey wrote, and Jane would not be permitted to go into the back country alone. Jane later explained, "In those days it was not thought at all safe for a young, single girl to go into the wilds of Africa and study animals." She selected her mother as her traveling companion, and the two were once again off for Africa.

The chimpanzee population to be studied was located in the Gombe Stream Game Reserve in Tanganyika. Because of some fighting among tribesmen in the bush country, the Goodalls were delayed for some time in Tanganyika before they could go to Gombe. Finally, in July of 1960 Jane arrived at Gombe for the first time. She got up at 5:30 each morning to observe the chimps. She soon discovered many characteristics of their behavior and social system, such as the fact that they lived in groups of six or less but were all part of a larger community. She began to recognize individual chimps, and gave them names, such as David Greybeard, the first chimp she observed regularly. Friends of David Greybeard she named Goliath, William, and Flo. Jane recognized that once one observes chimps for a while, they are as easy to identify as humans.

Jane's work was funded in part by the National Geographic Society, with Louis Leakey dispersing the funds. In the early 1960s, the Society sent a young photographer to Gombe to film the chimps: Hugo van Lawick, a Dutch baron who traced his ancestry back to the 13th century. In 1964, Jane and Hugo were married. Hugo remained in the bush with Jane and shot many hours of wonderful films for the National Geographic Society.

Within a few years, Jane was forced to leave Gombe to return to England and earn a Ph.D. The degree was something she had promised Leakey she would earn, and future funding likely depended on it. Although she had no college degree, Jane was accepted at Cambridge University after Louis Leakey again intervened on her behalf. At Cambridge, she studied animal behavior, usually termed "ethology," and in 1966 she received her Ph.D. and returned to Tanganyika.

In 1967, Jane experienced "the most important event of my life. I had a baby. . . ." She named her son Hugo Eric Louis van Lawick, after her husband, one of her uncles, and Louis Leakey. Although his parents nicknamed him "Grub," the infant did not seem to mind, and his indomitable spirit allowed Jane and Hugo to continue their work at Gombe.

Although Jane spent all of her time at Gombe, husband Hugo still worked for the National Geographic Society. He was assigned to various stories throughout the world, and was away from Gombe much of the time. Finally, they were divorced in the mid-1970s. Jane later said, "it was sad, especially for Grub. If I could live that part of my life over again, I would try very hard to work things out differently."

Jane soon remarried, to an Englishman named Derek Bryceson, who was the director of Tanzania National Park. Bryceson lived in Dar es Salaam, the capital of Tanzania (the name of Tanganyika had been changed when the country merged with the island of Zanzibar). He had been a fighter pilot in World War II, had been shot down, and was almost completely paralyzed from the waist down. Jane began spending some of the year in Dar es Salaam writing, and the remainder at Gombe. Sadly, Bryceson died of cancer only a few short years after he and Jane were married.

Many of the chimps Jane had first seen at Gombe had died, but some remained alive. Chimps often live to be 50 years old, and Jane had known many of the individuals at Gombe for so many years that when one occasionally died it was like losing a member of her own family. She continued her work at Gombe, continued writing in Dar es Salaam, and spent about four months a year raising money for further research at Gombe.

Jane was by this time using other avenues to inform the world of her research on chimps and of the dangers of the unrestricted advance of civilization. In addition to National Geographic magazine and television specials, she began authoring books, such as *My Friends, the Wild Chimpanzees* and *In the Shadow of Man*. In 1975, she established the Jane Goodall Institute for Wildlife Research, Education, and Conservation in Tucson, Arizona, to provide funding for continued chimpanzee research at Gombe and to lend support to further research on apes and other animals around the world. She took visiting professorships at universities, including Stanford University in California and the University of Dar es Salaam in Tanzania. In the mid-1980s, she began a new project called ChimpanZoo. The project called for students and volunteers to study chimpanzee behavior at zoos. By 1988, 14 zoos in North America were taking part in the project, and several zoos in Europe were about to begin.

Jane Goodall continues to live by herself in Tanzania, at Gombe and at Dar es Salaam. Although she has spent nearly 30 years studying the chimpanzees at Gombe, she feels that her work is far from over. In 1986, she wrote a book about her many years in Tanzania entitled *The Chimpanzees of Gombe.* She has won many of the most prestigious wildlife and conservation awards around the world, including the Golden Medal of Conservation from the San Diego Zoological Society, the Order of the Golden Ark from the Netherlands, and the J. Paul Getty Wildlife Conservation Prize. Her goals have always been to understand and preserve the chimpanzees, and her work has been invaluable in bringing the need for conservation to the minds of millions of people. Jane is now recognized around the world as one of the foremost animal behaviorists of our time.

Sources

▶ **Books**

Coerr, Eleanor, *Jane Goodall*, Putnam, 1976.

Goodall, Jane, *My Friends, the Wild Chimpanzees*, National Geographic Society, 1967.

Goodall, Jane, *In the Shadow of Man*, Collins, 1971.

Goodall, Jane, *The Chimpanzees of Gombe*, Belknap Press, 1986.

Goodall, Jane, *My Life with the Chimpanzees*, Pocket Books, 1988.

Green, Timothy, *The Adventurers: Four Profiles of Contemporary Travellers*, M. Joseph, 1970, pp. 157-208.

▶ **Periodicals**

Ms., "Into Africa," March, 1988, pp. 222-223.

National Geographic, "My Life among Wild Chimpanzees," August, 1963, pp. 272-308, "New Discoveries among Africa's Chimpanzees," December, 1965, pp. 802-831, "Life and Death at Gombe," May, 1979, pp. 592-621.

U.S. News and World Report, "Years of Watching Chimps Help Us to Understand Ourselves," November 5, 1984, p. 81.

Billy Graham

"Come as a little child, not as a doctor of philosophy or a doctor of law, but come as a simple human being to the Cross and your life can be changed."

Born on a farm near Charlotte, North Carolina, on November 7, 1918, and named William Franklin Graham, Jr., Billy Graham is a well-known evangelist.

Present address: 1300 Harmon Place, Minneapolis, Minnesota.

G raham is the son of Franklin Graham, a stern Scottish Presbyterian, and Morrow Coffey. Rowdy and mischievous as a child, he was filled with self-doubt but was determined to be a farmer. His chief interests were baseball and history. When Graham was fifteen years old he fell under the influence of a spellbinding evangelist named Mordecai Ham and began to feel the urge to be converted and to preach. He was soon "born again" and his future began to take shape. In 1936 he was deeply influenced by another evangelist from Alabama named Jimmie Johnson.

After graduating from high school, Graham enrolled in Bob Jones College in Cleveland, Tennessee, but after a year switched to Florida Bible Institute, near Tampa. He was still worried by self-doubt and concern for his future. One night in March, 1938, at Bob Jones College, Graham was again converted. "I remember getting on my knees," he later said, "and saying 'O God, if you want me to preach, I will do it.'" With tears streaming down his face he was told that God did call him, and he "made this great surrender to become an ambassador for Christ." His life now began to take on purpose, and he has said that this second conversion was when he began to mature. Graduating in May of 1940, Graham went on to Wheaton College outside Chicago to get further knowledge that would be useful in his calling. There he met and married Ruth McCue Bell, of Virginian parents, who had been born in China.

Throughout life Graham has developed his ministry with great organizational skills and has worked to promote his own spiritual growth and eliminate his self-doubt. He helped organize Youth for Christ International, his first religious movement, and in 1947 he became president of Northwestern Schools in Minneapolis, Minnesota. He continued to solve his own problems about the role he was to play in life, although friends told him his faith was too simple for today's world, and he half believed them. Finally he told God that he accepted the Bible "by faith as the Word of God," and he would abide by its teachings. Graham has kept that resolve ever since, and his career has been meteoric, with a faith and message simple and straight from the heart.

On November 5, 1950, he began the half-hour radio program "Hour of Decision," which was broadcast on one hundred fifty ABC radio stations around the world—three hundred fifty in the United States. In December, 1952, Graham started writing a newspaper column, "My Answer," modeled after First Lady Eleanor Roosevelt's column "My Day." By the end of 1953 it ran in seventy-three papers and brought some fifteen million readers.

Graham is undoubtedly best known for his numerous "Crusades," which have attracted people by the millions around the world. In 1954, when he planned one for England and Scotland, friends advised him against it because they felt that the attitude of Britons and the newness of his appeals would guarantee failure. Instead Graham won countless friends and converts. From 1956 to 1959 he crusaded throughout the world—in India, Philippines, Hong Kong, Argentina, Japan, Korea, Australia, and New Zealand—and again was a great success. He founded a magazine, *Christianity Today*, in 1955, and in 1957 he preached at Yankee Stadium to an audience totaling 2,357,000. Through the years Graham has reached out in films, books, sermons, magazines, and in his lifestyle and appearance. He has been an unofficial White House minister to U.S. Presidents Harry Truman, Dwight Eisenhower, Richard Nixon, John F. Kennedy, Lyndon Johnson, Jimmy Carter, and Gerald Ford, and he has associated with many foreign leaders and other government officials.

In 1963 Texas Governor John Connally spoke of Graham: "Billy Graham is more than a preacher, more than an evangelist, more than a Christian leader. In a greater sense he has become our conscience." As this conscience of a nation, Graham has maintained a simple, heart-felt Fundamentalist point of view. On racial problems he has always been direct and clear: "There's no racial distinction here. Here are white and colored alike, standing before the cross of Christ. The ground is level at the foot of the cross." On the question of resolving the conflicts between blacks and whites, Graham appeals to the heart: "The race question will not be solved by demonstrations in the streets, but in the hearts of both Negro and white. There must be genuine love to replace prejudice and hate. This love can be supplied by Christ and only by Christ."

Graham has always been a team player, backed by a large and enthusiastic group of fellow-workers and himself playing on Christ's team. Yet he has always appealed to the individual heart, not to the mass. To him living is the individual's responsibility. "Come as a little child, not as a doctor of philosophy or a doctor of law," he says, "but come as a simple human being to the cross and your life can be changed."

Called the most effective evangelist in the world today, Graham has preached before a hundred million people and has received numerous honorary degrees from colleges and universities. He is a tall, lanky, hawk-faced man, rather stern but smiling and ready to go to his knees to exhort the public to come to God. In 1970 he said: "I am going to preach a gospel not of despair but of hope—hope for the individual, for society and for the world." There was room for that message of hope in the America of the 1950s, 1960s, 1970s and 1980s, and perhaps will be in the years following President Ronald Reagan's administration.

Sources

▶ **Books**

Pollock, John, *Billy Graham: The Authorized Biography*, McGraw-Hill, 1966.

Pollock, *John Billy Graham: Evangelist to the World, World Wide Publications, 1979.*

▶ **Periodicals**

Christianity Today, "Billy Graham in China, Building Bridges," June 17, 1988, p. 52, "William Franklin Graham: Seventy Exceptional Years," November 18, 1988, pp. 17-25.

Time, "And Then There Was Billy," November 14, 1988, p. 86.

U.S. News and World Report, "Present at the Creation," December 19, 1988, pp. 60-61.

Dick Gregory

"*L*" *aughter is the best way to release tensions and fear. If I fall down three flights of stairs, you just stand there and hold your breath. But if I get up and laugh about it, you laugh too. Then we can get together and fix any bones that got broken.*"

Born October 12, 1932, in St. Louis, Missouri, Gregory became known as a comedian, social activist, and diet developer.

Address: c/o John Bellamy, Dick Gregory Health Enterprises, Inc., 38 S. La Salle St., Suite 825, Chicago, IL 60603.

Dick Gregory was one of the first black comedians to appear
before white audiences and to address the problems of segregation and racism in his comedy. During the early 1960s he
became very active in the civil rights movement, and even further
involved in politics as a candidate for mayor of Chicago in 1966, and a
presidential candidate of the Peace and Freedom Party in 1968. Though
he did not win either election, he drew attention to his political
concerns. After retiring from show business in the 1970s, Gregory
developed a diet drink mix called Slim-Safe Bahamian Diet, and
recently sold its distribution rights for $100 million. Gregory donated
much of the money to such charitable and humanitarian groups as the
Red Cross, the United Negro College Fund, and Amnesty International.

Dick Gregory was born on October 12, 1932, in St. Louis, Missouri. The
second of six children, his father deserted the family when Gregory was
a small boy. Gregory's mother, however, was a constant source of
warmth and security. She tried to instill pride in her children and find
humor in difficult circumstances. She told her children when the relief
truck arrived at their house, "Aren't we lucky to get such service.?"

Dick helped to provide for the family, scouring the streets of St. Louis
for food and fuel, doing odd jobs, and shining shoes in a billiard parlor.

While at Summer High School, Gregory became a track star because, he
said, "I knew getting ninety on my tests wouldn't get me what winning
the mile in the city meet would." In 1951 he won the Missouri mile
championship with the time of 4:28, again in 1952 with a 4:27, and was
offered twelve athletic scholarships to colleges and universities. He
decided on Southern Illinois University at Carbondale, Illinois, where
he excelled at track and was named the university's outstanding athlete
in 1953. At the university he studied business administration with the
intention of eventually becoming a teacher.

After a two-year stint in the United States Army where he performed
comic routines in G.I. shows, Gregory returned to Southern Illinois
University, but dropped out to work in a variety of jobs. In 1958 Gregory
became an entertainer at the Esquire Club, a small black night spot in
Chicago. For a chance to perform, Gregory gave the master of ceremo-
nies $5 to take his place one evening, and afterwards worked there three
nights a week for a small wage.

In 1959 he married his wife Lillian and shortly thereafter borrowed some
money to open his own night club, the Apex, in Robbins, Illinois, a
Chicago suburb. The club soon folded and Gregory was out of work
until he rented the Roberts Show Club on Chicago's South Side in July
1959 and put on a show for the visiting members of the Pan American
Games teams. The owner of the club liked the show and signed a

contract with Gregory. News commentator John Daly filmed part of Gregory's act in 1960 and included it in *Cast the First Stone,* a documentary about blacks viewed by 60,000,000 Americans. Gregory was soon hired for more comedy appearances, but still had to supplement his income as a Post Office employee and a car washer.

Gregory's big break came on January 13, 1961 at Chicago's Playboy Club, when he filled in for another comedian. He signed a contract two days later. On February 17, 1961, *Time* magazine published a profile of Gregory. He then joined Colpix records and released *Dick Gregory in Living Black and White.* Jack Paar, on whose show Gregory appeared several times, said of the comedian, "He is the first of his race to come on as an intelligent comedian without any of the stereotypes long associated with Negro comedy."

It is not surprising that Gregory, who satirized racism in his comic routines, soon became involved in the civil rights movement. He marched in protests with leaders such as Medgar Evers and Dr. Martin Luther King, Jr. and was jailed numerous times. He also began to emulate one of his role models, Mohandas Gandhi, by fasting for causes such as world hunger.

In 1973 Gregory left show business because he considered his lifestyle unhealthy: "I was drinking a fifth of scotch and smoking four packs of cigarettes a day," Gregory said. For moral reasons, he also became a vegetarian. Becoming more and more interested in health concerns, over a period of fifteen years Gregory developed the Slim-Safe Bahamian Diet formula. To demonstrate the diet's value, and at the same time protest against world hunger, Gregory fasted for seventy days while being monitored by physicians. After he had lost fifty pounds, Gregory drank a six-ounce glass of his sea-weed-based formula and then began a journey from New Orleans to Baton Rouge, Louisiana, on foot.

Gregory originally targeted his Slim-Safe Bahamian to black consumers, because he said, "there aren't many health food stores in the black community." The diet formula received attention as a subject on the *Phil Donahue Show* and has recently been reviewed in such publications as *People* and *U.S.A. Today.* Gregory also gained publicity when he worked as Walter Hudson's personal dietician. Hudson weighed 1200 pounds and hadn't left his bed in 18 years, but under Gregory's care, Hudson lost 400 pounds.

Gregory recently sold distribution rights to his Slim-Safe Bahamian Diet to Cernitin America Inc. for $100 million and gave $1 million apiece to about 15 civil rights and humanitarian organizations. Gregory said, "My commitment to black institutions and black organizations will increase as my profits increase. We'll spend huge amounts to go out to talk about how the effects of drugs, alcohol and caffeine have ruined our community."

A family man, Gregory loves to spend time with his wife of twenty-five years and ten children. "I love my work," Gregory said in a *Macleans* article, "and I expect to live past 100."

Sources

▶ **Books**

Gregory, Dick, *Nigger,* Pocket Books, 1973.

Gregory, Dick, *Up From Nigger,* Stein & Day, 1976.

▶ **Periodicals**

Black Enterprise, "A Natural Wonder," May, 1985, p. 20.

Maclean's, "A Comic's Road to Health," December 3, 1984, p. 8.

Newsweek, "Funny Man, Serious Money," October 17, 1988, p. 61.

Florence Griffith Joyner

"I work hard to keep things around me positive. At a basic level, my belief in God lets me believe that I can achieve almost anything."

Born around 1960 in Los Angeles, California, Florence Griffith Joyner is an Olympic medal-winning track athlete.

F amed runner Griffith Joyner burst into the international limelight in the 1988 Olympic Games in Seoul, Korea, with a winning mixture of athletic prowess and flamboyant running outfits, which earned her the nicknames "Flourescent Flo" and "Flo-Jo." Although she is principally known for her achievements on the track, where she won five Olympic medals and set a new world record for the women's 100-meter dash, her keen sense of style has made her a favorite of both fashion pundits and the public alike. She has since retired from running in order to pursue business and creative interests. "Throughout the history of track and field," asserted a writer in a 1988 *Ms* profile, "there have only occasionally been athletes whose personalities and performances transcended their sport. . . . Florence Griffith Joyner has joined the immortals, rising to their status on the force of her amazing athletic achievement, aided by the singular nature of her personality and approach to life." Griffith Joyner was born Florence Delorez Griffith, the seventh child in a family of eleven children. Her father, Robert, was an electronics technician, and her mother, Florence, was a seamstress. Nicknamed Dee Dee (to distinguish her from her mother), Griffith Joyner grew up in a housing project in the impoverished Watts district of Los Angeles. Her parents were divorced when she was four, and the children lived with their mother. "My mother had no choice but to be independent," recalled Griffith Joyner, "and I think I got that from her—being able to stand on my own two feet. She taught us all that nothing is going to be handed to you—you have to make things happen."

Her upbringing was strict, but the experience of living in a large and loving family offered the young Griffith Joyner a creative environment in which to grow. As well as inheriting her mother's independent spirit, Griffith Joyner shared her mother's love of clothes and clothing design. As a child, she loved to play dress-up and dreamed of one day becoming a famous clothes designer. "My mother always wanted me to be different," she remembered. "I always tried to create a different pattern. Something no one else had." In kindergarten Griffith Joyner would braid her hair with one braid sticking straight up or go to a shopping mall with her pet boa constrictor wrapped around her neck.

Griffith Joyner discovered running at the age of seven and began competing in foot races at the Sugar Ray Robinson Youth Foundation wearing her own home-made running outfits. She quickly discovered that she was faster than many of the boys, a quality she would later attribute to her habit of chasing jack rabbits in the desert.

She continued running in high school, but she never considered the sport anything other than a fun way to keep fit. Nevertheless, when she graduated from Los Angeles' Jordan High in 1978, she held school records in both sprints and long jump.

Griffith Joyner attended California State University at Northridge as a business major, working as a bank teller to support herself. At Northridge she met assistant track coach Bobby Kersee, and they formed a close coach-athlete relationship which was to last almost a decade. When Kersee got another job at UCLA in 1980, Griffith Joyner moved with him. "UCLA didn't even offer my major . . . but my running was starting up, and I knew that Bobby was the best coach for me."

By 1982, when she ran the 200-meter race in 22.39 seconds for the NCAA Championship, Griffith Joyner was becoming one of America's most promising collegiate athletes. She narrowly missed making the team for the 1980 Moscow Olympics and subsequently channelled all her frustrations into making sure she qualified in 1984. Chosen for that year's Olympic team, she took a silver medal in the 200-meter dash.

Following the 1984 Olympics, Griffith Joyner reduced her training schedule and went into semi-retirement, working full time as a secretary at a bank, with a lucrative sideline as a hair and nail stylist. But at Kersee's urging, she stepped up her training program in 1986 and shed some weight. At the following year's World Championship in Rome, however, she could still only place second in the 200-meter race. Failing to win the gold medal deeply hurt Griffith Joyner. "When you've been second best for so long, you can either accept it or try to become the best," she said. "I made the decision to become the best in 1988."

In October, 1987, she married Al Joyner, an acquaintance since 1980 and triple-jump gold medalist at the 1984 Olympic games. Joyner's sister, Jackie, was by this time married to Kersee.

Under the instruction of Kersee, Griffith Joyner prepared rigorously for the Seoul Olympics. She was still working a regular job during the days, and the schedule exacted a heavy physical toll from her. "There were times when I wouldn't sleep for forty-eight hours because of everything I was trying to do," she recalled. Nine months after her marriage, she replaced Kersee with her husband Al as her coach.

In July's 1988 trials for the upcoming Olympics, Griffith Joyner made world headlines when she smashed Evelyn Ashford's four-year-old world record 100-meter time of 10.67 by nearly three-tenths of a second, an enormous margin in a short-distance race. During the Olympic Games in Seoul, Griffith Joyner won gold medals in both the 100-meter and 200-meter finals, and she shared a gold with three U.S. teammates in the 400-meter relay. She also won a silver medal in the

1600-meter relay final. Some critics called her the "greatest woman sprinter the world has ever seen."

Aside from her success on the track, Griffith Joyner attracted the attention of the media and the public with her unorthodox and colorful running attire. Also possessing striking good looks and three-inch-long fingernails, "Flo-Jo" (as the world now knew her) proved that, in her own words, "you can sweat and still look nice doing it." A writer in a 1989 *Vogue* feature declared: "Blessed with speed and style and defiant sexuality, Florence Griffith Joyner has broken down the barrier between vanity and athletic prowess." Many critics noted that individuality allowed her to capitalize on her athletic success. "She's great looking, wears colorful costumes, and is a personality," declared a member of a New York advertising agency. Another observer commented, "She happens to be a character of sorts, that's where the appeal is."

Following the Olympics in Seoul, Griffith Joyner has been in great demand for endorsements, and her face has appeared on magazine covers the world over. She recently began negotiations for her own clothing line, cosmetics line, and a "Flo-Jo" doll. She also wants to venture into acting and writing children's books. "Track is moving down on my list," she said in a recent interview. "I've reached more than I've ever dreamed of . . . and now I'd like to get some of my work published, get some of my designs done." In February, 1989, Griffith Joyner announced her retirement from athletics.

"Running is just something else I do with my life," she explained. Griffith Joyner believes that her hard work, determination, and the love of her family have helped her overcome her disadvantaged background. "We learned something from how we grew up," she reflected. "It has never been easy, and we knew it wouldn't be handed to us, unless we went after it. We didn't know how poor we were. We were rich as a family."

Sources

▶ **Periodicals**

Essence, "Florence Griffith Joyner: Life in the Fast Lane," March, 1989, p. 48.

Ms., "Siren of Speed," October, 1988, pp. 34-35.

Newsweek, "A Star Blazes in the Fast Lane: World Record Holder Florence Griffith Joyner is a Winning Mixture of Dazzle and Determination," September 19, 1988, pp. 54-57.

People, "Flashy Florence Griffith Joyner Will Be One to Watch—and Clock—in the Women's Sprints," August 29, 1988, pp. 60-62, "Flo-

Jo: The Twenty-Five Most Intriguing People of the Year," December 26, 1988, pp. 30, 49.

Runner's World, "Speed Queen," October, 1988, p. 79.

Sports Illustrated, "Very Fancy, Very Fast," September 14, 1988, p. 158, "A Special Fire," October 10, 1988, p. 43.

Time, "For Speed and Style, Flo With the Go," September 19, 1988, p. 52.

Vogue, "Go With the Fio," April, 1989, p. 402.

Womens Wear Daily, "Flo-Jo: Beauty Comes From Within," December 16, 1988, p. 10.

Dag Hammarskjold

*"*N*o life was more satisfactory than one of selfless service to your community—or humanity."*

Born July 29, 1905 in Uppsala, Sweden, Dag Hammarskjold died in a plane crash in Northern Rhodesia in 1961. He was a Swedish statesman and was Secretary-General of the United Nations from 1953 until his death.

Dag Hammarskjold was the youngest of four boys, the son of a stern, hardworking father who was Governor of Uppland and of a gentle, kindly mother who liked to dream. Hammarskjold's family background shaped his political philosophy. "From generations of soldiers and government officials on my father's side" he remarked,"I inherited a belief that no life was more satisfactory than one of selfless service to your community—or humanity. This service requires a sacrifice of all personal interests, but likewise the courage to stand up unflinchingly for your convictions." From his mother Hammarskjold recalled, he learned that "all men were equals as children of God, and should be met and treated by us as our masters in God."

At Uppsala University, Hammarskjold was easily the strongest and brightest student. He strove to develop his personality and talents, working on weekends while others played. He was not loved by fellow students, but he was admired.

Like his father, Hammarskjold loved his native Sweden. He became a successful naturalist, and knew more about the countryside and the plants and animals than did any of the other students. He felt that to sink one's roots deeply enough into his native soil one could reach a kind of universal. "The more we see and the more we widen our contacts with our fellow beings in other parts of the world," Hammarskjold said, "the more it is also revealed to us that the essential beauties and the ultimate human values are equally present among the stones where as children we played as in those other, far larger, worlds." He concluded: "The road inwards can become a road outwards."

In 1930 Hammarskjold moved with his father to Stockholm, the Swedish capitol. The young Hammarskjold almost immediately went into government, becoming secretary of the Royal Commission on Unemployment. He remained in public service thereafter, seemingly the model government man. As one observer wrote: "Dag has such a purity of character and an intelligence of such a high order that I do not for a moment hesitate to write that he will be Swedish prime minister at an early age."

When Hammarskjold became Secretary-General of the United Nations in 1953, the organization had slipped in prestige and power. He sought to reverse the trend, drawing on all his skills as charming politician and as able administrator. He was a persuasive talker, silver-tongued and literary enough to sometimes sound more profound than he was. He was also a master at seeming to say more than he committed himself to. The French called him "master of the calculated imprecision."

Though considered a strong Secretary of the UN, Hammarskjold also encouraged the organization to develop along democratic lines. He searched for untried ways to improve the world, observing that "working at the edge of the development of human society is to work on the brink of the unknown." Hammarskjold did not fool himself into thinking that his solutions were ones that would last. "There is no excuse for the failure to act in accordance with our best understanding, in recognition of its limits but with faith in the ultimate result of the creative evolution in which it is our privilege to cooperate."

In all his attitudes and activities, Hammarskjold stood tall and fiercely independent. After his death in a plane crash in 1961 in Northern Rhodesia (now Zambia) while on a mission to the Congo (now Zaire), a brief statement was found in his private papers which summarizes his life and attitude: "I, Dag Hammarskjold solemnly swear . . . to . . . regulate my conduct with the interests of the UN only in view and not to seek or accept instructions in regard to the performance of my duties form any government or other authority external to the organization."

In our day, when government is criticized for being easily swayed by external forces, Hammarskjold's pledge was especially noteworthy and desirable.

Sources
▶ **Books**

Lash, Joseph P., *Dag Hammarskjold: Custodian of the Brushfire Peace*, Doubleday, 1961.

▶ **Periodicals**

Life, "And This Is Where and Why Dag Died," September 29, 1961, pp. 46-47.

Look, "Dag Hammarskjold: A Personal Portrait: Excerpt from 'Fighter for Peace: Dag Hammarskjold,'" October 24, 1961, p. 140.

Newsweek, "Man of Faith and Courage," October 2, 1961, p. 19.

Reader's Digest, "Day Dag Hammarskjold Rode in My Jeep," May, 1962, pp. 244-46.

Time, "Bear's Teeth," February 24, 1961, pp. 16-19, "Calculated Insolence: C'est Fini," August 4, 1961, p. 17.

Katharine Hepburn

"*Y*ou *can't survive without character for long. If you get handed . . . a tragedy . . . , you have to face it with character. You don't get eaten up with weakness. . . . To me it's thrilling to make an effort.*"

Born November 8, 1909, in Hartford, Connecticut, actress Katharine Hepburn has been called "the first lady of American cinema."

T hroughout her long and successful career, Hepburn has fought against the stereotyping of women in our culture by careful choices of roles, directors, and leading men, as well as by her independent attitude in dealing with studio and public-relation politics. Self-discipline and conscientious work habits were instilled early by her parents. Her mother was involved in the fight for women's rights, particularly reproductive rights, and Hepburn recalls that her father, a physician, "had no patience for self-pity." If one of the children complained of not feeling well, he would say, "Take an aspirin, go up to your room, and lie down. Don't inflict the way you feel on the rest of us." Reportedly a tomboy in her youth, she was educated by private tutors and, discouraged from a career in medicine by the social restrictions placed on women at that time, she instead studied drama at Byrn Mawr College.

She debuted on Broadway in 1928, and acted in a number of productions before scoring a hit with "The Warrior's Husband" in 1932, which brought her offers to work in Hollywood. Having signed with RKO she quickly established herself as a movie star to be reckoned with. For her portrayal of the tomboy who yearns to be on the stage in "Morning Glory" in 1933, she received her first Oscar for best actress from the Academy of Motion Picture Arts and Sciences. She played a number of roles that dealt with the idea of breaking down gender barriers in our society; for example, in 1935's "Sylvia Scarlet," she is disguised as a boy for much of the film. However, her biggest success came when she teamed up with Cary Grant in films like "Bringing Up Baby" and "Holiday," both from 1938. During this early period Hepburn gained a reputation for wanting things her own way; however, she confessed in a New York *World-Telegram and Sun* interview in 1962 that although many people thought she was "bold and fearless and even arrogant," inside she was "always quaking." The willingness to stand up for what she believes is right has become Hepburn's trademark. As she once stated, "I don't care how afraid I may be inside—I do what I think I should." Because of the resultant friction between her and the studio representatives, though, Hepburn left RKO. After making "Holiday" at Columbia, Katharine ended up at Metro-Goldwyn-Mayer—the studio with "more stars than there are in the heavens."

"The Philadelphia Story" illustrates both her power and charisma. She starred in the Broadway production, which was written specifically for her. After a successful stage run she took her role to the screen in 1940 and was nominated for an Academy Award and won a New York Film Critics Award. In 1942, she followed this success with the first of several films to team her up with Spencer Tracy, "Woman of the Year," which led to yet another Academy Award nomination. The long partnership of Tracy and Hepburn spanned many successful movies from "State of the Union" in 1948, in which Hepburn plays a lawyer who undermines the notion of male superiority, to "Guess Who's Coming to Dinner" in 1967, in which they portray parents whose liberal views are tested when their daughter announces her plans to marry a Black man. For her performance Hepburn received her second Oscar for best actress.

In 1952, Hepburn starred in the successful "The African Queen" with Humphrey Bogart under the direction of John Huston. According to *Variety*, Bogart never had "a more knowing, talented film partner than Miss Hepburn." The movie, adapted by James Agee from C.S. Forester's novel, is a story of an amusing mismatch of African river captain and proper lady missionary. The role gained Hepburn another Oscar nomination and marked a high point in her career.

Besides playing the role of the mother in Eugene O'Neill's autobiographical "Long Day's Journey into Night," a performance that critics described as "an eloquent representation of a lovely woman brought to feeble, helpless ruin," Hepburn took time off in the early 1960s to care for the ailing Spencer Tracy. Describing him as her "rock of protection," she turned down numerous parts until Tracy had somewhat recovered. After Tracy's death, she resumed a greater work schedule than ever before. In 1981, she received her third Academy Award, for her performance with Henry Fonda in "On Golden Pond." She continues to appear on television talk shows and has recently published her account of the making of the film "The African Queen."

Sources
▶ **Books**

Dickens, Homer, *The Films of Katharine Hepburn*, Citadel Press, 1968.

Freedland, Michael, *Katharine Hepburn*, Salem House, 1984.

Hepburn, Katharine. *The Making of the "African Queen"; or, How I Went to Africa With Bogart, Bacall, and Huston and Almost Lost My Mind*, Knopf, 1987.

Higham, Charles. *Kate: The Life of Katharine Hepburn*, 1971, revised edition, New American Library, 1984.

Marill, Alvin H. *Katharine Hepburn*, Galahad Books, 1973.

▶ **Periodicals**

New York Times, (interview with Cecelia Ager), June 18, 1967.

World-Telegram and Sun, (New York), (interview with Dave Balch),
    September 27, 1962.

Sir Edmund Hillary and Tenzing Norgay

*"*I*f my life finished tomorrow I would have little cause for complaint—I have gathered a few successes, a handful of honors and more love and laughter than I probably deserve."*

—Sir Edmund Hillary

Edmund Hillary, a New Zealander born July 20, 1919, and Tensing Norgay, a Sherpa born in 1914, were the first people to reach the summit of Mt. Everest, the highest mountain in the world.

On May 29, 1953, a New Zealander named Edmund Hillary and a Sherpa named Tenzing Norgay stepped onto the summit of Mt. Everest, the world's tallest peak, stayed for fifteen minutes, and then descended. They came down as international heroes, flooded by media attention and pressured by politicians. This success changed not only the lives of these two men but also increased the trickle of climbers to Everest and other Himalayan peaks to a flood, altering dramatically the environment and social fabric of this remote area of Nepal. Since their historic climb over 150 other men and women have reached Everest's summit, some without the use of oxygen supplements, and some by more difficult routes. In fact, the south-east ridge, the one followed by Hillary and Norgay, is now referred to as "the yak route" by some Sherpa climbers. Despite these advancements in mountaineering, the significance of that 1953 ascent is hard to overestimate. Edmund Hillary was born on July 20, 1919, in Auckland, New Zealand, and raised in nearby Tuakau. His father, who edited the local paper, treated his son strictly, but Edmund describes his mother as warm and affectionate. Edmund was a rebellious youth: "I was a restless, rather lonely child and even in my teens I had few friends." At an early age he and his brother became involved with their father's hobby of beekeeping, a hobby Edmund pursued intermittently for many years. At sixteen he developed a taste for the mountains when he went on a winter holiday with schoolmates.

In 1941 Hillary joined the New Zealand Air Force and flew search and rescue missions in the Pacific. One day the speed boat he was in blew up, severely burning the young aviator. He returned to beekeeping, but found the life unsatisfying: "I was always too restless and life was a constant battle against boredom." He fell in love with the mountains and made his first real friends while climbing New Zealand's Southern Alps. Hillary liked the excitement and challenge of climbing. "In a sense fear became a friend—I hated it at the time but it added spice to the challenge and satisfaction to the conquest."

In 1950 Hillary made his first trip to Europe to climb the Swiss Alps. Then in 1951 he traveled to the Himalayas, climbing for weeks along the Tibetan border with Nepal. He was next invited to join a British expedition to the south side of Everest, discovering a possible southern route up the mountain. In 1953 he was invited to join the British team attempting to climb Everest, a group that included the Sherpa Tenzing Norgay. The Sherpas are a people who came over the mountain passes from Tibet to the high valleys of Nepal centuries ago. Tenzing Norgay was born in Tsa-chu, near Mt. Makalu, where his mother was on pilgrimage, in 1914, and raised in Thami, Nepal, a village in the shadow of Mt. Everest. The eleventh of thirteen children, Tenzing spent his youth herding his father's yaks, and left home at eighteen to go to Darjeeling, India. He became involved in mountain-climbing expeditions, and to climb Everest (Chomolungma in the Sherpa language) became a lifelong dream. In all he took part in seven expeditions to Everest, including three before World War II on the north slope, and two in 1952 with a Swiss team that nearly reached the summit.

When he and Hillary stood on Everest's summit embracing, making offerings, and taking photos, Tenzing was nearly forty. "I went up a simple man, came down a hero," he recalls. The excitement and recognition after the climb were bewildering. Politicians and others tried to make Tenzing the hero of the East and to split him from Hillary. Having never been far from the mountains before, he now toured Asia and Europe, receiving honors and having audiences with Prime Minister Nehru of India and Queen Elizabeth of Great Britain. After the climb Tenzing set up the Himalayan Mountaineering Institute in Darjeeling, where he was Director of Field Training from 1954 to 1956. He never attempted to climb Everest again. "I have done it once, after joining in many attempts. What is the point of repeating such a climb?"

After climbing Everest Edmund Hillary was knighted by Queen Elizabeth, then returned to New Zealand and married Louise Rose. In 1954 he returned to Nepal to explore the Garun Valley east of Everest. After the birth of his two children, Hillary led the New Zealand team in a 1956-58 trans-Antarctic expedition from the Weddell Sea to the South Pole and on to McMurdo Sound, an exhausting and dangerous trip. His party became the first people to reach the South Pole in forty-six years. In 1960 Hillary returned to Nepal again, searching for the *yeti*, Abominable Snowman. After many interviews and months of searching he came away, convinced the *yeti* does not exist. There were also other Himalayan expeditions, and a second trip to Antarctica, which included the first ascent of Mt. Herschel in 1967.

Hillary lost his wife and daughter Belinda in a plane crash in Nepal in 1975. In 1977 he took a jet boat up the Ganges River in India from its mouth in the Bay of Bengal to find its source in the Himalayas, a trip completed by his son Peter after Hillary nearly died of pulmonary edema. "Of all the journeys I have undertaken the one that was left the most vivid memories in my mind is our trip up Mother Ganga (Ganges) in 1977 from the Ocean to the Sky." In 1982 Hillary returned to India, this time just to "go looking, looking." After all of his travels and numerous awards Hillary seems satisfied with his life: "If my life finished tomorrow I would have little cause for complaint—I have gathered a few successes, a handful of honors and more love and laughter than I probably deserve."

Hillary is the founder and director of the Himalayan Trust. Since the 1960s, the Trust has built dozens of schools, bridges, hospitals, water pipelines, and an airfield for the Sherpas of Nepal. Life has changed radically for the Sherpas since 1953. Many are abandoning their old ways to become porters for climbing expeditions and changing their values to support a cash-based economy. With better health care has come a growing population, resulting in massive deforestation and environmental degradation. In 1976, largely due to Hillary's efforts, Nepal created the 480 square mile Sagarmatha National Park, which includes Mt. Everest.

Over the years some coolness developed between Hillary and Norgay, largely fueled by outside pressure about who reached the summit first. The two were reunited as friends, and in 1978 Hillary said the question "is not of the slightest consequence." Tenzing remarked, "God knows who was first and that is enough." Interestingly, in recent years Hillary commented, "I don't think our ascent of Everest was terribly important to the world," adding that his most satisfying trip was his South Pole expedition. Never the sentimentalist, Hillary states, "What you're doing today or what you're planning tomorrow is of much more importance than what you did yesterday."

Sources

▶ **Books**

Hillary, Sir Edmund, *Nothing Venture, Nothing Win*, Coward McCann, 1975.

Hillary, Sir Edmund, and Peter Hillary, *Ascent: Two Lives Explored; The Autobiographies of Sir Edmund and Peter Hillary*, Doubleday, 1986.

Norgay, Tenzing, and James Ramsey Ullman, *Tiger of the Snows*, Putnam, 1955.

Norgay, Tenzing, *After Everest: An Autobiography*, Allen & Unwin, 1977.

▶ **Periodicals**

People, "25 Troubled Years Later: Hillary and Tenzing Say Everest Was Not the Peak of Their Lives," June 12, 1978, pp. 42-43.

Newsweek, "Sir Edmund Hillary's Himalayan Odyssey," March 12, 1984, pp. 9-10.

Bob Hope

"*I keep moving so much because with my kind of act it's safer*"

Born May 30, 1903, in Eltham, England, radio, television, and movie star Bob Hope is renowned for his stand-up comedy routines.

B ob Hope is perhaps the most widely known and loved standup
comedian in America. On July 13, 1969, long before Hope
reached his greatest fame, the *Milwaukee Journal* stated that Hope
had "undoubtedly been the source of more news, and more newspaper
feature stories than any other entertainer in modern history." In addition to his successes on radio, in movies, on television, and in live
shows, Hope has developed a reputation for his untiring efforts to
entertain and boost the morale of American military personnel stationed all over the world and for the numerous appearances he has
made in the name of various charities.

Born Leslie Townes Hope, Hope was one of seven surviving boys. By
the age of four he was a skilled mimic and loved to sing and dance. In
1908 Hope's family moved from England to Cleveland, Ohio. Hope's
father, Harry, was a hard-drinking stonemason whose income was
irregular. For Hope, who looked and sounded British, the Americaniza-
tion process was difficult. The Cleveland neighborhood in which he
lived was tough, and the neighborhood kids made fun of him. They
inverted his name, Leslie Hope, to create the nickname "Hopelessly."
When he shortened his name to Les, they countered with another
nickname, "Hopeless." Hope was a scrappy kid and to ward off the
ridicule he fought easily and sometimes successfully, developing into a
boxer of some skill.

As a youth Hope sold two-cent newspapers on the streets of Cleveland
to supplement his family's income. On one occasion a gentleman in a
long black limousine waited while Hope, who did not have change for a
dime, rushed into a nearby store to get change. When he returned he
received a lecture about the importance of keeping change in order to
take advantage of all business opportunities. The man was oil magnate
John D. Rockefeller, founder of Standard Oil Company.

As a teenager Hope once boasted that he'd rather be an actor than hold
an honest job, and he participated in all kinds of school and amateur
training groups, specializing in dancing and in the one-liner jokes for
which he ultimately became famous. He gained a great deal of experience in an act Hope formed with a comedian from Columbus, Ohio,
George Byrne. Adopting the name Lester, Hope went with Byrne to
New York City in 1926. He and Byrne performed in cities and towns
outside New York City, and finally appeared in a New York City
vaudeville production called "Sidewalks"; they were fired within a
month, however, because the show was a success and did not need the
short dancing act that Hope and Byrne performed.

Hope got his first trial as a solo act at Chicago's Stratford Theatre in 1928.
For this solo appearance he changed his name to Bob because he felt that

would be "chummier" and look better on a theatre marquee. In solo appearances, Hope always made his audience feel at ease and comfortable with his self-deprecating humor. He worked desperately hard and succeeded but soon left the Stratford to tour midwestern cities.

From 1920 to 1937 Hope performed in all kinds of shows in vaudeville both on and off Broadway. Vaudeville was hard work for Hope. A typical show consisted of comedians running a patter of one-liners around various kinds of variety acts ranging from dancing dogs to sword-swallowers but featuring mainly dancing. Hope is considered a master of the one-liner. In later years Hope sometimes employed up to three joke writers at a time. One standard line when he boards an airplane is, "I knew it was an old plane when I found Lindbergh's lunch on the seat." He used a line in 1970 when he met with the English Royal Family: "I've never seen so much royalty. . . . It looks like a chess game . . . live!" In 1932, when fifteen million Americans suffered the joblessness of the Great Depression, Hope was earning a thousand dollars a week in his particular kind of vaudeville act. But he was not satisfied. Hope was always ambitious and wanted to improve. He yearned, as he said, "to be the best," to be the outstanding comic in the business.

Hope met actor and singer Bing Crosby in 1932. They liked each other immediately because their personalities and styles of acting fitted well, and they started performing together in song and dance routines. Hope met aspiring actress Delores Reade in 1933 and later married her. Already well established as a comedian by 1935, Hope that year joined the "Ziegfield Follies" and performed in cities outside New York; then on January 30, 1936, he opened in the "Follies" at New York City's Winter Garden Theatre, with such stars as Fanny Brice and Eve Arden. The "Ziegfield Follies" was a new vaudeville high for Hope. The show was the musical highlight of Broadway, consisting of dazzlingly beautiful girls and costumes, witty lines between the actors and actresses, and music by such great composers as Vernon Duke and Ira Gershwin. During his years in vaudeville, Hope was on the stage with such actors as Jimmy Durante, Ethel Merman, Edgar Bergen and Charlie McCarthy, Al Jolson, and many others.

Although Hope had acted in some short motion picture comedies as early as 1934, he began his feature-length movie career in Hollywood in 1938, with the Paramount film "The Big Broadcast of 1938" starring Hope, W.C. Fields, Martha Raye, Dorothy Lamour, and Shirley Ross. This was the beginning of an active career in film entertainment for Hope, who went on to appear in fifty-two movies; six of these comprise the "Road to. . ." series featuring Hope, Crosby, and Dorothy Lamour.

Hope has always been fiercely patriotic about his adopted country. On

December 7, 1941, when Japanese attack planes bombed the American naval installation in Hawaii's Pearl Harbor, thereby provoking U.S. participation in World War II, Hope denounced the attack. On December 16, during a radio broadcast, Hope declared his patriotism and voiced optimism about the outcome of the war: "There is no need to tell a nation to keep smiling when it's never stopped. It is that ability to laugh the makes us the great people that we are . . . Americans!"

One of Hope's former stand-ins who had joined the armed forces knew of Hope's reputation for charitable work and in 1942 asked the comedian to make an entertainment tour of Alaskan Army bases. Hope enlisted Frances Langford, Jerry Colonna, Tony Romany, and other performers to put together a variety show for the troops stationed there. That was the beginning of a commitment on Hope's part that has never ended. Every year, especially during the Christmas season, Hope has spearheaded a drive to present shows to American men and women in the armed forces. His service to American troops added to Hope's established reputation for activity in the name of numerous charities and benefits, including political, cultural, and humanitarian causes. In fact, at the Academy Awards on February 21, 1941, Hope was given an honorary award "to pay tribute . . . to a man who has devoted his time and energy to many causes. His unselfishness in playing countless benefits has earned him a unique position in a hectic community where his untiring efforts are deeply, profoundly appreciated." Hope also won honorary Oscars in 1940, 1944, 1952 and 1965.

Hope has long been many Americans' favorite comedian, from the average radio-listener and movie-goer to the rich and powerful. He often enjoyed a close relationship with the men serving as President of the United States. From the administration of Franklin Delano Roosevelt through that of Ronald Reagan, Hope has appeared many times at the White House. President Jimmy Carter, in paying tribute to the man who had entertained America for so long, commented on Hope's role as White House guest: "I've been in office 489 days. . . . In three weeks more I'll have stayed in the White House as many times as Bob Hope has." Hope's seventy-fifth birthday party, held in the Washington Kennedy Center to honor the United Service Organization, was attended by members of Congress and many of Hope's acting friends, including John Wayne, Elizabeth Taylor, and George Burns. Another celebration was held at the Kennedy Center in 1983 when Hope turned eighty years old, this time hosted by President Ronald Reagan and his wife, Nancy. Again Hope's friends were present to honor the occasion, including models Cheryl Tiegs and Christie Brinkley. At the celebration Hope was still what *Time* magazine called "The All-American Wisecracker," and showed no signs of slowing down. In all Hope has received thirty-four honorary degrees and awards.

As Hope begins to look forward to his ninetieth birthday, he can look back upon a life that has been full to the brim. One of his writers, Larry Klein, once said: "You know, if you had you life to live over again, you wouldn't have time to do it." Hope answered: "I wouldn't want to live it over again. It's been pretty exciting up to now. The encore might not be as much fun." Behind all Hope's humor is a serious core that directs his life, as evidenced by his efforts to help others less fortunate than himself. Some of his charitable activities involve golf benefits. A twelve-stroke handicapper, Hope has played the game all his life, often joining presidents, Hollywood's greats, and golf's immortals on the links. Because of the benefits the game brings to charities, Hope agreed in 1964 to have the Palm Springs Classic golf tournament renamed The Bob Hope Desert Classic, and he has hosted it ever since. Hope's serious side was also apparent in the preface to his 1963 book *I Owe Russia $1200*, in which he wrote: "Yes, the conquest of space is within our grasp, but as we reach out we seem to have diminished the inward search. No significant breakthrough has yet been made in the art of human relations. So perhaps this is the precise moment in history for each of us to look into his heart and his conscience and determine in what way we may be responsible for our present dilemma."

Sources

▶ Books

Faith, William Robert, *Bob Hope: A Life in Comedy*, Putnam, 1982.

Hope, Bob, *I Never Left Home*, Simon & Schuster, 1944.

Hope, Bob, *Have Tux, Will Travel: Bob Hope's Own Story*, Pocket Books, 1956.

▶ Periodicals

Good Housekeeping, "Delores Hope: My Forty-Eight Wonder Years with Bob," July, 1982, pp. 107-130.

New York Times, "On the Road to the 19th Hole," January, 1985, p. 50.

Time, "All-American Wisecracker," May 30, 1983.

TV Guide, "The Night Bob Hope Got Dropped on His Head," May 21-27, pp. 83, pp. 14-16.

Lee Iacocca

"Get all the education that you can, but then, by God, do *something*."

Born October 15, 1924, in Allentown, Pennsylvania, Lee Iacocca is an automotive manufacturing executive and entrepreneur.

Current address: Chrysler Corp., 12000 Chrysler Dr., Highland Park, Mich. 48288.

I acocca's is one of America's outstanding success stories. The son of Italian immigrants Nicola and Antoinette Iacocca, Iacocca, rose to head two of America's automotive giants, Ford Motor Company and Chrysler Corporation. He's become so well known and respected that many of his supporters urged him to run for the presidency of the United States. Perhaps no greater reward could be offered to a person considered by many to be a truly American hero.

Iacocca was born and raised in Allentown, Pennsylvania. His father, a successful businessman who lost all his money at the onset of the Great Depression, subsequently opened a restaurant. Iacocca followed him in the food business; at the age of ten he waited outside supermarkets with his red wagon, offering to take bags of groceries home for shoppers, and as a teenager he earned two dollars a day hauling produce for a fruit market. Iacocca also worked in his father's restaurant, and says that at one time he considered going into the fast-food restaurant line of work. By the time he was fifteen years old, however, Iacocca realized that retailing automobiles was fascinating work, as well as profitable. From that time onward, he says, all of his energies were centered on the automobile industry.

Iacocca studied engineering at Lehigh and Princeton universities and joined Ford Motor Company upon his graduation in 1945. Unhappy with engineering, Iacocca transferred to the company's sales and marketing division. Innovative and hardworking, Iacocca rose quickly in the ranks. He became truck marketing manager in 1956, car marketing manager the following year, and vice-president of the company and general manager of the Ford division in 1960.

Iacocca's success at Ford was overwhelming. In the mid-1960s he vetoed the development of the Cardinal, a proposed European-styled car, and developed instead an automobile that he thought would better meet the needs of the American public. The Mustang's success was astonishing. It sold 418,812 units in its first year of manufacture, and company chairman Henry Ford II consequently promoted Iacocca to company president in 1970. Eight years later, however, a petulant—some say jealous—Ford fired the maverick president. Soon after leaving Ford, however, Iacocca was approached by representatives of the financially failing Chrysler Corporation to come to that company. He made his conditions of acceptance clear: Iacocca would be the head of the company, his own boss, and would have a free hand in overseeing development.

Calling for broad organizational and complex financial restructuring, Iacocca turned Chrysler around. As he appeared in television commercials for Chrysler, his reputation as a straight-talking, honest, and pro-

American entrepreneur whose products were reliable grew. Citing his success at Chrysler and his growing popularity, people suggested that Iacocca run for president. He admitted that if he were ten years younger he might go into politics; he turned to other causes instead. He tried to revolutionize the relationship between management and labor, believing that the future prosperity of American business—and America—depends on the ability of management and labor to work together, not against each other.

Though a busy man, Iacocca does not hesitate to take on new assignments. President Ronald Reagan asked him to chair the Statue of Liberty-Ellis Island Centennial Commission. Iacocca saw this job as a labor of love: his parents and grandparents had entered this country through Ellis Island. "The island was part of my being," Iacocca elucidated, "not the place itself, but what it stood for." He went on to note that at Ellis Island many found their American roots, "and roots," he said, "are what this country is yearning for. People are aching to return to basic values. Hard work, the dignity of labor, the fight for what's right—these are the things the Statue of Liberty and Ellis Island stand for."

Iacocca fits the pattern of the American hero. He is a symbol of how successful a person can become in America. His mottoes outline his success and express hope for all Americans: "Apply yourself. Get all the education you can, but then, by God, *do* something. Don't just stand there, make something happen. It isn't easy, but if you keep your nose to the grindstone and work at it, it's amazing how in a free society you can become as great as you want to be."

Sources
▶ **Books**

Iacocca, Lee and William Novak, *Iacocca: An Autobiography*, Bantam, 1984.

Iacocca, Lee, *Talking Straight*, Bantam, 1988.

▶ **Periodicals**

Business Week, "Digesting AMC: So Far, So Good," February 22, 1988, p. 130, "Chrysler's Next Generation," December 19, 1988, pp. 52-54.

Fortune, "Iacocca's Time of Trouble," March 14, 1988, p. 79.

Good Housekeeping, "Lee Iacocca: Straight Talk on His Kids, His Mother, His Divorce," November, 1988, p. 134.

New Yorker, "Extra Virgin," October 24, 1988, pp. 34-35.

Jesse Jackson

''I am somebody. . . . Respect me. . . . I am God's child.''

Born October 8, 1941, in Greenville, S.C., Jesse Jackson is an American political and religious leader.

Present address: National Rainbow Coalition, 2100 M St. N.W., Suite 316, Washington, D.C. 20037.

J esse Jackson is one of today's leading black heroes. Jackson was raised in a proud but impoverished household. Born our of wedlock, he was adopted at the age of two by Charles Jackson, who married Jackson's mother, Helen Burns, and gave the boy his surname. Commenting on Jackson's ambition and air of professionalism, one of his high school teachers suggested that he was, even from his early years, searching for a mission and a role to play in life.

Jackson was quarterback at the all-black Sterling High School and received a football scholarship to the University of Illinois. When the position of quarterback on the university's team was denied him because of his race, Jackson transferred to North Carolina Agricultural and Technical College, where he became a star quarterback, an outstanding student, and a key figure in the desegregation of Greensboro, North Carolina.

According to his natural father, Noah Robinson, Jackson was impressed by the example of American religious and civil rights leader Martin Luther King, Jr., and, by the age of fourteen, dreamed of becoming a preacher. Charles Carter, Jackson's college roommate, recounted a dream Jackson had while in school: "One night he woke up and said he had an odd dream. He said he had been called to preach. He was shaking. I never saw him look so serious before." Dr. Sam Proctor, the president of North Carolina Agricultural and Technical College, encouraged Jackson to pursue a religious vocation. In 1963, Jackson decided against a career in law and enrolled at Chicago Theological Seminary to study for the ministry.

In 1965, Jackson answered King's call to stage a march for black rights in Selma, Alabama. As a member of King's Atlanta-based Southern Christian Leadership Conference (SCLC), he joined in the 1966 fight against Chicago mayor Richard Daley's alleged discrimination against blacks. Jackson went on to play important roles in other organizations dedicated to correcting racial injustices, including the National Association for the Advancement of Colored People (NAACP) and Operation Breadbasket/PUSH (People United to Serve Humanity).

Following King's assassination in Memphis, Tennessee, in 1968, Jackson was ordained a Baptist minister. He continued working with King's SCLC for more than three years before focusing his attention on the U.S. presidency. By 1972, Jackson had gained the support of blacks and liberal whites committed to political, social, and economic ideals that would benefit the nation's oppressed people.

Jackson's direct run for the U.S. presidency began at the Democratic Convention in 1983. He formed a large political and cultural power base among the disadvantaged: "Women, Hispanics, workers, Indians,

Chinese, Europeans—we must all come together and form a rainbow coalition," Jackson declared. He offered his candidacy in order to "help restore a moral tone, a redemptive spirit and a sensitivity to the poor and the dispossessed of the nation." In one of his most inspiring statements, Jackson said: "These hands . . . These hands . . . these hands that picked cotton can pick the next president of the United States." His enthusiastic audience responded with the famous phrase that was to echo across the land: "Run, Jesse. Run." Jackson's coalition was not strong enough, however, to win the nomination of the Democratic party in 1984 or 1988.

Jackson blames racism for most of America's social problems. As he said at one of his PUSH meetings: "The resolution of the race question in this country would liberate us to liberate others around the world. For until white America is what it ought to be, black America cannot be what it ought to be. And until black Americans are no longer prohibited by race from achieving their potential, all Americans will be poorer as a result." Jackson opens weekly PUSH meetings with the proclamation: "I am somebody. I may be poor, but I am somebody. I may be uneducated, I may be unskilled, but I am somebody. I may be on welfare, I may be prematurely pregnant, I may be on drugs, I may be victimized by racism, but I am somebody. Respect me. Protect me. Never neglect me. I am God's child."

Jackson's career, like that of most conventional heroes, has not been without controversy. He has been accused of accepting political help from the very forces he wished to usurp, namely the white elite, and his lack of political experience has, at times, caused him too appear insensitive and unwise. Still, Jackson is unequivocally one of the strongest political forces at work in the United States today. His forces are heroic, and he is respected by political allies and opponents alike.

Sources
▶ **Books**

Barker, Lucius Jefferson, *Our Time Has Come: A Delegate's Diary of Jesse Jackson's 1984 Presidential Campaign*, University of Illinois Press, 1988.

Chaplik, Dorothy, *Up With Hope: A Biography of Jesse Jackson*, Dillon, 1986.

Collins, Sheila D., *The Rainbow Challenge: The Jackson Campaign and the Future of U.S. Politics*, Monthly Review Press, 1986.

Jackson, Jesse, *Straight From the Heart*, edited by Roger D. Hatch and Frank E. Watkins, Fortress, 1987.

Jackson, Jesse, *A Time to Speak: The Autobiography of the Reverend Jesse Jackson*, Simon & Schuster, 1988.

Quinn, Richard, and Thomas Landess, *Jesse Jackson and the Politics of Race*, Green Hill, 1985.

▶ **Periodicals**

Nation, "For Jesse Jackson and His Campaign," April 16, 1988, p. 517, "Jesse is History," June 20, 1988, p. 15-18, "Creating a Democratic Majority," December 26, 1988, p. 705.

New Republic, "Anything He Wants," April 25, 1988, pp. 10-11, "The Curse of Jesse," December 5, 1988, pp. 20-21.

Newsweek, "Jackson for Vice President?" June 20, 1988, p. 29, "Does Jackson Want the Job?" June 27, 1988, p. 72, "A Jackson Strategy for '92," December 19, 1988, p. 7.

Time, "The Jackson Problem," December 12, 1988, p. 29.

Ann Jillian

"[I *want it to be remembered 40 years from now] that Ann Jillian made somebody feel good, somebody smile."*

Born January 29, 1951, in Cambridge, Massachusetts, Ann Jillian is an actress, dancer, and singer.

Address: c/o William Morris Agency, 151 El Camino Dr., Beverly Hills, CA 90212.

Ann Jillian was born Ann Jura Nauseda, the second child born to Lithuanian parents. Her mother wanted to be an actress, but before her dream was fulfilled she had to flee Lithuania when the Soviet Union invaded the tiny Baltic nation. Transferring this stage desire to her daughter, Mrs. Nauseda had her daughter dancing and singing by the time she was four years old. Jillian made her big-screen debut at age ten, playing Little Bo Peep in the 1961 Walt Disney movie *Babes in Toyland*. Two years later, at twelve, she appeared opposite Natalie Wood and Rosalind Russell in the film *Gypsy*. Jillian continued to play teenage roles in other 1960s films and made several guest appearances in a variety of television series.

After finishing high school, Jillian went to Pierce Junior College and then attended the Los Angeles Civic Light Opera on a scholarship. While performing with a traveling troupe in Chicago, she met Andy Murcia, a police sergeant who was later to become her husband. After marrying Andy, Jillian took a hiatus from performing, but soon returned in Mickey Rooney's Broadway show *Sugar Babies,* for which she won the 1979 Dramalogue Award. Her performance in *Sugar Babies* caused her to be cast as Cassie, the loudmouthed, man-hungry blonde in the ABC comedy series *It's a Living.*

From that point on, Jillian's career skyrocketed. She starred in the 1982 ABC television movie *Mae West,* winning an Emmy Award nomination, a Golden Globe Award nomination, and the Bronze Halo Award. She also appeared in the movie *Mr. Mom* (1983), in the television series *Jennifer Slept Here* (1983-84), and in the made-for-TV movie *Ellis Island* (1984), for which she won another Emmy nomination.

While filming the television mini-series *Alice in Wonderland* in 1985, in which she played the Red Queen, Jillian discovered that she had breast cancer and underwent a double mastectomy. As she told *People* magazine, it was not easy making the decision: "I was about to lose my breasts, my most feminine attribute. I would stand in front of the mirror, look at myself and cry. I was thinking about what every woman facing a mastectomy must think about—of being a whole woman."

However, Jillian did have the support of her family to rely on. Her husband, her parents, and several close friends were there to help her through the ordeal. As Jillian told *People* magazine, "Cancer is a family affair. It affects the family so profoundly that it makes us re-evaluate what we hold dearest." Jillian also received strength and guidance from Betty Ford, wife of President Gerald Ford, who has also undergone a mastectomy. She told Jillian: "God gives us unexpected challenges sometimes, but you'll get through it. It's all right to cry, but not for too long."

Heeding the advice of the former first lady, Jillian returned to the set of *Alice in Wonderland* eleven days after surgery. In the next few weeks she received more than 40,000 letters of support. Joan Rivers sent her a card which said: "Cheer up! I've been flat-chested all my life and it never stopped me." Many of Jillian's other Hollywood friends were also very supportive. Writing for the *Detroit Free Press*, Jillian remarked, "Mention Hollywood and many images come to mind. Having spent nearly all of my life in show business, I've always been aware of one of those images: that Hollywood is a tough dog-eat-dog town. How far from the truth this notion is, I learned during my recent operation and recuperation."

After her surgery, Jillian wrote several articles for various magazines and newspapers detailing her ordeal with cancer, but she had shied away from writing a book or producing a film about it. That changed in 1987 when she played herself in the made-for-TV movie *The Ann Jillian Story*. She told *The Saturday Evening Post*, "that movie—in one nutshell statement—was the most difficult thing I ever had to do and it always will be. I thought I would be protected because of the time that had passed, and because I could attack it from an actress' point of view. But it wasn't that easy. In the movie scene where I was given the injection, I would taste the metal in my mouth again and feel the burning sensation and the fuzziness—then the sickness. And the *anger* would come back to me, all the *hate* I had toward this thing called cancer." The viewing public rewarded her courage by making *The Ann Jillian Story* the highest-rated original TV movie of the 1987-88 season.

Above all, it's Jillian's determination which has cemented her triumph over cancer. As she told *People* magazine, "Cancer is not going to interfere with my career. . . . I'd still love to have breasts—but let's face it, I've never seen a pair of breasts tap dance, belt out a song or play Lady Macbeth. I know that Hollywood loves cleavage. But I think Hollywood ultimately has to look to the people. And as long as people out there like me—and I'm blessed to have that acceptance—then Hollywood's just going to have to accept me the way I am."

Sources

▶ **Periodicals**

Ladies Home Journal, "Ann Jillian: Getting on with Her Life," January, 1986, p. 38.

People Weekly, "Ann Jillian Finally Can't Kick," October 5, 1981, pp. 63-65, "I'm Begging You Don't Let Me Die," August 19, 1985, pp. 56-61, "Words of Assurance for a Stricken First Lady," November 2, 1987, pp. 48-50.

Saturday Evening Post, "Cancer Can't Stop Her," April, 1988, pp. 50-53.

Steven Jobs

"*My self-identity does not revolve around being a businessman, though I recognize that is what I do. I think of myself more as a person who builds neat things.*"

Born in 1955, computer designer and corporate executive Steven Jobs is co-inventor of the "Apple II" home computer.

Born in 1955, Steven Jobs was adopted shortly thereafter by a California couple, Paul and Clara Jobs. Jobs showed an early interest in electronics and gadgetry. As a high school student, he boldly asked William Hewlett, co-founder and president of the Hewlett-Packard computer firm, for some parts he needed to complete a class project. Hewlett was impressed enough to give Jobs the parts and offer him a summer internship at Hewlett-Packard.

After graduating from high school in 1972, Jobs attended Reed College in Portland, Oregon, for two years before dropping out, partly to ease his family's financial burden and partly to find himself. He hoped to visit India and study eastern spiritualism, but lacking necessary funds, went to work for Atari Computers part-time. He was able to save enough money to finance a trip to India in the summer of 1974. While there, he practiced meditation, studied eastern culture and religion, and even shaved his head. But by the fall, he became ill with dysentery and was forced to return to the United States.

For a short time, Jobs lived in a California commune but soon became disenchanted with the lifestyle. In 1975, he began associating with a group of computer aficionados known as the Homebrew Computer Club. One member, a technical whiz named Steve Wosniak, whom Jobs had first met at Hewlett-Packard, was trying to build a small computer. Jobs became fascinated with the marketing potential of such a computer, and in 1976 he and Wosniak formed their own company. The team was content to sell circuit boards designed by Wosniak until the computer prototype was complete. That same year, Wosniak succeeded in designing a small computer, and using Jobs's parents' garage, the two men worked to refine and market the product.

Jobs saw a huge gap in the existing computer market, as no product was targeted for home use. Wosniak improved his initial computer while Jobs lined up investors and bank financing. Marketing manager A.C. Markkula eventually invested $250,000 and became an equal partner in the Apple Computer Company. With new capital, Jobs and Wosniak refined the prototype. The redesigned computer—christened the "Apple II"—hit the market in 1977, with impressive first year's sales of $2.7 million. In one of the most phenomenal cases of corporate growth in U.S. history, the company's sales grew to $200 million within three years. Jobs and Wosniak had opened an entirely new market, that of personal computers, bringing the computational speed of business systems into people's homes and beginning a new era in information processing.

By 1980, the personal computer era was well underway. Apple was forced to continually improve its products to remain ahead in a growing marketplace. Competitors such as Radio Shack, Commodore, and International Business Machines (IBM) were gaining sales from Apple's market. In 1980, Apple introduced the Apple III computer, and improved version of the Apple II, but the new model suffered technical and marketing problems. It was withdrawn from the market, but was later reworked and reintroduced.

Jobs continued to be the marketing force behind Apple. He admitted that mistakes were made with the Apple III, but looked for innovative ways to meet new and existing consumer needs. Early in 1983, Jobs unveiled Lisa, another new computer, aimed this time at business executives. Lisa was designed for people possessing minimal computer experience. The model did not sell well, however, because of its high price and increased competition from IBM personal computers. By 1983, it was estimated that Apple lost half of its market share to IBM.

Faced with a declining market share, Apple introduced the Macintosh in 1984. In designing the model, Jobs apparently paid more attention to appearances than function. Although the Macintosh had "user-friendly" software and on-screen displays, Jobs failed to equip it with either a letter-quality printer or a hard disk drive. Lacking these features, the Macintosh did not sell well to businesses. The failure of the Macintosh signalled the beginning of Jobs's downfall at Apple Computer Company. In 1985, following a highly publicized showdown at Apple, Jobs resigned from the company he had founded, though he retained his title as chairman of its board of directors.

It was not long before Steve Jobs resurfaced, however. Soon after leaving Apple, he hired some of his former employees to begin a new computer company. The company was called NeXT, and Jobs invested $7 million of his own money to get it started. For three years, Jobs and his employees worked to produce the first NeXT computer, which was aimed at the educational market. Late in 1988, the NeXT computer was introduced at a large gala event in San Francisco. Initial reactions were generally good; the product was user-friendly, with very fast processing speed, excellent graphics displays, and an outstanding sound system. Other innovations included an optical disk drive instead of floppy disks, and a special sound chip to provide the fidelity of a compact disc. Judging from initial reactions, many critics were convinced that Steve Jobs had brought another revolutionary product to American consumers.

Steve Jobs helped start a revolution in information-processing in America. With his vision of affordable personal computers, he launched one of the largest industries of the past decades while still in his early

20s. He remains one of the most inventive and energetic minds in American technology today.

Sources

▶ **Books**

Butcher, Lee, *Accidental Millionaire: The Rise and Fall of Steven Jobs at Apple Computer*, Paragon House, 1987.

Young, Jeffrey S., *Steve Jobs: The Journey Is the Reward*, Scott, Foresman, 1988.

▶ **Periodicals**

Esquire, "The Second Coming of Steven Jobs," December, 1986, pp. 84-101.

Fortune, "Apple Bites Back," February 20, 1984, pp. 86-88.

Newsweek, "It's the Apple of His Eye," January 30, 1984, pp. 54-57, "Showdown in Silicon Valley," September 30, 1985, pp. 46-50, "Steve Jobs Comes Back," October 24, 1988, pp. 46-51.

Time, "Seeds of Success," February 15, 1982, pp. 40-41, "The Updated Book of Jobs," January 3, 1983, pp. 25-27, "Apple Launches a Mac Attack," January 30, 1984, pp. 68-69.

Pope John Paul II

*"*W*ork is one of the characteristics which distinguish man from the rest of the creatures."*

Birth-given name, Karol Josef Wojtyla; born May 18, 1920, in Wadowice, Poland, Pope John Paul II is the highest official in the Roman Catholic church.

Present address: Apostolic Palace, Vatican City, Italy.

P ope John Paul is one of the most distinguished religious leaders of the twentieth century. The younger of two boys born to Emilia Kaczorowska and Karol Wojtyla, Sr., a retired army lieutenant, John Paul II was raised in a strict Catholic family. He was a gifted student, excelling in literature, theatre arts, and athletics. In 1938, John Paul II entered University of Kracow to study literature, the Polish language, and acting.

Although the University of Kracow closed following the Nazi invasion of Poland in 1939, John Paul II continued to study underground and began training for the priesthood. Throughout the early 1940s, he supported himself through manual labor, hewing stones in a quarry and transporting lime buckets on a wooden yoke around his neck. In his publication *Laborem exercens,* John Paul II wrote that work is one of the callings of all men: "From the beginning man is called to work. Work is one of the characteristics which distinguish man from the rest of the creatures."

John Paul II's mother and older brother had both died when he was a child. In 1941, when John Paul II was twenty-one, his father died; that same year, John Paul was involved in two life-threatening accidents, fracturing his skull and causing permanent damage to his shoulders. These accidents, in combination with the death of his father and the ongoing atrocities of World War II, are said to have contributed to John Paul II's concern for the fate of mankind.

On November 1, 1946, John Paul II was ordained a priest. He studied philosophy and moral theology at Rome's Pontifical University of the Angelicum and became Doctor of Divinity in 1948. John Paul II served as Archbishop of Kracow and as a cardinal before being elected pope in 1978.

John Paul II is widely known for his conservative theological stands against divorce, artificial birth control, pre-and extra-marital sexual activity, and abortion. A dedicated human rights activist, John Paul II believes that every human being is divine and therefore worthy of respect and love. He has indicated that his own religious ideas were influenced by those of sixteenth-century Spanish mystic St. John of the Cross: "I think that in order to understand the dignity and genius of the human person one has to look into the theology of St. John the Cross. His teaching gives us a vision of the nature and meaning of man which will preclude our ever forgetting the value of the human person."

John Paul II has brought a smouldering energy and passion to the papal office. He is the first Polish pope ever and the first non-Italian to hold the office in 450 years. He has dedicated himself to maintaining the tradition of the Catholic church, making it his "primary duty to preserve the faith" and defend "moral ideals." An active leader, John Paul II favors direct and personal contact with people and therefore prefers to make live—rather than televised—appearances. He made four major tours in 1979—to Latin American, Poland, Ireland, and the United States.

On May 13, 1981, John Paul II was seriously wounded in Vatican Square by Mehmet Ali Agca, a young Turkish escaped convict. Upon his recovery, John Paul II publicly forgave his assassin and subsequently talked with him. Through the 1980s, the pope has continued many tours around the world, speaking to people of numerous countries in their own languages and demonstrating his love for mankind.

John Paul II has been called the greatest force for good in the world today. Critics have lauded his communication skills and credited him with bringing comfort and reassurance to a world that is often steeped in anxiety and fear. John Paul II's official biographer, Lord Longford, calls him "a loving shepherd who cares for all his sheep, whether they live up to his standards or, being human, fall below them." Both Catholics and non-Catholics throughout the world today respect the pope's opinions on the affairs of humanity.

Sources

▶ **Books**

Craig, Mary, *Pope John Paul II*, Penguin (London), 1982.

Hogan, Richard M., and John M. Levoir, *Covenant of Love: Pope John Paul II on Sexuality, Marriage, and Family in the Modern World*, Doubleday, 1986.

Johnson, Paul, *Pope John Paul II and the Catholic Restoration*, St. Martin's, 1982.

Longford, Lord, *Pope John Paul II: An Authorized Biography*, Morrow, 1982.

Schall, J. V., *The Church, the State, and Society in the Thought of John Paul II*, Franciscan Herald, 1982.

▶ **Periodicals**

America, "A Letter to Move the World," October 8, 1988, pp. 211-212, "The Pope on Human Vocation," October 22, 1988, p. 267.

Christian Century, "Back to Basics: A Decade of John Paul II," October 12, 1988, pp. 886-887.

Commonweal, "The Pope in Austria," August 12, 1988, pp. 421-422, "Blaming the Villains, Not the Victims," October 21, 1988, pp. 555-559.

Nation, "Casting Out the People's Church," August 27, 1988, pp. 161-
162.

National Review, "True Christian Feminism," November 25, 1988, p. 24.

Barbara Jordan

"We only want, we only ask, that when we stand up and talk about one nation under God, liberty, justice for everybody, we only want to be able to look at the flag, put our right hand over our heats, repeat those words, and know that they are true."

Born February 21, 1936, in Houston, Texas, Barbara Jordan is a professor of political science and former United States congresswoman.

T he summer of 1974 was an anxious time for the people of the United States. President Richard Nixon was under investigation for grave offenses in the Watergate affair. The thirty-five members of the House Judiciary Committee had been meeting for weeks behind closed doors to consider the evidence and define the charges against the president. Then, in July, the hearings were opened to the public. Television cameras zeroed in on individual committee members as they summarized their opinions. The speeches went on interminably, a formality in prelude to the important public hearing, with each congress member making the most of fifteen minutes on national television.

Then, at last, Barbara Jordan had her say. Looking solemn and tired, the freshman congresswoman from Texas stunned the nation with her intelligent, carefully considered comparison between Nixon's actions and the criteria for impeachment set down by writers from Thomas Jefferson to Alexander Hamilton. With her strong voice and forceful presence, Jordan put a mass of questions into a clear perspective. Basing her argument squarely on the Constitution, she reminded a confused and angry nation that lucid reasoning and consideration of the evidence should be the order of the day. "I believe hyperbole would not be fictional and would not overstate the solemnness that I feel right now," she said. "My faith in the Constitution is whole. It is complete. It is total. I am not going to sit here and be an idle spectator to the diminution, the subversion, the destruction of the Constitution." Reaction to the brief speech was overwhelming. People believed in Barbara Jordan; she—a black woman from the South—had spoken to each and every one of them.

Barbara Charline Jordan was the youngest of three daughters in a poor family. In her autobiography, she speaks of her Grandfather Patten as one of her closest friends during childhood. Her mother, Arlyne Patten Jordan, was trained at an early age as an orator in the Baptist Church, but devoted herself to her family in adulthood. Benjamin Jordan, her father, was extremely strict, demanding academic excellence while forbidding entertainment like dancing and movies. Watching her mother work from dawn to dark, washing, cooking, and keeping house, the young Barbara assumed her life would follow a similar course. "I don't know that I ever thought: 'How can I get out of this?' I just know that there were some things that I did not want to be a part of my life, but I had no alternatives in mind at that point. Since I didn't see movies, and we didn't have television, and I didn't go any place with anybody else, how could I know anything else to consider?"

But as she grew older, Jordan began to come into contact with new possibilities. A powerful orator, even while young, she was the star of the Phyllis Wheatley High School debate team. After listening to a talk by Edith Sampson, a black Chicago lawyer, during a high school "Career Day," Jordan decided to become a lawyer, though at the time, she said, "I believed I was going to be a lawyer, or rather something called a lawyer, but I had no fixed notion of what that was." She and her fellow students, she recalled, were still firmly fixed in the small world of their black, Houston ghetto. Jordan remarked, "What I'm saying is, at the time when I decided that I was not going to be like the rest, my point of reference was other black people. It seemed an impossibility to make any transition to that larger world out there."

After high school, Barbara Jordan went on to the all-black Texas Southern University, in Houston in 1952. Again she was a star debater, and the team's travels around the country plunged her for the first time into the prejudices and discrimination of the world at large. On the road in the deep South, blacks generally had to go to the back door of a restaurant to ask for a meal, and it was all but impossible to find a public restroom to use. But, she recalls, in the North things were somewhat different: " . . . we could at least go in front doors to get something to eat. That was the main point: we could go in the front door."

Throughout college, Jordan excelled in academics, and was accepted into Boston University Law School in 1956. It was there that she first truly began to learn to think instead of depending on her powerful speaking abilities. "I cannot, I really cannot describe what that did to my insides and to my head. I thought: I'm being educated finally." Law school was difficult and Jordan read long into the night to try and catch up to her fellow students who were mostly white. "I realized that the best training available in an all-black instant university was not equal to the best training one developed as a white university student. Separate was not equal; it just wasn't. No matter what kind of face you put on it or how many frills you attached to it, separate was not equal. I was doing sixteen years of remedial work in thinking."

Receiving her degree in 1959, Jordan returned to Houston to practice law. For the first three years, she used her parents' dining room table as her desk, but eventually saved enough money to open an office with another lawyer. Along with her private practice, she worked as an assistant to a county judge and became active in the Harris County Democratic Party. She ran twice for a seat in the Texas House of Representatives, losing both times. After the second loss, she said "I intended to devote my full attention to figuring out the way to succeed. And the first thing I knew was that it was not to let anybody else get inside my head. It was not to let anybody else make the decisions again."

The third time around, Jordan did succeed. She was elected to the state senate in 1967, making her the first black woman in the Texas Legislature. Shortly after her election, she was invited to the White House to confer with President Johnson on his Fair Housing legislation. A practical, no nonsense politician, she knew that to be an effective legislator, "Your work and you learn the rules and you keep your mouth shut until it is time to open it." She was readily accepted into the all-male, all-white Senate, and set to work on legislation such as the state's first minimum wage law, which especially aided "the really poor people, laundry workers, domestics, farm workers." Unopposed in 1968, she was reelected to a second term. In June of 1972, the Senate honored Jordan by naming her the traditional "Governor for a Day."

Barbara Jordan decided in 1971 to run for the United States Congress. She soundly defeated her opponent and took office on January 3, 1973. She was immediately named to the House Judiciary Committee, an extraordinary appointment for a freshman member of Congress, and thus was a major participant in the momentous impeachment hearings. Criticized by some for not being more of a leader in Civil Rights matters, Jordan consciously limited her role to that of legislator, believing that she could most effectively bring about change through her work as a lawmaker.

In 1976, Jordan's keynote speech set the Democratic National Convention on fire. Across the nation, people called for her to be named Jimmy Carter's vice-presidential candidate, or even to run for president. But believing the country was not yet ready for a black, woman president, Jordan, always the practical politician, threw support behind Carter and campaigned heavily for him.

When Jordan announced in 1977 that she would not seek a fourth consecutive term in the House, the political world was shocked. Why had this "rising comet" on the political scene so inexplicably decided to withdraw? Jordan explained that, as a firmly established national figure, "I thought that my role now was to be one of the voices in the country defining where we were, where we were going, what the policies were that were being pursued, and where the holes in those policies were. I felt I was more in an instructive role than a legislative role." To that end, she accepted a position at the Lyndon B. Johnson School of Public Affairs at the University of Texas. While not completely ruling out the possibility of a return to politics, her devotion to teaching is total at present. "When I leave these classes," she remarked, "I'm just—I'm on the ceiling, and all I want to do is talk about what went on in class and how my students responded."

Sources

▶ **Books**

Haskins, James, *Barbara Jordan*, Dial Press, 1977.

Jordan, Barbara and Shelby Hearon, *Barbara Jordan: A Self-Portrait*, Doubleday, 1979.

Stineman, Esther, *American Political Women: Contemporary and Historical Profiles*, Libraries Unlimited, 1980.

▶ **Periodicals**

Ms., "Barbara Jordan Talks about Ethics, Optimism and Hard Choices in Government," April, 1985, pp. 75-76.

Jackie Joyner-Kersee

"I *remember where I came from, and I keep that in mind. . . . If the young female sees the environment I grew up in and sees my dreams and goals come true, they will realize their dreams and goals might [also] come true."*

Born March 3, 1962, in East St. Louis, Illinois, Olympic gold medal winner Jackie Joyner-Kersee is considered one of the world's greatest athletes.
Address: P.O. Box 21053, Long Beach, CA 90801.

Often referred to as the world's greatest living woman athlete, Jackie Joyner-Kersee is the undisputed champion of the heptathlon, track and field's grueling seven-event sport which consists of the 200-and 800-meter dash, the 100-meter hurdles, and four field events: the high jump, long jump, shot put, and javelin throw. Among her accomplishments, Joyner-Kersee has finished first in numerous competitions, including two gold medals in the 1988 Seoul Summer Olympics for both the heptathlon and long jump, has broken her own heptathlon world record several times, and is the only heptathlete to break the 7,000-point barrier, a feat she has accomplished five times. Joyner-Kersee has never been one to rest on her laurels, however. She was once quoted: "People look at my marks and say 'You can't go any faster.' I don't believe that. I believe you can go faster in the hurdles and I believe I can throw farther and jump farther."

Joyner-Kersee's achievements are particularly inspiring considering the circumstances she had to overcome. Born Jacqueline Joyner on March 3, 1962, in East St. Louis, Illinois, an economically depressed industrial city along the Mississippi River, Jackie grew up in a neighborhood that was ravaged by street crime. Daily life was also one of economic struggle for Jackie, her three siblings, and her parents, Alfred and Mary Joyner, who were only teenagers when Jackie was born. The Joyner family lived in an inadequate house, sleeping in the kitchen because the stove was the only source of heat. Even getting enough to eat was a major concern. Jackie recalls, "We would have no food in the house, so we would eat mayonnaise sandwiches."

In spite of the bleak circumstances of her youth, Jackie strove to succeed. She has said, "Being able to go through the struggle is the reason why I am where I am today." At the age of nine she entered her first track meet and, although she finished last, "the next week in practice I could feel improvement," she once said. Soon Jackie began winning meets, especially in the long jump, where she displayed prowess. By the time she was twelve, Jackie had already leaped over seventeen feet. Her family, always a source of support, helped install a long jump pit at the end of their porch by bringing home sand from a local playground in potato chip bags. Jackie's successes in track and field served as an inspiration to her brother, Alfred, Jr., who would himself one day become an Olympic gold medalist in the triple jump.

Joyner-Kersee did not allow her achievements in sports to harm her academically. Her parents ensured this by grounding her for any Ds or failures in school. Jackie kept excellent marks in school and continued to develop her athletic skills. Joyner-Kersee excelled as an athlete in high school. At the age of fourteen, she won her first National Junior Pentathlon Championship, a feat she would duplicate for three more consecutive years. In her junior year, she set an Illinois state high school record of twenty feet, seven and one-half inches in the long jump. Jackie also played volleyball and basketball, and was part of the Lincoln High School girls basketball team which accumulated a record of 62-2 in her last two years of school.

Jackie graduated in the top ten percent of her class in 1980 and accepted a basketball scholarship to the University of California at Los Angeles (UCLA). Before her freshman year began at UCLA, she earned a spot on the United States Olympic team in the long jump. Joyner-Kersee's Olympic hopes would have to wait another four years, however, as the United States voted to boycott the 1980 Moscow Summer Olympics in protest of the Soviet Union's invasion of Afghanistan. Then another, more serious blow came to Jackie. Midway through her freshman year, her mother died of meningitis.

Along with the grief over her mother's death came a new sense of determination. She soon met Bob Kersee, later to be her husband, who convinced her to start competing in the heptathlon. She qualified for the 1983 world track and field championships in Helsinki, Finland, but unfortunately suffered a pulled hamstring and was unable to compete. Another hamstring injury the following year during the 1984 Los Angeles Summer Olympics caused her to fall behind the lead in the heptathlon by thirty points on the first day of competition. She regained the lead with a phenomenal javelin throw, setting the stage for a showdown in the competitions final event, the 800-meter run. The gold was not to be Joyner-Kersee's this time, however, as she finished .06 seconds behind the time she would have needed to win.

After her silver medal performance at the 1984 Olympics, Joyner-Kersee's determination helped her continue to improve in heptathlon competition. At the 1986 Goodwill Games in Moscow she broke the world record in amazing fashion, the first athlete in history to surpass the 7,000 point mark in the heptathlon. Less than a month later, she broke her own world heptathlon record at the United States Olympic Festival in Houston, Texas. Those two outstanding performances resulted in her winning the 1986 Sullivan Award, the 1986 Jesse Owens Award, and the *Track and Field News* "Athlete of the Year" Award.

Joyner-Kersee's achievements have continued at a record pace. In 1987 she won gold medals in both the heptathlon and long jump at the Rome world track and field championships and later the same year was named McDonald's amateur sportswoman of the year. The 1988 Seoul Summer Olympics marked one of Joyner-Kersee's greatest performances as she won gold medals in both the heptathlon and long jump, breaking her heptathlon record in the process. Joyner-Kersee shared the spotlight with her sister-in-law Florence Griffith Joyner who herself won three gold medals. Since then the accolades and honors have been numerous. Joyner-Kersee was selected McDonald's amateur sportswoman of the year for the second year in a row and the city of St. Louis named a day in her honor. More importantly, she has never forgotten her roots. In a recent trip to her hometown of East St. Louis she raised $40,000 to reopen the Mary Brown Community Center where she began her track and field career. During the visit she was introduced to 2,000 shrieking teenagers at the Kiel Opera House as "outstanding, beautiful, one of the fastest running and jumping and stomping women in history!" Joyner-Kersee responded by speaking about goals and dreams and of the importance of "bringing something back to this community [and those who] helped you on the way."

Sources

▶ **Periodicals**

Ebony, "The World's Greatest Woman Athlete," October, 1986, pp. 77-79.

Life, "Wonder Woman," October, 1988, pp. 89-93.

Maclean's, "Ghetto Goddess," September 12, 1988, pp. 66-67.

Ms., "Go, Jackie, Go," October, 1988, pp. 30-33.

Rolling Stone, "Bound for Glory," September 22, 1988, pp. 92-93.

Sports Illustrated, "Our Woman in Moscow," July 21, 1986, pp. 12-17, "Way Out Where No One Can Join Her," August 11, 1986. pp. 20-21, "Ties that Bind," April 27, 1987, pp. 76-85, "On Top of the Worlds," September 14, 1987, pp. 18-23, "Proving Her Point," October 3, 1988, pp. 28-31, "A Special Fire," October 10, 1988, pp. 43-47.

Vogue, "Winning Style," April, 1988, pp. 340-43.

Helen Keller

"**I** knew then that 'w-a-t-e-r' meant the wonderful cool something that was flowing over my hand. That living word awakened my soul, gave it light, hope, joy, set it free!"

Born June 27, 1880, in Tuscumbia, Alabama, author, lecturer and social activist Helen Keller promoted social reforms to improve the education and treatment of handicapped individuals. She died June 1, 1968, in Westport, Connecticut.

I n February, 1882, Helen, the nineteen-month-old daughter of Arthur and Kate Keller, was rendered unconscious by a severe fever. Helen Keller describes the incident in her autobiography, *The Story of My Life:* "They called it acute congestion of the stomach and brain. The doctor thought I could not live. Early one morning, however, the fever left me as suddenly and mysteriously as it had come. There was great rejoicing in the family that morning, but no one, not even the doctor, knew that I should never see or hear again."

Despite her loss of sight and hearing, Keller learned to do many small tasks such as folding the laundry and fetching objects for her mother. In fact, she devised an effective though limited system of signs to make her wishes known. Keller knew she was different from other people; understandably, the girl's frustration was uncontrollable at times. "Sometimes I stood between two persons who were conversing and touched their lips. I could not understand, and was vexed. I moved my lips and gesticulated frantically without result. This made me so angry at times that I kicked and screamed until I was exhausted."

The Kellers were unable to provide Helen with the specialized training required by a child with her handicaps. As the years passed, she became more willful and less responsive to the guidance of her protective parents. "I was strong, active, indifferent to consequences. I knew my own mind well enough and always had my own way, even if I had to fight tooth and nail for it." When Helen was about six years old, her father took her to Washington, D.C., to be examined by Dr. Alexander Graham Bell. Dr. Bell urged him to write the Perkins Institution for the Blind in Boston requesting that a competent teacher be sent to Tuscumbia to undertake Helen's education.

In answer to this request, twenty-year-old Anne Mansfield Sullivan, a recent graduate of the Perkins Institution, arrived at the Keller home on March 3, 1887. Sullivan was the daughter of poor Irish immigrants. At an early age she and her younger brother were sent to the infamous Tewksbury almshouse in Massachusetts. She was nearly blind as a result of an eye disease, and had entered the Perkins Institution in 1880.

Sullivan knew from her own experience that firmness and determination would be required to teach the undisciplined, though intelligent, Helen. Tempering firmness with love, she spent hours each day teaching Helen the manual alphabet, which the child imitated quickly. It took a great deal of time and perseverance, however, for Sullivan to impress upon Keller the significance of the finger symbols. The moving scene of Keller's discovery that everything has a name has been reenacted time and time again in motion pictures, plays, and dramatizations. Her own description of the incident is quite eloquent: "We walked down the path to the well-house, attracted by the fragrance of the honeysuckle with which it was covered. Some one was drawing water and my teacher placed my hand under the spout. As the cool stream gushed over one hand she spelled into the other the word 'water,' first slowly, then rapidly. I stood still, my whole attention fixed upon the motions of her fingers. Suddenly I felt a misty consciousness as of something forgotten—a thrill of returning thought; and somehow the mystery of language was revealed to me. I knew that that 'w-a-t-e-r' meant the wonderful cool something that was flowing over my hand. That living word awakened my soul, gave it light, hope, joy, set it free! There were barriers still, it is true, but barriers that could in time be swept away."

From that time forward, Keller's curiosity was insatiable and Sullivan's patient perseverance unflagging. Little by little, Keller learned to express herself through the manual alphabet and to read Braille. When Keller was ten years old, Mary Swift Lamson, one of Laura Bridgman's teachers, told Keller about Ragnhild Kaata, a deaf and blind Norwegian child who had been taught to speak. Keller immediately resolved to learn to speak. Sullivan took her to Sarah Fuller, principal of the Horace Mann School for the Deaf. Keller made remarkable progress and eventually learned to speak French and German as well as English. While attending the Wright-Humason School for the Deaf and the Cambridge School for Young Ladies, Keller also studied history, mathematics, literature, astronomy, and physics. Her determination to possess as much knowledge as possible took her to Radcliffe College, from which she graduated, cum laude, in 1904.

Keller's triumph over ignorance was followed by her triumph over public indifference to the welfare of the handicapped. She devoted the rest of her life to the promotion of social reforms aimed at bettering the education and treatment of the blind, the deaf, the mute, and, in effect, all handicapped individuals. The recipient of innumerable humanitarian awards and citations, Keller is credited with prompting the organization of many state commissions for the blind. Her efforts were also very influential in putting an end to the practice of committing the deaf and the blind to mental asylums. In addition, she was a pioneer in informing the public in the prevention of blindness of the newborn. Her candid articles in the *Kansas City Star* and *Ladies' Home Journal* were among the very first public discussions of venereal disease and its relationship to newborn blindness. Keller carried her campaign to improve the condition of the handicapped throughout the world, completing several extensive lecture tours in Europe, Asia, North and South America, and Africa. Keller is universally recognized as one of the foremost humanitarians of the century.

Through all the triumphs and trials, Keller's constant companion was her teacher, Anne Sullivan. Even the older woman's marriage to John Albert Macy, the literary critic and editor of Keller's autobiography, did not interrupt the friendship. Sullivan assisted Keller all through her school and college days, manually spelling the lectures and reading assignments into Keller's palm. Later, she accompanied Keller on her lecture tours, giving full support to her pupil and their joint cause of aiding the handicapped. The partnership was ended only at Sullivan's death in 1936.

A play and several films have been based on the story of Keller's life. "The Miracle Worker" by William Gibson was originally written as a play and was later made into a film. The film version starred Anne Bancroft and Patty Duke, who were named best actress and best supporting actress by the Academy of Motion Picture Arts and Sciences in 1962.

Sources

▶ **Books**

Johnson, Ann D., *The Value of Determination: The Story of Helen Keller*, 2nd edition, 1976.

Keller, Helen, *The Story of My Life*, edited by John Albert Macy, Doubleday, Page, 1903, revised and enlarged edition, Hodder & Stoughton, 1966.

Keller, Helen, *Midstream: My Later Life*, Doubleday, Doran, 1929, reprinted, Greenwood Press, 1968.

Ross, Ishbel, *Journey into Light*, Appleton, 1951.

Wilkie, Katherine E., *Helen Keller: From Tragedy to Triumph*, new edition, Bobbs Merrill, 1983.

John Fitzgerald Kennedy

" $\mathbf{A}$ sk not what your country can do for you, but what you can do for your country."

Born May 29, 1917, in Brookline, Massachusetts, John Fitzgerald Kennedy was the thirty-fifth president of the United States, and was assassinated November 22, 1963, in Dallas, Texas.

K ennedy was one of nine children born to mega-millionaire Joseph P. Kennedy and his wife, Rose. He was raised at the family's Hyannis Port, Massachusetts, compound on Cape Cod, where he was encouraged to develop a directness of manner and keen sense of competition. Because of the family's size, each member had to vie for attention, and no one could expect preferential treatment. "I grew up in a very strict house," Kennedy once said, "where there were no free riders."

Although Kennedy also proved a competitive student at such exclusive institutions as the Choate Preparatory School for Boys, he was always aware of his privileged status and the obligations that it imposed upon him. "Of those to whom much is given, much is required," he reasoned. Therefore, after completing studies at Harvard University, he began a career of public service.

He had been early introduced to the world of politics when his father served President Franklin Delano Roosevelt as U.S. ambassador to England. In 1939, while Kennedy was with his father at the American Embassy in England, the British ship *Athenia*, with many Americans aboard, was sunk near Glasgow, Scotland, by the German navy. Kennedy was sent by his father to investigate the sinking and assist the surviving American passengers. Kennedy's father later contended that his son obtained valuable experience from this assignment.

During World War II Kennedy continued to devote himself to the good of others by serving in the armed forces. A serious back injury (sustained while playing football at Harvard) had jeopardized his enlistment, but successful treatment eventually enabled him to join the U.S. Navy and become commander of a torpedo motorboat in the Pacific Theater. When his boat was destroyed by Japanese forces, Kennedy survived by swimming three miles to safety, and he saved a crew member by biting into his life belt and towing him. For his conduct, which he forever downplayed, Kennedy earned a medal for heroic action.

While recuperating back in the United States, Kennedy learned that his older brother, Joseph, Jr., had died in the war. The death was particularly shattering to Kennedy's father, who had intended Joseph, Jr., for a political career. Once the war ended, however, Kennedy assumed his brother's aspirations and ran as his district's Democratic candidate for the House of Representatives. Though somewhat uneasy courting voters, Kennedy won the election. He continued to hold office in the House of Representatives for two more terms, distinguishing himself as a relatively independent Congressman with allegiance principally to his own working-class constituency.

In 1952 Kennedy decided to oppose incumbent Republican Henry

Cabot Lodge for the Senate. By this time, Kennedy has matured as a politician, using his wit, warmth, and intelligence to great effect in appealing to voters. Ted Sorensen, one of Kennedy's closest friends and confidants, later remarked: "[Kennedy] had a great capacity for growth . . . , willingness to learn . . . , [and] determination to explore and to inquire and to profit by experience. He was always interested in a new challenge for competition." Despite formidable opposition from Lodge and the Republican Party, Kennedy won the election.

In the Senate Kennedy continued to distinguish himself as a supporter of the working class, particularly through his membership in the Labor and Public Welfare Committee. Within the Democratic party, he also showed himself a confident, concerned politician, and by the late 1950s, when Kennedy was in his third Senate term, he was being considered a likely presidential prospect. In 1960 he submitted his candidacy for party nomination, which he won following a string of primary victories in the spring. In opposing Republican nominee Richard M. Nixon, Kennedy waged an enterprising campaign. He was especially success- ful in exploiting the television medium, and during a nationally broad- cast debate his wit, grace, and physical appeal overwhelmed his oppo- nent. The election was ultimately a close one, but Kennedy emerged triumphant.

As president, the charismatic Kennedy quickly became a symbol of a new spirit in America, one of hope and prosperity in which every American would have to contribute in order to reap the benefits. "Ask not what your country can do for you," he proclaimed at his inaugura- tion, "but what you can do for your country." He was characterized in the press as a knight in shining armor—indeed, some journalists even referred to America as Camelot—and his family was likened to royalty. Kennedy appeared particularly engaging when speaking to reporters, with whom he often exchanged quips and goodnatured banter. On one such occasion, he was asked if he thought the presidency were a good job and if he would recommend it to others. Kennedy answered that the presidency was indeed a good job but that he would not recommend it to anyone else, at least not for four more years.

Kennedy called his political program the New Frontier, and he envi- sioned an America free of racism, poverty, and disadvantage. During his administration civil-rights measures were introduced and social programs were developed. In addition, organized crime was more forcefully opposed, and equality was vigorously emphasized. On the international level, Kennedy faced other problems. Early in the admin- istration he was drawn into a CIA-organized plot to invade communist Cuba with anti-communist Cuban refugees. The resulting action, often referred to as the Bay of Pigs Incident, proved disastrous—the invaders were easily defeated—and Kennedy was blamed for the defeat. Later, he proved more successful in handling international affairs, particularly the Cuban Missile Crisis, when Soviets established nuclear weapons in Cuba. Kennedy, realizing that World War III might be possible, was firm, but not antagonistic, in demanding the withdrawal of Soviet weaponry. After minimal deliberation, the Soviets dismantled the missiles and returned home.

The Cuban Missile Crisis was a key moment in the Kennedy administration, for at that point Kennedy proved himself a capable—as opposed to merely charismatic—world leader. Unfortunately, his presidency ended abruptly. On November 22, 1963, while touring downtown Dallas in a motorcade, he was shot twice and killed. A suspect, Lee Harvey Oswald, was captured, but he too was shockingly murdered. Kennedy was buried at Arlington Cemetery during a ceremony attended by the world's most important dignitaries.

Historians now speculate that Kennedy's death was a turning point in American history. Some see the assassination as an end of innocence and naivete—an end to the belief in an America that could actually rival the mythical Camelot in prosperity. Some historians even perceive the killing as the beginning of a period of social unrest that swept America throughout the remainder of the decade. Among the more violent aspects of that period were race riots and the shooting deaths of such leaders as Martin Luther King, Jr., Medgar Wiley Evers, and Kennedy's own brother, presidential candidate Robert Kennedy.

If John F. Kennedy left an enduring legacy, it is probably one of fairness. He had hoped to see the elimination of injustice and inequality in America, and though his own efforts were violently abbreviated, others have persevered in continuing his efforts. Economist John Kenneth Galbraith, a longtime friend of Kennedy, wrote: "The best way to serve his memory is to redeem and revindicate the values of decency, of rationality, of civility, of honor—those values for which he stood through his life and to which in the end he gave his life."

Sources

▶ **Books**

Brown, Thomas, *JFK: History of an Image*, Indiana University Press, 1988.
Carr, William H., *JFK: The Life and Death of a President*, Lancer Books, 1964.
David, Jay, *The Kennedy Reader*, Bobbs-Merrill, 1967.
Donovan, Robert J., *PT 109: John F. Kennedy in World War II*, Fawcett, 1961.
Lasky, Victor, *J. F. K.: The Man and the Myth*, Arlington House, 1966.
Sorensen, Theodore, *Kennedy*, Bantam, 1966.

Martin Luther King, Jr.

"C ertainly I don't want to die. But if anyone has to die, let it be me."

Martin Luther King, Jr., a Baptist minister and civil rights leader was born January 15, 1929, in Atlanta, Georgia, and assassinated April 4, 1968, in Memphis, Tennessee.

T here was always something special about Martin Luther King, Jr., even as a child, according to his father. He loved books and liked to keep them around him, even before he could read. King early recognized his talent as an orator and sought ways for its best use. He deliberated for years about becoming a minister like his father but felt that the ministry was not sufficiently intellectual to allow him to speak on contemporary problems. He then considered medicine, law, and other professions, but he remained unable to make up his mind.

In 1940 King entered Morehouse College, having skipped a year in high school. He majored in sociology and in his junior year decided to enter the ministry. Voicing his opinion on the role of education, he wrote, "The function of education . . . is to teach one to think intensively and to think critically. But education which stops with efficiency may prove the greatest menace to society. . . . The most dangerous criminal may be the man gifted with reason, but with no morals."

After graduating from Morehouse College in 1948, King entered Crozer Theological Seminary to further his training for the ministry. While there he attended a lecture by Modecai Johnson, president of Howard University, on Indian pacifist Mahatma Gandhi. Johnson's lecture provided King the direction he needed for his life. "His message was so profound and electrifying," King later said, "that I left the meeting and bought a half dozen books on Gandhi's life and works."

After graduating from Crozer in 1951 with the highest grade average in his class, King entered Boston University as a doctoral student. In Boston he met his future wife, Coretta Scott, who was studying voice at the New England Conservatory of Music. King received his doctorate from Boston University in 1955, then became pastor of the Dexter Avenue Baptist Church in Montgomery, Alabama. The future course of his ministry became apparent when he joined the supporters of Rosa Parks, a black woman who had been arrested in Montgomery for quietly refusing to give up her bus seat to a white person. King also began his relationship with Ralph Abernathy, a minister with whom he would work for the rest of his life.

In 1957 King and Abernathy were instrumental in founding the Southern Christian Leadership Conference, one of several groups King helped start. On January 14 that year, King's home and church in Montgomery were bombed as violence against black protesters continued.

After this bombing King began to reveal more of the dual nature of his personality—the desire to live and fight for the rights of black people, but also the resignation to die and thus become a martyr. William Robert Miller, one of King's biographers, commented on this nature: "When he did obey what seemed to be an occasional irresistible inner compulsion, he said that he felt seriously called to be a martyr—but he found it extremely difficult, and equally difficult to admit that he was worried about what he regarded as his inadequacy for the destiny that God had given him. After the Montgomery bombing, King had said: "Lord, I hope no one will have to die as a result of our struggle for freedom in Montgomery. Certainly I don't want to die. But if anyone has to die, let it be me."

Though always conscious of the possibility of death, King was steadfastly dedicated to nonviolence because of its power over violence. "Nonviolence can touch men where the law cannot reach them," he felt, because nonviolence allows the just consciences of the "great decent majority" of people to shine through, as Gandhi had demonstrated.

He knew black people would have to suffer while adopting the role of nonviolence. "The Negro all over the South must come to the point that he can say to his white brother: 'We will match your capacity to inflict suffering with our capacity to endure suffering. We will meet your physical force with soul force. We will not hate you, but we will not obey your evil laws. We will soon wear you down by pure capacity to suffer!'"

King's life was filled with confrontations, for he was always ready to rush to a city or a scene where he could help demonstrate the power of nonviolence. In March of 1963, the scene was Birmingham, Alabama. A *New York Times* reporter had said that Birmingham was a city that was culturally and racially backward: "The striking thing about Birmingham," he wrote, "is that it seems so advanced industrially and so retarded politically." Into this fray King threw himself. He was one of the black leaders whom most people watched and from whom the most was expected. He led with stirring oratory and insistence on nonviolence: "If you don't go," he said of the proposed march, "don't hinder me! We will march nonviolently. We shall force this nation, this city, this world, to fact its own conscience. We will make the God of love in the white man triumph over the Satan of segregation that is in him. . . . The struggle is not between black and white. But between good and evil."

These were the days when King began to use the language and wisdom of the visionary. In Detroit he had used the "I have a dream" motif which was to carry him to his greatest heights of persuasiveness. Speaking at the March on Washington, August 28, 1963, from the Lincoln Memorial, he began the litany that would sound in the hearts of every listener: He dreamed of that day, he said, when "my four little children . . . will not be judged by the color of their skin but the content of their character." It was a note that touched the very heart of America.

King ended is talk with the stirring lines: "Free at last! Thank God Almighty, we are free at last!"

Through the years King continued to be the center around which a whirlwind of events made history. In 1963 he became *Time* magazine's Man of the Year. In 1964 he was awarded the Nobel Peace Prize, becoming the youngest recipient of that prize in history. And through the years he was always willing to demonstrate for civil rights, as he did in leading a march across Pettus Bridge in Selma, Alabama, on March 21, 1965. His resulting speech, delivered from the steps of Alabama Capitol in Montgomery, demonstrated again King's unequaled gift for oratory. How long, he asked, would it take for justice to take over the world? "How long? How long? Because mine eyes have seen the glory of the coming of the Lord," he quoted from "The Battle Hymn of the Republic."

Though himself a nonviolent person, King was surrounded by violence and by allies who preached violence on his part. In Harlem while autographing copies of his book *Stride Toward Freedom* he was stabbed. King was frequently jailed, but he regarded this as a realistic and practical way of symbolizing his willingness to suffer and sacrifice for the common good. He expected no less of fellow sympathizers, black and white. Nonviolence "may mean going to jail," he said. "If such is the case the resister must be willing to fill the jail houses of the South. It may even mean physical death. But if physical death is the price a man must pay to free his children and his white brethren from a permanent death of the spirit, then nothing could be more redemptive." Further, King's marches were not always successful. In 1966 he had taken on militancy in Chicago, further arguing for nonviolence, but did not win. Such radical leaders as Stokely Carmichael criticized King for his stand. Congressman Adam Clayton Powell of Harlem derisively called the great leader Martin "Loser" King. And at times even his closest friends, such as Andrew Young and Ralph Abernathy, began to feel that King was becoming so visionary as to be ineffective. King's wife, Coretta, remarked on her husband's demons in life: "My husband was what psychologists call a guilt-ridden man. He was so conscious of his awesome responsibilities that he literally set himself the task of never making an error in the affairs of the Movement."

In the violent America of the 1960s, perhaps it was inevitable that the driven civil rights leader would meet fatal violence. He went to Memphis, Tennessee, to help out striking garbage workers in their push toward better salaries. Perhaps it was fitting that King see his highest and most tragic goal in this setting. "Well, I don't know what will happen now," he said in his speech. "But it doesn't matter with me now. Because I've been to the mountaintop. I won't mind. Like anybody, I would like to live a long time. Longevity has its place. But I'm not concerned about that now. I just want to do God's will. And He's allowed me to go up to the mountain. And I've looked over, and I've seen the promised land." He darkened his vision with strong hints of his own doom: "I may not get there with you, but I want you to know tonight that we as a people will get to the promised land. So I'm happy tonight. I'm not worried about anything. I'm not fearing any man." And he ended this emotional climb with the words: "Mine eyes have seen the glory of the coming of the Lord!"

King was assassinated April 4, 1968, on the balcony outside his Memphis motel room. Perhaps no more fitting tribute could be raised to the slain believer in the power of nonviolence than one of his own statements: "If a man hasn't found something he will die for, he isn't fit to live."

Sources

▶ **Books**

Branch, Taylor, *Parting the Waters: America in the King Years, 1954-63*, Simon & Schuster, 1988.

Davis, Lenwood G., *I Have a Dream: The Life and Times of Martin Luther King, Jr.*, Negro Universities Press, 1969.

King, Martin Luther, Jr., *Stride Toward Freedom*, Harper, 1958.

King, Martin Luther, Jr., *Strength to Love*, Harper, 1963.

King, Martin Luther, Jr., *Why We Can't Wait*, Harper, 1964.

King, Martin Luther, Jr., *Free at Last*, 1977.

Lewis, David Levering, *King: A Biography*, University of Illinois Press, 1978.

Walton, Hanes, *The Political Philosophy of Martin Luther King, Jr.*, Greenwood Press, 1971.

▶ Periodicals

American History Illustrated, "Trumpet of Conscience: A Portrait of Martin Luther King, Jr.," April, 1988, pp. 18-27.

Christian Century, "Incorporating the Dream of Martin Luther King, Jr.," April 6, 1988, pp. 332-333.

Department of State Bulletin, "The International Legacy of Martin Luther King, Jr.," November, 1988, p. 17.

Mother Jones, "A Challenge in King's Memory," February/March, 1988, p. 60.

Newsweek, "The Explosive Power of Good," November 28, 1988, pp. 84-85.

Time, "Martin Luther King, Jr.," January 11, 1988, p. 22.

Henry Kissinger

"I am always convinced of the necessity of whatever I'm doing. And people feel that, believe in it."

Born May 27, 1923, in Furth, Germany, Henry Kissinger, former U.S. Secretary of State, is a scholar of international policy.

K issinger, a recipient of the Nobel Peace Prize, may have been the single most important American political individual of the twentieth century. At the height of his popularity—during the administration of President Richard M. Nixon—Kissinger enjoyed immense public recognition. A joke circulated that the superhero Superman was even seeing a psychiatrist because he kept imagining that he was Kissinger, and one commentator speculated that Kissinger had actually replaced Uncle Sam as the most appropriate symbol of America.

Kissinger was the son of a teacher who was, in turn, also the son of a teacher. The Kissingers lived in Germany until the Nazis proved an overwhelming threat to virtually all European Jews, whereupon the family fled to England, then moved to the United States. In his youth, Kissinger was greatly interested in sports, though he also distinguished himself in mathematics. During World War II he served in the U.S. Army as a member of the intelligence corps, and when the war ended he entered Harvard University, where he eventually graduated *summa cum laude.*

After completing his studies Kissinger remained at Harvard to teach. Upon the election of John F. Kennedy to the presidency, however, Kissinger was called to Washington, D.C. But the two men apparently had disagreements, so Kissinger returned to Harvard. During the Nixon administration, Kissinger finally enjoyed substantial power in the American government, becoming a key adviser during the Vietnam conflict. After the war ended Kissinger remained in the administration as Secretary of State in 1973. He was valued for his shrewd analysis and straightforward assessments of political problems. "When one persuades or conquers someone, one mustn't deceive them," he confided to journalist Oriana Fallaci.

The political demise of President Nixon hardly altered Kissinger's impressive stature. He has served as a consultant to other presidents, and he has remained prominent on the social scene, where he is prized as a powerful, brilliant thinker. "The nature of power has never been easy to assess," he once acknowledged. As a German-born academician, Kissinger continues to occupy a unique position in international politics.

Sources
▶ **Books**

Mazlish, Bruce, *Kissinger: The European Mind in American Policy*, Basic Books, 1976.
▶ **Periodicals**

Foreign Affairs, "Bipartisan Objectives for American Foreign Policy," summer, 1988, pp. 899-921.

Nation, "Minority Report," April 2, 1988, p. 452.

Newsweek, "An Agenda for 1989," June 6, 1988, pp. 31-34.

Time, "Kissinger the Pessimist," March 7, 1988, p. 40.

C. Everett Koop

"*When you approach the 70 percent of sexually active teenagers and tell them to just say no, they laugh at you.*"

Born October 14, 1916 in Brooklyn, New York, C. Everett Koop began serving as U.S. Surgeon General in 1982 and has made notable strides in such health care areas as AIDS education and anti-smoking campaigns.

C Everett Koop was about to retire as surgeon in chief at Children's Hospital in Philadelphia when he was selected in 1981 by President Reagan to become U.S. Surgeon General. In his more than 30 years as chief surgeon at Children's Hospital, Koop had become famous in medical circles for innovative surgical techniques and his care for children. He pioneered early efforts to repair intestinal obstructions and to correct undeveloped esophaguses, and established the nation's first hospital neonatal unit. When Koop arrived in Washington in 1981 to await Senate confirmation as Surgeon General, however, he met unexpected resistance from a number of quarters. Because of his fundamentalist Christian beliefs and staunch opposition to abortion, many leading liberals and civil rights groups opposed his nomination. Criticism mounted that Koop was being selected on the basis of his political viewpoints, rather than his medical credentials. After nearly nine months of bitter conflict on Capitol Hill, Koop was narrowly confirmed by a Republican-controlled Senate. During his tenure as Surgeon General, however, Koop became a strong and compassionate leader in several of America's most important health care arenas, winning the support of many of the groups who had initially opposed him. Koop displayed an ability to separate his personal feelings from his professional duty, making him an effective and responsible leader in this nation's health care movement.

Charles Everett Koop, the only child of John and Helen Koop, knew he wanted to be a doctor by the time he was five years old. As a child, he had several serious accidents, including a brain hemorrhage suffered while playing football, which kept him in bed for over a year. By the time he was fifteen, he was so enthralled by medicine that he would sneak into Columbia Presbyterian Hospital in New York, don a white lab coat, and sit in the amphitheater of operating rooms posing as a medical student. Following high school, Koop attended Dartmouth College in Hanover, New Hampshire, and graduated with a bachelor's degree in 1937 at the age of 20. From there he went on to attend Cornell University Medical School, where he majored in pediatric surgery. As Koop later said, "Children weren't getting a fair shake in surgery, getting giant incisions . . . and being sewn up like a football when a tiny hole would do. I saw the chance to make a difference." After training at Boston Children's Hospital, Koop did his graduate work at the University of Pennsylvania Medical School. He then took a position at Children's Hospital in Philadelphia.

When Koop began practicing pediatric surgery in the early 1940s, there were only about five pediatric surgeons in the entire United States. The field was clearly underdeveloped, and Koop would get his chance to make a difference. "On call" 24 hours a day, Koop quickly established himself at Children's Hospital as a compassionate and tireless surgeon. Once he was slowed by a peptic ulcer, and was forced to spend two weeks in the hospital as a patient. Rather than spend more time in the hospital, he constructed a device which treated him at home so that he could work during the day. The device consisted of an intravenous tube containing milk which he pushed through his nose and down his throat so that his ulcer could be treated as he slept.

Koop was chosen to become chief surgeon at Children's Hospital in 1948. He soon became one of the real pioneers of children's medicine. After founding the first neonatal surgical care unit in the United States, Koop began his pioneering work in operating on undeveloped esophaguses in newborn infants. In 1965, he operated on a severely deformed baby, David Sweeney, whom other doctors had given very little chance of survival. For the first 20 years of Sweeney's life, Koop operated on the child 37 times, and Sweeney not only survived but became a functioning member of society. In 1974 Koop supervised a surgical team that successfully operated on a pair of Siamese twins, joined at the abdomen, who had been pronounced inoperable by other physicians. These twins also survived.

When Koop was selected by President Reagan to become Surgeon General, he had the backing of many conservative and religious organizations, who supported his views on abortion, family life, and religion. Koop's appointment ran into trouble, however, with a well-organized and ferocious attack from liberal groups, in particular leading women's rights organizations. Many people feared that Koop's positions against abortion and euthanasia, and his condemnation of homosexuality would make him a rigid right-wing proselytizer as Surgeon General. For his part, Koop was saddened and angered by the charges leveled against him, at one point saying to his wife, "I don't need this! I've never been treated this way before!" Koop attempted to defuse many of the criticisms of his conservative beliefs by promising to keep his own personal beliefs separate from what he saw as best for public health. After nine often bitter months, Koop's confirmation process finally came to a close with Koop being approved as Surgeon General by the narrowest of margins in the Senate.

Koop's actions in office during the ensuing years would largely reverse many of the apprehensions raised in his confirmation hearings. One of his earliest actions as Surgeon General was to lead an all-out assault against the tobacco industry. In May of 1984, Koop issued a report condemning all uses of tobacco, and pointed out the dangers of "passive smoking," where bystanders inhale smoke from someone else's cigarette. Koop proposed a "smokeless society by the year 2000," indicating his hope that America as a nation could "kick the habit."

Koop's report alienated some conservative supporters, including Senator Jesse Helms of North Carolina, a state with a thriving tobacco industry, while other realized perhaps for the first time that Koop was not just a "knee-jerk" conservative.

Koop further alienated conservatives with a report concluding that there was no evidence of adverse psychological effects of abortion. Although Koop himself remained opposed to abortion, he softened his views considerably; when asked once what medical advice he would give to a pregnant woman with AIDS, he responded, "If you want to give her all the possibilities that were available to her, you would have to mention abortion." Anti-abortionists were appalled, some calling for Koop's resignation. Other groups were glad to see Koop's delicate handling of difficult issues.

Perhaps Koop's greatest impact as Surgeon General came in response to the AIDS crisis. Although the exact genesis of AIDS is still subject to some question, it became a world-wide crisis in the mid-1980s. At first confined largely to homosexuals, by the mid-1980s AIDS was recognized as a disease affecting all individuals. Conservatives had wanted the Reagan administration to use AIDS as a way of condemning homosexuality. In 1984, public pressure to take action prompted Reagan to ask Surgeon General Koop to prepare a report on the disease.

Koop began to investigate the disease with leading experts and researchers around the world. The results of his two-year investigation were published in October of 1986. Koop had written 27 drafts of the report before he was satisfied with it. More than 107 million copies of the report were mailed to American households. The main findings of the report were that the best methods for controlling AIDS were sex education at an early age and the use of condoms during sexual intercourse. Koop concluded that sex education regarding AIDS must begin for school children "at the lowest grade possible." Koop's approach was nonjudgmental, calling for sympathy for all AIDS victims, be they homosexual or heterosexual, drug addicts or infant children. His call for increased use and availability of condoms infuriated the Reagan administration and conservatives, who had supported abstinence. Koop concluded, "When you approach the 70 percent of sexually active teenagers and tell them to just say no, they laugh at you."

Koop's report on AIDS has been credited by many citizens as opening up a responsible discussion about the disease. Many fears and misconceptions about the disease were repudiated by the report, while the real concerns were delineated. C. Everett Koop's tenure as Surgeon General has rarely been without controversy, but the awareness of health care issues among American citizens has likely never been higher. Koop's sensitivity toward all victims of pain and disease, and his ability to effectively separate his personal beliefs from his job as America's leading health official, have helped him leave a significant mark on all American citizens.

Sources

▶ **Periodicals**

New Republic, "An Officer and a Gentleman," January 23, 1989, pp. 19-22.

Newsweek, "Koop Controversy," June 8, 1981, p. 101, "Koop Makes Waves in His War on AIDS," March 2, 1987, p. 31.

People, "C. Everett Koop," April 21, 1986, pp. 91-92.

Time, "The Missionary Doctor," June 8, 1987, p. 22, "A Doctor Prescribes Hard Truth," April 24, 1989, pp. 82-84.

U.S. News & World Report, "A Fall from Grace on the Right," May 25, 1987, pp. 27-28, "Rebel with a Cause: Koop," May 30, 1988, pp. 55-63.

Candy Lightner

"I 'd much rather have my daughter back, but the fact that I've given some positive meaning to her death and that others have lived as a result makes me feel good. If you care enough, you can accomplish anything."

Born May 30, 1946, in Pasadena, California, Candy Lightner is a social activist and author.
Address: Suite 1-289, 22653 Pacific Coast Hwy., Malibu, California 90265.

S ince the 1980 death of her teenage daughter in a traffic accident involving a drunk driver, Candy Lightner has been a vocal advocate of tougher laws against people who drink and drive. "The public," she says, "doesn't perceive drunk driving as a crime, yet more people are killed each year in this manner than they are by handguns." Inspired by the anger she felt after her daughter's death, Lightner founded Mothers Against Drunk Drivers (MADD; now Mothers Against Drunk Driving), which has grown from a one-woman crusade into an organization of national significance. Lightner and MADD have successfully lobbied for legislation restricting the sale of alcohol to minors and increasing the penalties for drunk driving; showing that, as a 1986 *Vogue* profile commented, "one passionate woman can change the world."

Candy Lightner was born Candy Lynne Doddridge, the daughter of Dykes, a career serviceman in the U.S. Air Force, and Katherine, a civilian Air Force employee. She was educated in Fairfield, California, and attended American River College in Sacramento after graduating from high school.

Lightner's upbringing and early adult life gave little indication of the path she was eventually to follow. After graduating from high school in 1964, she worked as a dental assistant in various private offices in California, where she met and married Steve Lightner, a U.S. Air Force serviceman. They had three children before they divorced, and Lightner embarked on a fresh career as a real estate agent in Fair Oaks, California.

The stable routine of Lightner's family life came to an abrupt end one sunny Saturday in May of 1980 when her thirteen year-old daughter Cari was struck and killed by a car as she walked her bike to a church carnival. The driver of the car, who was drunk, never even stopped, and was only arrested after a call from his conscience-stricken wife. Just two days before the fatal accident, the man, Clarence Busch, had been arrested for another hit-and-run incident and had been released on bail. Although he had several previous convictions for drunk drioving, his most severe punishment had been forty-eight hours in jail, and his driver's license had been reissued after each offence.

When she learned the facts behind her daughter's death, Lightner's grief turned to anger. "This was not an unfortunate accident," she later observed. "Cari was the victim of a violent crime. If my daughter had been raped or murdered, no one would say of the killer, 'There but for the grace of God go I'".

Determined to make Cari's death meaningful, Lightner resolved to end the public thinking which sees "death caused by drunk drivers [as] the only socially acceptable form of homicide." Her anger transformed her from an apolitical real estate agent not even registered to vote, into a national figure who considers the victims of drunk drivers to be her "constituency".

Lightner founded Mothers Against Drunk Drivers on the eve of her daughter's funeral. "I remember sitting in the bar with all these people and saying out loud, 'I'm going to start an organization. . . .' There was a big moment of silence, and then my girlfriend pipes up and says, 'And we can call it Mothers Against Drunk Drivers.'"

Lightner quit her job and, using her savings plus insurance money from Cari's death, she managed to fund 60% of MADD's first year budget of $41,000. Fuelled by her energy, MADD grew quickly, taking everyone by surprise. "I had in mind twenty women marching on the Capitol in California" she said, "but within two months we were about one hundred people marching on the White House in Washington."

One of Lightner's first successes was persuading Governor Jerry Brown of California to appoint a state commission to study drunk driving. It took months of daily visits to his office, but in the fall of 1980 he finally agreed, and Lightner was appointed as the commission's first member. By the following year, MADD had grown into a five state, twenty-five chapter organization. "We've kicked a few pebbles," Lightner told a *Time* reporter, "we'll turn a few stones, and eventually we'll start an avalanche."

She was encouraged in 1981 by the approval of new laws in nine states allowing law enforcement agencies to pursue drunk drivers more rigorously than before, and at her prompting, her native state of California passed a tough drunk driving code which caused alcohol-related traffic accidents and deaths to fall dramatically.

Lightner's cause was helped by the staggering number of fatalities due to drunk driving. In the first two years of the eighties alone, more Americans died as a result of drinking and driving than had died in the Vietnam war. Lightner's refusal to let such statistics escape the public eye, and her constant pressure on legislators and Congressmen led eventually to the establishment in 1982 of the National Commission on Drunk Driving, to which she was appointed by President Reagan.

By 1982, MADD had eighty-nine chapters in twenty-nine states and operated on a budget of $160,000. Two years later, these figures had grown to 325 chapters in forty-seven states, with a budget of several million dollars and a new headquarters in Hurst, Texas.

Twenty-seven states toughened their drunk driving laws in 1982 as a direct result of Lightner and MADD, and with each new legislative measure, the numbers of alcohol-related traffic deaths fell and the numbers of drunk drivers arrested rose.

One of Lightner's primary concerns has always been the education of the young, and in 1980 she founded Students Against Driving Drunk (SADD). She also urged Congressmen to raise the national legal drinking age to twenty-one, saying "we just don't feel that kids at eighteen, many of whom are just learning to drive, should be allowed to drink too." Her efforts bore fruit in 1984 when, after a lengthy campaign, she succeeded in attracting enough support to ensure the passage of Representative James Howard's bill raising the minimum drinking age to twenty-one. "Our intent was not to punish the minority, the youth of our nation who are under twenty-one," said Lightner of the new National Minimum Drinking Age Act. "We hope to give them a chance—an even better opportunity to live, to prosper, and to enjoy all that life has to offer."

In 1985, Candy was included among *Time* magazine's "Seven Who Succeeded", and the following year was also elected the YWCA "Woman of the Year" and ranked in the top twenty-five of America's most influential women by the *World Almanac and Book of Facts*. Lightner left MADD in 1985 following criticism of her financial management. She is now a frequent speaker at college campuses and on television and radio talk shows.

Lightner's achievements have been won through commitment to her beliefs and years of single-minded determination. While some people have accused her of obsessiveness, many others thank her for her efforts. As President Reagan's Secretary of Transportation, Elizabeth Hanford Dole stated, Lightner has awakened "America to the menace of the drunk driver."

"You have to believe in your cause above everything else," claims Lightner. "I can't stand apathy. I cannot tolerate people who tell me that they don't vote because it won't make a difference." Although nothing can erase the painful memories of that spring day in 1980, she believes that by campaigning against drunk driving she is helping make Cari's death less pointless. "I believe that for every problem there is a solution. . . . We are changing the way people think about drinking and driving. But more than that, we have caused people to change their behavior, and this is saving lives. I believe in the rights of victims. And I do believe that if you believe in something badly enough, you can make a difference."

Sources

▶ **Periodicals**

Broadcasting, "MADD as Hell and Not Going to Take It Anymore," April 15, 1985, p. 54.

Consumers Digest, "Putting a Stop to Drunk Driving," November-December, 1982, pp. 20-22.

Nation's Restaurant News, "Interview: MADD's Lightner, the Founder of Mothers Against Drunk Drivers Talks about How the Restaurant Industry Can Help Curb Alcohol Abuse," November 25, 1985, pp. 533-535.

Newsweek, "Curbing Drunk Drivers," January 25, 1982, p. 30.

People, "A Grieving, Angry Mother Charges That Drunk Drivers Are Getting Away with Murder," June 29, 1981, pp. 24-26, "Already the Conscience of a Nation, Candy Lightner Prods Congress Into Action Against Drunk Drivers," July 9, 1984, pp. 102-103.

Vogue, "One Woman Can Make a Difference," April, 1986, p. 170.

Charles A. Lindbergh

*"*A*s our civilization advances . . . I feel sure we will realize that progress can be measured only by the quality of life—all life, not human life alone. The accumulation of knowledge, the discoveries of science, the products of technology, our ideas, our art, our social structures, all the achievements of mankind have value only to the extent that they preserve and improve the quality of life."*

Born February 4, 1902, in Detroit, Michigan; died of cancer, August 26, 1974, in Maui, Hawaii. A pioneering aviator, scientist, and social commentator, Charles A. Lindbergh was the first pilot to make a nonstop solo flight from New York to Paris.

C harles A. Lindbergh was born at a time when the United States was shedding its rural, humanistic roots and fast becoming an urban, technological society. As a witness to the revolutionary changes occurring in the first half of the twentieth century, he became one of America's greatest heroes.

Lindbergh was the only son of Charles Augustus Lindbergh, a Minnesota congressman, and Evaline Lodge Land. Though born in Detroit, he was taken as an infant to Lindholm, his father's farm, on the west bank of the Mississippi River. Here Lindbergh developed a strong love of the country and roamed the landscape free and unrestrained, dreaming that he could "ride on the wind and be part of the sky." His father believed that children should be self-reliant and unbroken by adults, reasoning, "The more child life is dominated, the easier adults are influenced."

An indifferent student in high school, Lindbergh preferred to spend his time drawing mechanical gadgets and asking scientific questions. He tried college at the University of Wisconsin but did not like it. Instead, he pursued an interest in flying and airplanes and by 1922, was barnstorming through Nebraska and performing parachuting and piloting stunts. On March 19, 1924, Lindbergh started formal training in the Army Air Corps. He graduated the next year as a second lieutenant in the Army Air Service Reserve. In addition, he started an airmail service from St. Louis to Chicago. With hazardous landing strips, weak planes, and no lights, the work was dangerous for Lindbergh and his pilots.

Lindbergh soon decided to try for the Orteig Prize, a $25,000 purse awarded to the first person to fly from New York to Paris. He arranged for his plane to be built in San Diego and flew it back to New York via St. Louis, setting a transcontinental record in the flight. In preparing the plane—called the *Spirit of St Louis*—for the flight to Paris, Lindbergh lightened it in every possible way. He reduced the weight of his clothing, took only minimal food, and even threw away all the unnecessary pages from his flight book, replacing every pound he saved with gasoline. Early on the morning of May 20, 1927, Lindbergh took off from a soggy field into a heavy drizzle. He flew by way of Nova Scotia, Newfoundland, and Ireland, constantly reminding himself of what would occur if he fell asleep: "death and failure, death and failure." Thirty-three and one-half hours later, Lindbergh landed at Le Bourget Field, Paris, to a hero's welcome. Shy and unassuming, he captured America's heart and gained international fame.

Lindbergh married Anne Morrow on May 27, 1929. Two years later, their first child, Charles, was kidnapped from their home in Hopewell, New Jersey. On May 12, 1931, the baby was found dead. The loss of his son and subsequent harassment by the press drove him to leave Hopewell; he donated the house to a nonprofit organization "to provide for the welfare of children . . . without discrimination in regard to race of creed."

Kept constantly in the public eye, Lindbergh finally bent under the pressure and moved to England in 1935, commenting, "We Americans are a primitive people. . . . Americans seem to have little respect for the law, or the rights of others." He returned to the United States four years later, at the dawn of World War II, whereupon he expressed unpopular opinions about the implications of the war effort. He denounced France and England's lack of military readiness and spoke out against American involvement in the war, but after the United States was attacked at Pearl Harbor, he demonstrated loyalty to his country. Lindbergh worked as a consultant to Henry Ford at the Willow Run plant near Detroit and to the U.S. War Department, helping to design the B-24 Liberator bomber. He flew fifty missions in the Southwest Pacific as an "indefatigable" volunteer pilot for the U.S. Air Force.

In addition, Lindbergh contributed to the advancement of several scientific fields, including aeronautics and cryogenics. Later in his life, however, he reassessed his devotion to science. In his 1948 book *Of Flight and Life,* the aviator recounted an incident in which an improper reading of a faulty gauge nearly led to his death. "In worshipping science," he wrote, "man gains power but loses the quality of life."

During the last decade of his life, Lindbergh was active in many conservation causes. He contributed to the preservation of Peruvian whales, the tamarau and monkey-eating eagles of the Philippines, and the Stone Age Tasaday people on Mindanao Island. While suffering from cancer in the summer of 1974, he flew to Maui. He died there on August 26 and was buried in a humble cemetery. Throughout his lifetime, Lindbergh was the inspiration for hundreds of popular creative works, including symphonies, songs, dances, operas, poems, novels, sculptures, and cartoons. But many historians agree that his greatest gift to America and humanity as a whole was his recognition of spiritual life in a world of technology.

Sources
▶ **Books**

Crouch, Tom D., editor, *Charles A. Lindbergh: An American Life,* Smithsonian, 1977.

Gray, Susan M., *Charles A. Lindbergh and the American Dilemma: The Conflict of Technology and Human Values,* Bowling Green State University, 1989.

Lindbergh, Charles A., *Of Flight and Life*, Scribner, 1948.

Luckett, Perry D., *Charles A. Lindbergh: A Bio-Bibliography*, Greenwood, 1986.

▶ **Periodicals**

Life, "Lindbergh: Stubborn Young Man of Strange Ideas Becomes a Leader of Wartime Opposition," August 11, 1941, pp. 64-70.

New Republic, "High Cost of Fame," June 12, 1929, pp. 87-88.

Reader's Digest, "The Thrill That Swept the World," June, 1948, pp. 7-12.

Saturday Evening Post, "The Facts About Lindbergh," December, 1940, pp. 12-13, 50-53.

Time, "American Epic," September 14, 1953, p. 116, "Lindbergh: The Way of a Hero," May 26, 1967, pp. 22-23, "Charles A. Lindbergh: Pragmatist and Pioneer," February 18, 1974, p. 18.

Greg Louganis

"*I like to have a sense of command up there, a psychological edge—like everyone else is a step behind me before they start, like they'll have to wait until I miss.*"

Born c. 1960, Greg Louganis is an Olympic gold medal-winning diver.

L ouganis is widely considered the greatest diver in the world. Of Samoan and European ancestry and adopted shortly after birth by American parents, Louganis refined his natural athletic ability and grace at an early age with dance lessons and gymnastics. Soon an accomplished junior diver, he qualified at age sixteen for the 1976 American Olympic diving team, winning a silver medal in the platform event in Montreal. Louganis went on to earn three world diving championships before competing in the 1984 Olympic games in Los Angeles, where he won gold medals in both the platform and the springboard events. Competing in his third Olympic competition—the 1988 summer games in Seoul, Korea—he again won both the springboard and the platform events, despite suffering a head injury in the process. Louganis thus became the first man to win two gold medals in diving in successive Olympics games.

Peter and Frances Louganis of San Diego, California, adopted Greg when he was nine months old. Peter Louganis was a bookkeeper at the time and later worked as a tuna-boat controller. Before the young Louganis was two years old, he was doing headstands and other acrobatics. His parents enrolled him in a tap-dancing class when he was about three, and by the time he was eight, Louganis was an outstanding gymnast. When he performed acrobatic jumps into the Louganis pool, his father signed him up for diving lessons.

Louganis' life in school as a child was unpleasant. Subjected to racial slurs because of the dark Samoan skin, he suffered further name-calling because of a stutter and a reading disorder diagnosed as dyslexia. The treatment he received from some of his classmates, coupled with his natural shyness, led him to largely withdraw into his own shell.

Two years after Louganis began taking diving lessons, coaches around the nation were already in awe of his performances. At age eleven, he was spotted at a diving competition in Fort Lauderdale, Florida, by Ron O'Brien, then a coach at Ohio State University, and later Louganis' personal coach. O'Brien later commented on Louganis' performance at that competition: "The moment I saw him dive, I thought this was a kid who someday could win the Olympics, that's how impressive he was even then." The same year, Dr. Sammy Lee, the American diver who had won gold medals at both the 1948 and 1952 Olympics, saw Louganis at a diving meet in Colorado Springs, Colorado. Lee later said, "When I first watched him, I said to myself, 'My god, that's the greatest talent I've ever seen.'"

At age fifteen, Louganis began studying under Lee, who did not charge the Louganises anything for lessons; Lee said, "I do it for love." Louganis, however, did have to follow two rules that Lee felt necessary for success: no drinking, and no smoking. Louganis also had to clean Lee's pool. One year later, in 1976, Louganis qualified for the Summer Olympic games in Montreal. He won the silver medal in platform diving, barely losing the gold to Italy's Klaus Dibiasi. Although the silver medal was not actually a disappointment to Louganis, both he and his coaches knew he could do better.

In 1978 Louganis enrolled as a student at the University of Miami. He had just won the World Championships in platform diving that summer in Berlin, Germany, and he was interested in studying drama and dance in addition to competing in diving. After two years at Miami, Louganis transferred to the University of California at Irvine, which was near his training facilities at Mission Viejo and coach O'Brien, Louganis' new trainer.

Louganis was unable to compete in the 1980 Olympics in Moscow because the United States and other free world nations boycotted the games to protest the Soviet invasion of Afghanistan. Louganis kept training, however, hoping to compete in the 1984 Olympic games in Los Angeles. By the early 1980s, Louganis was recognized as the world's greatest diver; He had won twenty-six U.S. championship events, four events in the Pan American Games, and three world championship events, in addition to his silver medal in Montreal. Having added the springboard event to his repertoire, Louganis was acknowledged to be the best in the world in both springboard and platform diving; he was to compete in the two events in Los Angeles' 1984 Olympic games.

In Los Angeles, Louganis not only won the gold medal in the springboard event, he won by more than ninety-two points over his nearest rival. Louganis' former coach, Lee, said, "I have been around diving for 50 years, and no one I have seen past or present, or whom I see coming in the future, will equal [Louganis'] performance." In the platform competition, Louganis went into his last dive with a score so much higher than his competitors' that he almost could have fallen into the water and still won the event. Nonetheless, on his final dive he received five scores of 9.0, one of 9.5. and one of 10.0 from the judges, winning the gold medal by sixty-seven points and setting a new world record for points scored. He became the first man in fifty-six years to win gold medals in both springboard and platform events in an Olympic competition.

Following the 1984 Olympics, many members of the diving community speculated Louganis would retire from international competition, He was twenty-four years old and had many other interests, including acting, which would require a great deal of time. As with any sport, diving necessitates rigorous practice to stay in top form, leaving little time for anything else. Louganis decided to stay with diving and prepare himself for the 1988 Olympics in Seoul.

By 1988, Louganis was twenty-eight years old, ancient by diving standards. Some of his competitors in the upcoming Olympic games would be half his age. Louganis, though, was still the premier diver in the world. Unfortunately, he arrived in Seoul with physical problems: in addition to an injured wrist suffered during a practice dive he had a fever, falling ill with a sore throat soon thereafter. Undaunted, Louganis prepared himself for the springboard competition, his first event. One of Louganis' strengths in diving is his ability to jump higher off the springboard (up to nine feet) than any of his competitors. This great height allows Louganis to do more complex and difficult dives than many of his opponents. It also entails more risks. During one of his springboard competition dives, Louganis miscalculated his distance from the board, and on the way down from the jump struck his head on the board. He sustained a three-inch gash that required stitches. In what many considered a truly heroic effort, Louganis returned to finish the springboard competition and won the gold medal.

Several days intervened between the springboard and platform events, and Louganis had some time for his head wound to begin healing. In the meantime, however, the media began to sensationalize his injury, as well as the pressure on Louganis to win the second gold medal. Louganis later said, "I just freaked out. The pressure was really getting to me like never before." He withdrew from the spotlight, remaining in his room alone.

The platform competition began, and Louganis built a comfortable lead through the first few dives. Then Xiong Ni of China, only fourteen years old, began to close in on Louganis' lead. At his tenth and final dive, Louganis needed a superior dive and a total of 85.57 points to win the gold medal. Louganis later recalled his thoughts as he walked down the platform for his final dive: "No matter what happens, my mother will still love me." He succeeded in scoring 86.70 points and winning his second gold medal of the 1988 Olympics, his fourth gold overall. Recalling that last dive, he said, "In a way, it was the same as any other dive. You hear the tremendous crowd noise, then you enter the water and suddenly you are surrounded by silence." The dive, in fact, was extraordinary, for it not only won for Louganis the gold medal, but rendered him the first man in history to win two gold medals in diving at two successive Olympic games. For his heroism despite the injury to his head, Louganis was honored with the Olympic Spirit Award, the highest honor bestowed upon an Olympic competitor.

Following the 1988 Olympic games, Louganis said he intended to compete in one more world championship and then pursue a career in acting. Regardless of what he does in the future, Louganis—to many the essence of grace, form, and strength—will be remembered as the greatest diver of his time and, perhaps, of all time.

Sources

▶ Periodicals

Newsweek, "True to the Olympic Ideal," October 10, 1988, pp. 63-64.

People, "Primed and Ready for Seoul," September 19, 1988, pp. 48-55.

Reader's Digest, "Greg Louganis: High Diver with Heart," June, 1988, pp. 163-64.

Rolling Stone, "Arc of a Diver," September 22, 1988, pp. 86-91.

Sports Illustrated, "Winging On toward Immortality," May 11, 1981, pp. 32-37, "Best is Getting Better," August 29, 1983, pp. 10-15, "It's a Bird, It's a Plane, It's Supergreg!," August 20, 1984, pp. 80-83.

Time, "A Soaring, Majestic Slowness," August 20, 1984, pp. 62-63.

Sean MacBride

"The Republic of Ireland Act which resulted in the official declaration of Eire as the Republic of Ireland, is a great event for which our joy is marred by the fact that six of our northeastern counties remain arbitrarily cut away from us."

Born January 25, 1904, in Paris, France, Sean MacBride died in Dublin, Ireland on January 15, 1988. He was the founder of the Irish Republican Party and co-founder of Amnesty International.

S ean MacBride was the Republic of Ireland's Minister for External Affairs from 1948 to 1965. He came into office as a member of then Prime Minister John Costello's Cabinet in February, 1948. He entered the Irish Republican Army in his early youth and fought in the Irish Independent movement. In 1947, MacBride organized the Clann na Poblachta (Republican) party to work for the establishment of the Republic of Ireland and for the end to the partition of the country. The Republican party was responsible for the fall of De Valera's government, which was replaced by a Coalition government in 1948. In 1949, MacBride, a member of the nine Ministers on the steering committee of the Office of European Economic Cooperation, saw the Republic of Ireland proclaimed. In the early 1960s, MacBride helped to found Amnesty International, an organization that works to free political prisoners around the world. MacBride worked in the early 1970s to liberate Southwest Africa from the grasp of South Africa, for which he was awarded the Nobel Peace Prize in 1974. In 1977, he was awarded the Lenin Peace Prize. MacBride died on January 15, 1988.

Sean MacBride was born to John and Maud (Gonne) MacBride. His father founded the Irish Brigade in the 1890s, and fought with it as a major against the British in the Boer War. His mother was a supporter of the Irish revolutionary movement. His parents separated shortly after MacBride's birth. His father returned to Dublin, Ireland, and his mother remained in Paris. In 1916 MacBride's father was executed by the British for his part in the Easter Rebellion. MacBride was educated at the Jesuit Institution St. Louis de Gonzague in Paris until he was 12 years old, and later at Mount St. Benedict in Gorey, County Wexford, Ireland. At the age of 13, he joined the Irish Republican Army as a junior volunteer. He spent the next 20 years working in the political underground. Sean was an officer in B Company of the Third Battalion of the I.R.A. Brigade, and later became a member of the GHQ staff during the 1919-21 struggle with the Black and Tan constabulary. He also became a junior member of the Irish delegation which negotiated the Anglo-Irish Treaty of 1921.

The Anglo-Irish Treaty ended the strife between Britain and Ireland and established the Irish Free State with dominion status at home, but with Crown control abroad. In the summer of 1922, MacBride joined De Valera in attempting to seize power in Dublin and was captured and imprisoned in Mountjoy Prison. He escaped while being transported from Mountjoy to another jail. An amnesty was declared for political prisoners at the end of 1923, but MacBride continued to work underground. In 1925 he became adjutant general to Liam Lynch, then commander-in-chief of the Irish Republican Army.

MacBride enrolled at Dublin National University, and despite the amnesty for political prisoners, he was arrested the second day he went to classes. Throughout this period he wrote for journals in support of Irish independence. Once out of prison, in 1926, he married Catalina Bulford, an Irish girl born in Argentina. Under assumed names, the couple spent time in France and returned to Ireland in 1927 for the birth of their daughter Anna. MacBride later went to the United States to enlist support for the Irish Republican Army, returning within a short time. In 1936, he became commander-in-chief of the I.R.A., but resigned a year later because of a policy dispute with other leaders. He withdrew from the I.R.A. in September 1937, and after completing his law school studies, was admitted to the Irish bar. He soon became known as the most successful trial lawyer in Dublin, and after seven years of practice, was called to the Inner Bar with the title of Senior Counsel, an accomplishment that usually took 15 years.

At the end of World War II, MacBride was pressured to form a new political party. A year later he founded the Clann na Poblachta, or Republican Party, and worked for a New Deal-type economic program, the establishment of an Irish Republic, and an end to the partition of Ireland. MacBride was elected to the Dial as a member for Dublin County. De Valera, in an attempt to weaken the new party, called for a general election in February 1948. But MacBride's forces won ten seats from Fianna Fail, De Valera's group, which ended De Valera's majority in the Dial. A new Coalition Government was formed, with John Costello of the Fine Gael (United Irish) party as Prime Minister, and MacBride as Minister for External Affairs, a post previously held by De Valera.

MacBride met in Paris with ministers of the 19 Marshall Plan countries in July, 1948, to establish the office for European Economic Cooperation. MacBride's efforts at this meeting established the principle that membership of the organization's permanent council be composed of Foreign Ministers, not of civil servants (France and Great Britain favored technical experts) with no power to make policy decisions. MacBride was one of those largely responsible for the Republic of Ireland Act, which resulted in the official declaration of Eire as the Republic of Ireland.

MacBride remained active in Ireland's government until the mid-1960s. At about that time, he met 39 year-old Peter Benenson, a British attorney who specialized in defending people persecuted for their political or religious beliefs. Because of the high number of political prisoners around the globe, Benenson realized his effect as an attorney was limited, so he declared 1961 a year of an "Appeal for Amnesty." That year MacBride joined forces with Benenson, and together they planned the first missions of the newly named "Amnesty International" to help individual prisoners.

In 1972, Amnesty began a worldwide "Campaign for the Abolition of Torture." "The growth of torture has been described as epidemic," said MacBride. "To control dissent and maintain power, governments have submitted torture to intellectual analysis and produced progressively more sophisticated methods of cowing, punishing, and eliminating real or imagined opponents of their regimes." For the next several years, MacBride, as chairman of Amnesty International's Executive Committee, worked closely with the United Nations to keep tabs on, and hopefully reduce, the numbers of political prisoners. MacBride resigned his chairmanship in 1974, just one month before he was awarded the Nobel Peace Prize "in recognition of his lifelong work for human rights." MacBride continued to work behind the scenes in human rights cases until his death in Dublin on January 15, 1988.

Sources

▶ **Periodicals**

Life, "Old Maude Sends Her Boy Out To Beat Devil," February 23, 1948, pp. 40-41.

Newsweek, "Surprise, Surprise," October 21, 1974, p. 49.

New York Times, January 25, 1988.

New York Times Magazine, "Rebel With Portfolio," March 11, 1951, p. 17.

Saturday Evening Post, Ireland's New Man of Destiny," *April 23, 1949, p. 31.*

Time, "Phoenix," December 1, 1947, p. 34, "Portrait," February 28, 1949, p. 27.

Nelson and Winnie Mandela

"[I *would] gladly go and water that tree of liberation with my blood, if it meant that the children I am bringing up under [present] conditions will not lead my kind of life . . . I find myself strength from the knowledge that each step I take the nation is behind me."*
—*Winnie Mandela*

The Mandelas—Nelson, born in 1918 in Transkei, South Africa, and Winnie, born in September, 1936, in Transkei—are perhaps the best known political activists protesting South Africa's racially biased laws.

N elson Mandela, a lawyer and leader of the outlawed African National Congress (ANC), and his wife Winnie, originally a social worker, have been called "the first family of South Africa's freedom fight" for their efforts to end the South African government's segregationist policy of apartheid and to gain equal rights for all South Africans. Although Nelson has been imprisoned for more than a quarter of a century, he continues to be the focal point of much anti-apartheid protest; and Winnie has also survived prison terms and government harassment in her efforts to win representation for the seventy-five percent of South Africa's population that is denied the right to vote and forced to live rigidly segregated from the white ruling class.

Nelson Rolihlahla Mandela was born in 1918, in the Transkei region of South Africa's Eastern Cape Province, the son of an important tribal chieftain. Nelson renounced his hereditary right of succession when he left home to avoid an arranged marriage and to seek a career in Johannesburg, a booming commercial region. Attracted to the study of law, he attended University College at Fort Hare, but was expelled for his role in the student strike of 1940. He later worked as a policeman while taking correspondence courses, and earned his law degree from the University of South Africa in 1942. In 1944, Nelson joined the African National Congress (ANC), an organization that since 1912 had worked to find ways to alleviate racial tensions.

Recognizing that the ANC's approach to the racial problem was inadequate, Nelson helped organize the Congress Youth League (CYL), an ANC splinter group. The CYL advocated non-violent resistance like that pioneered by Mohandas Gandhi: boycotts, general strikes, and civil disobedience. In 1956, the government brought charges against Nelson and, in a four-and-a-half year action known as the "Treason Trial," tried to show that he and the other leaders of the ANC were guilty of having violated anticommunist and treason laws. Nelson's able defense of the ANC's motives and activities resulted in the presiding judge acquitting all the defendants in March of 1961. When he helped organize a three-day general strike later that year, he was again threatened with arrest, and had to go undercover.

On August 4, 1962, Nelson Mandela was apprehended by the South African police, after eighteen months in hiding. Brought to trial in October, he turned his defense into a ringing indictment of the apartheid system. In an eloquent statement to the presiding judge, the ANC leader rejected the right of the court to hear the case on the grounds that—as a black man—he could not be given a fair trial under a judicial system intended to enforce white domination, and furthermore, he considered himself neither legally nor morally bound to obey laws created by a parliament in which he had no representation. Nelson vigorously cross-examined prosecution witnesses on the inequities of apartheid and delivered a stirring pre-sentencing statement in which he described his personal career and political education, and explained why he felt justified in having taken "extra-legal" (as opposed to illegal) action. Despite his able defense, he was given a five-year suspended sentence.

In 1964, Nelson was again arrested, this time for his role in organizing an undercover military organization dedicated to governmental sabotage. In June he was sentenced to life in prison. All his books and public speeches were banned, and possessing them was made a criminal offense in South Africa. He has remained in prison ever since.

After her husband's imprisonment, Nlosikazi Nobandle Nomzamo Madikzela—named "Winnie" by her father out of respect for Christian missionaries—emerged as a leader of the liberation struggle in her own right. She had married Nelson, eighteen years her senior, in 1958, and recognized both the necessity and the morality of his struggle. Her commitment to his ideals helped sustain her after Nelson's arrest. "I rediscovered," she said, "the value of my soul in relation to my religious beliefs and most of all to the cause of my people. . . . I had ideas and views of my own. I had my own commitment and I wasn't just a political ornament." In May, 1969, Winnie was arrested under a new law that allowed police to detain people suspected of terrorism indefinitely. She spent eighteen months in jail without trial, much of the time in solitary confinement, deprived of any contact. After her release, she was placed under house arrest, and in 1977 was forced to move to a small town in the Orange Free State. After the small house in which she and her daughters lived was firebombed in 1985, Winnie returned to the Johannesburg area, continuing to speak out against government oppression.

Although officially considered a "non-person," Nelson Mandela remains the symbolic leader of the Black nationalist struggle in South Africa. Restrictions on Nelson's imprisonment have eased over the past twenty-five years. In 1980 some 58,000 South Africans petitioned their government to "Free Mandela," and in 1984 the government offered to release him if he would agree to settle in the "tribal homeland" of Transkei. Nelson rejected their terms, stating that he would only accept unconditional freedom and would not participate in the "homelands" policy.

On July 5, 1989, he met with South African President P.W. Botha—a meeting that gave instant legitimacy to a man the government has consistently labelled a terrorist—fueling speculation that his release was imminent. However, after a five hour seventy-first birthday celebration with sixteen members of his family, Nelson told them that he would not be freed immediately. Winnie Mandala, quoting her husband, said, "His exact words were: 'There will be no release, definitely not this year.'" She went on to add that "on his personal agenda his release will be the last item. He wants freedom for his political views."

Nelson and Winnie Mandela are committed to achieving a non-racial socialist state where South Africa's seventy-three percent majority has its rightful role, in a society that includes all races. "Whites in South Africa belong here. . .," Nelson has said. "We want them to share power with us." South African archbishop Desmond Tutu, recipient of the Nobel Peace Prize, has said of the Mandelas: "[They] have become a symbolic couple with their incredible strength and refusal to be broken."

Sources

▶ Books

Benson, Mary, *Nelson Mandela: The Man and the Movement*, Norton, 1986.

Harrison, Nancy, *Winnie Mandela*, Braziller, 1986.

Mandela, Nelson, *No Easy Walk to Freedom*, Basic Books, 1965.

Mandela, Nelson, *The Struggle Is My Life*, Pathfinder Press, 1986.

Mandela, Winnie, *Part of My Soul Went with Him*, Norton, 1984.

▶ Periodicals

Ms., "Winnie Mandela," January, 1987, pp. 82-83.

Newsweek, "Mrs. Mandela's Disgrace," February 27, 1989, p. 44, "Teatime in Pretoria," July 24, 1989, p. 24.

Wisconsin State Journal, "Mandela Says No Release," July 19, 1989.

World Press Review, "Behind the Mandela Myth," September, 1986, pp. 30-31.

Mickey Mantle

*"*T *he only thing that's gonna make me retire is if I feel like I can't play any more. I know that every February I get an itch to play."*

Born October 20, 1931, in Spavinaw, Oklahoma, switch-hitting Mickey Mantle won four home-run championships, a Triple Crown, and three Most Valuable Player awards during his eighteen-year career with the New York Yankees.

Mickey Charles Mantle was born in Spavinaw, Oklahoma, to Elvin ("Mutt") and Lowell Mantle. A former semi-pro baseball player, Mutt Mantle was so fond of baseball he named his first child after Detroit Tiger catcher Mickey Cochrane. Mickey was barely out of diapers before he was practicing baseball with his father. Mutt believed that the only way to excel in the major leagues was as a switch-hitter, so he taught his son to swing from both sides of the plate. Mickey would use his natural right-handed swing against his left-handed father, then would turn around and bat left-handed against his right-handed grandfather.

Mantle played baseball and basketball at his high school in Commerce, Oklahoma. He was also a star halfback on the football team. During one game, however, he was kicked in the leg and developed osteomyelitis, a bone marrow disease that would affect his future baseball career. While playing high school baseball, Mantle impressed New York Yankee scout Tom Greenwade, who signed him to a contract with a $1000 bonus—a bargain even in the days of low salaries in professional sports.

Mantle reported to the Yankees' minor league team in Independence, Kansas, in 1949 as a switch-hitting shortstop. After two years in the minor leagues, the Yankees invited him to their major league spring training camp. He earned a place on the roster, and the New York media soon began comparing him to Babe Ruth and other past Yankee greats. Only 19 years old and two years out of high school, Mantle did not immediately live up to the public's high expectations. He started slowly in his new position—right field—and was sent back briefly to the minors. Mantle's first year in the majors was marred by inconsistent play and jeering from fans both in New York and around the league. His difficulties continued when, early in 1952, Mutt Mantle died of Hodgkins disease at the age of thirty-nine. Mantle had been very close to his father, and he took his father's death hard.

Mantle was moved to center field when Joe DiMaggio retired from the Yankees following the 1951 season. He began to adjust to big–league play, and in 1952 batted .311 with twenty-three home runs and eighty-seven Runs Batted In (RBIs). That season Mantle began to establish himself as one of baseball's premier power hitters. During one game against the Washington Senators, Mantle hit a ball completely out of Griffith Stadium in Washington, D.C. Measured at 565 feet the home run is believed to be the longest ever hit. The New York Yankees won the American League pennant and World Series during each of Mantle's first three seasons, from 1951 to 1953. During the 1952 World Series against the Brooklyn Dodgers, Mantle batted .345 with two home runs.

In the 1953 Series, again against the Dodgers, he batted only .208, but hit two more home runs.

Mantle's talents led the Yankees as they dominated the American League throughout the late 1950s. They won the pennant each year from 1955 to 1958, taking the World Series in 1956 and 1958. Mantle became a genuine superstar in 1956 when he won baseball's Triple Crown, with a .353 batting average, fifty-two home runs, and 130 RBIs. He was also selected the American League's Most Valuable Player (MVP). In 1957 he hit .365 and was again named the league MVP.

Mantle's success at the plate continued as the Yankees remained strong well into the 1960s. After losing the pennant to the Chicago White Sox in 1959, the Yankees came back to win it the next five seasons, joined by new stars such as Tony Kubek, Bobby Richardson, Ryne Duren, Bill Skowron, and Roger Maris. Mantle captured the home run title again in 1960 with forty round-trippers, and he led the competition for the title again in 1961—the most dramatic home run season in the history of the game. By early August Mantle already had hit forty-three home runs and Maris forty-two. The record for home runs in a season was held by the legendary Baby Ruth, who had blasted sixty in 1927. Although Mantle ended the year with fifty-four home runs (his all-time high), Maris hit sixty-one homer's and established the new all-time record.

Mantle continued to excel even though his legs hurt most of the time from the osteomyelitis and other injuries. In 1962 he was named American League MVP for the third time. Although the Yankees continued to win pennants, their days of glory were waning. They lost the 1963 World Series to the Los Angeles Dodgers and were swept in the 1964 World Series by the St. Louis Cardinals. By 1965 the Yankees' heyday was finished. Mantle became frustrated with his pain and with his many strikeouts. During the 1965 season he said, "It isn't any fun when things are like this. I'm only 33, but I feel like 40." Mantle continued to play through the 1968 season; he announced his retirement in the spring of 1969.

Mantle left the Yankees with many great achievements. In addition to hitting 536 lifetime home runs, he led the American League in homers four times and was chosen as its Most Valuable Player three times. He is one of only a few players to win a Triple Crown. He played on twelve pennant-winning and seven World Series–winning teams. He still holds the all-time record for home runs in World Series play (eighteen) as well as numerous other World Series records. As much as DiMaggio before him, Mantle symbolized the Yankees and their dominance of baseball. In 1974, Mantle was elected to baseball's Hall of Fame in his first year of eligibility—an honor bestowed on few players in the history of the sport. Mantle has since pursued a business career, and he occasionally provides color commentary for televised Yankees games.

Epitomizing home run power greater than any man's since Babe Ruth, Mantle's name was on the lips of every would-be slugger on the sandlots of America during the 1950s and 1960s. Mantle's outstanding abilities and courage in the face of pain made him a hero to a generation of youngsters and adults alike.

Sources

▶ Books

Gallagher, Mark, *Explosion! Mickey Mantle's Legendary Home Runs*, Arbor House, 1987.

Mantle, Mickey, *Education of a Ball Player*, Simon & Schuster, 1967.

Mantle, Mickey, and Herb Glick, *The Mick*, Doubleday, 1985.

Mantle, Mickey, and Ben Epstein, *The Mickey Mantle Story*, Holt, 1953.

Schaap, Dick, *Mickey Mantle: The Indispensible Yankee*, Bartholomew House, 1961.

Schoor, Gene, *Mickey Mantle of the Yankees*, Putnam, 1959.

Silverman, Al, *Mickey Mantle, Mister Yankee*, Putnam, 1963.

▶ Periodicals

Life, "Last Innings of Greatness," July 30, 1965, pp. 47-53.

Look, "Mickey Mantle: Oklahoma to Olympus," February 23, 1965, pp. 71-75, "Mickey Mantle's Decision," March 18, 1969, pp. 29-32.

Newsweek, "Oklahoma's Mickey Mantle," June 25, 1956, pp. 63-67, "Home Runs . . . 61 in '61?" August 14, 1961, pp. 42-46.

Margaret Mead

"I n the summer of 1925, when I said goodbye to my family . . . I had the courage of almost complete ignorance. . . . In fact, I had never spent a day in my life alone."

Born December 18, 1901, in Philadelphia, Pennsylvania, Margaret Mead was an internationally known and widely respected anthropologist and documenter of human social behavior whose work revolutionized the field of anthropology itself. Her studies have given us valuable knowledge of the world's primitive peoples and cultures.

W hen *Coming of Age in Samoa*, a study of adolescent behavior in a Polynesian society, was published in 1928, it became a bestseller due to its novelistic style and its subject matter, which included sexual patterns among Samoan females. It also brought its author, Margaret Mead, to the forefront of American anthropology, a position she would occupy for the next fifty years. Numerous field trips and books followed, as did studies of American nutrition patterns and changing social values. Margaret Mead pioneered research methods which helped turn social anthropology into a major science and made anthropology relevant to public policy. She specialized in the study of gender role conditioning, cross-cultural communication, cooperation and competition among various cultures, and in comparative child psychology. From her long-term analysis and commentary on American culture Mead achieved preeminence in education, in environmental and women's movements, and other socio-political issues. She served on various international commissions on ecology, nutrition, and science. Her frequent commentaries on contemporary social mores—the family, sex, the generation gap, and moral issues—made her into a figure scorned by some and revered by millions.

Mead was the oldest of four children. Both of her parents were educators, and the family moved a great deal during her youth, away for summers and back to Philadelphia for the winters. Her mother, a suffragette, and grandmother instilled in Mead the belief that women could have their own profession. She was encouraged to play with children of all racial and economic backgrounds, and was taught early to closely observe others, to use her hands, and to paint and dance. She recalls that she "took pride in being unlike other children and in living in a household that was in itself unique."

While attending Barnard College, Mead developed an interest in anthropology. In a class with the famous anthropologist Franz Boas she was persuaded of the importance of studying cultures that were rapidly disappearing around the world. "That settled it for me. Anthropology had to be done *now*. Other things could wait." After graduating in 1923 Mead married Luther Cressman and entered Columbia University graduate school. Two years later she left for Samoa to study adolescence and biological and cultural influences on behavior. Mead spent nine months in Samoa, "suspending for the time one's beliefs and disbeliefs, and of simultaneously attempting to understand mentally and physically this other version of reality." Margaret lived with the villagers. "Living in the village by night as well as by day and for long uninterrupted months, the field anthropologist witnesses thousands of small events which never would have become visible, let alone intelligible, at a greater distance." Her most important work in Samoa was on courtship patterns in adolescents. Monogamy and jealousy were not valued or understood by the Samoans. Divorce occurred simply by "going home."

Mead's second field trip was in the late 1920s, when she went with her second husband Reo Fortune to study the Manus culture of the Admiralty Islands off the coast of New Guinea. She was studying the fantasy worlds of younger children and the development of social behavior. She wrote *Growing Up in New Guinea* (1930) about her findings among the Manus. In 1935 Mead published *Sex and Temperament* about her New Guinea studies of the Arapesh, Mundugumor, and Tchambuli peoples. In it she stressed the impermanence of human values and their dependence on time and environment.

In 1936 Mead went to Bali with Gregory Bateson, her third husband, originally planning to study the presence or absence of schizophrenia. Franz Boas had told Mead "If I were going to Bali I would study gesture," and that is one of the things they did. In fact, they took 38,000 photos in their study of Balinese character, resulting in their important 1941 book *Balinese Character: A Photographic Analysis.*

After having been told by a doctor years earlier that she could never have children, and after several miscarriages, Mead gave birth to a daughter, Mary Catherine Bateson, in 1939. During World War II Mead served on the government's Committee on Food Habits. She also worked on a national character study, which took anthropology and personality theory and applied them to members of national political units. Her work was on Anglo-American relations. In 1942 she published *And Keep Your Powder Dry: An Anthropologist Looks at America,* showing U.S. culture outlined against the cultures of seven other countries.

Mead seemed always to return to studying the family. Every few years she commented on the problems facing American families amid changing social conditions, including the loss of extended families and urbanization and its resulting isolation. An early feminist, she wrote about the need for changing gender roles as early as 1946. Perhaps her most profound impact was as a counselor to American society. Through a monthly column in *Redbook,* which she wrote from 1961 to 1978 with Rhoda Metraux, Mead offered advice and information to American women. Though married and divorced three times, Mead firmly stated, "I don't consider my marriages as failures. It's idiotic to assume that because a marriage ends, it's failed." But for all her support Mead also criticized the women's movement when it became too stridently anti-male. She called for a truly revolutionary vision of gender relations.

During the 1960s Mead wrote on a number of social and moral issues, especially the so–called generation gap. She also wrote on the environ-mental crisis and the population explosion. On the latter topic she advocated a philosophy of educating and nurturing all the world's children as our own, rather than focusing just on having more. She was also an early and vocal proponent of birth control, for the repeal of anti-abortion laws, for the right to die, civil disobedience, and liberal sexuality laws. But she was also a strong believer in people being moral and responsible in their lives, illustrated by her phrase "sex is not like beefsteak."

Margaret Mead lived life fully and tirelessly. "I am glad that I am alive. I am glad that I am living at this particular very difficult, very dangerous and very crucial period in human history." Her list of published works is huge and her honors numerous. In 1969 *Time* named her "Mother of the Year." She was president of the American Academy for the Ad-vancement of Science among others. She taught at Columbia, New York University, and other schools. Her association with the American Museum of Natural History dates from 1926, when she became Assist-ant Curator, through 1964 (Curator) to 1969 (Curator Emeritus). Marga-ret Mead died of cancer on November 15, 1978, in New York City. Her colleague Barry Commoner said her work set the "sciences in relation-ship to human life." The way she lived her life is perhaps epitomized in her statement: "Life in the 20th century is like a parachute jump—you have to get it right the first time."

Sources
▶ **Books**

Cassidy, Robert, *A Voice for the Century*, Universe Books, 1982.

Howard, Jane, *Margaret Mead: A Life*, Simon & Schuster, 1984.

Mead, Margaret, *Blackberry Winter: My Earlier Years*, Morrow, 1972.

Mead, Margaret, *Letters from the Field, 1925-75*, Harper, 1977.

Golda Meir

"*Our generation reclaimed the land, our children fought the war and our grandchildren should enjoy the peace.*"

The fourth prime minister of Israel, a country she helped found, Golda Meir was born on May 3, 1898, in Kiev, Ukraine, Russia (now U.S.S.R.), and died while suffering from leukemia on December 8, 1978, in Jerusalem, Israel.

From her childhood in a poor Ukrainian Jewish family facing persecution, Golda Meir dreamed of a homeland for her people, a place where Jews could be "masters, not victims, of their fate." Once she immigrated to Palestine, the ancient center of Jewish culture, she would live only there—on a kibbutz, in the crowded city of Tel Aviv, and finally in Jerusalem. She worked for years in labor organizations, suffered through the trauma of World War II, and experienced the subsequent heady days of Israel's founding, saw the country through several wars with Arab neighbors, and finally became prime minister. Through it all, her duty was to the establishment and preservation of a state where Jewish people could prosper, a duty that took precedence over her family and other personal concerns.

Originally named Golda Mabovitch by her parents, carpenter Moshe Mabovitch and his wife Blume, Meir spent the first eight years of her life in the Ukraine amidst anti-Semitic Cossacks and peasants, nurturing her dream of a haven for Jews. During three of those years her father lived and worked in Milwaukee, Wisconsin, and in 1906 she, her mother, and her two sisters immigrated there also. Though the move could not satisfy her dream, it helped the family avoid anti-Semitism and gave Meir the opportunity for education. Her parents opposed her going to high school, however, so she ran away to live for a time with her married sister in Denver, Colorado, returning when her parents came to support her decision to become a teacher. Meir's stay in Denver exposed her a number of Jews interested in socialism and Zionism—the right of the Jewish people to have a nation of their own—and sparked her own interest. Upon her return to Milwaukee she began to promote Zionism as a street-corner speaker.

In 1917 Meir's life turned fully to Zionism. Though she graduated from Milwaukee Teachers' Training College that year, she abandoned teaching to take a job with Poale Zion, a socialist Zionist group. In the same year she married Morris Meyerson (whose surname she hebraized to Meir in 1956), whom she had met in Denver, and secured his promise that they would try living on a kibbutz, or collective settlement, in Palestine. The couple immigrated to the British territory in 1921, to a kibbutz south of Nazareth. When Morris's health began to suffer under the difficult kibbutz life, husband and wife moved to Tel Aviv and later to Jerusalem. With two children to support and care for, Meir quit her job with the Jewish labor organization, the Histadrut, and stayed at home, taking in laundry for a small income. These years were among her worst; she later recalled thinking, "Was this what is was all about—poverty, drudgery and worry?" The family finally assumed secondary status in 1928, when she rejoined the Histadrut as women's labor council secretary. In 1933 Meir and her husband separated.

Meir continued to work for the Zionist cause through the 1930s, traveling in Europe and the United States to raise money for Palestine, taking part in various political enterprises, and serving as a delegate to the World Zionist Congress. Among her responsibilities was administering mutual aid programs and medical services. In 1940 she added foreign relations to her growing political involvement when she took charge of the political department of the Histadrut.

By the end of World War II Meir was a member of the Jewish Agency for Palestine, fighting the British decree that limited the number of Jewish refugees allowed to immigrate. She won a small victory in 1947 after visiting a refugee camp in Cyprus, where she was told the children could not survive the winter; thanks to her negotiations, the restrictions were relaxed for children. According to Meir, the immigration rules only increased the Jews' desire for nationhood: "Political independence was not something that we could go on regarding as a distant aim." Meir, who had supported Jewish leader David Ben-Gurion's strategy of acting as if a Jewish state already existed, finally saw the Zionist goals realized on May 14, 1948, when she and other Jewish leaders signed Israel's declaration of independence. In the same year she became Israel's minister to the Soviet Union, and in 1949 she was elected to the Israeli parliament, the Knesset, where she remained for the next twenty-five years.

Meir held a variety of posts in the new government. From 1949 to 1956 she was minister of labor in Prime Minister Ben-Gurion's cabinet, introducing legislation to improve housing, education, and insurance for Israelis, and in 1956 she became foreign minister, a post that allowed her to meet many world leaders and expand Israel's influence. By the time she was elected prime minister in 1969, Meir had more that forty-five years of political experience behind her.

Chosen in part to avoid dividing the country between the two other candidates, Moshe Dayan and Yigal Allon, Meir proved to be a strong unifying force for Israel as prime minister. Among her cabinet she was never outvoted on major issues, and the citizens saw her "as a kind of Mother Courage, radiating confidence and faith, the very personification of the Jews' will to survive as a people in the aftermath of the Nazi holocaust and in the face of repeated Arab attacks." Such attacks, spurred by unrest in territories occupied by Israel that had once belonged to Arab nations, Meir was usually able to overcome by military strength or face-to-face talks with Arab leaders. In October of 1973, however, rare indecision regarding the buildup of Arab troops near Israeli borders resulted in a war for which many Israelis blamed Meir; in the aftermath of the war, in 1974, she resigned, though she continued to be a strong voice in the labor party.

Living a wholly dedicated life, Meir became one of the most influential women of the twentieth century. Though tough and determined, demanding "secure, recognized and agreed boundaries" with the Arab countries, Meir sought peace rather than war. "We don't want wars even when we win," she said. "We do not rejoice in victories. We rejoice when a new kind of cotton is grown and when strawberries bloom in Israel." She was awarded the Freedom of Jerusalem, an honor she said was probably her greatest tribute, in 1971. At her death in 1978 she was mourned internationally and hailed as a "stalwart lioness" and "the conscience of the Jewish people." Among the Israelis she was affectionately remembered as "Our Golda."

Sources

▶ **Books**

Meir, Golda, *A Land of My Own*, Putnam, 1973.

Meir, *My Life*, Putnam, 1975.

Shenker, Israel and Mary Shenker, *As Good as Golda*, McCall, 1970.

Syrkin, Marie, *Golda Meir: Israel's Leader*, Putnam, 1969.

▶ **Periodicals**

New York Times, "Golda Meir Dies in Jerusalem: Israelis Acclaim 'Stalwart Lioness,'" December 9, 1978.

James Howard Meredith

" $\mathbf{T}$ he price of justice is indeed high, but the price of
holding it back is much higher."

American civil rights activist James Howard Meredith was born
near Kosciusko, Mississippi, on June 25, 1933, and became the first
black student to attend the University of Mississippi.

Present address: 427 Eastview St., Jackson, Miss. 39209.

J ames Howard Meredith grew up in Kosciusko, Mississippi, and graduated from high school in 1950. He enlisted in the U.S. Air Force and served for nine years, attaining the rank of staff sergeant before returning to Mississippi to pursue a college education.

Meredith attended the all-black Jackson State College for a year before he applied early in 1961 for admission to the University of Mississippi, an institution that had excluded blacks during its entire 114-year history. Denied admission, Meredith obtained the aid of the National Association for the Advancement of Colored People (NAACP) to begin legal procedures against the university and its discriminatory policy. After a legal battle lasting more than eighteen months, Meredith was granted admission by a U.S. Court of Appeals, only to be prohibited from entering the university by then Mississippi governor Ross Barnett. President John F. Kennedy intervened in September, 1962, by personally contacting Barnett, making a televised appeal to the citizens of Mississippi to respect the court's ruling, and finally, calling in the National Guard to protect Meredith after he moved into a campus dormitory. Three hundred federal marshals and a force of Mississippi state troopers protected Meredith at the University of Mississippi for the next three semesters. Despite riots and continual harassment from his white classmates, Meredith obtained his political science degree on August 18, 1963.

Meredith left Mississippi after graduation and went to New York City, where he enrolled in Columbia University's law school. In June, 1966, however, Meredith returned to the South to participate in a civil rights march from Memphis, Tennessee, to Jackson, Mississippi, for the purpose of encouraging black voter registration and challenging what he called the "all-pervasive and overriding fear that dominates the day-to-day life of the Negro in the United States—especially in the South and particularly in Mississippi." On June 5, the second day of the march, Meredith was shot by an unseen assailant, just ten miles inside the Mississippi state line. Although he suffered some sixty superficial shotgun wounds, Meredith returned to the march on June 24, and completed it.

After earning his law degree in 1968, Meredith continued to work for increased opportunity for blacks. He entered the business world and, a year later, walked from Chicago to New York City to "promote Negro pride and positive goals in the black community." In February of 1972, Meredith ran for the Republican senate nomination in Mississippi but lost the primary election.

Meredith believes he was chosen by God to help end racial tension in his state and country. "Because of my 'Divine Responsibility' to advance human civilization," Meredith said, "I could not die. If one places society above self, and I do, life never ends. Everything I do, I do because I must; and everything I must do, I do."

Sources

▶ Books

Meredith, James, *Three Years in Mississippi*, Indiana University Press, 1966.

▶ Periodicals

Bookweek, April 24, 1966.

Nation, "Is Meredith Right?," June 27, 1966, p. 765.

National Review, "How Guilty is the South?," June 28, 1966, p. 611.

Newsweek, "Proud Man," April 18, 1966, p. 112, "Hometown Advice," March 27, 1967, pp. 39-40.

New Yorker, May 21, 1966.

New York Times Book Review, "In Brief," July 3, 1966.

Mother Teresa

"*F or all kinds of diseases there are medicines and cures. But for being unwanted, except there are willing hands to serve and there's a loving heart to love.*"

Born August 27, 1910, in Skopje, Serbia (now Yugoslavia), Mother Teresa has won the Nobel Peace Prize for a lifetime of dedication to serving the poor.

I n 1952 Mother Teresa and a few other Catholic sisters opened the Nirmal Hriday ("Pure Heart") Home for Dying Destitutes in Calcutta, India, in a former temple hostel to the Hindu goddess Kali, more recently a denizen of gamblers, to be "a shelter where the dying poor may die in dignity." So began a service to "the poorest of the poor", in one of the more afflicted areas of the world, which has since taken in thousands of orphaned and abandoned children, lepers and dying adults, and has provided medical treatment to millions, a service which has since expanded all over the world. Mother Teresa, now a citizen of India, has become not only accepted, but honored and revered by millions in this vast Hindu and Muslim country. She remains very clear about her commitment and the nature of her mission. "I am not a social worker," she says. "We do it for Jesus."

Mother Teresa was born Agnes Gonxha Bojaxhiu, one of three children of Albanian parents. She discloses little about her childhood, except to say that because it was happy, it was hard for her to leave home. She attended a Catholic school, and at the age of twelve, knew that she wanted to be a missionary serving the poor. Six years later she joined a group of Irish nuns, the Sisters of Loreto, in their Calcutta mission. Her first position there was teacher in a high school for girls—a position she enjoyed, and would have kept indefinitely. However, in 1964, she felt an involuntary calling "to leave the convent and help the poor, while living among them," she said. Two years later, she received permission from the Archbishop and the Vatican to begin a school for destitute children.

Others joined her in the work, which became the religious order known as the Missionaries of Charity. Like other members of this order, Mother Teresa took a vow of poverty; in addition, she promised to give "whole-hearted free service to the poorest of the poor." Distressed to see the homeless dying in the streets, she founded Nimral Hriday, a hospice where the dying could find the medical care and affirmation of individual worth that was not available to them elsewhere. In 1964, the sisters, who had started treating lepers from Calcutta slums in 1957, organized a colony for lepers in West Bengal, using money from the auction of a limosine given to Mother Teresa by Pope Paul VI. Though Mother Teresa has never solicited funds, donations have allowed the mission to open branch houses in more than thirty countries around the world. The missions provide shelter for orphans, lepers, the terminally ill, drug addicts, alcoholics, and people from third world countries, such as the aborigines in Australia, who are displaced by encroaching modernization. Mother Teresa was instrumental in forming a religious order for men, the Missionary Brothers of Charity, but she declined to oversee it, believing that the Bible prohibits women from having authority over men. Her own order answers directly to the Vatican since 1965 when it was made a society of pontifical right.

Mother Teresa's vow to accept no reward for her service has been severely tested. In 1979, she agreed to accept the Nobel Peace Prize on behalf of the poor. "I am happy that the award recognizes that the works of love were works of peace," she said. To diffuse the attention from admirers after receiving the award, she observed a self-imposed month of silence. The $6000 set aside for the Nobel banquet was deferred at her request to be given to the poor, as was the entire financial award accompanying the prize. She fends off mentions of her accomplishments by explaining that she is motivated solely by her personal devotion to Jesus Christ. In a 1986 documentary of her activities, she said, "Jesus said I have chosen you. Every day you have to say 'yes' in total surrender and acceptance. . . . It is not how much we do, but how much love we put into the doing." She points out that the rich also are in need: "All experience pain, loneliness. You must have the courage to recognize the poor in your own family, in loving."

Mother Teresa was hospitalized for treatment of a heart ailment in September, 1989, at which time more than forty thousand people were serving her cause in ninety-two countries.

Sources
▶ **Books**

Doig, Desmond, *Mother Teresa and Her Work*, Harper, 1976.

Egan, Eileen, *Such a Vision of the Street*, Doubleday, 1985.

Muggeridge, Malcolm, *Something Beautiful for God: Mother Teresa of Calcutta*, Perennial Library, 1986.

▶ **Periodicals**

Christian Century, "Love in Action and Contemplation," March 18-25, 1987, pp. 260-261.

New York Times Magazine, "The World of Mother Teresa," December 9, 1979, pp. 2-98.

Ralph Nader

″ **T** *he most important question that can be asked about any society is how much effort do citizens spend exercising their civic responsibility. We can't possibly have a democracy with two hundred million Americans and only a handful of citizens.″*

Born February 27, 1934, in Winsted, Connecticut, Ralph Nader is a consumer advocate, lawyer, and author.
Address: P.O. Box 19367, Washington, D.C. 20036.

R alph Nader first achieved public recognition in 1965 with the publication of his hard-hitting book *Unsafe At Any Speed*, which attacked the Detroit auto industry for its emphasis on style rather than safety, and has in the more than twenty years since continued his uncompromising and often highly successful defense of consumer rights and civic responsibility.

He was born the youngest of five children, February 27, 1934 to Lebanese parents in Winsted, Connecticut. Nader's lifelong interest in social issues and the responsibilities of citizenship began with the reading of such social tracts as Upton Sinclair's *The Jungle*, an expose of Chicago's slaughterhouses, and intensified through noisy family debates around the kitchen table. After graduating from high school in 1951, Nader enrolled at Princeton University, where he studied government and economics at the Woodrow Wilson School of Public and International Affairs. Upon graduation from Princeton in 1955, he attended Harvard Law School, where he edited the *Harvard Law Record*. It was in the *Record* that Nader published "American Cars: Designed for Death," which voiced his growing concern about the automotive industry's emphasis upon style rather than safety. Nader earned his LL.B. degree from Harvard in 1958, graduating with distinction. After spending six months as a cook in the U.S. Army, he established a small legal practice in Hartford, Connecticut, and travelled widely through Asia, Africa, and the Americas as a free-lance journalist. Disturbed by the corporate greed and indifference that he witnessed, Nader was convinced of the need for some form of public protection for the average citizen.

By the mid-1960s, Nader's dissatisfaction with his role as a lawyer prompted him to move to Washington. "I had watched years go by and nothing happened," Nader later recounted. "Before that, decades had gone by. I decided it took total commitment." Concerned primarily with the issue of auto safety, he was hired as staff consultant on highway safety by the Assistant Secretary of Labor, Daniel Patrick Moynihan. The complex legislative background report that he authored became the basis for his 1965 book *Unsafe at Any Speed: The Designed-In Dangers of the American Automobile*, a stinging indictment of the safety record of the automobile industry in general and General Motors Corporation in particular. Nader achieved instant recognition and helped shift the emphasis of the debate over road safety away from the roads and the road-users to the manufacturers. When GM tried to discredit Nader, however, the maneuver backfired and GM President James M. Roche was forced to publicly apologize for his company's "harrassment."

Although depicted by the press as a "zealous consumer crusader," Nader nevertheless inspired admiration, particularly among the young, with his ceaseless advocacy of the rights of the average American in the face of powerful giant corporations. He became, in the words of one commentator, "a national symbol for taking on the big guys, an indication that one man could still make a difference." By the end of the decade, Nader had taken the battle to many fronts, and his efforts were instrumental in ensuring legislation that improved safety standards in the automobile, oil, and food industries. His teams of associates, many of them young law students, were dubbed "Nader's Raiders" by the press; and their efforts helped to change the public's perception of their own rights as consumers.

In 1969, Nader founded the Center for Study of Responsive Law, a consumer action group designed, as Nader put it, "to represent the public against . . . an unholy alliance between corporations and the government." The following year, as the result of a lawsuit, Nader received a substantial out-of-court settlement for invasion of privacy from GM, money which he used to found the Corporate Accountability Research Group, the Public Interest Research Group (a campus-based consumer action organization), and, in 1971, Public Citizen, Inc. Perceived as a consumer rights counterforce to the powerful corporate lobbies in Washington, Public Citizen, Inc. became the parent organization of Congress Watch, Retired Professionals Action Group, and the Tax Reform Research Group. Nader continued to score major successes with the passage of a bill establishing the Environmental Protection Agency in 1970, and the Freedom of Information Act of 1974. And the creation of the Occupational Safety and Health Administration in 1976 owed much to Nader, but two years later, Congress rejected his proposed Consumer Protection Agency.

With his high public profile and his staunch opposition to corporate power, Nader earned powerful enemies, though. He was condemned by then U.S. Supreme Court nominee Lewis F. Powell, Jr., as "perhaps the single most effective antagonist of American business," and was portrayed as a menace. Others criticized his refusal to compromise and his "combative nature." Although Nader rejected such condemnations ("Is it so implausible, so distasteful, that a man would believe deeply enough in his work to dedicate his life to it?"), by the end of the decade, it was clear that his fortunes and influence were on the decline. His attacks on the economic power of corporate America and the insidious violence and criminality stemming from that power alienated many would-be supporters who felt his zealous campaigns were fundamentally anti-capitalist.

With the election of Ronald Reagan to the presidency in 1980, Nader's ideas lost further favor with the general public, and by 1985, he headed just two of the many consumer organizations he had founded. He has made significant contributions in such areas as meat inspection, mental health, care of the elderly, environmental pollution, and technological data gathering. And although he continues to investigate, among other things, the postal service, the insurance industry, and nuclear power, he resigned as president of Public Citizen, Inc. in 1980 to help organize grass roots consumer rights groups such as Citizen Utility Boards and Buyers Up. He still funds his Corporate Accountability Research Group by lecturing and writing. He has written, edited, and co-authored nearly a dozen books on consumer-related topics, and remains a powerful voice in national affairs. "You can disagree with Nader here and there," said a 1985 *Washington Monthly* profile. "But on what really counts—a commitment to making democracy work and a willingness to that end—he is profoundly right." "Nader's concept of a new democratic politics of citizen participation has revolutionized the conduct of civic affairs in America," declared a 1985 *Nation* article. With his highly individual style and tireless enthusiasm, Nader has been instrumental in ensuring legislative protection for the consumer, and his accomplishments—from seat belts to shatterproof windshields—are such an integral part of our modern lives that we take them for granted. "I'm no longer seen as the Lone Ranger," Nader said recently. "I consider myself a public citizen. I enjoy achieving justice in society."

Sources
▶ **Books**

Nader, Ralph, *Unsafe at Any Speed: The Designed-In Dangers of the American Automobile*, Grossman, 1965.

Nader, Ralph, *The Big Boys: Styles of Corporate Power*, Pantheon Books, 1986.

▶ **Periodicals**

Nation, "Citizen Nader," November 30, 1985, pp. 572-573.

New Republic, "Saint Ralph," December 9, 1985, p. 4.

Newsweek, "Has Nader Gone Soft?" June 2, 1986, p. 51, "The Aging of Ralph Nader," December 16, 1986, p. 57.

Washington Monthly, "Ralph Nader Reconsidered," March, 1985, pp. 12-21.

Patricia Neal

*"*I* realized I was, in fact, living and was starting to like the experience again."*

Born January 20, 1926, in Packard, Kentucky, Patricia Neal overcame a series of personal crises that nearly ended her award-winning career as a stage, screen, and television actress.

Address: Gypsy House, Great Missendeb, Buckinghamshire, England.

P atsy Louise Neal was born in 1926 in a Kentucky mining camp. Her family moved to Tennessee, where, with support from her parents and the experience of singing in religious activities, she became interested in acting. Neal went on to enroll in acting school at Northwestern University. She never completed the program, however, choosing rather to gain first-hand experience by working as an understudy in the road company of John Van Druten's production of "The Voice of the Turtle." She adopted the stage name Patricia Neal in 1945, just before she was called to fill in for the play's lead actress, Vivian Vance. Neal's performance was good enough to earn her the part during the play's two-week Broadway run.

Encouraged by her success, Neal remained in New York City to pursue her acting career in earnest, supporting herself by working at odd jobs. During this time she met artistic and influential people, notably playwright Eugene O'Neill, who helped her obtain a role in the Theatre Guild production of "Devil Take a Whittler." Neal's performance in the play led to a leading role in Lillian Hellman's "Another Part of the Forest," which opened in New York in November of 1946. For her portrayal of the greedy and amoral Regina, Neal received rave reviews and numerous honors, including a Tony award. Soon afterward, she signed a Hollywood contract with Warner Bros. studios.

Neal's first big role in movies was Dominique Francon in the 1949 adaptation of Ayn Rand's *The Fountainhead*, playing opposite Gary Cooper, with whom she reportedly had a love affair. She learned much about acting in front of the camera, and her strong, independent personality blended well with that of her characters; critics also admired Neal's distinctive voice—her trademark. In 1950 she performed in "Three Secrets" and the following year, in the cult classic "The Day the Earth Stood Still." Neal returned to the stage in 1952, when she acted in another acclaimed Hellman play, "The Children's Hour"; she made her London debut in the 1958 production of Tennessee William's "Suddenly Last Summer."

During the early 1960s Neal appeared in her best-known Hollywood roles. She played the woman next door ("2-E") in a bohemian apartment building in the 1960 "Breakfast at Tiffany's," a love story starring George Peppard and Audrey Hepburn. Among other prestigious acting awards, Neal won the 1964 Best Actress Oscar for her portrayal of housekeeper Alma Brown in "Hud," the story of a Texas ranching family that also featured Paul Newman and Melvyn Douglas.

Although Neal's professional life has been enormously successful, her personal life has been marred by tragedy. During the making of "Breakfast at Tiffany's" her infant son Theo suffered a severe brain injury in an automobile accident, and shortly afterward, her eight-year-old daughter Olivia died of complications of the measles. And early in 1965, at perhaps the height of her career, she suffered a series of strokes that left her—with blurred vision, diminished memory, and paralysis—unable to care for herself. During this time Neal relied heavily on the love and support of her husband since 1953, Roald Dahl, as well as that of her friends. Neal has described this time in her life as a period during which she learned the value of humility and came to regard her misfortune as an opportunity to reevaluate her life and its meaning. With courage and perseverance, Neal overcame her sorrow and her disability, emerging from her trials with a new self-knowledge and determination.

Neal's recovery took two years. At Dahl's urging she returned to the screen, resuming her career in the 1968 movie "The Subject Was Roses." Her work in the film earned her a second Academy Award nomination. Three years later Neal starred in "The Night Digger," which has been described by some as her most impressive late work. In the movie she portrayed a woman who redeems, and then inadvertently destroys, a young psychopathic killer. Among Neal's more recent films are "The Passage," "All Quiet on the Western Front," and "Ghost Story." The actress has starred in several television movies as well, including "The Eleanor and Lou Gehrig Story," "Things in Their Season," "Shattered Vows," and "The Homecoming," the pilot movie for the popular television series "The Waltons." Neal has also written the 1989 autobiography *As I Am*, describing in detail her early years on stage and screen, as well as her stroke and the difficulties she experienced in her inspiring recovery.

Sources
▶ **Books**

Burrows, Michael, *Patricia Neal and Margaret Sullavan*, Primestyle, 1971.

Neal, Patricia, *As I Am*, Simon & Schuster, 1989.

▶ **Periodicals**

Films in Review, "Patricia Neal," April, 1983, pp. 203-220.

Sandra Day O'Connor

"**I** was very fortunate in my life to have some opportunities to do work which was particularly interesting. I might not have felt the same way if the work hadn't been so interesting, but for me it always was."

Born March 26, 1930, in El Paso, Texas, Sandra Day O'Connor is the first woman to serve as a U.S. Supreme Court justice.
Address: 3651, East Denton Lane, Paradise Valley, Arizona 85253.

When President Reagan nominated Sandra Day O'Connor to serve on the U.S. Supreme Court in 1981, he broke tradition of male exclusivity stretching back nearly two centuries. As the first woman to be appointed as Supreme Court justice, O'Connor is well aware of her position as a role model for women and as a symbol of women's improving status in society. This awareness has led her to publicly caution her Supreme Court colleagues against making "traditional, often inaccurate assumptions about the proper roles of men and women." A judicial conservative, O'Connor believes that she is "obligated to recognize that others have different views." Her refusal to become an ideologue and her willingness to retain an open mind on such controversial judicial and social issues as abortion have earned her the widespread respect of her peers in the legal profession. Says a friend, "Just remember that Sandra O'Connor has been concerned about all good things—and she is scrupulously fair."

Sandra Day O'Connor, the oldest of three children, was born the daughter of Harry and Ada Mae Day in El Paso, Texas. She was raised on the family's Lazy B ranch in southeastern Arizona.

Although the ranch offered a great way of life, educational opportunities were limited, so O'Connor was sent to live with her maternal grandmother in El Paso. There she attended Radford School, a private institution for girls, before studying at Austin High School. After graduating from high school in 1946, she began majoring in economics at Stanford University and had no thoughts of law as a career until she took a law course in her senior year. She entered Stanford Law School in 1950 and graduated third in her class two years later. It was while she was at Stanford that she met John Jay O'Connor III, whom she married upon her graduation.

Although qualified as a lawyer, O'Connor had difficulty finding a job. She finally found work as a deputy county attorney in San Mateo, California, while waiting for her husband John to graduate from law school, and when he was drafted to serve as an army lawyer in Frankfurt, West Germany, O'Connor followed. She worked in Frankfurt as a civilian lawyer for the Quarter-master Corps before returning to Phoenix, Arizona, in 1957, where she opened her own law firm two years later.

Between 1960 and 1965, O'Connor devoted herself to raising her three sons and doing volunteer work, although she did find time to serve on the Maricopa County Board of Adjustments and Appeals and the Governor's Committee on Marriage and Family.

She returned to the legal profession as assistant attorney general for Arizona before entering the state Senate in 1969 on the Republican ticket. While serving three terms in the Senate she became concerned with issues such as sex discrimination and the problems of families at the poverty line. As state senator, she initially supported the Equal Rights Amendment, and she unsuccessfully introduced a bill calling for a statewide referendum on the issue. She also pushed for revision of discriminatory Arizona statutes, and she developed legislation that allowed women to manage jointly property held with their husbands.

In 1972, Sandra Day O'Connor became the Arizona Senate's majority leader. She was the first woman to hold that office in any state Senate. In 1974, after serving five years in the Senate, she decided to return to the judiciary. She won election to the Superior Court of Maricopa County, and for four years she served as a trial judge, earning a reputation for toughness tempered by genuine concern.

In 1979, Arizona governor Bruce Babbitt named her to the Arizona Court of Appeals. She once again earned respect as a compassionate reasoning judge. In the Court of Appeals, she was concerned with such issues as divorces, bankruptcies, appeals from criminal conviction, and tenant-landlord disputes.

When campaigning for the presidency, Ronald Reagan pledged that he would appoint a woman to fill one of the first vacated seats on the Supreme Court, and when associate justice Potter Stewart announced his retirement in June, 1981, an exhaustive search for a successor began. It ended with Reagan's nomination of O'Connor on July 7, 1981.

Her nomination was confirmed by the Senate Judiciary Committee, and she became the first woman to serve on the Supreme Court in its 191-year history. Her appointment aroused protests from some right-wing groups who remembered her support of the ERA and who accused her of favoring abortion, but it was generally praised as being an astute decision on Reagan's part. "Sandra Day O'Connor will bring to the Supreme Court a solidly grounded understanding of the real lives of women in contemporary society," declared a 1981 profile in *Ms.* magazine. "She will bring to the Court's deliberations of [women's] issues the touchstone of reality that has been so glaringly absent."

Since her appointment she has won a reputation as a judicial conservative who upholds the law rather than rewrites it. O'Connor is prepared to defend the rights of those who have differing views, and although she tends to ally herself with the conservative wing of the Supreme Court, she is her own person.

Of her career, O'Connor says, "I worked hard to try to eliminate what I saw or judged as legal impediments in the way of letting women progress and meet their career goals. . . . It wasn't until the '60s that women began to bring to the forefront the continuing concerns that they had about equal opportunity. I am sure that but for that effort, I would not be serving in this job."

When asked how she balances her home life with her position as justice on the Supreme Court, she admits that there is "no balance . . . it's all at court." But her earlier years of parenting and homemaking have, in her view, influenced her professional life. "Having family responsibilities and concerns just has to make you a more understanding person."

Despite the exhausting demands of her position, O'Connor continues to earn recognition as an accomplished leader, a fair-minded, compassionate, and extremely competent judge.

Sources
▶ Books

Woods, Harold, and Geraldine , *Equal Justice: A Biography of Sandra Day O'Connor*, Dillon Press, 1985.

▶ Periodicals

Ms., "Sandra O'Connor and the Supremes: Will the First Woman Make a Difference?" October, 1981, pp. 71-72, "Supreme Court Justice O'Connor: The Woman Whose Word is Law," December, 1982, p. 52.

People, "Up at 4 a.m. to Read Briefs, She Learns That a Woman Justice's Work Is Never Done," December 28, 1981, pp. 84-85.

Saturday Evening Post, "Her Honor: The Rancher's Daughter," September, 1985, pp. 42-47.

Time, "Establishing Her Independence," May 12, 1986, p. 85.

Working Woman, "Justice!" September, 1981, pp. 80-82, "Personal Priorities: Sandra Day O'Connor Talks About the Skill (and Stress) of Juggling Work, Kids, Car Pools—and Why She Spent Five Years as a Career Dropout," January, 1986, pp. 89-91.

Georgia O'Keeffe

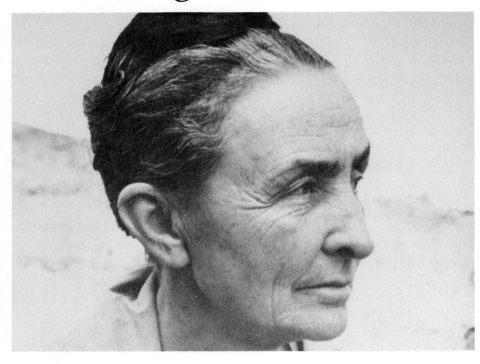

" W hen you take a flower in your hand and really look at it, it's your world for the moment. I want to give that world to someone else."

Born November 15, 1887, near Sun Prairie, Wisconsin, Georgia O'Keeffe revolutionized the role of women in art with her fresh, vivid paintings of desert scenes and oversized flowers.

I n the early part of the twentieth century the art world in America was dominated by men. Women artists were not taken very seriously either by critics or male artists. One woman who began to challenge this prejudice was Georgia O'Keeffe, whose highly original paintings of New York's skyline, and later of desert mountains, flowers, plants, and bones, in stark yet lyrical abstractions, amazed, perplexed, and impressed the New York art establishment. Beginning with the first exhibition of her drawings in 1916 in the gallery of her future husband Alfred Stieglitz, and continuing throughout her long and extraordinary life, she continued to paint without regard to art trends and outside pressure, remaining true to her own inner vision.

Georgia O'Keeffe was born November 15, 1887, near Sun Prairie, Wisconsin, a small farming community a few miles outside the state capital of Madison. She was the second of seven children of Francis and Ida O'Keeffe. Her father farmed several hundred acres of land. Her mother was an intelligent and serious woman, and worked to develop intellectual curiosity in her children. Georgia liked to entertain herself, and later in life remarked: "I've never been bored." Georgia apparently did not like school very much, although she was a good student. She was a highly individualistic child. "I decided that the only thing I could do that was nobody else's business was to paint," she said. "I could do as I chose because no one would care."

Francis O'Keeffe, concerned that he would contract the tuberculosis that had claimed the lives of his three brothers, sold his farm in 1903 and moved his family to the warmer climate of Williamsburg, Virginia. Already a self-confident, independent teenager, Georgia maintained her individualism and refused to conform to Southern society's expectations of a young lady. In 1905 she began attending the Art Institute of Chicago. When she returned to Williamsburg the following summer she contracted typhoid fever. After several months of recuperation Georgia traveled to New York to study at the Art Students League. After her extensive illness she loved the sensations and freedom of the city life.

Meanwhile, her father's business ventures in Williamsburg were failing, and Georgia realized she would have to support herself. She returned to Chicago where she worked as an illustrator, drawing lace and embroidery for advertisements, in 1908-09. Then she got measles, which weakened her eyesight, and she had to return to Virginia, where she worried she would no longer be able to paint if her eyesight did not return. Discouraged, for a time she gave up painting. After her family moved to Charlottesville, Virginia in 1912, Georgia enrolled in an art class, where she was exposed to a new form of art. To date Georgia had painted representational art, or that which tries to reproduce what is seen. This style had grown quite stale for her, however. "If one could only reproduce nature, and always with less beauty than the original, why paint at all?" Her exposure, at this time, to the abstract work of mainly European artist, re-ignited her passion and opened up new inner vistas for her to explore.

The following year Georgia received an offer to teach art in Amarillo, Texas. Having always dreamed of the West, she accepted. "That was my country [Texas]—the terrible winds and wonderful emptiness", she later said. She stayed four years in Amarillo supervising art instruction. While there she mailed a number of drawings to a friend with instructions not to show them to anyone. Her friend, however, did show the drawings to Alfred Stieglitz, a pioneering photographer, owner of the 291 gallery in New York and an influential art critic. Stieglitz liked the drawings and immediately decided to show them. He called them "the purest,' finest, sincerest things that have entered 291 in a long while." His view on women in art was an exception to the prevailing views at the time. He believed that women experienced the world in a different way than men, and were freer of societal inhibitions and more able to vividly express personal visions. In 1916 Stieglitz mounted an exhibition of Georgia's drawings without her permission and using the name Virginia O'Keeffe. When Georgia found out about the showing she was furious, and went to the gallery to confront Stieglitz. "For me the drawings were private", she said, "and the idea of their being hung on the wall for the public to look at was just too much." Finally Stieglitz was able to persuade her to accept the showing, and Georgia privately confided to a friend: "I believe I would rather have Stieglitz like something—anything I had done—than anyone else I know of."

Georgia returned to Texas and her teaching job, but the next year returned to New York for a second showing of her drawings. It was clear there was a growing attraction between her and Stieglitz, and in 1918 Georgia moved back to New York and began to spend a lot of time with him. Later they moved in together, though Stieglitz was still married. Georgia later described those first years with Stieglitz as some of the happiest of her life. He photographed her in almost every conceivable pose, often in front of her paintings, and people began to wonder who she was. In 1923 Georgia held her first major showing at Stieglitz's gallery "291," and the following year Stieglitz, having gotten a divorce, married her. She was thirty-seven and he sixty-one.

In 1924 Georgia began painting huge flower blossoms, something no one had done before, conveying her understanding of the significance of the flower. "When you take a flower in you hand and really look at it, it's your world for the moment. I want to give that world to someone else," she said. Her 1926 showing of these paintings caused a great stir and prompted one critic to call her a "raging, blazing soul." In the summer of 1929, after a winter in which Stieglitz had suffered a heart attack, Georgia felt a need for a change and accompanied a friend to Taos, New Mexico. There she began painting scenes of the desert, and also met the Sierra Club photographer Ansel Adams. She returned to New Mexico the following two summers, as well, and began her series of skull and bone paintings which later caused quite a sensation in New York art circles.

Meanwhile, Georgia's marriage was having problems, and she was under a lot of stress. In 1933 she suffered a nervous breakdown and, after her recovery, she returned to New Mexico. "I'm frightened all the time. . .", she said, "but I've never let it stop me." That year she found the Ghost Ranch and moved into a house there. She began spending each summer there, and did some of her most famous work in those early years, including *Blue River* (1935), *Ram's Head, White Hollyhock* (1935), and *Red Hills and Pedernal* (1936). In 1937 she stayed at Rancho de los Burros, near Ghost Ranch, and loved it. "As soon as I saw it, I knew I must have it," she said, and three years later did buy the house for $6000, the cost of one of her major oil paintings. Meanwhile, her professional career in New York was thriving, and Stieglitz kept her work before the public with yearly showings at his gallery. In 1942 Georgia received an honorary doctorate from the University of Wisconsin, an honor that pleased her very much.

By the time Stieglitz died in July, 1946, Georgia had decided to move to New Mexico full-time. In 1949 she was elected to the prestigious National Institute of Arts and Letters, and in 1963 to the fifty-member American Academy of Arts and Letters. In 1959, at the age of seventy-one, O'Keeffe embarked on a trip around the world. She liked Asia the best: "I like the dirty parts of the world", she said. The yearly showings of her work had ended with Stieglitz' death, and Georgia was all but forgotten by the fickle New York art world. A cover story in *Life* magazine in 1968, coupled with a 1970 retrospective exhibition in New York, brought her work to the attention of a whole new generation of admirers. She continued to paint, drawing her inspiration from the silence of the desert. When asked about her qualities as an artist, she responded: "I don't think I have a great gift, it isn't just *talent*. . . . It's mostly a lot of nerve and a lot of very, very hard work."

Georgia continued to paint, and did some sculpting as well, right up to the end of her life. Reflecting on her mortality she said: "When I think of death, I only regret that I will not be able to see this beautiful country anymore, unless the Indians are right and my spirit will walk here after I'm gone." Georgia died on March 6, 1986, at the age of ninety-eight. She helped to define modern art, a domain formerly exclusive to men.

Always, she remained true to her inner vision: "I find that I have painted my life—things happening in my life—without knowing." It is this expression of her vision through art that, for Georgia O'Keeffe, counts the most: "The meaning of a word—to me—is not as exact as the meaning of a color. . . . Where I was born and where and how I have lived is unimportant. It is what I have done with where I have been that should be of interest."

Sources

▶ **Books**

Bachman, Donna, and Sherry Piland, *Women Artists: An Historical, Contemporary and Feminist Bibliography*, Scarecrow Press, 1978.

Berry, Michael, *Georgia O'Keeffe*, Chelsea House, 1988.

Gherman, Beverly, *Georgia O'Keeffe*, Atheneum, 1986.

Lisle, Laurie, *Portrait of an Artist: A Biography of Georgia O'Keeffe*, Seaview Books, 1980.

O'Keeffe, Georgia, *Georgia O'Keeffe*, Penguin, 1976.

Rosa Parks

"There was not much I could do except struggle on. There were times when it would have been easy to fall apart or to go in the opposite direction, but somehow I felt that if I took one more step someone would come along to join me."

Born in Tuskegee, Alabama, on February 4, 1913, Rosa Parks helped initiate the civil rights movement of the 1950s and 1960s by refusing to give up her bus seat to a white patron.

I n 1957 the United States Congress passed a civil rights act, the first such legislation since 1875. The law created the Civil Rights Commission, an agency solely concerned with the protection of civil rights, and increased the size and power of the Justice Department's civil rights branch. Some called the act revolutionary, others a sham, but there was no doubt that it effectively called national attention to the issue of civil rights as never before. Congress had been prompted to action by a wave of protests across the nation, but especially in the segregated South. Led by people like Dr. Martin Luther King, Jr., blacks were pushing for an end to centuries of discrimination. It was a time when seemingly minor actions could take on great significance—a black drinking from the "wrong" drinking fountain, voting in a local election, or, in the case of Rosa Parks, refusing to give up a bus seat after a hard day's work.

Rosa Parks's parents, James McCauley, a carpenter, and Leona McCauley, a school teacher, separated while she was quite young. She spent her early years living on a farm near Pine Level, Alabama, with her mother, her grandparents, and her brother. The family was very poor and worked hard to raise enough food to feed themselves. To earn money Leona sewed for her neighbors, worked as a hairdresser, and, when the rare opportunity arose, taught school. Parks's grandparents also picked crops on nearby plantations with the young girl working along beside them gathering corn, peanuts, and sweet potatoes. It wasn't unusual for a child to do this; in fact Parks's school closed three months earlier than the school for white children so that she and the other black children would be free to work all day. "I never had more than five or six months of education a year while the white children went to school for nine months," she recalled.

Unlike the school for white children, the school Parks attended was little more than a shack; there were no windows or desks and few books. When school was dismissed the children took the books they did have home to protect them in case the school was attacked by the Ku Klux Klan during the night. The education the students received was minimal, leaving most of them poorly qualified for anything but menial jobs. Finally, when Rosa was eleven, her mother had saved up enough money to send her to a private school in Montgomery.

On the farm, Parks's grandfather kept a shotgun handy to protect the family. Alabama was a dangerous place for blacks. There was always the threat of churches being burned, lynchings, and other horrors. Some nights Parks was so frightened she couldn't sleep. In later life she developed chronic insomnia, which she associated with those long nights of terror during childhood.

Life for a Southern black in those days was harsh and full of injustice. But it was clear, even from an early age, that Parks was not one to endure acts of injustice without responding. While walking one day through a white neighborhood in Montgomery, she was pushed from behind by a white boy. Instead of walking on and trying to ignore the action, as it might have been prudent to do, Parks turned around and shoved the boy back. When the child's mother exclaimed, asking how a black girl would dare touch a white boy, Parks responded, "I don't want to be pushed by your son or anyone else," and calmly walked away.

At fifteen Parks graduated from Booker T. Washington Junior High School and, with financial help from her parents, took courses at the Alabama State College for Negroes. In December, 1932, she married Raymond A. Parks, a local barber she had met the previous year. Out of school, Rosa Parks worked for a time as an office clerk, then as a saleswoman for a black insurance agency, and then as a tailor's assistant. She spent years working as a youth adviser for the NAACP and joined the Montgomery Voters League. Her work in getting blacks registered to vote was especially difficult. She recalled later: "Even if we succeeded in getting applications filled out, the registrars would take them and tell us we would hear from them by mail if we passed. Very few ever heard of course. Whites got their certificates right away. If ever you did get registered, you had to pay poll tax. . . . But hardship or not, almost every Negro finally found some way to get the money and have his name on the books."

Of all the indignities blacks had to suffer in everyday life in the South, one of the most frustrating was the treatment they received on the city bus system—a system that depended on black riders for a great part of its revenue. Martin Luther King, Jr., described the situation: "Frequently Negroes paid their fares at the front door, and then were forced to get off and reboard the bus at the rear. Often the bus pulled off with the Negro's dime in the box before he had time to reach the rear door." If the "whites only" section filled up with more whites waiting to be seated, blacks were told to stand and give up their seats. If they refused— which happened very rarely—they were arrested.

Parks could not easily accept the treatment she received on the city buses. Whenever possible she walked. When she did ride she often argued with bus drivers who demanded that she use the rear entrance. "You died a little each time you found yourself face to face with this kind of discrimination," she commented later. "The question of where we had to sit on the bus wasn't a little thing."

But the day of December 1, 1955, was an especially tiring one for Mrs. Rosa Parks, and she decided to take a bus home instead of walking. The hours she'd spent pressing pants and putting cuffs in hems left her weary with a sore neck from bending over all day. She hoped she'd be able to get a seat and not have to stand all the way home. Luckily, when she climbed into the crowded bus she found one empty seat in the front of the "colored" section.

As the bus picked up more riders the front of the bus—the white section—quickly filled up until there were no seats left at all. When the driver noticed a white man standing in the aisle, he ordered four people, including Rosa Parks, to give up their seats. At first no one moved. But then the bus driver said, "You all better make it light on yourselves and give me those seats." At this point three of the riders stood up, but Parks quietly refused. Giving up her seat just then was more indignity than she could bear. "I was just plain tired," she said later, "and my feet hurt." As a result Parks was arrested, taken to the police station, fingerprinted, and charged with disobeying the segregation laws.

Word of the arrest of this highly respected black woman spread quickly through the black community in Montgomery with momentous results. It touched off the thirteen-month Montgomery bus boycott that brought the young Dr. Martin Luther King, Jr., to the forefront of the civil rights movement and resulted in the Supreme Court ruling outlawing segregation on the buses. Because of her calm but firm refusal to submit to yet another example of injustice, she became known as "the Mother of the civil rights movement." Years later Dr. King wrote of her: "She was anchored to that seat by the accumulated indignities of days gone by and the boundless aspirations of generations yet unborn."

After suffering threats and harrassment at their home in Montgomery, Rosa Parks and her husband moved in 1957 to Detroit, where she worked as a congressman's assistant. In 1987 the couple established the Rosa and Raymond Parks Institute for Self Development to provide leadership training for underprivileged youth. She travels widely around the nation, speaking to audiences of every age, race, and background, concerning herself especially with voter registration programs. Upon being presented with a donation for the first Rosa Parks Scholarship, she said, "I am grateful that I have endured and lived to see this day. We have to continue our struggles against all obstacles."

Sources

▶ Books

King, Martin Luther, Jr., "Stride Toward Freedom: The Montgomery Story," in *A Testament of Hope: The Essential Writings of Martin Luther King, Jr.*, edited by James Melvin Washington, Harper, 1986.

Metcalf, George R., *Black Profiles*, McGraw-Hill, 1968.

Robinson, Jo Ann Gibson, *The Montgomery Bus Boycott and the Women Who Started It,* edited by David J. Garrow, University of Tennessee Press, 1987.

Thomas, Arthur E., *Like it Is: Arthur E. Thomas Interviews Leaders on Black America,* edited by Emily Rovetch, Dutton, 1981.

Linus Pauling

"For many years it has not been respectable to work for peace. Perhaps the . . . Nobel Prize committee's action will help to make it respectable."

Born February 28, 1901, in Portland, Oregon, Linus Pauling is an American chemist and peace activist.

P auling has been one of the world's preeminent chemists for more than half a century. His work on chemical bonding forms the basis for many concepts in modern chemistry. He helped discover the structure of hemoglobin, which led to advances in the treatment of sickle-cell anemia. His work on the structure of protein molecules laid the foundation for the discovery of the structure of DNA. Pauling has been more than a scientist, however. As an opponent of nuclear testing in the 1950s and 1960s, he was both criticized and lauded for helping to lead the movement against the deployment of nuclear weapons. For his efforts, Pauling was awarded two unshared Nobel prizes; he is the only person ever to be so honored.

Pauling was born in Portland, Oregon, the son of a pharmacist. As a child, he was an insatiable reader. When he was a teenager, he discovered chemistry one day in a friend's makeshift home laboratory, and he vowed to make a career of the subject. Pauling attended Washington High School in Portland but left without graduating because his curriculum had not included the proper courses.

In 1917 Pauling entered Oregon State Agricultural College in Corvallis. He majored in chemistry and physics, graduating in 1922 with a Bachelor's degree. He then went to the California Institute of Technology (Caltech) in Pasadena, and received his Ph.D. in 1925. He stayed at Caltech the following year as a research fellow, and in 1926 he was awarded a Guggenheim Fellowship to study for a year in Europe. There he worked with Erwin Schroedinger and Niels Bohr, two pioneers of quantum mechanics. This exposure to the theory of quantum mechanics had a profound influence on Pauling's later work in chemistry.

Pauling returned to Caltech where he became an assistant professor of chemistry. He began investigating the nature of crystals, and from there he moved on to study the structure of molecules and the nature of chemical bonds. His previous experience with quantum mechanics allowed him to make a crucial insight: ideas from quantum mechanics could be combined with principles of chemistry to gain knowledge about chemical bonding. His major discovery is known as the "resonance theory," in which Pauling explained the structure of certain molecules that had previously baffled scientists. This theory helped scientists understand complex substances and helped in the development of new drugs and synthetic fibers.

Becoming a full professor at Caltech in 1931, Pauling became the chairman of the chemistry department and the director of the university's chemistry laboratories in 1937. During World War II he worked for the U.S. Government on the National Defense Research Committee; for his efforts, he was awarded the Presidential Medal of Merit in 1948. Following the war, Pauling returned to complex topics in chemistry, most notably the area of organic proteins. He was interested in the structure of amino acids and peptides, the building blocks of protein. In 1949 Pauling and Harvey Itano discovered the biochemical structure of hemoglobin, which led to dramatic breakthroughs in the study of sickle-cell anemia. In 1950 Pauling and Robert Corey reported that many protein molecules were arranged in the form of a helix; this discovery had profound implications in chemistry, and helped lead to the discovery of the structure of DNA by James Watson and Francis Crick a few years later.

Because of his extraordinarily valuable work, Pauling was awarded the 1954 Nobel Prize in chemistry. In making the announcement, the Nobel committee emphasized Pauling's applications of quantum mechanics to chemistry as his most important contribution to the advancement of science. It was about this time that Pauling began to involve himself in anti-nuclear weapon activities. As a result, he was accused of being a communist by Senator Joseph McCarthy and was twice denied a passport. It was only after the announcement of his Nobel Prize that his passport was reinstated, allowing him to travel to Sweden to accept the award.

In the late 1950s, while still at Caltech, Pauling became increasingly concerned about the testing of nuclear weapons and the possibility of nuclear war. In 1958 he participated in the now-famous television debate with a developer of the atomic bomb, Edward Teller, over the wisdom of continued nuclear testing. In the same year he published a book deploring nuclear testing entitled *No More War* and presented a petition to the United Nations signed by more than eleven thousand scientists calling for an end to testing. In 1960 the U.S. Senate Internal Security subcommittee subpoenaed Pauling, demanding that he turn over the list of scientists who had signed his United Nations petition. Pauling refused, saying, "I am convinced that these names would be used for reprisals against those believers in the democratic process. . . . As a matter of conscience, as a matter of principle, as a matter of morality, I have decided that I shall not conform to the request." Although the subcommittee threatened to hold Pauling in contempt for his refusal, he escaped unpunished.

For his efforts in attempting to discourage nuclear testing and war, Pauling was awarded the 1962 Nobel Peace Prize, thus becoming the first person in history to win two unshared Nobel prizes. When asked which of his Nobel prizes was more important to him, Pauling replied,

"[The Peace Prize], I think, perhaps because I feel so strongly about the need for peace and an end to human suffering from wars."

In 1963 Pauling left Caltech and worked with the Center for the Study of Democratic Institutions in Santa Barbara, California, until 1969. In addition, he was on the faculty of the University of California at San Diego from 1967 to 1969 until he moved to Stanford University. In the early 1970s Pauling began concentrating on orthomolecular psychology, the effect of specific concentrations of natural substances on mental disease. He studied individual biochemical differences between human beings, hoping to apply the resulting information to dietary therapy. His measurement of Vitamin C levels in schizophrenics led not only to his well-known book, *Vitamin C and the Common Cold*, but to a great deal of criticism from the medical community. Critics charged that the evidence supporting Pauling's claim that large quantities of Vitamin C shorten and prevent colds and may even prevent cancer were laden with anecdotal stories rather than scientific proof. In the years that followed, many studies were conducted, some supporting Pauling's view, others casting doubt on it.

Pauling's brilliance and hard work led to his Nobel Prize in chemistry. His courage and determination in championing a then-unpopular cause led to his Nobel Peace Prize. Throughout his life, he has worked to reduce human suffering, both from diseases that could be better understood by improved knowledge of chemical structure and from humans themselves who threaten nuclear war. Through both work and inspiration, Pauling led humankind to a better understanding of ourselves.

Sources

▶ **Books**

Gray, Tony, *Champions of Peace*, Paddington Press, 1976, pp. 266-270.

Pauling, Linus, *No More War!*, Dodd, 1958.

Pauling, Linus, *Vitamin C, the Common Cold, and the Flu*, W. H. Freeman, 1976.

White, Florence Meiman, *Linus Pauling: Scientist and Crusader*, Walker, 1980.

Wintterle, John and R.S. Cramer, *Portraits of Nobel Laureates in Peace*, Abelard-Schuman, 1971, pp. 223-228.

▶ **Periodicals**

Saturday Evening Post, "Linus Pauling: Molecular Artist," fall, 1971, pp. 14-16.

Newsweek, "The Timeless Honor," November 15, 1954, pp. 72-74, "Deadline for Dr. Pauling," July 4, 1960, p. 17, "A Second Nobel,"

October 21, 1963, p. 38, "Nobelist Promotes Vitamin C Therapy," October 27, 1980, pp. 18-23.

Omni, "Interview," December, 1986, pp. 102-104.

Itzhak Perlman

"You can tell your age by the repertory you're asked to play. At 19, I had Paganini, Tchaikovsky, Wieniawski coming out my ears. Now I play Mozart, Beethoven, Brahms, Bartok, Stravinsky. I'm getting old!"

Concert violinist Itzhak Perlman was born August 31, 1945, in Tel Aviv, Palestine.

I tzhak Perlman was born in Tel Aviv, the largest city in Palestine, in 1945. At that time, Palestine had not yet been granted the status of nationhood by the United Nations; a few years after Itzhak's birth it became the nation of Israel. Itzhak's father was a barber, and the family lived a middle class existence. When he was still very young, Itzhak fell in love with the violin, and began playing on a toy instrument when he was only three years old. When he was four years old, however, Itzhak was stricken by polio, the dreaded disease which often left the victim paralyzed. Itzhak caught the disease only a few years before Dr. Jonas Salk developed an effective vaccine to prevent polio.

Although he could no longer walk without crutches, Itzhak continued to practice the violin, perhaps all the more because many other activities were no longer possible. His parents did all they could to allow Itzhak to continue to develop. Itzhak later recalled, "The tendency was to send handicapped kids away. But my parents instinctively did things right. They treated me in a natural way." In time, Itzhak became an accomplished young violinist. He began playing at the Tel Aviv Academy of Music at a young age, where he soloed for such eminent musicians as Arthur Rubenstein, conductor Leonard Bernstein, and violinist Isaac Stern. He also was heard on radio broadcasts while performing in Jerusalem.

In 1958, the popular American television program "The Ed Sullivan Show" was assembling a group of international performers to appear on the program. Young Itzhak Perlman auditioned to represent Israel, and was selected. His first trip abroad, at age thirteen, was quite an experience. His mother accompanied him to the United States, and following the appearance on the Sullivan show, the group toured the U.S. for several months. Itzhak later recalled, "We were still kosher then, so we lived on nothing but bread and butter and sardines. I'll never forget when we hit Los Angeles and found a Jewish delicatessen."

After the tour ended, Itzhak and his mother settled in New York City. His father moved to the United States a year later to join his family. Itzhak was by this time studying violin with some of the greatest teachers in the world, including Ivan Galamian and Dorothy DeLay. Of DeLay, Itzhak later said, "[She's] the kind of teacher who doesn't tell you what to do but inspires you to tell her what you want to do." Itzhak was able to spend the equivalent of high school in the Juilliard School of Music in New York, and later entered Juilliard at the collegiate level.

In 1963, Perlman debuted at Carnegie Hall in New York City, performing Wieniawski's "Violin Concerto No. 1" with the National Orchestra. At this performance he became reacquainted with violinist Isaac Stern and other prominent violinists of the day. In 1964, Perlman won the prestigious Leventritt Foundation music competition, which led to solo performances with orchestras in New York, Cleveland, Detroit, Pittsburgh, and other cities during the next several years. Isaac Stern became Perlman's mentor, which gave Perlman a kind of instant credibility. Perlman later said of Stern, "It was wonderful having an established violinist behind me. . . . [O]rchestras . . . tend to be leery of competition winners: after all, you haven't proven yourself to *them*."

In 1967, Perlman married Toby Friedlander, a fellow violinist and one of Itzhak's biggest fans. By this time, Perlman's career was really beginning to blossom. He played with the great orchestras in America, under directors such as George Szell, Zubin Mehta, Lorin Maazel, and others. In the early 1970s, Perlman appeared in hundreds of concerts throughout the United States and Canada, playing works by Mozart, Beethoven, Mendelssohn, Ives, Faure, Bach, Paganini, and many others. He purchased a Stradivarius violin, one of a small number of instruments produced by the man whom many musicians consider the greatest violin-maker who ever lived. The instruments are so valuable, and the sounds produced so exquisite, that Perlman paid $60,000 for his Stradivarius.

Although the amount of violin music written is not particularly large (it is far smaller than the repertory for the piano, for example), Perlman has attempted to expand his repertoire into areas not explored by many violinists. Perlman is not a snob about music, and he often plays the violin like a fiddle at informal gatherings, playing numbers such as "Turkey in the Straw." He also plays Scott Joplin rag tunes, and has performed much of the violin duet material with instruments such as the viola and the piano.

Perlman credits much of his joy in playing the violin to his relationship and duets with Pinchas Zukerman, a fellow Israeli and master violinist. Perlman and Zukerman first toured together in 1976 in Europe, where they played duets from Mozart, Bach, Prokofiev, and others. In 1979, they again appeared together in eleven concerts in eleven different U.S. cities. Although among the three or four best violinists in the world, Zukerman is also one of the top violists as well. In some of the duets, Perlman plays violin to Zukerman's viola. Perlman says of his duets with Zukerman, "There is such electricity, and yet this homogenous element. It's such a rare thing, two people with such an effortless rapport." Zukerman and Perlman knew each other vaguely as children in Tel Aviv, but Zukerman, three years younger, claimed to have always been in awe of Perlman. Age and experience have narrowed the gap between the two men, and today they are often called the two greatest violinists in the world.

Perlman's playing style is very intense. Although he must play sitting down, he has such presence that he controls the very atmosphere of a concert hall. Although he often clowns around off-stage, on-stage he is all business. One European critic once said Perlman has "demonic power," a reference to his intensity in concert. Conductor Zubin Mehta has said of Perlman, "It is a great pleasure to accompany him. He molds his own voice so closely to the orchestra's. The result is intensive music making."

Perlman has many other interests in addition to the violin. Although it requires a great deal of work to remain at the top of his profession, Perlman tends to do most of his mental work in advance, often requiring a year to learn new pieces of music. After he has mastered a piece, it requires little time to maintain, and leaves time for other pursuits. Perlman is an excellent cook, even having taken cooking lessons. He is also a well-informed financial investor and a collector of art. Perhaps his most celebrated outside interest, however, is sports. Although he is severely limited in his own participation, he does swim, play ping pong, and even a bit of tennis (although he is not mobile on the court). He is mostly a sports *fan*, particularly of the New York Yankees baseball team, but also of basketball and even the sumo wrestlers of Japan.

Perlman spends as much time as he can with his family. He and Toby have four children, Noah, Navah, Leora, and Rami. Because he is so often on concert tours, he worries that his children do not see enough of him, and often visits home even while he is on tour. Perlman says, "If you're not careful, the children will grow up on you and you'll miss the most glorious part of life."

In recent years, Perlman has used his position to further the rights of handicapped persons. He has served on commissions to increase handicapped access to public places, and often visits handicapped children in hospitals. Wherever he goes, his enthusiasm and love of life inevitably shine through, giving hope to many.

Itzhak Perlman remains today one of the world's greatest violinists. That he has accomplished so much despite his physical handicap is testament to his determination and hard work. His friend and mentor Isaac Stern once said, "I remember the first time I saw [Itzhak]. . . . [He] touched me with his indomitable courage, his invulnerable spirit. He never looked at himself in the same light as other people might see him, and by his refusal to do so, he became Itzhak without qualifications."

Sources

▶ **Periodicals**

Glamour, "To Help the Handicapped, Talk To Them," March 1987, p. 64.

Hi Fi, "Itzhak Perlman, Superstar," August 1979, pp. MA18-20.

Newsweek, "Itzhak Perlman, Top Fiddle," April 14, 1980, pp. 62-72.

People, "Itzhak Perlman Drew His Bow and . . . Zing! Went the String of His Violin," May 26, 1980, p. 28; "Itzhak Perlman is the Fiddler Going Through the Roof," June 8, 1981, pp. 55-56.

Reader's Digest, "Perlman, Prince of Fiddlers," August 1980, pp. 33-34.

Sally Ride

"**I** did not come to NASA to make history. It's important to me that people don't think I was picked for the flight because I am a woman and it's time for NASA to send one."

Born May 26, 1951, in Encino, California, Sally Ride is an American astronaut.

I n the 1960s, the United States was in the midst of a technological revolution, with rapid advances occurring in many fields, including electronics and space flight. By the conclusion of the decade, two American astronauts would walk on the moon. As a teenager growing up in the '60s, Sally Ride became fascinated with science. As a young adult, she became an astrophysicist, and in 1978 she was admitted to the National Aeronautics and Space Administration (NASA) astronaut training program. In 1983, she became the first American woman in space.

Sally Ride grew up in Encino, California, a suburb of Los Angeles. As a youngster, she loved to read the "James Bond" and "Nancy Drew" as well as science fiction stories. Her father was a political science professor at Santa Monica Community College, and her mother stayed at home to care for Sally and her sister while they were growing up. The Ride children were raised in a liberal, nonjudgmental atmosphere. Her father said, "We might have encouraged, but mostly we let them explore." Ride's early love was tennis, and by the time she was a teenager she was a nationally ranked amateur player. She took tennis lessons from well-known coaches and traveled around the country to play in tournaments. She received a partial scholarship to Westlake School, a private high school, as a result of her tennis skills. Tennis pro Billie Jean King later saw Ride play and suggested that she join the professional circuit.

By her mid-teens, however, Ride had also developed a love for science. Following high school, she enrolled at Swarthmore College in Pennsylvania; after several semesters, she transferred to Stanford University. As an undergraduate at Stanford, she eventually branched out of math and science, taking classes in the humanities as well. She graduated in 1973 with a Bachelor of Science degree in physics and a Bachelor of Arts degree in English.

To continue her scientific studies, Ride began graduate work in astrophysics. Remaining at Stanford, Ride studied X-ray astronomy and theories on the behavior of free electrons in a magnetic field. She received her Ph.D. in 1978. She had not yet found a job when she saw an advertisement in a student newspaper asking for applicants to NASA's astronaut training program. Although she had never imagined herself as an astronaut, Ride decided to apply.

There were more than 8,300 applicants to the NASA training program, the first of its kind in ten years. Among the applicants were more than one thousand women. Following preliminary interviews, Ride was among approximately 200 finalists who were interviewed at the Johnson Space Center near Houston, Texas. The candidates were given extremely thorough mental and physical tests. Finally, 35 candidates, Ride among them, were selected to become astronauts. She speculated that she was chosen because she possessed a good educational background and one that showed "I could learn new things readily." Her former husband, fellow astronaut Steve Hawley, believes otherwise. He claims that all successful applicants answered the NASA psychiatrist's question about whether they had ever had amnesia by saying, "I don't know, I can't remember" [Newsweek, June 13, 1983].

As a young astronaut, Ride became a "mission specialist," an astronaut-scientist who often performs specific scientific tasks unrelated to the actual flying of the spacecraft. Ride became a specialist in maneuvering the space shuttle's remote manipulator arm, a device used to grasp and manipulate objects outside the shuttle. She worked for three years to learn how to operate the arm in every conceivable situation, and to know how to perform corrective procedures should they become necessary in space.

Ride was selected to serve as the capsule communicator for the second flight of the space shuttle. The capsule communicator relays the instructions of the flight director from mission control in Houston to the astronauts aboard the shuttle. She performed in the same capacity for the third shuttle mission. Then, in 1982, the crew for the seventh space shuttle mission was announced, with Ride among the five astronauts selected. Although she would be the first American woman to fly in space (two Soviet women had preceded her), she made it clear that she was there because of her qualifications, not simply because she was a woman. She said, "I didn't become an astronaut to become a historic figure or a symbol of progress for women." She went on to say, "It's too bad this is such a big deal. It's too bad our society isn't further along."

Ride's assignment during the flight of the space shuttle *Challenger* was to perform several tasks with the remote manipulator arm. With John Fabian, another remote arm specialist, Ride was scheduled to release and later attempt to catch a specially designed payload in space. If the maneuver were successful, it would greatly improve astronauts' ability to repair damaged satellites in space. Ride would also serve as a flight engineer, monitoring the instrument panel and offering input in the case of an emergency during take-off or landing.

On June 18, 1983, *Challenger* lifted off from Cape Canaveral, Florida, for its 6-day, 196-orbit mission in space. The commander, Robert Crippen, had piloted the first shuttle mission several years before. The rest of the crew consisted of pilot Frederick Hauck and physician Norman Thagard. Their voyage would later be described by the head of NASA's shuttle program as "nearly a perfect mission." The crew deployed two satellites and worked with the remote manipulator arm. On the fifth day of the mission, Fabian released into space a West German–built Shuttle Pallet Satellite (SPAS) from the *Challenger's* cargo bay. Fabian and Ride then used the remote manipulator arm to recapture the SPAS several different times. The crew tested the recapturing maneuvers under various conditions to prepare for future missions when the arm would be used to capture and repair real damaged satellites. By all accounts, the remote manipulator arm was a success.

On June 24, the *Challenger* was scheduled to re-enter the earth's atmosphere and land at Cape Canaveral. However, poor weather in Florida forced the shuttle to land instead at Edwards Air Force Base in southern California. Therefore, the hero's welcome scheduled for Ride and the rest of the crew at Cape Canaveral had to be postponed. Although only about 125 people witnessed the landing at Edwards Air Force Base, Ride and the crew nevertheless emerged from the spacecraft with joy and pride. Shortly after landing, Ride said, "The thing that I'll remember most about the flight is that it was fun. In fact, I'm sure it was the most fun that I will ever have in my life."

Following her historic flight, Ride continued to be active in the U.S. space program. In 1985 she began compiling the "Ride Report," which assessed America's future in space exploration and called for increased education for all Americans on issues involving space travel. The following year she served on the presidential commission investigating the Space Shuttle *Challenger* accident. Ride left NASA in 1987 to accept a position as physicist at Stanford University's Center for International Security and Arms Control. On July 1, 1989, she was appointed director of the California Space Institute at the Scripps Institution of Oceanography and a professor of physics at the University of California at San Diego.

Regardless of what else she does in the future, Ride has already left her mark in space history. By becoming the first American woman to travel in space, she has sent a message to young people throughout the nation: It is not gender which is important in doing a job; it is qualifications and desire.

Sources
▶ **Books**

O'Connor, Karen, *Sally Ride and the New Astronauts: Scientists in Space,* Watts, 1983.

Ride, Sally, with Susan Okie, *To Space and Back,* Lothrop, Lee & Shepard, 1986.

Ride, Sally, *Leadership and America's Future in Space,* NASA, 1987.

▶ **Periodicals**

Ms., "Sally Ride, Astronaut," January 1983, pp. 45-52.

Newsweek, "Sally Ride: Ready for Liftoff," June 13, 1983, pp. 36-51, "Challenger: Ride Sally Ride," June 27, 1983, pp. 20-21, "Challenger's Happy Landing," July 4, 1983, pp. 68-70.

People, "NASA Picks Six Women Astronauts," February 6, 1978, p. 28.

Time, "Sally Ride's Joy Ride into the Sky," June 13, 1983, pp. 56-58.

Jackie Robinson

" The Hall of Fame is tremendously important to me, but if it meant I had to give up anything I did or said, the Hall of Fame would have to go its own way. I did what I thought was right and, to me, right is more important than any honor."

Born a sharecropper's son in rural Cairo, Georgia, on January 31, 1919, John Roosevelt (Jackie) Robinson was the man who broke the color barrier in major league baseball. He died October 24, 1972 in Stamford, Connecticut.

W hen Jackie Robinson was a year old, his father left the family; his mother moved her children from rural Georgia to Pasadena, California, in hope that Pasadena would bring relief from the hard life and racial bigotry of Georgia—but that was not to be. Mrs. Robinson had to work many long hours of manual labor to feed her family. As for race relations, Robinson later said, "Pasadena regarded us as intruders. My brother and I were in many a fight that started with a racial slur on the very street we lived on. . . . In certain respects Pasadenans were less understanding than Southerners and even more openly hostile."

Fortunately, athletics provided a safe release from racial tensions. On the ball field, race did not seem to make much difference to anyone; Robinson was an outstanding athlete, and later recalled that "other boys brought me sandwiches and dimes so they could play on my team." He attended Muir Technical High School in Pasadena, and starred in basketball, football, and track. After graduating from high school, Robinson enrolled at Pasadena Junior College, and later at UCLA where he played four sports. During one football season, he led the nation in overall yardage gained. In basketball, he led the Pacific Coast League in scoring for two years, and he was also an outstanding tennis player.

Robinson had no thoughts of playing major league baseball, which was for whites only. After college, Robinson played a season of professional football with the Los Angeles Bulldogs, and then joined the U.S. Army. He served 31 months in the Army, spending time at Fort Riley, Kansas, and Camp Hood, Texas, where he was a lieutenant in the cavalry. While in the army, Robinson met a man who pitched for the Kansas City Monarchs in Negro League baseball. The pitcher suggested that Robinson try out for the team, and although he did not like the idea, Robinson agreed. The salary was excellent—$400 per month—and Robinson hoped to use his exposure to land a job in the East or Midwest as a social worker to help underprivileged boys.

The Monarchs were a strong team during the 1945 season, thanks to Robinson and a pitcher named Satchel Paige. The team was being scouted for talent by the Brooklyn Dodger organization. One day in Chicago, Brooklyn scout Clyde Sukeforth told Robinson that Branch Rickey, general manager of the Dodgers, wanted to see him. Robinson was suspicious, but agreed to the meeting. Rickey, who had been secretly planning to break the color barrier in the major leagues for several years, knew that the man for the job would have to be tough and disciplined as well as talented. He found his man in Jackie Robinson. During that first meeting, Rickey told Robinson what it would be like to be the first black man in the major leagues. Playing the role of bigoted fans, of insulting hotel clerks, and generally saying to Robinson what others were sure to say, Rickey finally asked, "Can you do it?" Robinson answered by asking Rickey if he wanted a ballplayer who was "afraid to fight back?" And Rickey told him he wanted "a ballplayer with the guts not to fight back." Robinson left Rickey's office that day with a $3500 signing bonus and a $600 per month contract to play for the Dodger farm club in Montreal.

Robinson spent the 1946 season with Montreal of the International League. The league's reaction to Robinson was a curious blend of enthusiasm, curiosity, and bigotry. Montreal's attendance for road games tripled that year because of Robinson's presence, but they had to cancel an exhibition road trip through the southern United States because southern cities forbade whites and blacks to play baseball on the same field. Robinson thrived on International League pitching, leading the league in hitting with a .349 average and in fielding with a .985 average. Montreal won the league pennant, and after one game the fans carried Robinson around the field in celebration.

The next season, Robinson was brought to spring training by the Dodgers. After he made the major league club, rumblings were heard around the league. Some baseball people predicted that Robinson would not make it simply because he was black. One New York reporter said, "Robinson may be going good now, but colored boys have no endurance. He won't last the season out." One of Robinson's own teammates, star catcher Dixie Walker, said he would rather be traded than be on the same team as a black man. The St. Louis Cardinals and Philadelphia Phillies threatened to boycott games with the Dodgers. It was at this time that National League president Ford Frick stepped in. He said that if players went on strike, they would be kicked out of the league. He said he did not care if half the league went on strike; he would kick them all out. With the league behind the Dodgers, some of the whirlwind subsided.

Branch Rickey organized committees of leading black citizens in every National League City to advise both Rickey and Robinson how to handle Robinson's introduction to baseball. Mainly, Robinson was advised to keep his mouth shut and not show anger at racial slurs, which, as Rickey had told Robinson in their first meeting, took a lot more courage than to fight back.

Robinson did have his share of supporters among other major leaguers, however small. He later gave a great deal of credit to Kentucky-born shortstop Pee Wee Reese, a Dodger teammate, for helping him through the first season. In every park he visited, when opposing players would start yelling things at Robinson, Reese would go over to Robinson, put his arm around him, and talk to him in a friendly manner, smiling and laughing. That ususally quieted the opposition. Once when Robinson was on first base, future Hall-of-Famer Hank Greenberg, then the Pirates' first baseman, turned to Robinson and said, "A lot of people are pulling for you to make good. Don't ever forget it." And the one constant support Robinson had was his wife Rachel, whom he had married several years earlier. He always credited his wife's patience and understanding with getting him through that first season.

The nation's media generally labeled Robinson's entrance into baseball a great "social experiment." He received a great deal of attention throughout the nation, not only from baseball fans, but from educators and civic leaders as well. National magazines such as *Newsweek* and *Time* reported on Robinson's progress fairly and without condescension. Robinson was on the cover of *Time* in September of 1947. On the field, Robinson's first year was a great success. Although he was forced to move from his regular shortstop position to first base, he gradually learned to field the position. At the plate he was outstanding, leading the team with a .297 batting average. For his efforts, he was selected the National League Rookie of the Year. He also helped lead the Dodgers to the National League pennant.

After Robinson's first season, things began to get a little easier for him. Other black players cracked the major leagues, including several more for the Dodgers. Robinson soon established himself as one of baseball's top hitters and base stealers. In 1949 he led the National League in batting with a .342 average and was named the league's Most Valuable Player. Robinson helped lead the Dodgers to pennants in 1947, 1949, 1952, 1953, 1955, and 1956. In the first four World Series, however, they lost to their cross-town rivals, the New York Yankees. Finally, in 1955, they defeated the Yankees in the Series to bring the first-ever championship to Brooklyn.

Robinson's skills began to deteriorate in the mid-1950s, and he decided to retire after the 1956 season at the age of 38, with a lifetime batting average of .311. Immediately after his retirement he was named vice president for personnel of the Chock Full O' Nuts restaurant chain. In 1960, he took on the additional job of writing a newspaper column appearing three times a week in the New York *Post,* in which he commented on sports but primarily on politics and civil rights.

The baseball community took a step toward repaying Jackie Robinson in January of 1962. In his first year of eligibility, he was elected by the Baseball Writers of America to the baseball Hall of Fame. Few players in history have been elected in their first year, and it is the ultimate honor in baseball. The week before the vote, Robinson said, "The Hall of Fame is tremendously important to me, but if it meant I had to give up anything I did or said, the Hall of Fame would have to go its own way. I did what I thought was right and, to me, right is more important than any honor."

During the 1960s, Robinson continued to stay active in civil rights issues. In business affairs, Robinson eventually resigned from the Chock Full O' Nuts company, but later worked for Harlem's Freedom National Bank (a black-owned bank), a Brooklyn-based construction company, and a life insurance company. He was also a special assistant for community affairs to New York Governor Nelson Rockefeller.

Jackie Robinson's later life was not all joy, however. His eldest son, Jackie Jr., was arrested for possession of drugs in 1968, and was killed in an automobile accident in 1971. Robinson himself began to experience physical problems, including a heart ailment, arthritis, and diabetes, which caused blindness in one eye. On October 24, 1972, Jackie Robinson suffered a heart attack at his home in Connecticut and died at the age of 53. The world mourned his loss. His funeral was attended by thousands of people, including athletes, civil rights leaders, and politicians. Perhaps the most moving eulogy was delivered by Reverend Jesse Jackson, who said, "When Jackie took the field in 1947, something unusual rose up in all of us. For he'd demonstrated to us that something could be done." Jackie Robinson took courageous steps for all of us. In a world still torn by racial hatred, he symbolizes judging people on merit rather than physical characteristics. His legacy is in the hope he offered to millions of black Americans and the enlightenment to millions of others.

Sources
▶ **Books**
Allen, Maury, *Jackie Robinson: A Life Remembered*, Watts, 1987.

Robinson, Jackie, *Baseball Has Done It*, Lippincott, 1964.

Robinson, Jackie, and Alfred Duckett, *I Never Had It Made*, Putnam, 1972.

Robinson, John R., and Wendell Smith, *My Own Story*, Greenberg, 1948.

▶ **Periodicals**
Ebony, "Black America Says Goodbye," December, 1972, pp. 174-198.

Life, "Life Goes to Jackie Robinson's Jam Session: $15,000 for Civil Rights," July 5, 1963, p. 79.

Look, "Now I Know Why They Boo Me," January 25, 1955, pp. 23-28, "A Kentucky Colonel Kept Me in Baseball," February 8, 1955, pp. 83-90,

"Your Temper Can Ruin Us," February 22, 1955, pp. 78-86, "Why I'm Quitting Baseball," January 22, 1957, pp. 91-92.

Newsweek, "Royal Robinson," August 26, 1946, pp. 71-72, "Batting at Robinson," May 19, 1947, pp. 88-90, "Negro Outspoken," January 29, 1962, p. 80.

Time, "Jackie Makes Good," August 26, 1946, pp. 63-64, "Rookie of the Year," September 22, 1947, pp. 70-76, "Keeping Posted with Jackie," April 11, 1960, p. 93, "A Hard Out," November 6, 1972, pp. 90-91.

Oscar Romero

*"*H*e who wants to withdraw from danger will lose his life. But the person who gives himself to the service of others will be like a grain of wheat that falls to the ground and dies—but only apparently dies, for by its death, its wasting away in the ground, a new harvest is made."*

Born August 15, 1917, near Ciudad Barrios, El Salvador, Oscar Arnulfo Romero y Galdames was a Catholic priest and human rights advocate who spoke out against his native country's repressive and violent military dictatorship. He was assassinated March 24, 1980, in San Salvador, El Salvador.

W hen Nobel Peace Prize nominee Archbishop Oscar Romero was assassinated as he celebrated mass in the small chapel of the hospital where he lived in El Salvador's capital, the plight of the tiny Central American republic, suffering under a brutal and repressive military regime, was catapulted into the international spotlight. As a fearless opponent of the violent activities of the government armed forces and right-wing death squads, Romero became a champion of the poor and a strong advocate of civil rights. He continued to denounce El Salvador's bloody regime despite numerous threats to his life. "I do not believe in death without resurrection," Romero told a reporter shortly before his assassination. "If they kill me, I will arise in the Salvadoran people."

Romero was born to lower middle-class parents in a remote village in the mountainous San Miguel region of eastern El Salvador. Romero's father was the telegraph operator in Ciudad Barrios and the village in which young Oscar spent his childhood years was so isolated that it could be reached only by foot and horse trail until he was twenty-three years old.

A devout Roman Catholic all his life, Romero attended seminary schools in San Miguel, San Salvador, and Rome, Italy, before entering the church as parish priest in San Miguel, where he was to spend most of his life. In later years, he returned to the capital where he served as editor of *Orientacion*, the archdiocese newspaper, and as secretary of the Catholic Bishop's Conference. "In those years I lived a very private life, anonymous you might say," recalled Romero in a 1979 *Fellowship Magazine* interview. He seemed destined to spend the remainder of his days as a minor church functionary until he was swept up in the wave of political and social unrest that engulfed El Salvador in the mid-1970s.

In 1975 Romero was appointed auxiliary bishop in the town of Santiago de Maria, and in the course of his work among the people, he became increasingly exposed to the injustices suffered by the peasants at the hands of the repressive military government of colonel Arturo Molina. Romero had earned a reputation as a conservative: as editor of *Orientacion*, he had chosen to avoid the controversial political issues of the day and editorialized against the dangers of a politicized priesthood. He was described by associates as "churchy, a lover of rules and clerical discipline," and yet his experiences of the desperate plight of the poor and those seeking democratic change in El Salvador gradually opened his eyes to the killings and repression being conducted by the military. "I would say I evolved rather than changed," said Romero later. "The circumstances of the country led me to overcome my timidity and come closer to the people."

Romero was to prove receptive to the ideas of those members of the church who advocated adopting a radical stance toward the government. By 1976 the government had become alarmed at the growing power of this "liberation theology" among the people, and pressured the Vatican into retiring the hostile archbishop of San Salvador, Luis Chavez y Gonzalez; government officials were delighted when the reputedly conservative Romero was named in his place. His traditionally deferential attitude toward those in power, even when in disagreement with them, undoubtedly led the government to believe he would be easy to manipulate, and Romero's ordination was lavish.

Thus it came as something of a surprise when the politically inexperienced new archbishop made a stand just three weeks later when one of the most distinguished jesuit priests in his diocese, Father Rutilio Grande, was murdered along with two of his parishioners. Grande had helped organize the first-ever strike at a sugar mill just north of San Salvador, and his death was widely attributed to right-wing death squads acting at the behest of the government.

Romero was outraged at Grande's murder and closed church schools for three days, announcing that the church would boycott all official government events until the cause of Grande's death was "clarified." In May, 1977, another priest was murdered, and the following month the military attacked Aguilares, the parish where Grande had helped organize the strike. In July Romero refused to attend the inauguration of the new president, General Carlos Humberto Romero (no relation), and it was announced that all Jesuits in El Salvador would be assassinated if they did not leave the country immediately.

Romero began to use the very pages of the archdiocese newspaper he had used to condemn the politicization of the clergy to list the names of those people who had been arrested by government security forces and had subsequently disappeared. He also began to use the pulpit as a forum for his attacks against the military and its reign of violence, and his Sunday masses became a focal point for El Salvador's opposition forces. Romero was liked and respected by the poor and the peasants, and they packed San Salvador's Metropolitan Cathedral to hear him speak.

Despite his popularity, he was condemned as a "communist" by some clergy who remained sympathetic to the government and denounced him to the Vatican. A Papal inspector advised the archbishop to tone down his political attacks. Romero didn't, and was eventually summoned to Rome for "consultations."

In November, 1978, a priest, Ernesto Barrero, was killed while fighting alongside guerillas of the Popular Forces of Liberation. Romero attended the funeral and declared later: "When a dictatorship seriously violates human rights and attacks the common good of the nation, when it becomes unbearable and closes all channels of dialogue, of understanding, of rationality, when this happens, the church speaks of the legitimate right of insurrectional violence."

General Romero was deposed by a coup in 1979, and although the new government was comprised of some civilians, Archbishop Romero refused to give his unqualified support to the new regime. Also that year, Romero was nominated for the Nobel Peace Prize by the U.S. Senate and members of the British Parliament, a nomination which signified "very great moral and international support for our struggle." Romero was certain he would not win the Prize itself, saying the nomination alone was prize enough.

The threats against him increased, and he became convinced his life was in danger. Yet he continued to courageously read out the names of those who had disappeared while in military custody. On March 23, 1980, Romero addressed his sermon to El Salvador's soldiers: "No soldier is obliged to obey an order contrary to the law of God. It is time that you come to your senses and obey your conscience rather than follow sinful commands."

The next evening, while celebrating mass in the small chapel of a hospital for terminally-ill cancer patients in San Salvador, Romero was shot and killed by a lone gunman. His funeral was attended by many foreign bishops and clergy, who heard him praised as a "beloved, peacemaking man of God." The ceremony was tragically marred, however, as gunmen opened fire on the estimated fifty-thousand mourners, killing as many as a hundred people and shocking nations worldwide.

Revered among ordinary El Salvadorans and fellow churchmen alike, Oscar Romero will be remembered as a courageous defender of human rights and a man of great compassion, "a pastor," as Pope John Paul II declared in 1983, "celebrated and venerated by his flock who tried . . . to stop the violence and to reestablish peace."

Sources

▶ **Books**

Brockman, James R. *The Word Remains: A Life of Oscar Romero*, Orbis Books, 1982.

Erdozain, Placido, *Archbishop Romero: Martyr of Salvador,* translated by John McFadden and Ruth Warner, Orbis Books, 1981.

Keogh, Dermott, *Romero: El Salvador's Martyr*, Dominican Publications (Dublin), 1981.

▶ **Periodicals**

America, "El Salvador's Agony and U.S. Policies," April 26, 1980, pp. 360-363, "Five Years After Romero," May 18, 1985, p. 403.

Fellowship Magazine, "Oscar Romero: Archbishop of the Poor," November, 1979, pp. 10-11.

Nation, "Who Killed Archbishop Romero," October 13, 1984, pp. 337, 350-354.

Time, "Something Vile in This Land: Panic and Death Defile a Peacemaker's Funeral," April 14, 1980, p. 61.

Eleanor Roosevelt

"O ur own success, to be real, must contribute to the successes of others."

Born in New York City in 1884, Eleanor Roosevelt was a lecturer, columnist, writer, public speaker, and social reformer who became First Lady, Representative to the United Nations, and Chairman of the Commission for Human Rights. She died in Hyde Park, N.Y., in 1962.

Eleanor Roosevelt's mark on American and international society developed from her open mind and her wide range of interests. In all her public roles she remained simple in approach and philosophy, direct and outspoken in manner, and democratic and humanitarian in social attitude. Throughout her life she served as an excellent example of how adversity and opportunity allow the best to develop in individuals.

Eleanor, the oldest of three children, was born into the "Four Hundred Families" of New York City society, of which her mother, Anna Hall Roosevelt, was a prominent member. Her father Elliott, younger brother of Theodore Roosevelt, came from a family involved in community issues. By the time she was ten, both of Eleanor's parents had died. An unattractive and clumsy child, Eleanor became lonely and alienated, feelings that lingered into her adult life. In 1905 Eleanor married Franklin Delano Roosevelt, a distant cousin; but her new husband intimidated Eleanor, as did his mother, Sara, who dictated Eleanor's life as she dictated her son's. Eleanor believed, however, that the dominating influences of both Sara and FDR made her develop a strength she did not know she possessed. "Perhaps," she wrote, "it was that having two such personalities as my husband and his mother I had to develop willy-nilly into an individual myself."

Relying on herself, Eleanor soon discovered that she had an intelligence and character of her own. "I was learning," she later remembered, "to have certain confidence in myself and in my ability to meet emergencies and to deal with them." Perhaps because of her own earlier weaknesses, Eleanor came to appreciate and accept other points of view. "I think I learned particularly," she later remembered, "that no one in the world was entirely good, and that motives are often more important than actions." Eleanor applied this understanding to her own life, and gradually pushed her mother-in-law out of her life and assumed responsibility for herself.

In the 1920s, Eleanor began to realize how important reform movements could be in politics. She thought that women's suffrage in particular would serve as a tool for social reform, and she worked for the League of Women Voters. "Women must not be content until they are as independent within the [Democratic] party as men are, which isn't saying much," she wrote. When FDR was elected President of the United States in 1932, Eleanor was wary that her accomplishments would be overshadowed by her role as First Lady. But she overcame her fears by working actively in various political efforts, and she began to develop a political agenda of her own, assisting FDR.

Eleanor was effective in pushing through many of the programs of the New Deal. She was concerned about the "forgotten woman" who was cast out on the streets and into the parks, and wanted equal access to jobs and relief for them. She was especially anxious about the youth of America, and she joined with others in drawing up plans for the National Youth Administration (NYA), and convinced FDR to approve it. She was praised for these efforts: "The intensive and sympathetic work you have been doing for the youth has in a large measure made this new venture possible."

During the 1930s and throughout her life, Eleanor took it upon herself to champion the rights of blacks. She believed that by working step by step against injustice, blacks could eventually achieve equality. Speaking out for civil rights cost Eleanor popularity, and FDR many votes in the South; nevertheless, she was effective. Roy Wilkins, Executive Director of the NAACP, said of Eleanor: "The personal touches and the personal fight against discrimination were Mrs. Roosevelt's. That attached to [President] Roosevelt also—he couldn't get away from it—and he reaped the political benefit from it." She used World War II legislation to fight for the rights of blacks, especially through the Fair Employment Practices Commission. Her goals for blacks were the "Four Freedoms": equality of opportunity in education; equality before the law; equality in getting jobs; and the right to vote.

After World War II and the death of her husband, Eleanor was appointed a member of the U.S. delegation to the United Nations. She believed that her work on the Human Rights Covenants of the United Nations was one of her most significant contributions to the nation's social development, for the promotion of equality and justice was important to her. As Frances Perkins, Secretary of Labor in the Roosevelt Administration and first woman to hold a Cabinet position, said of the First Lady: "She *lived* equality, freedom, and democracy. . . . She put those ideals into flesh." To the end Eleanor associated herself with youth, tomorrow, and the promise of development and growth. She was always impatient; for her, evolution was too slow. "Tomorrow is now," she was famous for saying.

Eleanor also believed that individual accomplishment could be applied to the greater good of all: "The motivating force of the theory of a democratic way of life is still a belief that as individuals we live cooperatively, and to the best of our ability serve the community in which we live," she once wrote. Although she was sometimes a controversial figure, Eleanor Roosevelt helped bring about changes in American society and set a new standard for public service in government.

Sources

▶ **Books**

Caroli, Betty Boyd, *First Ladies,* Oxford University Press, 1987, pp. 184-202.

Hareven, Tamara K., *Eleanor Roosevelt: An American Conscience,* Quadrangle, 1968.

▶ **Periodicals**

Life, "Great Lady Is Dead," November 16, 1962, p. 50.

Look, "Eleanor Roosevelt 1884-1962," December 18, 1962, pp. 124-5.

National Review, "Mrs. Roosevelt, RIP," January 29, 1963, p. 58.

Newsweek, "Her Glow Warmed the World," November 19, 1962, p. 47.

New Yorker, "Notes and Comment," November 17, 1962, pp. 41-2.

Time, "Too Busy to Be Sick," November 16, 1962, p. 67.

Bill Russell

"All I have finally asked is for everybody to succeed or fail on their own merits. . . . I have never worked to be well-liked or well-loved, but only to be respected. . . . I have my own ideas for the future. . . . I believe that I can contribute something far more important than mere basketball."

Born February 12, 1934 in Monroe, Louisiana, Bill Russell has been a professional basketball player, coach, executive, and television commentator.

346

W hen Bill Russell arrived to play professional basketball with the Boston Celtics in 1956, he found himself the only Black player on the team. Russell was an outspoken critic of racial prejudice and was often surrounded by controversy. Nevertheless, his efforts helped pave the way for many other Blacks to enter the National Basketball Association. Through his years with the Celtics, Russell's teams achieved a pinnacle unmatched in any professional sport: they won eleven world championships in thirteen seasons. In 1966, Russell was named player-coach of the Celtics, the first Black head coach of any team in major professional sports history.

Russell was born into a poor family in a small town in Louisiana. When he was a small child, his father left a factory job in Monroe, Louisiana and eventually moved the family to Oakland, California. There the Russells lived in a house that held nine families—one in each room and one in the garage. But Russell later said, "Oakland, compared with Louisiana, was paradise." Russell's mother died when he and his brother were still young, and his father gave up a successful trucking job in the San Joaquin Valley to be near his sons.

Russell entered McClymonds High School in Oakland as a gangly young man who did not seem to do anything well. As a sophomore, he was the sixteenth man on the fifteen–man basketball team. The coach saw some potential in Russell, so he expanded the team to 16 players; Russell and the fifteenth player had to share the last jersey. The coach, George Powles, was one of Russell's strongest supporters in school. Russell would later say, "By [keeping me on the team], I believe that man saved me from becoming a juvenile delinquent. If I hadn't had basketball, all my energies and frustrations would surely have been carried in some other direction." Russell continued to work hard at the game, and by his senior year he was a starter. He was also six and one-half feet tall.

During one game against an arch-rival high school in Oakland, a scout from the University of San Francisco's basketball team was in the audience to watch a player from the rival high school. The scout was so impressed with the play of Russell, however, that Russell was offered a scholarship rather than the rival player. It was the only such offer that Russell received, and he knew it was his only opportunity to attend college. He accepted the scholarship and vowed to do his best.

In high school, Bill had been a poor shooter and consequently not much of a scorer. But he had compensated for his weak offense by blocking shots, rebounding, and playing excellent defense. At the University of San Francisco he began to hone these skills, skills which would later lead him to glory in the professional ranks. At USF, his roommate was a quiet young man named K. C. Jones, who would later star on the same professional team as Russell. With Russell, Jones, and others, the USF Dons were transformed into a national basketball power. During his junior and senior years, Russell led USF to two consecutive NCAA national basketball championships and was twice named an All-American. During that time the Dons won fifty–six consecutive games. Also at that time, the NCAA initiated two rule changes, largely because of Russell's defense: the free–throw lane was widened to keep centers from guarding the basket, and shots could no longer be blocked after they had started a downward trajectory to the basket. The era of the defensive center had begun.

Because of his success in college, Russell was drafted by the National Basketball Association's Boston Celtics, who had done some wheeling and dealing to secure the draft rights to Russell. First, however, Russell was selected for the 1956 U.S. Olympic basketball team. He travelled with the team to Melbourne, Australia, and helped lead the United States to a gold medal. Following the Olympics, he returned to the United States to begin his professional career.

When Russell came to the Celtics, he joined a team of great players such as Bob Cousy, Bill Sharman, Frank Ramsey, and Tom Heinsohn. The coach was the legendary Red Auerbach. Despite all the talent, the team had never won an NBA championship. In his first season, Russell averaged 14.7 points per game and 19.6 rebounds. He was second in the Rookie-of-the-Year balloting to teammate Tom Heinsohn. More importantly, Russell led the Celtics to their first NBA championship, and began to change the way the game was played with his defense.

During Russell's second year, the Celtics lost the championship when Russell was injured during the playoffs. The following year, however, the Celtics began a string of eight consecutive world championships, a record unmatched in American professional team sports history. In all of Russell's thirteen seasons, the Celtics won eleven NBA titles. Russell was named the NBA's Most Valuable Player five times. Players joined and left the Celtics during that period; the one constant was Bill Russell. With his defense and rebounding, Russell redefined the game of basketball. A generation of young people emulated Russell, realizing that team play is more important than individual statistics.

Perhaps Russell's most difficult task during his years in the NBA was dealing with racial prejudice. While white players were free to concentrate on the game, black players were constantly reminded of the bigotry which was still explicitly tolerated in much of American society. Russell was the only black player on the Celtics during his first year, but it was not a problem because the Celtics' owner, Walter Brown, was unconcerned with the color of a player's skin. The other Celtic players seemed to be concerned only with winning, not race. However, there was considerable prejudice around the league, and black players were harassed by bigoted fans almost everywhere. Furthermore, there seemed to be an unwritten quota in the league that no team could have more than one or two black players. In 1958, Russell told newspapers that he believed teams had quotas. He was widely criticized for his statements, but his actions helped pave the way for more blacks to enter the sport, and soon any remnants of a quota system began to disappear.

Some of Russell's most memorable confrontations came with giant center Wilt Chamberlain, perhaps history's greatest individual player. Although Chamberlain's statistics were generally more specatacular than Russell's, especially in scoring, only once did Chamberlain's team, the Philadalphia '76ers, win an NBA title during Russell's career. Time and again the two men met in the championship series, and Russell won every head-to-head competition in the finals, causing Chamberlain understandable frustration.

In 1966, Red Auerbach retired as coach of the Celtics and selected Bill Russell as his successor. Russell thus became the first black head coach in NBA and American professional sports history. Although Russell's Celtics did not win the NBA championship in the 1966-67 season, his first year as player-coach, they came back to win the title the following two years. Players such as K. C. Jones, Bob Cousy, and Bill Sharman had retired, but Russell was joined by younger stars such as Sam Jones, Bailey Howell, Larry Siegfried, Don Nelson, and John Havlicek. The last two championships were rather remarkable because Russell and the Celtics were in decline and had to battle their way past younger and more physically talented teams.

Russell coached the Celtics until his retirement as a player in 1969. He later coached the Seattle Supersonics for several years, and most recently, the Sacramento Kings in 1987 and 1988. He is currently an executive with the Kings. Between coaching and executive jobs, he was an analyst for NBA games on television with ABC, CBS, and cable television.

The years from the mid-1950s to the late 1960s are known in basketball lore as the "Bill Russell Era." There were arguably greater players during those years, such as Oscar Robertson, Jerry West, Elgin Baylor, and Wilt Chamberlain, but the era is named for Russell because he put the team and winning above all else, above all personal goals. Los Angeles Laker great Jerry West once said, "They can talk about individual players in any sport, but I tell you that when it comes to winning, there is no one like Bill Russell. This guy is the greatest of them all."

Sources
▶ **Books**

Greenfield, Jeff, *World's Greatest Team*, Random House, 1976, pp. 88-101.

Heuman, William, *Famous Pro Basketball Stars*, Dodd, 1970, pp. 73-81.

Hirshberg, Albert, *Bill Russell of the Boston Celtics*, Messner, 1963.

Libby, Bill, *The Coaches*, Regnery, 1972, pp. 23-28.

Pepe, Phil, *Greatest Stars of the NBA*, Prentice-Hall, 1971, pp. 33-50.

Richardson, Ben, and W. A. Fahey, *Great Black Americans*, Crowell, 1976, pp. 318-26.

Russell, Bill, and William McSweeney, *Go Up For Glory*, Coward-McCann, 1966.

Russell, Bill, and Taylor Branch, *Second Wind: The Memories of an Opinionated Man*, Random House, 1979.

▶ **Periodicals**

Life, "Best Big Man on View," January 16, 1956, pp. 12-14.

Look, "Bill Russell, the Antenna With Arms," January 10, 1956, pp. 66-68.

Newsweek, "Coach Russell," May 2, 1966, pp. 72-73. "Boston's Old, Old Pros: Championship," May 19, 1969, p. 77, "Parting Shots," June 2, 1969, p. 67.

Anwar Sadat

*"*M*y contemplation of life . . . had taught me that he who cannot change the very fabric of his thought . . . at a deeper and perhaps subtler level than the conscious level . . . will never be able to change reality, and will never, therefore, make any progress."*

Born December 25, 1918, in Talah Monufiya, Egypt (now Arab Republic of Egypt), Anwar Sadat was President of his country from 1970 until his assassination on October 6, 1981, in Cairo, Egypt.

A nwar Sadat was born into poverty in a small village in the Nile delta region of Egypt, between Alexandria and Cairo, in 1918. His father worked as a clerk, and when Sadat was six years old, the family moved to Cairo where his father took a position at a military hospital. Sadat's family was devoutly religious, and he studied the Koran, the holy book of the Moslem religion, at high school in Cairo. As a young man, Sadat became obsessed with the idea of driving the British from Egypt. The British held Egypt as a colonial possession until 1936 and had significant influence thereafter.

In 1936 Sadat entered the Abbassia Military Academy. At that time, only young men from privileged families were generally allowed to attend military schools; children of lower-class families had to be sponsored by wealthy patrons to enroll. Sadat later recalled his experience with a patron: "The [patron] looked at my father and said very haughtily: 'Oh, yes. You're the senior clerk of the Health Department, and that's your son. . . . ' It was an experience that has remained with me all my life. I don't think I shall ever forget it."

Sadat did well in school and graduated in 1938, during the rise of Nazi Germany; he was then stationed at a garrison in northern Egypt. Because the Nazis represented the downfall of numerous former European colonial powers, such as France and the Netherlands, Sadat was sympathetic to the Nazi cause, despite the fact that Germany itself had been a colonial power of some repute. He began aiding German spy operations in Egypt in an attempt to undermine the British influence there but was arrested in 1942. Imprisoned, he was stripped of his military rank and expelled from the Egyptian army. While in prison, Sadat sustained himself with visions of an Egyptian revolution, in which Egypt's corrupt monarch and all vestiges of British rule were removed. He later said, "I discovered my real self in Cell 54, Cairo Central Prison."

Escaping from prison in 1944, Sadat went into hiding. He assumed a variety of disguises and identities and worked at menial jobs including selling used tires. In 1946 he was again captured and imprisoned for carrying out terrorist activities against the British and served three more years in prison. Finally, in 1952, Sadat joined his former classmate Gamal Abdel Nasser and a number of other military leaders in overthrowing the monarchy of King Farouk. Nasser assumed power and Sadat began a long career in various government positions. Although Nasser and Sadat had plotted the revolution together, Nasser did not completely trust any of his subordinates, and he kept Sadat at some political distance. Sadat faded into the metaphorical woodwork, holding government jobs that were significant but never colorful.

In 1964 Nasser appointed Sadat to a visible but largely ceremonial post as one of Egypt's four vice-presidents. Nasser's distrust of his political rivals continued, and though most men did not last long in important positions, Sadat remained, apparently because Nasser became convinced that Sadat posed no threat to his power. Following the disastrous 1967 six-day war with Israel, in which Egypt lost territory to the Israelis, Nasser temporarily abolished the office of vice-president. He reestablished the office in 1969, making Sadat the sole vice-president.

Nasser died of a heart attack in 1970 after several years of illness. Shortly thereafter, Sadat was selected as his successor by the Arab Socialist Union party, reportedly because he was viewed as the least objectionable choice. Sadat inherited a nation-filled with tensions and bitterness. Under Nasser, Egypt had continued sparring with Israel and had established close ties with the Soviet Union. Sadat had been a nearly fanatic opponent of Israel, and many western observers wondered whether new hostilities would erupt after Sadat took over. Sadat, however, surprised his doubters by immediately extending the cease-fire Nasser had established shortly before his death. Furthermore, Sadat soon distanced Egypt from the Soviet Union by expelling seventeen thousand Soviet technicians and advisers in 1972.

In 1973, hostilities between Israel and Egypt again flared. Over a period of two weeks in October of 1973, more than twenty thousand people were killed in fighting between the Arab nations of Egypt and Syria and the nation of Israel. For a few days it appeared that the Israeli army would overrun Egypt, but Egyptian forces finally pushed the Israelis back into the Sinai Peninsula. The result of the conflict was clearly in doubt, although Israel yet appeared to hold the upper hand, when Sadat seized the opportunity to call for a historic peace treaty. Had the Egyptians failed to drive the Israelis back, there could have been no peace proposal because Sadat would have had no strong position from which to bargain, but he acted quickly with his first chance. Sadat proposed that Israel withdraw from the Sinai Peninsula and restore to Egypt the land captured during the 1967 war and occupied ever since. In exchange, Egypt would attend an international peace conference sponsored by the United Nations and re-open the Suez Canal, a vital shipping link for all the world's cargo ships. Negotiations between Sadat and the Israelis, spearheaded by U.S. Secretary of State Henry Kissinger, were front-page news around the world. It was at this point that the world began taking Anwar Sadat seriously. Journalist Gail Sheehy reported that when asked where he would rank Sadat on a scale of visionary statesmen, Kissinger replied, "Sadat is the greatest since Bismarck."

Despite Sadat's efforts in 1973, the Arab-Israeli problems were not over.

In 1977, following new aggressions and posturings by the two countries, Sadat again reflected on a plan for peace. Discussing the matter privately with American president Jimmy Carter, a man he deeply trusted, Sadat realized that bold action was necessary. Sheehy reported that during a flight from Romania, Sadat said, "How am I going to make this bold act that I promised Carter? It was then that I drew, almost unconsciously, on the inner strength I had developed in Cell 54 of Cairo Central Prison—a strength, call it a talent or capacity, for change. . . . My contemplation of life and human nature in that secluded place had taught me that he who cannot change the very fabric of his thought . . . at a deeper and perhaps subtler level than the conscious level . . . will never be abel to change reality, and will never, therefore, make any progress."

Sadat's solution to the dilemma reflected the flair for the dramatic that he had displayed ever since taking office. Changing the rules of the game, the "very fabric of his thought," Sadat boldly offered to address the Israeli parliament in Jerusalem, disregarding the dangers he faced from both Arab and Zionist extremists. It would be the first visit by an Arab leader to Israel, and the offer stunned the world. In his address in Jerusalem, Sadat offered to guarantee Israel's security in the troubled region in exchange for the return of the remaining Egyptian lands occupied by Israel. The trip was applauded throughout the free world as a gesture of courage and humanity. Unfortunately, the talks between the two nations broke down shortly thereafter. Then in September of 1978, U.S. Secretary of State Cyrus Vance arranged a summit between Sadat and Israeli prime minister Menachem Begin with President Carter at Camp David, Maryland. The result, ironed out in a largely secret summit, was an agreement known as the "Camp David Accord," which promised new hope for peace in the Middle East.

Although it was still some time before a workable plan for peace was devised and a formal peace treaty signed, in the end Sadat's efforts were rewarded. Israel returned most of the land occupied since 1967 as well as the oil fields and military bases that went with it. Egypt, for its part, promised a normalization of relations between the two nations and security for Israel in the region. In November of 1978, even before the final peace treaty was signed, the Nobel Prize committee voted to award the Nobel Peace Prize to Sadat and Begin. Many political commentators felt that it was Sadat who deserved the prize, but the Nobel committee did not want to risk offending Begin and Israel at that critical juncture in Middle East history, and so honored him as well.

Sadat's bold steps to forge a peaceable relationship with Israel were not universally well received in the Arab world. In fact, many Arabs resented Sadat's bargaining as mortgaging the future of the Palestinian refugees who had been displaced by Israel's nationhood in 1948. The more fanatic elements of Arab lands began to plot against Sadat, and the culmination of the plots occurred in October of 1981, when members of the Egyptian army assassinated the president during a parade in Cairo.

Although Sadat died before his time, his legacy lives on. He emerged in nearly a decade of leadership as a bold and courageous leader, contrary to what his past career might have seemed to promise—he had had a relatively undistinguished military career, and after his important role in the overthrow of the monarch, he served as an unspectacular government official for nearly twenty years. Even his appointment as president appeared to have been by default. After assuming office, however, Sadat seemed transformed. Rather than be changed for the worse, as have many who gained power, Sadat was reborn as a resolute, courageous leader who realized the great power of peace. The ability to change oneself that Sadat had spoken of turned him into one of the great leaders of the twentieth century. His efforts to bring peace to an area of the world war-torn for millennia made him a symbol of peace throughout the world.

Sources

▶ **Books**

Heikal, Mohamed, *Autumn of Fury: The Assassination of Sadat*, Random House, 1983.

Hirst, David, and Irene Beeson, *Sadat*, Faber & Faber, 1981.

Israeli, Raphael, and Carol Bernstein, *Man of Defiance: A Political Biography of Anwar Sadat*, Barnes & Nobel, 1985.

Sadat, Anwar, *In Search of Identity: An Autobiography*, Harper, 1977.

Sadat, Camelia, *My Father and I*, Macmillan, 1985.

▶ **Periodicals**

Esquire, "The Riddle of Sadat," January 30, 1979, pp. 25-39.

New Republic, "Anwar Sadat's Legacy," October 21, 1981, pp. 7-10.

Newsweek, "A New Leader and an Uneasy Truce," October 19, 1970, pp. 53-54, "A Timely Award?," November 6, 1978, pp. 67-71.

Time, "Arabs Vs. Israelis in a Suez Showdown," October 29, 1973, pp. 22-34, "Sadat Shouts an Angry No," January 30, 1978, pp. 35-38, "The Sealed Lips Summit," September 18, 1978, pp. 18-21, "How It Happened," October 19, 1981, pp. 14-18.

Carl Sagan

"*We make our world significant by the courage of our questions and by the depth of our answers.*"

Born November 9, 1934, in New York City, Carl Sagan is an astronomer and popularizer of science.

Address: Laboratory for Planetary Studies, Center for Radiophysics and Space Research, Cornell University, Ithaca, NY 14850.

Of those who have tried to make science comprehensible to the American public, surely one of the most successful is astronomer Carl Sagan. Because of their technical nature, scientific disciplines traditionally have been largely outside the public domain, partly because scientists have had difficulty making ideas accessible to the popular press. Although many of his colleagues grimace when he simplifies aspects of science, Sagan has succeeded in popularizing a number of areas of science, particularly astronomy. Through his books, essays, and television series "Cosmos," he has informed and enlightened millions of people on a wide range of scientific subjects.

Sagan was born in 1934 in New York City. His father was a Russian immigrant who worked in a textile factory. As a young boy, Sagan was fascinated with stars—one day he asked his friends what they were, and was told they were "lights in the sky." Not satisfied with that explanation, he began checking out library books on stars and became even more intrigued with the subject. With these books, he later recalled, "I got my first sense of the immensity of the universe. I was hooked."

When he was ten years old, Sagan discovered science fiction books, notably Edgar Rice Burroughs's tales of adventures on Mars. He became very interested in astronomy and began studying simple mathematical relationships involving stars and planets. Sagan's family later moved to Rahway, New Jersey, just west of Staten Island, and he entered Rahway High School. An excellent student who took a strong interest in science courses, Sagan decided at Rahway to become a professional astronomer, graduating in 1951 as the student most likely to succeed.

Sagan wanted to attend a university that was strong in the humanities as well as physics and astronomy. He finally decided on the University of Chicago because "In the early 1950s, [it] was a very exciting place to be." The university faculty included several Nobel prize winners in the natural sciences, and Sagan was eventually introduced to Dr. Harold Urey, winner of the 1934 Nobel Prize in Chemistry. He studied with Urey and worked one summer with Nobel laureate Hermann Muller at Indiana University. In 1954 Sagan graduated with a Bachelor's degree from the general college; in 1955, he received a Bachelor of Science degree in physics. Assisted by a grant from the National Science Foundation, Sagan earned a Master's degree in physics in 1956. It was at this time that he began to develop ideas about life on other planets and in other galaxies. He moved to Madison, Wisconsin, and met geneticist Joshua Lederberg, another Nobel laureate. Lederberg shared Sagan's interest in extraterrestrial life, and the two began speaking at conferences together. Sagan later received a predoctoral fellowship and in 1960 graduated from the University of Chicago with a Ph.D in astronomy.

Following his graduation Sagan began postdoctoral work at the University of California at Berkeley. He demonstrated his continued interest in the solar system by publishing an article covering the planet Venus. In 1962 he took posts as an astrophysicist at the Smithsonian Astrophysical Observatory in Cambridge, Massachusetts, and as a lecturer at Harvard University. During the next few years Sagan conducted significant studies of Mars, which culminated with an article for *National Geographic* magazine, and began working with the National Aeronautics and Space Administration (NASA).

Despite his accomplishments, Sagan was not offered tenure by Harvard University; in 1968 he went to Cornell University in Ithaca, New York, to serve as director of Cornell's Laboratory for Planetary Studies. At Cornell, he began studying the planet Jupiter and was asked to advise the NASA astronauts who would be landing on the moon. Winning NASA's Apollo Achievement Award in 1970, Sagan continued to work on NASA projects, including the Pioneer 10 and 11 explorations of Saturn and Jupiter and the Mariner 9 and Viking expeditions to Mars.

It was during this time that Sagan began the endeavor for which he will probably be best remembered: bringing scientific ideas to the public arena. In 1973, Sagan, a prolific writer who has contributed more than two hundred articles to scientific journals, published his first book intended for general readership, *The Cosmic Connection*. The book was very successful, and Sagan was invited by television talk-show host Johnny Carson to appear on NBC's "Tonight" show. Sagan impressed the audience and Carson (himself an astronomy buff) enough to be invited back for numerous appearances. In the late 1970 Sagan began producing a thirteen-week television series for the Public Broadcasting System (PBS) entitled "Cosmos." The series, one of the most popular in PBS history, took three years to finish, during which time Sagan travelled around the globe to bring home his messages about scientific progress, the evolution of life on earth, and exploration of space. With easily understood words and examples, "Cosmos" made science accessible to more than 250 million viewers around the world. This was not science for intellectuals only, it was for everyone to understand and appreciate. As Sagan notes, "There is nothing about science that cannot be explained to the layman."

Sagan continue to write books for the general reader. In 1978 he wrote about the evolution of the human brain in *The Dragons of Eden*, which won a Pulitzer Prize. He later wrote *Cosmos*, a companion book to the television series, and *Murmurs of Earth: The Voyager Interstellar Records*. These and other subsequent books have all attempted to further his ideal of bringing science into the popular imagination. Sagan's first novel, *Contact,* was published in 1985 and provided a fictional account of the search for extraterrestrial civilizations. To date, Sagan's books have sold nearly ten million copies and have been translated into a dozen languages.

Sagan teaches and conducts research at Cornell and is working on more books that he hopes will create greater public enthusiasm for science. Concerning his efforts to popularize scientific concepts, Sagan insists, "Science is a joy. It is not just something for an isolated, remote elite. It is our birthright."

Sources

▶ Books

Cohen, Daniel, *Carl Sagan: Superstar Scientist,* Dodd, 1987.

Sagan, Carl, *The Cosmic Connection: An Extraterrestial Perspective,* Anchor Press, 1973.

Sagan, Carl, *The Dragons of Eden,* Random House, 1977.

Sagan, Carl, and others, *Murmurs of Earth: The Voyager Interstellar Record.* Random House, 1978.

Sagan, Carl, *Contact: A Novel,* Simon & Schuster, 1985.

▶ Periodicals

Newsweek, "Seeking Other Worlds," August 15, 1977, pp. 46-47.

New Yorker, "Profiles: A Resonance With Something Alive-I," June 21, 1976, pp. 39-83, "Profiles: A Resonance With Something Alive-II," June 28, 1976, pp. 30-61.

People, "Up Front," December 15, 1980, pp. 42-45

Time, "The Cosmic Explainer," October 20, 1980, pp. 62-69.

Andrei Sakharov

*"*I*ntellectual freedom is essential to human society— freedom to obtain and distribute information, freedom for open-minded and unfearing debate, and freedom from pressure by officialdom and prejudices."*

Born May 21, 1921, in the Soviet Union, Soviet physicist and political dissident Andrei Sakharov is known for both his pioneering work in thermonuclear fusion and his advocacy of human rights.

Andrei Sakharov first gained international fame in the 1950s as one of the developers of the Soviet Union's hydrogen bomb. A premier physicist, he was the youngest person ever elected to the Soviet Academy of Sciences, and was decorated three times with the Soviet's highest civilian honor, the Order of the Red Banner of Labor. During the 1960s, however, Sakharov became disenchanted with the nuclear arms movement. "Civilization," he wrote, "is imperiled by universal thermonuclear war." By the early 1970s, a time when most dissenters in the U.S.S.R. were immediately imprisoned or exiled, he began a mounting dissent against Soviet nuclear proliferation and political suppression. Only internationally known figures who expressed these opinions—such as Sakharov, writer Aleksandr Solzhenitsyn, and a few others—were tolerated because of the worldwide disgrace that would follow their censure. In recognition of his efforts to bring about greater political freedoms in the U.S.S.R., Sakharov was awarded the Nobel Peace Prize in 1975.

In 1980, despite the international pressures, Sakharov was seized from his home in Moscow and sent to the Soviet city of Gorki, a fortressed city closed to foreigners. For six years Sakharov was held prisoner there and suffered torture and a number of hunger strikes. He was finally released in 1986 by Soviet leader Mikhail Gorbachev, but not before agreeing to curtail his dissident activities. Today Sakharov remains the chief symbol of Soviet dissent even as the country experiences *glasnost,* a policy of political reform and openness implemented by Gorbachev in the 1980s—due in part to Sakharov's efforts over the past two decades.

Andrei Sakharov was born in 1921 and grew up in Moscow. His father was a physics teacher who wrote textbooks. Sakharov found a love for science, particularly physics, at an early age, and his family nourished his intellectual development. He later said, "I lived in an atmosphere of decency, mutual help and tact, a liking for work and respect for the mastery of one's chosen profession." In 1942, Sakharov graduated with honors from Moscow State University, and went to work as a researcher in the field of hydrogen fusion. Exempted from military duty during World War II, he continued work in atomic physics, receiving a Ph.D. in physics and mathematics in 1947.

During the early 1950s, Sakharov made major contributions to the Soviet development of the hydrogen bomb. He later commented: "When I began working on this terrible weapon, I felt subjectively that I was working for peace, that my work would help foster a balance of power." It was Sakharov, in collaboration with Igor Tamm, who first developed controlled thermonuclear fusion, the basis for the nuclear generation of electricity. In 1953, at the age of 32, Sakharov was named to the Soviet Academy of Sciences, the youngest person ever to be elected. He three times won the Red Banner of Labor medal in addition to many scientific awards.

By the late 1950s, Sakharov began questioning the prudence of developing nuclear weapons. He later said, "I developed a moral consciousness in the 1950s. I suppose the turning point came when I sent a letter of protest [in 1961] to the government against our atomic tests." The comment stunned former Soviet chief Nikita Khrushchev, who was angered by Sakharov's interference. This marked the beginning of the break between Sakharov and the Soviet political establishment.

In 1968, Sakharov published a manuscript entitled *Progress, Peaceful Coexistence, and Intellectual Freedom*. In the book, Sakharov pressed the Soviet government for greater political freedoms, freedom of speech, and demilitarization. The book was received with anger and hostility by Soviet officials, who barred Sakharov from further scientific research. Although the reaction from Sakharov's scientific colleagues was also generally cool, he was allowed to retain his post in the Academy of Sciences and was able to live off the income from the membership.

From the mid-1960s into the 1970s, many Soviet dissidents were put on trial, deported, or sent to Siberia. Sakharov wrote many letters to government officials protesting harsh treatment of dissidents. Sakharov himself seemed immune to such interference because of his scientific standing, but by the early 1970s, his telephone was tapped and he was generally followed wherever he went.

In 1973, Solzhenitsyn nominated Sakharov for the Nobel Peace Prize. In his nominating letter the Soviet author wrote, "And may the Nobel committee be in no doubt because of Sakharov's former, quite considerable achievement in the area of weapons, nor see here something paradoxical; the human spirit's admission of earlier mistakes, its cleansing and breaking free from these mistakes—precisely here is to be found greater justification of man's existence on this earth." In 1975, Sakharov was awarded the Nobel Peace Prize, the first ever awarded to a Russian. Upon hearing the news of the award, Sakharov characteristically remarked, "I hope this will help political prisoners." Because of his position as a dissident, however, the Soviet government would not allow him to travel to Stockholm to receive the award (the Soviets had similarly refused permission in past years for writers Boris Pasternak and Solzhenitsyn to accept their Nobel prizes). Sakharov's wife Yelena Bonner, who had been undergoing surgery abroad at the time, accepted the award for him.

In 1975 Sakharov published *My Country and the World* in which he continued his criticism of nuclear armament. In the book he said, "The unchecked growth of thermonuclear arsenals and the buildup toward confrontation threaten mankind with the death of civilization and physical annihilation." He went on to say, "Thermonuclear warfare has already become a dark reality of modern times, like Auschwitz, the Gulag, and famine." Through the late 1970s, Sakharov pressed for freedom for political prisoners and greater civil rights.

In January of 1980, the Soviet government took definitive antidissident action: on a routine visit to a university seminar, Sakharov was intercepted by Soviet police. He was taken to a state prosecutor's office and sent with his wife to the Soviet city of Gorki, a military-controlled city far east of Moscow. Sakharov's banishment was generally seen as a crippling blow to Soviet political dissent. One Muscovite scholar said, "[The government] has eliminated the main figure in the movement. The message is clear: the Soviet government has decided that it will tolerate no more opposition."

Sakharov spent nearly seven years in exile at Gorki. During that time he was subjected to much abuse from the KGB, the Soviet secret police. Sakharov went on several hunger strikes while in Gorki, to protest his wife's conviction for distributing "anti-communist" materials, and later to protest the Soviets' refusal to allow his wife to travel abroad for eye and heart treatments. He was then force fed by the KGB, a procedure so painful that it left his face "badly bruised." At the same time, the Soviets created a campaign to attempt to show the West that Sakharov was being treated humanely and was in good health.

Early in 1985, Sakharov wrote a letter to Gorbachev promising "to cease completely my public activities (apart, of course, from exceptional cases)." Viewing further conflict as a futile gesture, he was allowed to return from exile to Moscow in 1986. As stipulated, he remained more on the sidelines than he had prior to his exile.

In the late 1980s, nationalist feelings prompted unrest in areas of the Soviet Union near Asia Minor, particularly in the provinces of Armenia and Azerbaijan. Despite the new official policy of *glasnost* the Soviet government arrested numerous nationalist dissidents in Armenia in 1988. Because of these arrests, Sakharov was again compelled to speak out against the Soviet government. In 1989 Sakharov criticized Gorbachev's actions in Armenia and took the opportunity to question the degree of freedom advanced by Gorbachev's overall policies. Sakharov said, "Gorbachev has acted courageously in the international arena. He has made some intelligent moves at home as well, but there are some very serious shortcomings in his domestic policies. In particular, I am referring to political democratization and interethnic relations." Sakharov also said that human rights "are not getting any better in the U.S.S.R. but in fact have taken a step backward."

In the period of *glasnost*, the Soviet Union is now a freer society than it has been in nearly seven decades. That *glasnost* is a reality at all is due in large part to the heroic actions of Sakharov and dissidents like him.

Sources

▶ **Books**

Bonner, Yelena, *Alone Together*, Knopf, 1986.

Le Vert, Suzanne, *The Sakharov File: A Study in Courage*, Messner, 1986.

Sakharov, Andrei, *My Country and the World*, Knopf, 1975.

Sakharov, Andrei, *Progress, Peaceful Coexistence, and Intellectual Freedom*, Norton, 1970.

▶ **Periodicals**

Newsweek, "Thinking the Unthinkable," August 5, 1968, p. 41, "A New Kind of Cold War," October 8, 1973, pp. 56-68, "An Exile in His Own Country," February 4, 1980, pp. 50-55.

Time, "Climax of a Lonely Struggle," October 20, 1975, p. 44, "Pilgrim of Conscience," February 21, 1977, pp. 21-30, "Battening Down the Hatches," June 4, 1984, pp. 32-35.

U.S. News & World Report, "Sakharov's Painful Triumph," March 3, 1986, pp. 34-38, "Sakharov's Bold Challenge," January 30, 1989, pp. 49-50.

Jonas Salk

‘‘I don't feel like a hero, but I know that's how people feel about me.''

Born October 28, 1914, in New York City, American epidemiologist and medical researcher Jonas Salk is noted for having developed the vaccine that induces the building of antibodies against several types of polio.

J onas Salk was born in New York City in 1914, the son of a garment manufacturer. As a child, Salk was an average student, not good at sports, and generally ignored by his school classmates. He worked hard, however, and eventually entered a high school for "accelerated" students, graduating at the age of sixteen. He then went on to the College of the City of New York, earning a Bachelor of Science degree at the age of nineteen. During the summers between school years, he worked as a technician in a laboratory and developed a keen interest in scientific research. After college, he entered medical school at New York University, where his interest in applied research was further kindled. Salk interned at Mt. Sinai Hospital in New York, where he was called "the most stable young man in the place. . . . Nobody ever saw Jonas ruffled." Rejecting a medical practice to pursue a career in research, Salk attended the University of Michigan in Ann Arbor on a research fellowship; in 1947, he was chosen by University of Pittsburgh Medical School to begin work in a new virus laboratory.

It was at Pittsburgh that Salk was to achieve his greatest fame. His initial work was directed toward the influenza virus, but in 1949 he began to work on poliomyelitis, a dreaded viral disease that usually caused paralysis and often resulted in death. The disease was generally referred to simply as "polio," or "infantile paralysis," since it most commonly attacked children. There was no method of predicting whom it would strike or when, except that there was a "polio season" every summer, with August being particularly bad. Salk's first work involved the classification of one hundred different types of the polio virus. He then began working with the data of Dr. John Enders and his associates, who had developed the theoretical basis for a polio vaccine. Working sixteen hours a day, six days a week, Salk studied the various strains of polio and worked to develop a vaccine that would stimulate the human body to produce antibodies to ward off the disease. He finally developed a vaccine that used dead polio cells to induce the production of antibodies. The vaccine was initially tested on monkeys; finally, in 1952, after several revisions of the formula, Salk was confident that he had found a vaccine that would be safe and effective for human beings. He first tested it on people who had already had polio but had fully recovered because these people would have antibodies present to ward off the disease if the vaccine should prove ineffective. Following a successful trial with these subjects, Salk published the results of his experiments in the spring of 1953. That same year, he successfully tested the vaccine on 700 students; and in 1954, with a sponsorship from the March of Dimes, the vaccine was administered to 440,000 children throughout the United States. Salk's mentor at New York University and the University of Michigan, Dr. Thomas Francis, Jr., calculated the results of the mass inoculation in 1954, and announced in Ann Arbor in

1955 that the program had been nearly 90% effective in immunizing patients against polio. Salk became a folk hero in American popular culture, a doctor who had brought the end to a "plague." The medical community and American citizens hailed Dr. Salk's achievement. Over the next six years, it was reported, the Salk vaccine prevented more than 300,000 cases of polio in the United States alone. The vaccine represents on of the premier achievements of applied science in American history.

Despite his success, Salk suspected that all of the publicity surrounding it would probably hurt him professionally. He later said, "The worst tragedy that could have befallen me was my success. I knew right away that I was through, cast out [by my contemporaries]." Salk was criticized for not doing more testing before announcing his discovery, for not publishing more of his results, and for releasing his results to the popular media before publishing them in "scholarly" journals. Although Salk was nominated for the Nobel prize in medicine, he did not win; instead, the prize went to Dr. Enders and his associates, for their work in developing the theoretical basis for the vaccine. Neither did Salk make any money from his discovery; the money went to the suppliers of the vaccine, such as Eli Lilly & Co. When asked who owned the patent for the vaccine Salk said, "The people. . . . Could you patent the sun?"

In the late 1950s, Albert Sabin developed a polio vaccine that could be taken orally on sugar cubes, largely replacing the Salk vaccine, which must be administered via four shots. Because Sabin vaccine carries live polio cells, it runs the risk of causing the disease in patients—although this has occurred very rarely. Recently, the Salk vaccine has made something of comeback in less developed countries where polio is still a devastating disease.

Throughout the 1950s, Salk continued his work in immunology, but by the early 1960s, he had a new idea. He wanted to create a research institute in which scientists could work unhindered by the pressures of academia, and where funding for work was easily obtained. In 1963, that idea became reality with the founding of the Salk Institute for Biological Studies in La Jolla, California, near San Diego. Funded by federal grants, private endowments, corporate sponsorships, and organizations such as the March of Dimes, the Institute has a group of research fellows working on whatever projects they like, free from pressures of the outside world. Just prior to the opening of the Institute, Salk acknowledged the potential pitfalls from having scientists work with complete freedom, "This is an experiment, after all, and certainly one of the great questions to be answered in the experiment is whether or not it is possible to institutionalize freedom." The first research fellows of the Institute read like a "Who's Who" of science; Jacob

Bronowski, Francis Crick, Warren Weaver, and Jacques Monod were just a few of the scientists-in-residence, in addition to Salk himself. While Salk's work at the Institute has mainly concerned cancer research and human immunology, he has also attempted to find a cure for multiple sclerosis, and has written several books on subjects as diverse as the evolution of human problem solving and the effects of world population growth.

Jonas Salk saved thousands of people's lives with his development of the polio vaccine in 1952, and saved millions more from a life of paralysis. "I don't feel like a hero," he later said, "but I know that's how people feel about me." His efforts in applying basic research to the real needs of people, moving from theoretical results to reality, helped Salk achieve lasting fame as the conqueror of one of the earth's most dreaded diseases.

Sources
▶ **Books**

Carter, Richard, *Breakthrough: The Saga of Jonas Salk*, Trident Press, 1965.

Rowland, John, *Polio Man: The Story of Dr. Jonas Salk*, Roy, 1960.

Salk, Jonas, *The Survival of the Wisest*, Harper, 1973.

Salk, Jonas, and Jonathan Salk, *World Population and Human Values: A New Reality*, Harper, 1981.

Salk, Jonas, *Anatomy of Reality: Merging of Intuition and Reason*, Columbia University Press, 1983.

▶ **Periodicals**

Esquire, "The Summer before Salk," December, 1983, pp. 40-45.

Life, "The Great New Dream of Dr. Salk," February 8, 1963, pp. 78-90.

Newsweek, "A Quiet Young Man's Magnificent Victory," April 25, 1955, pp. 64-67, "Polio Pioneers Are Still Busy," May 19, 1980, p. 19.

Psychology Today, "A Conversation with Jonas Salk," March 1983, pp. 50-56.

Time, "Closing In on Polio," March 29, 1954, pp. 56-58.

Jan C. Scruggs

"T*he wounds of the war still require a political healing, a healing on many different levels.*"

Student, soldier, and fund raiser Jan C. Scruggs was born around 1950 in Bowie, Maryland, and currently lives in Columbia, Maryland. A dedicated person who capitalized on his experiences to achieve his goals, Jan was able to spur a nation and a government into action.

J an, who grew up in a small rural community in Maryland, graduated from high school in 1968 and immediately enlisted in the Army to serve in Vietnam. He came home in March of 1970, changed by the memory of fallen friends and his own injuries. Almost ten years later, Jan saw the film *The Deer Hunter,* and its graphic realism made his memories of the war resurface. Similar to many other vets, Jan felt that Vietnam and those who fought there had been forgotten, so he envisioned a memorial that would list the 58,156 names of those who had lost their lives in the war.

It took a while to get the project going; Jan collected less than $150 dollars in the first month. He said that "you got the feeling of what it's like to be a mad scientist who has an idea that you know is right, but the world won't listen." With two other veterans, Bob Doubek and John Wheeler, Jan founded the Vietnam Veteran Memorial Fund. He worked eleven hours a day, six days a week, and his efforts brought about a change in his personality, as his wife Becky described: "He went from being a passive person to a very intense, ambitious man. He always seemed to be anxious." His intensity paid off, however, for Jan ultimately helped raise more than eight million dollars from private donors. Jan believed that because most of the funds came from outside the government, the project had a more personal quality. He noted: "As it turned out, the monument has more of an import being done privately. It was Vietnam veterans taking care of their buddies."

The Wall was dedicated in 1982 and since has become the capital's most popular memorial, drawing up to 25,000 people a day. Added to the wall in 1984 was Frederick Hart's seven-foot bronze statue of three soldiers who gaze knowingly in the direction of the names of those who will never return from the battlefield. Jan spoke fondly of this additon, which satisfied those who wanted a more traditional monument: "If this isn't an example of a perfect Washington compromise, I don't know what it is."

Coupled with the success of the Memorial was that of Jan's book, *To Heal a Nation,* which was made into a movie by NBC in 1988. Jan was facing new frustrations, however. He left the VVMF, the organization he had helped found, and decided to go to law school out of "desperation," still feeling unable to find his place in American society. "It took a lot of the bitterness out of the Vietnam debate," says Scruggs, "but I wouldn't say the memorial healed the nation." Some Americans, Jan thought, considered the problems of the vets solved with the construction of the Memorial. He remarked that "veterans may get solace from the memorial, but they need real programs to help them—programs for job counseling, psychological counseling, aid for homeless vets." He hopes that rather than an ending, the Wall is just a beginning.

While it has not resolved the debate over Vietnam, the Wall has moved the country in the right direction. Navy vet Everett Alvarez, Jr., the first pilot to be shot down over North Vietnam, commented that "the monument makes the final step of dedicated effort to overcome the past." The Wall fulfills what Jan C. Scruggs had envisioned, enabling vets to vent their feelings for their dead comrades, and giving the American people a sacred place at which to mourn. In addition, the Wall remains a constant reminder of a country's turmoil.

Sources

▶ **Books**

Scruggs, Jan and Joel L. Swerdlow, *To Heal a Nation: The Vietnam Veterans Memorial,* Harper, 1985.

▶ **Periodicals**

Esquire, "The Wall," September, 1985, p. 3.

Newsweek, "The Final Touch," November 12, 1984, p. 20.

People, "His Dream Was to Heal a Nation. . .," May 30, 1988, p. 21.

Time, "Healing Vietnam's Wounds," November 26, 1984, p. 22.

Alan Shepard

"Wow it's really wild up here. . . . It's a beautiful day in the land of Fra Mauro."

Born November 18, 1923, in East Derry, New Hampshire, Alan Shepard was the first American astronaut in space.

A lan Shepard was born in East Derry, New Hampshire, a small village a few miles south of Manchester, the son of an army colonel. As a small child, Shepard attended school in a one-room schoolhouse, where he was a good student, particularly in mathematics. He graduated from the Pinkerton Academy in Derry, New Hampshire, and entered the U.S. Naval Academy in Annapolis, Maryland, in 1941.

During World War II, Shepard served as an ensign aboard the destroyer *Cogswell* in the Pacific. Following the war, he began flight training and qualified as a pilot in 1947. As a Naval pilot, Shepard served in Norfolk, Virginia, Jacksonville, Florida, and aboard several aircraft carriers in the Mediterranean. In 1950, he became a test pilot, and over the next eight years he tested a variety of aircraft and worked as a flight instructor. He was also assigned to duty aboard a carrier in the Pacific and eventually earned an appointment to the staff of the Atlantic fleet's commander in chief.

In 1958, Shepard was one of 110 test pilots chosen by NASA as prospective astronauts. NASA planned to judge the applicants based on physical and mental criteria, looking, as NASA administrator T. Keith Glennan stated, for "men of vision . . . with a practical, hard-headed approach to the difficult job ahead." After a battery of physical and psychological tests, seven men were selected as the nation's first astronauts: John Glenn, M. Scott Carpenter, Virgil Grissom, Donald Slayton, Leroy Cooper, Walter Schirra, and Alan Shepard. Following the announcement Shepard said, "My feelings about being in this program are really quite simple. . . . I'm here because it's a chance to serve the country. I'm here, too, because it's a great personal challenge: I know [space travel] can be done, that it's important for it to be done, and I want to do it."

Shepard began intensive training for space flight. Courses in biology, geography, astrophysics, astronomy, and meteorology supplemented his physical training, which included exposure to conditions much more severe than were anticipated during space travel. Shepard also spent long hours performing weightlessness tests, preparing for the weaker gravitational pull outside the earth's atmosphere.

Early in 1961, NASA chose Shepard over Glenn and Grissom, the two other finalists, to be the first American in space. The astronauts themselves had attempted to downplay the importance of the selection of the first astronaut. John Glenn said, "We have tried to do away with a lot of this talk about who is going to be first on this, because we feel very strongly that this is so much bigger than whose name happens to be on the first ticket." Preparations for America's first manned space flight therefore commenced in a spirit of cooperation. Glenn acted as Shepard's back-up, ready if Shepard became unable to fly, and Slayton served as Shepard's radio contact at the Mercury Control Center. The other astronauts also had responsibilities during Shepard's flight.

On May 5, 1961, *Freedom 7* lifted off from Cape Canaveral, Florida. Shepard piloted the Mercury capsule 115 miles above the earth's surface and 302 miles across the Atlantic Ocean. After landing safely in the Atlantic, Shepard was picked up from the water by helicopter pilot; his first words were, "Man, what a ride!" Although the trip lasted for only about fifteen minutes, Shepard's journey was almost technically perfect, and it paved the way for many more flights by U.S. astronauts. Shepard returned to ticker-tape parades, and he received a medal from President John F. Kennedy.

After his historic flight Shepard looked forward to future missions. In 1963, however, he was diagnosed as having Meniere's syndrome, a disease of the inner ear that produces nausea, vertigo, and hearing impairment. NASA removed Shepard from active flight duty and re-assigned him to NASA's Houston, Texas, facility, where he became chief of the Astronaut Office. Although he became quite wealthy as a result of real estate and banking investments during the next few years he yearned for space flight. In 1968, he underwent a successful operation in which a small drain tube was implanted in his inner ear. Shepard applied for readmission to active duty, and in 1969 his patience and determination were rewarded when NASA chose him to command the Apollo 14 flight to the moon. "I think if a person wants something badly enough," Shepard once said, "he's just got to hang in there and keep at it."

Apollo 14 became an important mission for the U.S. space program. Apollo 13 had been a disappointment; technical difficulties had prevented it from landing on the moon as planned, and the space program was losing public support. The Apollo 14 astronauts were scheduled to test new equipment on the moon's surface and to spend longer periods outside the space capsule. Shepard and Edwin Mitchell were assigned to land on the moon while Stuart Roosa orbited the moon in the command module, the *Kitty Hawk*.

On January 31, 1971, Apollo 14 blasted off from Cape Kennedy, nearly ten years after Shepard's first space flight. Five days later Shepard and Mitchell landed on the moon's surface, the third group of astronauts to do so. From their lunar module, the two astronauts stepped out into the Fra Mauro Highlands, as the world watched on television. Shepard said, "Wow, it's really wild up here. . . . It certainly is a stark place." The astronauts had brought a lunar cart with them, and during two trips outside the lunar module, each lasting more than four and a half hours, they conducted experiments and gathered rock specimens. On one excursion Shepard hit a golf ball across the moon's surface. In addition, the astronauts left behind a multi-million dollar mini-scientific station that would continue to send messages to scientists on earth. Thirty-three and a half hours after they landed, the two astronauts completed a successful docking with *Kitty Hawk*. The 240,000–mile journey back to earth ended with a splash-down near Samoa in the South Pacific on February 9. By all accounts, the voyage was a big success.

Shepard retired from NASA in 1974. Always a successful entrepreneur, he developed a wholesale beer distributorship and a real estate firm in the Houston area. He has been married for over forty years and has two daughters. Although no longer active in the space program, Alan Shepard will be remembered both as the first American in space and as one of a handful of men to walk on the moon.

Sources

▶ **Books**

Caiden, Martin, *The Astronauts: The Story of Project Mercury*, Dutton, 1961.

Carpenter, M.C., and others, *We Seven, By the Astronauts Themselves*, Simon & Schuster, 1962.

MacMillan, Norman, *Great Flights and Air Adventures*, St. Martin's, 1965, pp. 202-203.

Silverberg, Robert, *First American Into Space*, Monarch Books, 1961.

▶ **Periodicals**

Life, "Shepard and U.S.A. Feel 'AOK,'" May 12, 1961, pp. 18-27.

Time, February 1, 1971, p. 46, October 3, 1980, pp. 40, 58.

U.S. News and World Report, "After Letdowns, a Lift: First American in Space," May 15, 1961, pp. 53-59, "First Americans in Space—Most Are Doing Well, Thank You," May 10, 1976, p. 49, "Probing the Lunar 'Badlands,'" February 15, 1971, pp. 29-31.

Karen Silkwood

" "A s I remember Karen, she was the kind of person who, if something was wrong, was not going to stand by and ignore it. She was not afraid to stick her neck out."

Born February 19, 1946, in Longview, Texas, Karen Silkwood, a nuclear plant laborer who died while investigating safety violations made by her employer, is viewed as a martyr by anti-nuclear activists.

On the night of November 13, 1974, Karen Silkwood, a technician at the Kerr-McGee Cimarron River nuclear facility in Crescent, Oklahoma, was driving her white Honda to Oklahoma City. There she was to deliver a manila folder full of alleged health and safety violations at the plant to a friend, Drew Stephens, a *New York Times* reporter and national union representative. Seven miles out of Crescent, however, her car went off the road, skidded for a hundred yards, hit a guardrail, and plunged off the embankment. Silkwood was killed in the crash, and the manila folder was not found at the scene when Stephens arrived a few hours later. Nor has it come to light since. Although Kerr-McGee was a prominent Oklahoma employer whose integrity had never been challenged, as a part of the nuclear power industry it had many adversaries. The controversy ignited by Silkwood's death regarding the regulation of the nuclear industry was intense, with critics finally finding an example around which to focus their argument. The legacy of the Silkwood case continues to this day in the on-going debate over the safety of nuclear technology.

Silkwood seemed an unlikely candidate to have had such a dramatic impact on American society. One biographer commented that "most of her life was distinguished by how ordinary it was, as ordinary as her death was extraordinary." Silkwood grew up in Nederland, in the heart of the Texas oil and gas fields. The oldest of three daughters of Bill and Merle Silkwood, Silkwood led a normal life. In high school she played on the volleyball team and flute in the band, and was an "A" student and a member of the National Honor Society. She excelled in chemistry and, upon graduation, went to Lamar College in Beaumont to become a medical technician.

After her first year of college, Silkwood eloped with Bill Meadows. They moved around Texas, where Meadows worked in the oil industry and Silkwood took care of their three children. After years of financial struggle (they finally declared bankruptcy), Silkwood left him in 1972 when she discovered Meadows was having an affair with her friend. Giving Bill custody of the children, she moved to Oklahoma City. There she found a job at Kerr-McGee's Cimarron River plant in Crescent, thirty miles north of Oklahoma City, soon joined the Oil, Chemical and Atomic Workers Union, and walked the picket line during their largely unsuccessful nine week strike in 1972.

The Cimarron facility manufactured fuel rods that were used in nuclear fission reactors. Contained within these fuel rods were particles of plutonium, an element created from uranium atoms, and the most toxic substance then known. Even pollen-sized grains of plutonium can cause cancer, as had been shown in animal experiments, but the workers at the plant were not alerted to any danger. Nonetheless,

Silkwood became increasingly concerned about health and safety violations that went uncorrected by management, and as 1974 drew on, got
involved with the bargaining committee for the union. The Cimarron
plant was experiencing sixty percent employee turnover a year, was
using second-hand equipment, and was behind on production. Desperate to avoid another strike, which was looming, Kerr-McGee
organized a union de-certification vote which, though ultimately
failing, galvanized the union into bringing the safety violations to the
attention of federal officials. Silkwood and two other local union officials went to Washington, D.C., to confer with national union leaders
and the Atomic Energy Commission. Chief among their allegations
were the lack of training given employees, failure to minimize contami-
nations, and poor monitoring, including the finding of uranium dust in
the lunchroom. At this meeting Silkwood secretly agreed to obtain
before and after photomicrographs of faulty fuel rods showing where
they were being ground down to disguise faults.

After this meeting Silkwood began carrying around notebooks to
document a variety of safety violations at the plant. Her assertion was
that people were being contaminated by plutonium all the time, and
indeed there were at least seventeen acknowledged incidents of exposure involving seventy-seven employees in the recent past. Silkwood's
concern was obsessive. As her friend Stephens remarked: "She just
lived it, couldn't let it go and relax, particularly in the last month she
was alive." On November 4 and 5, 1974, for two consecutive days,
Silkwood was contaminated by radioactivity, detected by plant elec-
tronic monitors when leaving work. By November 7, her urine showed
very high levels of radioactivity. When tested, her apartment also
showed high levels, especially in the refrigerator. At this time Silkwood
was convinced she was going to die of plutonium poisoning. She and
her roommate and Stephens were sent to Los Alamos, New Mexico, to
be more thoroughly tested. The exposure level was deemed not serious.

On November 13, Silkwood attended a local union meeting then got
into her car to drive to Oklahoma City to deliver the manila folder of
evidence, the results of her seven week vigil, to *New York Times* reporter
David Burnham. Ten minutes later her car went off the road and
Silkwood died. The state patrol ruled it an accident, saying "it's pretty
clear she fell asleep at the wheel. She never woke up." While blood tests
showed a small amount of alcohol and methaqualone (a prescription
sedative) in her system, it is doubtful the amount was sufficient to
induce sleep in ten minutes. A subsequent investigation by a private
detective concluded that she had likely been forced off the road by
another car; a dent in the rear bumper showed metal and rubber
fragments, as if another car had rammed her from behind. The manila

folder was not recovered from the site of the crash, though other personal effects were. A subsequent Justice Department investigation also ruled it an accident. Congressional hearings, along with a lawsuit on behalf of Silkwood's children, however, have revealed an intriguing and bizarre story to discredit critics, involving the FBI, newspaper reporters, and the nuclear industry, a story largely left untold. It is possible Silkwood's phone had been tapped and that she had been under surveillance for awhile. Union official Jack Tice has said the Silkwood had been alarmed prior to her death: "She was starting to think someone was out to get her."

The truth of what happened the night of November 13, 1974, may never be known. What is clear is that the death of Silkwood has become a rallying point for anti-nuclear activists and put the nuclear industry on the defensive. The Atomic Energy Commission confirmed three violations at the Cimarron plant, which eventually shut down. And a major questioning of the nuclear industry has occurred as a result of the revelations which have come to light. In a suit filed by Bill Silkwood on behalf of his grandchildren, a jury in May, 1979, awarded the Silkwood estate over ten million dollars in punitive damages and cleared Silkwood of the allegation that she had stolen plutonium from the plant. It also found that Kerr-McGee had been negligent and that someone had planted plutonium in her apartment. Though an appeals court overturned the decision, the Supreme Court eventually agreed with the lower court, reinstating the victory for the Silkwood Family and saying that punitive damages could be awarded in cases involving the nuclear industry, effectively allowing state and jury regulation. Though many mysteries remain surrounding the death of Silkwood, the public has gained much awareness about nuclear issues and has pressured the industry to become more responsible to health and safety concerns. As former Congresswoman Bella Abzug has commented, the issues stemming from the Silkwood case are "a matter of concern both in regard to public safety and the rights of individuals."

Sources

▶ **Books**

Kohn, Howard, *Who Killed Karen Silkwood?*, Summit Books, 1981.

Rashke, Richard, *The Killing of Karen Silkwood*, Houghton, 1981.

▶ **Periodicals**

Ms., "The Case of Karen Silkwood," April, 1975, pp. 59-76.

Newsweek, "The Silkwood Case," September 9, 1978, p. 26.

Science News, "Silkwood—the Legal Fallout," February 4, 1984, pp. 74-79.

Mitch Snyder

"I *had learned that ... you could make things change if you were willing to stick by what you believed in."*

Born August 14, 1943, in Brooklyn, New York, Mitch Snyder is an activist and spokesperson for the American homeless.
Home and office: 425 Second St. NW, Washington, D.C. 20001.

T he son of Jewish parents, Snyder was nine years old when his father, then the vice-president of an engineering firm, abandoned his wife and young son and daughter. Their situation changed suddenly from one of comfort and security to a life of living hand-to-mouth, never sure where the next meal would come from. The young Snyder soon began to get into trouble; for breaking into parking meters, he was placed in a juvenile detention center. At age fifteen he quit school and worked at various jobs and eventually attented night school. There he met Ellen Kleiman, whom he later married.

By 1969, when Snyder was twenty-five, he had a wife, two sons and a well-paid positon at a management-consultant agency. Nevertheless, he was terribly unhappy. He recalled in an *Esquire* article by Gwenda Blair that he woke up one morning "in a cold sweat. In about a second the rest of my life passed before my eyes, and I didn't like what I saw. It didn't make any sense." So Snyder took to the road, "looking for myself," and Ellen and the boys went back to her parents' home. Mitch traveled for a year until he was arrested in California and charged with car theft. Snyder, however, claimed he was an innocent passenger in a vehicle which he did not know was stolen. While serving a three–year jail sentence, he met a group of political prisoners—among them, priests Philip and Daniel Berrigan, who had been convicted of destroying draftboard records—who exposed him to radical Christianity, nonviolent protest, and anarchist political theory. "It was a very intense process," Snyder told Blair. "It helped to focus everything and clarify where I was going, which was toward resistance to values that don't mean anything." Snyder then rejected all governments, educational institutions, and salaried employment.

In prison Snyder began the first of his many fasts, consuming only water in protest to the Vietnam War, U.S. prison conditions, and other issues. The fast lasted thirty-three days and when it ended successfully, Snyder realized that he could change things by his actions. Upon his release, he realized it would be impossible to resume normal life with his family. "Who I am does not allow me to do things other people do," Snyder remarked to Blair. "I think anyone who works for money is stark raving mad, because prostitution is bad, and it doesn't matter whether you're standing on Fourteenth Street or in a boardroom for AT&T."

In 1973, Snyder joined a local group of social activists called the Community for Creative Non-Violence (CCNV) and proceeded to live with and work for homeless people. Until Snyder's actions brought about government funding in February of 1986, CCNV's shelter for the homeless depended on private donations, which also funded free food and clothing centers, a soup kitchen, and a health clinic. Snyder and other activists in the group have also tried to dramatize the plight of the homeless, employing such tactics as letting cockroaches loose in the White House, living in cardboard boxes on the mayor's front steps, staging a march in which they carried the body of a street dweller who froze to death, and creating a monument to the homeless: a sculpture of a family sleeping on a steam grate.

Snyder's main tool, however, for drawing attention to his cause has been his self–imposed starvations. He estimates that he has spent more than two years of his life not eating, mostly as a means to get the government to meet his demands or revise its policies. His fasts, he explained to Blair are simply "part of the job, which is to make the world a better place to live. It's an expensive job. There's a high price attached to it." Several times it has brought him close to death, yet he insists it is worth it. The federal government is "going to move the moment there's enough pressure put on them to move," he told Blair. "Now the only question is whether I live or die before that happens."

These extreme measures for the sake of the homeless have nominated Snyder in the eyes of some people as a candidate for "sainthood," while others see him as more of a stunt man, using dangerous methods to gain publicity. Some of his critics have accused him of "moral terrorism," by placing his opponents in the position of being murderers if they do not comply with his extreme demands.

However controversial his actions may be, he has been successful in bringing the plight of the homeless into the consciousness of the American public and the U.S. government.

Sources

▶ **Books**

Hombs, Mary Ellen, and Mitch Snyder, *Homelessness in America: A Forced March to Nowhere,* Community for Creative Non-Violence, 1983.

▶ **Periodicals**

Esquire, "Saint Mitch," December, 1986, pp. 222-231.

▶ **Other**

"Samaritan: The Mitch Snyder Story," a made-for-television movie, was aired by CBS in May, 1985.

Aleksandr Solzhenitsyn

"I do not block anyone from the path of truth; for its course I am ready to accept death."

Born December 11, 1918, in Kislovodsk, U.S.S.R., Aleksandr Solzhenitsyn is an author and Soviet dissident.

In February, 1945, while serving on the German front in the Russian Army, Aleksandr Solzhenitsyn was arrested for writing letters to a friend criticizing Soviet leader Josef Stalin. He spent the next eight years in various detention camps for political prisoners, known as the GULAG; it was a period in which, among other hardships, he nearly died from cancer. Solzhenitsyn's sojurn in Soviet prisons, writing about camp conditions and Russian history, and graphically illustrating the repression of free speech and other rights that then existed in Soviet society, has served as an inspiration to other Soviet dissidents and has brought awareness to the West of these conditions. His writings, and the honors bestowed on him by Western countries, have pressured the Soviet government to lighten some of the repressive constraints on their citizens' rights to express themselves. Solzhenitsyn's outspokenness on East-West relations in the 1970s triggered a debate over the wisdom of detente. His writing, though stark in its style and uncompromising in its position, has always stood boldly and passionately in support of the freedom of Soviet people.

While in prison Solzhenitsyn was to write in *The First Circle:* "one's ability to perform a heroic deed, a deed beyond the strength of an ordinary individual, partly arises from one's will and partly seems to be inborn." Both of these, an iron will and an inborn strength, are certainly hallmarks of Solzhenitsyn's life.

Solzhenitsyn was born on December 11, 1918, in Kislovodsk, in the Soviet Union. While his motherTaisiya was still pregnant with him, his father was killed in a hunting accident. Known only through photographs and stories, his father was nonetheless a permanent symbol in Solzhenitsyn's thoughts, manifested especially in his passion and the pursuit of excellence. Solzhenitsyn lived in dire poverty for much of his childhood, waiting in food lines in the early 1930s, and living in a reconstructed stable in the town of Rostov-on-Don, where conditions did not provide adequate protection from the cold climate.

Solzhenitsyn graduated in 1936 from intermediate school in Rostov, where he studied Russian and Science. Already aspiring to be a writer, he unsuccessfully submitted work to various magazines. At the University in Rostov he did very well in physics and math, and then completed a two-year course in literature in Moscow in 1940. That same year, he married Natalya Reshetovskaya, his childhood sweetheart. In 1941, Solzhenitsyn was drafted into the Soviet Army; and it would be nearly fifteen years before he would see Natalya again. Serving first as a transport wagon driver, he was later transferred to an artillery division. Although from an early age, Solzhenitsyn had questioned the personality cult surrounding Soviet leader Josef Stalin, there was nothing to indicate he was a controversial officer; nonetheless, in February, 1945,

Solzhenitsyn was arrested by Soviet counter-espionage agents. "I was arrested for naivete," Solzhenitsyn later recalled. His anti-Stalinist thinking, expressed in letters to a friend, formed the basis of the case against him, and he was sentenced to eight years in a "Correction Camp." For four years Solzhenitsyn worked as a mathematician at the "Mavrino" prison in Moscow, "in good circumstances." He was then sent to "the lowest circle", a labor camp for political prisoners in Kazakhstan in Soviet Central Asia, "an island in the Gulag Archipelago." Working as a bricklayer and construction worker, Solzhenitsyn chronicled the conditions of the camp in the events of one day in January, 1951, in *One Day in the Life of Ivan Denisovitch*.

On March 5, 1953 Solzhenitsyn awoke to the news that Stalin had died, describing that moment as a "release to freedom." Settling in the village of Kok-terek in Kazakhstan, Solzhenitsyn taught school, but became increasingly ill with cancer. Near death, he was finally granted permission to travel to Tashkent for treatment. Against his own prediction he survived. He described that spring of 1955 as "the most agonizing and most beautiful of my life." During this period Solzhenitsyn was once again seized by the desire "to create," and began to write again.

In 1956, Nikita Khruschev gave his famous speech denouncing Stalin's atrocities, and Solzhenitsyn's exile to Kok-terek was annulled and his earlier sentence reversed. Settling at Riazon in European Russia, Solzhenitsyn was reunited with his wife Natalya. No one but she knew of his literary work, though, until 1961. Late in that year he sent the manuscript of *One Day in the Life of Ivan Denisovitch* to the editor of the magazine *Novy Mir*. After a year of political maneuvering the story was finally published. This publication caused a further polarization in Communist Party circles between the liberal anti-Stalinists and the conformists—a struggle that a year later would topple Khruschev. After *One Day* became public, the KGB began collecting evidence against Solzhenitsyn, and a slander campaign was begun that would last the next six years, culminating in 1969 when Solzhenitsyn was expelled from the Union of Soviet Writers. Self-disciplined and perfectionistic in his art, he sometimes wrote for twelve hours a day during this period. He has written that "conscience, truth and steadfastness" are what guides his work and his life. Believing that "conscience is given to us only once," Solzhenitsyn wrote often of the awakening of conscience in his characters, as with Volodin in *The First Circle*. The KGB leaked copies of this manuscript and that of *The Cancer Ward* to the West where they were published, and used as a tool in campaigns against him. Despite, or perhaps because of, the persecution Solzhenitsyn faced at home, he was awarded the Nobel Prize for Literature in 1970.

The battle between Solzhenitsyn and the KGB continued for the next three years. In 1973, he hurriedly published *The Gulag Archipelago*—a stinging portrayal of life in a series of political prison camps in the Soviet Union—in the West after the KGB had discovered a copy. In response, the Soviet press branded Solzhenitsyn a traitor in January, 1974. Expecting arrest, Solzhenitsyn got all of his literary files in order; barely a month later, he was detained and summarily deported to West Germany without his wife and children. Solzhenitsyn settled in Zurich for a year, and then began to travel widely, including a trip to the United States. He became a vocal critic of the policy of detente, saying that the West did not understand the Soviet Union and were being duped into giving up too much. In 1976, he settled in Vermont, and continued to criticize friendlier Soviet-American relations, lamenting the "collapse of courage" of the West. His vocal conservative ideology polarized people, and may have caused splits among those critical of the Soviet Union.

Solzhenitsyn's writings revealed to the West the horrors of the Soviet political prison system. His dedication to literature and to revealing the truth as he sees it are reflected in his statement: "I do not block anyone from the path of truth; for its course I am ready to accept death." In a letter to the Fourth Writer's Congress of the Soviet Union, shortly before he was expelled from that body, Solzhenitsyn wrote "my literary task I will fulfill under all conditions, and from the grave even more successfully and indisputably than when alive."

Sources
► **Books**

Bjorkegren, Hans, *Aleksandr Solzhenitsyn: A Biography*, Third Press (New York), 1972.

Burg, David, and George Feifer, *Solzhenitsyn: A Biography*, Stein & Day, 1972.

Rzhevshy, Leonid D., *Solzhenitsyn: Creator and Heroic Deed*, University of Alabama Press, 1978.

Scammell, Michael, *Solzhenitsyn: A Biography*, Norton, 1984.

Solzhenitsyn, Aleksandr, *A Pictorial Autobiography*, Farrar, Straus, 1974.

► **Periodicals**

Newsweek, "The Limits of 'Glasnost,'" December 12, 1988, p.6.

Steven Spielberg

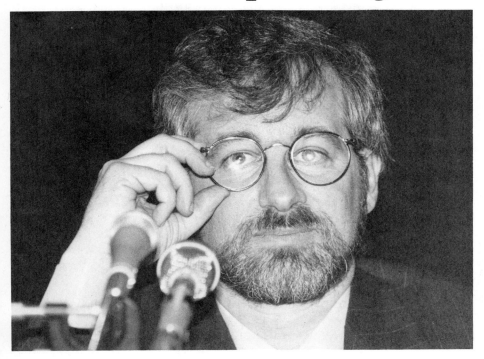

"I feel fortunate that I've lucked into an art form that allows me to make life as perfect as I can within the time parameters and the amount of money I'm given to spend on a picture."

Born December 18, 1947, in Cincinnati, Ohio, Steven Spielberg is one of the most successful motion picture producers and directors of all time.

As many film journalists are fond of pointing out, Steven Spielberg's surname translates from the German into "play mountain," an apt image for a writer/director and producer of some of the most popular (and highest-grossing) movies in cinema history. A Spielberg production has come to gain the reputation as a visually compelling, multilayered mythic tale, as epitomized by the director's most famous offering, "E.T. the Extra-Terrestrial."

The eldest of four children, Spielberg enjoyed an extraordinary childhood. In interviews, he describes growing up in a world of humor and fantasy. A relentless practical joker whose favorite victims were his three sisters, the young boy discovered an eight-millimeter camera in the family garage and promptly began his career. From the beginning, the youngster had a knack for getting actors and crew to respond: At Steven's request, a *Time* profile relates, his mother, Leah, "boiled cherries jubilee in a pressure cooker until it exploded, and Steven filmed the messy crimson walls and floor." Spielberg has credited his accommodating family partly for his success. In a magazine article, Spielberg admits: "From age twelve or thirteen I knew I wanted to be a movie director."

By the time Spielberg was out of high school, he was already winning student awards for his short films. One of them, "Firelight," even had a real premiere at a local movie theatre. But college held little appeal for the young man, who preferred to spend his days on a particular movie lot. "I remember taking a bus tour through Universal Studios," Spielberg tells an interviewer. "I remember getting off the bus; we were all let off to go to the bathroom. Instead, I hid between two soundstages until the bus left, and then I wandered around for three hours. I went back there every day for three months. I walked past the guard every day, waved at him, and he waved back. I always wore a suit and carried a briefcase, and he assumed I was some kid related to some mogul, and that was that."

Persistence finally paid off. At twenty, after an executive viewed some of Spielberg's films, the young director was signed to a seven-year contract for Universal television. Journeyman work in several weekly series led to Spielberg's first television movie, "Duel." The story of a motorist pursued by an unseen driver in a menacing truck, the film gained much critical attention. In fact, according to Hirschberg, "Duel" was released as a feature in Europe and Japan and became a worldwide hit.

Spielberg's next big success was "Jaws," a film released in the summer of 1975. Based upon a best-selling novel, cast with mostly unknown actors, and filmed with a daunting (for 1975) $8 million budget, "Jaws" exploded into American theatres and instantly became the most talked-about movie of its time—making its 26-year-old director a star in his own right. "Jaws" concerns a homicidal great white shark who terrorizes an American beachfront community; it quickly became the highest-grossing movie to its date. As *Time* points out, "If the great white shark that terrorizes the beaches of an island summer colony is one of nature's most efficient killing machines, *Jaws* is an efficient entertainment machine."

Many wondered how the young filmmaker could top the commercial appeal of "Jaws." Spielberg answered the challenge in 1977 with another blockbuster, "Close Encounters of the Third Kind." The title was an unfamiliar phrase to American ears, but soon everyone knew that a close encounter of the third kind meant physical contact with alien life forms. Mainstream films had long portrayed aliens as menacing monsters from beyond; to Spielberg, the thought of inter-planetary co-existence held a much more benevolent promise. Spielberg's inspiration resulted in the story of how a series of UFO sightings in Indiana leads to revelation and awe. The sweeping satellites draw in a number of people—a group of scientists, a family man, and five-year-old boy with his mother. The ultimate landing of the brightly colored "Mother Ship" at Devil's Tower in Wyoming bestows a message of hope and goodwill that helped vault "Close Encounters of the Third Kind" to the top-ten moneymakers and brought further acclaim for the director.

Spielberg's interest in aliens also inspired his biggest film yet, and the number-one box office draw of all time, "E.T. the Extraterrestrial." The germ of the story came to Spielberg in 1980 when he was in the Tunisian desert making "Raiders of the Lost Ark," a homage to old-time adventure serials he made in collaboration with "Star Wars" director George Lucas. "I was kind of lonely at the time," Spielberg explained. "My girlfriend was back in Los Angeles. I remember saying to myself, 'What I really need is a friend I can talk to—somebody who can give me *all* the answers.'" That friend turned out to be a nameless visitor from the heavens who is left stranded on Earth when his spaceship leaves without him. Finding his way into a typical suburban American neighborhood, the little alien—"a squat-looking creature with an expandable neck that sort of looks like an eggplant on a stick," according to one critic—meets a lonely boy, Elliott. Once the two overcome their mutual apprehension, they become great allies.

Since the success of "E.T.," Spielberg has made such hit films as "The Color Purple," "Empire of the Sun," and, with George Lucas, the Indiana Jones series of adventure films. He also directed the immensely successful "Back to the Future" and "Who Framed Roger Rabbit?"

Spielberg's company Amblin Entertainment has produced "Young Sherlock Holmes," "Gremlins," and a number of other films.

The continuing popularity of Spielberg reflects the tastes of his target audience—young children and their young parents—in the opinion of one critic. "Spielberg's first hits," writes the critic, "struck the baby boomers at a precise, very difficult stage in their development. Though cresting into adulthood, the baby boomers of the late '70s—a middle-to-late-20s age group—still wanted to prolong the golden adolescence they had experienced in the prosperous '60s." But the filmmaker's works "also function on a deeper level," the critic continues. "In film after film the same pattern is repeated: A weak, unstable family, burdened with an absent or irresponsible father, is strengthened and saved through the intervention of a supernatural force—a force that can be either sweet and benign ('E.T.,' 'Close Encounters') or evil and destructive ('Jaws,' 'Poltergeist'). There is in these films a yearning for authority, a powerful need to feel protected and watched over (or, the dark films, a demand for discipline and strength) that has an obvious nostalgic appeal for young adults freshly booted out of the family nest." To his associates, Spielberg represents the new Hollywood, "a regular guy whose detractors, if any, all seem to have been abducted by aliens," as one critic puts it. A man who believes in loyalty and friendship, Spielberg is often described as a family type even at work. "Sure he drives a Porsche," states one observer, "but he'll still pull into a 7-11 and buy a Slurpie. How much more regular can you get?"

Sources

▶ Books

Mutt, Donald R., *Steven Spielberg*, [Boston], 1986.

Sinyard, Neil, *The Films of Steven Spielberg*, Bison Books, 1986.

▶ Periodicals

Action, "Tell the Shark We'll Do It One More Time," July/August, 1974, pp. 4-12.

American Cinematographer, "Spielberg Speaks about Close Encounters," January, 1978, "The Mind behind Close Encounters of the Third Kind," February, 1978.

American Film, "Close Encounters with Steven Spielberg," November, 1977, pp. 24-29.

Film Comment, "Interview with Steven Spielberg," January/February, 1978, pp. 49-55.

Focus on Film, "Steven Spielberg," winter, 1972.

Jounal of Popular Film and Television, "Steven Spielberg: Gore, Guts, and PG-13," spring, 1986.

Newsweek, "Close Encounter With Spielberg," November 21, 1977, pp. 98-99.

Millimeter, "From Television to Features," March, 1975.

Rolling Stone, "Steven Spielberg," October 24, 1985, pp. 22-24.

Time, "I Dream For a Living," July 15, 1985, pp. 54-58.

Benjamin Spock

"We know enough now to begin making our world over, if we only had the vision. All studies in child development from the first half century point in the same direction. A child is born with a greater capacity to love than to hate, to build than to destroy, to profit from every chance to learn and mature. The greater part is done through the love and care of the parents."

Physician, author, and peace activist Benjamin Spock was born May 2, 1903, in New Haven, Connecticut.

B enjamin Spock was the eldest of six children. His father was an attorney, and the family lived in upper-middle class surroundings. Although his parents were loving, Spock later said his mother was a "fiercely opinionated, moralistic, rather tyrannical person." As a child, Spock was shy and a bit withdrawn. His conservative upbringing did not lend itself to a self-indulgent lifestyle, and he attended all the "right" schools and was a young gentleman. After graduating from Andover prep school, he attended Yale University, where he became an expert on the rowing team. He was on the gold medal-winning rowing team at the 1924 Summer Olympics in Paris. After receiving a Bachelor of Arts degree, Spock entered Yale Medical School, but later transferred to the Columbia University College of Physicians and Surgeons, where he received his M.D. in 1929.

Spock's chosen area of specialization was pediatric medicine, a field he had become interested in while observing physicians treating children with polio. He served several residencies at hospitals in New York City, and then set up private practice in pediatric medicine in New York. During the 1930s and early '40s, he also taught medicine at Cornell University Medical School.

The business of raising children in America during the early years of the 20th century was a strict exercise in discipline and manners. Parents were advised to avoid spoiling children at all costs, and corporal punishment to erase bad habits was encouraged. Children were to be self-disciplined and independent at as early an age as possible, and were really never allowed to be "children" at all. The eminent behavioral psychologist John B. Watson advised parents to "Never, never kiss your child." Another child-raising manual told parents to shake hands with their children in the morning. The result of all this was that in "sophisticated" families it was not much fun to be a child.

In 1943, the editor of Pocket Books, Donald Geddes, approached Spock about authoring a book on caring for babies. Although Spock at first turned him down, Geddes persisted, and Spock finally agreed to make an attempt. Geddes had said that the book did not have to be very good because at 25 cents a copy it would sell easily. Spock later said, "That hit the spot. The fact that he didn't say, 'We want the best damned book in the world'—I figured, Why not take a try?" From 1944 to 1946, Spock worked as a psychiatrist for the U.S. Navy Reserve, and during this time wrote his book. First published in 1946 under the name *The Commonsense Book of Baby and Child Care* (now entitled *Baby and Child Care*), the book was roundly praised by critics as a much-needed change of direction for child-rearing. The book was written in an informal, easy-going style which had the effect of calming nervous parents. Spock later said, "I wanted to be supportive of parents rather than to scold them. Instead of just telling a parent what to do, I usually tried to explain what children are like at different stages of development, what their drives are, so that the parent would know what to expect and could act on his own knowledge."

Dr. Spock's book quickly became a best-seller, as Geddes had predicted. For Spock, the timing could not have been better. World War II had just ended, and hundreds of thousands of children would soon be born. The "baby boom" was about to hit the United States, and most of the new parents were armed with Dr. Spock's new book. Spock's book, with its relaxed style and home-spun advice, offered the perfect opportunity to change the way Americans raised their children.

In 1947 Spock moved to the University of Minnesota at Minneapolis to continue teaching and lecturing in psychiatric medicine and to consult at the Mayo Clinic. In 1951 he moved to the University of Pittsburgh, and in 1955 he became professor of child development at Western Reserve University in Cleveland.

Through his research, Spock came to understand the importance of school in a child's development. Although parents are of primary importance, schools and teachers played an important secondary role. In 1959 Spock said, "We know that when schools are good, when they meet a child's emotional and social as well as intellectual needs, they can do wonders. It's sad, and hard to explain, why America, which loves its children and counts on them for the future, spends a smaller proportion of its income on public education than other poorer, 'backward' nations."

In 1962, Spock became convinced that the only way to solve significant world problems was through peaceful coexistence. This period marked the height of the "Cold War," and was the era of incidents such as Francis Gary Powers' U-2 disaster and the "Cuban Missile Crisis." Spock's position was not yet shared by many people, although there was even then a fledgling peace movement. In 1967, Spock retired from Western Reserve University to devote all of his time to peace activism.

In 1967, the United States was in the throes of the Vietnam War. Spock and other supporters of the peace movement escalated their efforts to bring the war to an end. They distributed anti-war materials and urged young Americans to burn their draft cards. In 1968, Spock and several other "co-conspirators" were arrested and charged with conspiring to counsel draft resistance, a federal crime. Lawyers for the prosecution were able to successfully bar all women from the jury by arguing that they would be biased by Dr. Spock's baby book. During the trial Spock said, "What is the use of physicians like myself trying to help parents to bring up children healthy and happy, to have them killed in such numbers for a cause that is ignoble?" The times were such that Spock was convicted, but his conviction was overturned in 1969. A New York *Post* commentator said at the time that the appeals court's ruling overturning Spock's conviction probably caused a sigh of relief at the U.S. Justice Department. "The thought of sending the grandfatherly Dr. Spock to prison for two years would have stirred up a major national reaction that at the very least would have been embarrassing and at the worst explosive."

Spock's dissatisfaction with American political leaders led him to seek the presidency in 1972. Although he was clearly not a serious threat to win, he was able to raise the issues he thought were important to American voters. Running for the People's Party, he finished fourth in the election with over 78,000 votes.

Spock continued to voice political opinions through the 1970s and '80s, particularly his concerns over the nuclear arms buildup. His baby book continued to flourish, and he released a fourth edition in 1976 and a fifth edition in 1985. In his later editions, Spock attempted to rectify superficial problems with the earlier books; the basic psychological problems he had championed in the 1940s remained essentially unaltered. He said in 1976, "I don't mean to sound smug, but I haven't had to swallow any words so far. The book is sensible and sensitive, and it's not very easy to criticize." He attempted to erase the sexism in the earlier editions, replacing the automatic "he" pronoun with alternating "he" and "she," acknowledging the husband's role in child-raising, and including new chapters on breast-feeding, diet, adoption, marijuana use, child abuse, and violence on television. By the time his fifth edition was published in 1985, previous editions had already sold more than 30 million copies. Commenting on the success of the book, Spock said, "The main effect of the book is to give parents confidence, and I think I succeeded better than I ever thought I could."

In the mid- and late 1980s, Spock has remained in vigorous health, and has continued to lecture, particularly on political topics. A strong supporter of liberalism, Spock is still in high demand as a speaker. Although his interests in political topics has increased through the years, he remains committed to the philosophy that prompted him to write his child development book in the first place—that people possess unique capacities for self-improvement and should always strive to be the best they can be. Dr. Spock's book has touched the lives of millions of people in the United States and around the world. In many ways, Spock was in the enviable position of influencing American values and beliefs and attitudes in ways which no politician or other leader ever could. By influencing the *development* of children, Spock reached them before their attitudes were set, and left a lasting impression. His legacy will likely live on through many more generations of parents and their children.

Sources

▶ **Books**

Bloom, Lynn Z., *Doctor Spock: Biography of a Conservative Radical*, Bobbs-Merrill, 1972.

Michalek, Irene R., *When Mercy Seasons Justice: The Spock Trial*, Branden Press, 1972.

Spock, Benjamin, *Decent and Indecent: Our Personal and Political Behavior*, McCall Publishing Co., 1970.

Spock, Benjamin, and Michael B. Rothenberg, *Baby and Child Care*, Dutton, 1985.

▶ **Periodicals**

Esquire, "Benjamin Spock's Baby Bible," December, 1983, pp. 520-526.

Look, "A Visit with Doctor Spock," July 21, 1959, pp. 23-26.

Newsweek, "Updating Dr. Spock," May 3, 1976, p. 86.

Post (New York), September 9, 1969.

Time, "Free Speech or Conspiracy?", May 31, 1968, pp. 16-17; "Bringing Dr. Spock Up To Date," April 8, 1985, pp. 76-77.

Gloria Steinem

"One full revolution is not complete until it has passed through the superficiality of novelty and even law to become an accepted part of the culture. Only when we look back over a long passage of time do we see that each of these cycles has been moving in a direction. We see the spiral of history."

Born in Toledo, Ohio, on March 25, 1934, Gloria Steinem is a journalist, the founding editor of *Ms.* magazine, and a leading activist for women's rights.

I n 1972 the United States Congress passed the Equal Rights Amendment, an addition to the Consitution which stated simply "Equality
of rights under the law shall not be denied or abridged by the
United States or by any states on account of sex." Passage of that piece
of legislation was counted a success by leaders of the women's rights
movement, but they were well aware that they were about to embark on
a much more difficult, ultimately unsuccessful struggle—the ratifica-
tion of the amendment by three-fourth of the states within the seven-
year time limit imposed by Congress. In that same year *Ms.* magazine, a
new national publication devoted to the advancement of feminist
causes, was launched. Described by one writer as the "journalistic
linchpin of the American feminist movement," the magazine sold out
its first 300,000 copies in just eight days. Gloria Steinem, a founding
editor of *Ms.*, had been in the forefront of the women's movement for
several years and gained prominence as she traveled the country
speaking in support of women's rights and the ERA. Advocating action
on every level, Steinem stirred up support for the movement wherever
she appeared. "We are all organizers," she wrote later, "and no
organizer should ever end a meeting or a book or an article without
ideas for practical action. After all, a movement depends on people
moving. What *are* we going to do differently when we get up tomorrow?"

Steinem was the second daughter of Leo Steinem and Ruth Nunevillar
Steinem. For the first twelve years of her life, the family traveled the
country in a house trailer while Leo tried to earn a living from a variety
of trades. Throughout this time Steinem's mother—a bright, educated
woman, who had once pursued a career in journalism—suffered from
crippling bouts of depression and anxiety. When her parents divorced,
in about 1946, Steinem returned alone with her mother to Toledo, Ohio,
where she began to attend school regularly for the first time in her life.
But living in a rat-infested house, with little money, and an almost
helplessly incapacitated mother to care for, the young girl's life was
anything but normal. Later on she was to write about her mother in her
moving account,"Ruth's Song (Because She Could Not Sing It)": "She
was just a fact of life when I was growing up; someone to be worried
about and cared for; an invalid who lay in bed with eyes closed and lips
moving in occasional response to voices only she could hear; a woman
to whom I brought an endless stream of toast and coffee, bologna
sandwiches and dime pies, in a child's version of what meals should be.
She was a loving, intelligent, terrorized woman."

Finally, in her senior year of high school, Steinem moved to Washington D.C. to live with her sister. Though her school grades were low, she
was accepted to Smith College in 1952 based on her high entrance
examination scores. There, free at last from the great emotional de-

mands of her earlier years, Steinem became an excellent student, majoring in government. She spent her junior year abroad in Geneva, Switzerland, was elected to Phi Beta Kappa, and graduated magna cum laude in 1956. She once remarked, "I loved Smith. I couldn't understand women who weren't happy there. They gave you three meals a day to eat, and all the books you wanted to read—what more could you want?" She then went on to India to study at the universities of Delhi and Calcutta on a Chester Bowles Asian Fellowship. But finding the prescribed coursework "pointless," she spent much of her time traveling throughout southern India during a time of great social upheaval. She later recalled "walking through village caste riots with nothing but a cup, a sari, and a comb."

Back in the United States, Steinem set about making a career for herself as a journalist. She gained a modest amount of notice when *Esquire* published her first article in 1962, a piece dealing with the sexual revolution entitled "The Moral Disarmament of Betty Coed." In 1963 Steinem published "I Was a Playboy Bunny," an expose of Hugh Hefner's Manhattan Playboy Club. From then on she wrote for a variety of magazines such as *Vogue* and *McCalls*, becoming, in the meantime, something of a celebrity in her own right. During this time she found her glamorous writing assignments at odds with her own more serious political concerns: "I was . . . traveling in 100 degree heat with Cesar Chavez and his Poor People's March to the Mexican border in order to organize press coverage, but reporting on tropical vacations; raising bail and collecting clothes for migrant workers organizing on Long Island, but interviewing James Coburn about some James Bond-type movie."

It wasn't until 1968, when Steinem began writing a weekly column, "The City Politic," for *New York* magazine, that her personal and professional interests combined. "For the first time," she commented, "I wasn't writing about one thing, while caring for something else." She traces her first strong interest in the women's movement to time spent on assignment for *New York* at a radical feminist pro-choice meeting. Listening to other women speak about their experiences with illegal abortion, she wrote, "was like the 'testifying' I had heard in southern churches and civil rights meetings of the earlier sixties: emotional, rock-bottom, personal truths. Suddenly, I was no longer learning intellectually what was wrong, I knew." That meeting prompted Steinem to publish her first openly feminist essay, "After Black Power, Women's Liberation."

Capitalizing on her celebrity status, Steinem soon became a high-profile spokesperson for the feminist movement. She became active in political organizations like the National Women's Political Caucus and helped establish the Women's Action Alliance, a group which mobilized minority men and women to work against social and economic discrimination. Along with over fifty other well-known women who had had abortions, Steinem signed a full-page petition for safe and legal abortions published in the inaugural issue of *Ms.* magazine in 1972.

Though almost overwhelmed by a fear of public speaking, she lectured around the country, and appeared frequently on television talk shows. In the introduction to *Outrageous Acts and Everyday Rebellions*, a collection of twenty years-worth of writing, she recalls months spent traveling as a speaking team with a succession of black feminist partners. At that time, she wrote "There was little public understanding that feminism, by its very definition, has to include females as a caste across economic and racial boundaries, just as a movement against the racial caste includes each individual marked by it, regardless of sex or class." Speaking in high school gyms, church basements, and union halls in almost every state in the country, Steinem and her partners galvanized men and women from all walks of life with her forceful, articulate, and sometimes humorous call for equal rights under the law.

In 1977 Steinem was appointed to the National Committee on the Observance of International Women's Year by President Carter, and was awared a fellowship to study feminist theory at Woodrow Wilson International Center for Scholars. She continues to write and edit, while maintaining her active involvement in political causes through her many speaking engagements. "As an itinerant organizer," she writes, "my own two biggest rewards are still a sense of making a difference and the birth of ideas. The first would be enough in itself, for that is how we know we are alive, but the second is magic. On a good night, a roomful of people can set off a chain of thought that leads us all to a new place—a sudden explosion of understanding, a spontaneous invention. We hear ourselves saying things we had felt but never named. It will take a lifetime to write them all down."

Sources

► **Books**

Diamonstein, Barbaralee, *Open Secrets*, Viking, 1973.

Henry, Sondra and Emily Taitz, *One Woman's Power: a Biography of Gloria Steinem*, Dillon Press, 1987.

Kostman, Samuel, *Twentieth-Century Women of Achievement*, Richards Rosen Press, 1976.

Steinem, Gloria, *Outrageous Acts and Everyday Rebellions*, Holt, 1983.

► **Periodicals**

Esquire, "Liberation's Next Wave According to Gloria Steinem," June, 1984, pp. 202-206.

Margaret Thatcher

*"*T*he younger generation doesn't want equality and regimentation, but opportunity to shape their world while showing compassion to those in real need."*

Politician, stateswoman, and prime minister of Britain Margaret Hilda Roberts Thatcher was born October 13, 1925, in Grantham, England.

Address: 10 Downing Street, London, England.

T hatcher is the second daughter of a grocer and a dressmaker; and while her family was not rich, neither was it poor. A clever child whose father was an ardent worker in local politics, she decided early in life to become a member of Parliament. She began her political career at the age of twenty-three when she was nominated for office from Dartford in Kent. During these early days, she developed her political philosophy. To socialist Britain she said: "You cannot have the dream of building up your own fortune by your own hopes, your own hands, and your own British guts," and then set out to create the conditions that would allow one to make his or her own fortune. Later, she added another "freedom" to her list: "The freedom to use one's talents as one wished and to develop one's own ideas."

In 1951, Margaret Roberts married Denis Thatcher, a successful director of a paint firm; and in 1959, she was elected to Parliament. Analytical, articulate, and ambitious, she quickly became prominent among other politicians. An excellent debater, she was frequently called upon by fellow Conservatives to answer, criticize, and denounce Labour policies. Thatcher's career in politics has not always been well-regarded. In 1972, for example, when she was at the Ministry of Education, she was referred to in the *Sun* newspaper as "the most unpopular woman in Britain." However, she is described as warm and genial by her friends, who point out that Thatcher likes to do her own grocery shopping and laundry, and used to invite out-of-town friends to stay with her in Chelsea to save on their hotel bills. She enjoys cooking and, reportedly, prepares breakfast for her family; she drives her own car and has never received a parking ticket. And while she has never been widely liked, she has won three elections in ten years. "Although a populist," writes biographer Hugo Young, "she is the ultimate argument against the contention that a political leader needs, in her person, to be unpopular." On May 4, 1989, Thatcher became the twentieth-century's longest-serving prime minister of Britain and will probably continue to serve as prime minister for as long as she desires the position. Perhaps she has surprised even herself, since she claimed never to aspire to anything higher politically than Chancellor of the Exchequer—the equivalent of Secretary of the Treasury in the United States.

Throughout her career, Thatcher has ruled with a stern determination to bring about change in Britain. Her medicine for curing Britain's troubles has always been painful. "After almost any major operation," she contends, "you feel worse before you convalesce. But you do not refuse the operation." Fiercely patriotic, she wants freedom of choice for all people. Some people have seen her as a true political revolutionary in that she has broadened the base of the Conservative party, especially to include the sturdy middle-class and wealthy. Although some people have accused her of rediscovering and promoting the past in an effort to recreate a Britain of yesteryear, others believe that she has restored pride in being British. "She is," one biographer, Russell Lewis, writes, "the embodiment of many hopes." Regardless of the length or extent of her success in politics, Thatcher exemplifies how a woman can succeed through hard work, ambition, and the drive to succeed.

Sources

▶ **Books**

Lewis, Russell, *Margaret Thatcher: A Personal & Political Biography*, Routledge & Kegan Paul, 1975.

Young, Hugo, *One of Us: A Biography of Margaret Thatcher*, Macmillan, 1989.

▶ **Periodicals**

Business Week, "Thatcher's Crackdown Could Be a Boon to the IRA," November 7, 1988, p. 59.

Current History, "Britain Moves Toward 1990," November 1988, pp. 369-72.

Fortune, "A Year to Shout About," January 4, 1988, pp. 34-5.

Nation, "Thatcher's Inglorious Revolution," January 30, 1988, p. 109.

National Review, "Capturing the Moral Initiative," December 30, 1988, p. 43.

Time, "And Marxism's Had It," November 28, 1988, p. 46, "Thatcher for President," May 15, 1989, p. 90.

U.S. News & World Report, "You Never, Never Drop Your Guard," December 19, 1988, pp. 18-19.

Desmond Tutu

*/ /*I am committed to working for a non-racial, just and democratic South Africa. Transfer of power to the people of South Africa means exactly that.''*

Born October 7, 1931, in Klerksdorp, Transvaal, South Africa, Desmond Tutu is the Nobel Peace Prize-winning black Anglican archbishop who advocates democracy to replace the apartheid government of South Africa.

I n 1925 the Prime Minister of South Africa, General Hertzog, made a speech in the Orange Free State calling for segregation of the races, to protect "civilized" from "uncivilized labour"—meaning the separation of white from black laborers. The succeeding laws implementing these ideas became known as the "Hertzog Bills." While racial segregation and exploitation were already well-established in South Africa, ever since the Dutch, French, and German settlers arrived to colonize, the white government was looking for ways to legalize their beliefs in racial superiority. In 1948 the National Party was elected to power in South Africa by promising apartheid, a word meaning "apartness" in the Afrikaans language. A system explicitly designed to mandate white supremacy, apartheid separates blacks from whites in all spheres, giving blacks no rights, no political power, and no protection. The system kept the 8.5 million Africans (now 23 million), plus the one million "coloreds" and one-half million Indians, under the control of 2.5 million whites, with no possibility of majority rule. The struggle for justice and freedom for blacks in South Africa has been long and tragic, and today is nowhere near resolution. One of the leading voices in the struggle has been that of Desmond Tutu, now the Archbishop of Capetown. Choosing a central path between the proponents and opponents of apartheid, Tutu has struggled for the liberation of his people while preaching non-violence and racial tolerance.

Born October 7, 1931 in the goldmining town of Klerksdorp in Transvaal province, Desmond Mpilo Tutu was given a middle name meaning "life" in the Sotho language. His father, Zachariah, was a schoolteacher from the Xhosa tribe, while his mother Aletha was a domestic servant of the Tswana tribe. Desmond says he had a happy childhood, though perhaps was a little spoiled by his sisters. They had no toys, but were constantly inventing games to play. He was baptized a Methodist, but later the family became Anglican. When Desmond was twelve the family moved to the township slum at Krugersdorp, near Johannesburg. While in missionary school there Desmond was greatly moved by the stories of serving the disadvantaged. While suffering from a long bout with tuberculosis Desmond first met Father Trevor Huddleston, now a leading anti-apartheid activist in England, who was to visit Tutu almost daily and have a profound impact on the teenage boy.

After high school Desmond wanted to go to medical school but his family could not afford it. He instead went to school to become a teacher, receiving a degree from the University of Johannesburg. Tutu taught high school from 1954-57. He resigned in protest when the government instituted a policy of giving blacks a second class education, the so-called "Bantu education" program. Tutu then turned to religious ministry. He was "grabbed by God by the scruff of the neck in order to spread his word, whether it is convenient or not." When he first started on this path Desmond admits he was "not moved by very high ideals", but his faith deepened. Communion, prayer, and meditation became essential parts of his life. Tutu received his licentiate in theology in 1960 from St. Peter's Theological College in Johannesburg, and was ordained an Anglican priest in 1961. He went to England where he received a master's degree in theology. From 1967 to 1969 Tutu lectured at the Federal Theological Seminary in the tribal homeland of Ciskei, and then at a university in the independent tribal enclave of Lesotho. In 1972 he returned to England, where for three years he administered scholarships for the World Council of Churches, and traveled widely in Asia and Africa. In 1975 Tutu returned to South Africa as the Anglican dean of Johannesburg, and the following year became bishop of Lesotho.

Tutu was already becoming very involved in the struggle for equal rights for blacks. In 1976 he wrote a letter to the prime minister, warning of impending violence in the township of Soweto. The letter was ignored, and 600 blacks were shot to death in the ensuing riots. In 1978 Tutu became secretary general of the South African Council of Churches (SACC), which became an important vehicle for protest. He infuriated government officials by protesting the forced removal of blacks to the so-called "tribal homelands," and the deplorable conditions most blacks were living in. Even more serious in the government's eyes was Tutu's support for Western countries' economic divestment from South Africa. In 1981 he toured the United States and Europe. Tutu's message was clear; "If you want to see fundamental change in South Africa by peaceful means, you must give assistance by applying pressure on the South African government, political, diplomatic, but above all, economic." For his outspokenness Tutu's passport was twice seized by the government.

Tutu's message is one of peace and harmony among the races. He supports the African National Congress's (ANC) struggled for a "truly democratic", non-racial South Africa. Recognizing the bondage that apartheid places on both blacks and whites, Tutu says "oppression dehumanizes the oppressor as much as, if not more than, the oppressed." In October, 1984, Desmond Tutu received the Nobel Peace Prize. In bestowing the award the chairman said: "This year's award should be seen as a renewed recognition of the courage and heroism shown by black South Africans in their use of peaceful methods in the struggle against apartheid." A month later Tutu was elected the first black Anglican bishop of Johannesburg. He continued to be outspoken, however, criticizing the Reagan administration's policy of "constructive engagement" with South Africa, saying "to be impartial (as the U.S.) . . . is indeed to have taken sides already.

Though firmly committed to non-violence, Tutu is perhaps a little harder than he once was. "I will never tell a man to pick up a gun", he says, "but I will pray for the man who picks up the gun, pray that he will be less cruel than he might otherwise have been, because he is a member of the community." Though more patient than most younger blacks, Tutu is also realistic about the struggle. "There are two things we need to say to our people. That the liberation is certain and that it is going to be costly." The latest South African constitution, passed in 1984, gives limited representation to Asians and mixed race people, but excludes seventy-three percent of the people (blacks) from participating in the political process. Tutu's response is to ask: "How much time has been wasted and how many lives lost trying to beautify apartheid through cosmetic improvements while the pillars of a vicious system still remain firmly in place?"

In 1986 Tutu was elected Archbishop of Capetown, the highest position in the Anglican Church in South Africa. He continues to speak out, such as calling for the 1500 children held in detention during the state of emergency to be released, and calling on the West to support the ANC. He has also renewed his call for economic sanctions against South Africa, and asked all nations to break diplomatic relations with the country. He continues to highlight the cruelty and hypocrisy of the apartheid system. Tutu remarked: "If Christ returned to South Africa today he would almost certainly be detained under the present security laws, because of his concern for the poor, the hungry and the oppressed."

Sources

▶ **Books**

Du Boulay, Shirley, *Tutu: Voice of the Voiceless*, Eerdmans, 1988.

Tutu, Desmond, *Crying in the Wilderness*, Eerdmans, 1982.

Tutu, Desmond, *Hope and Suffering*, Eerdmans, 1983.

▶ **Periodicals**

Harper's, "Botha's Bible—and Mine," July, 1988, pp. 25-26.

New York Times Magazine, "South Africa's Bishop Tutu," March 14, 1982, pp. 22-25.

Lech Walesa

"**N**o matter what the system, if it is not based on truth, on morality, on honesty, it hasn't a chance."

Born September 29, 1943, Lech Walesa is the leader of Solidarity, the Soviet bloc's only independent trade union. He is also the main force behind the creation of Poland's first democratically-elected government since the Second World War.

I n the summer of 1980, workers in cities across Poland staged a series of major strikes that crippled the communist government's shaky economy. By August, one man had emerged as the clear leader of the strikers, Lech Walesa, organizer and chairman of Solidarity, an outlaw union of Polish workers. Walesa's leadership of the strike resulted in a historic victory. On August 21, 1980, he met with Poland's Deputy Premier and negotiated the world's first union agreement with a communist government, an agreement which also guaranteed the legal recognition of Solidarity as an independent trade union. Since that initial victory, Walesa has endured an 11-month prison sentence, the banning of Solidarity, and a martial law crackdown. But in 1989, the communist government of Poland was forced to agree to the first free elections in Poland since the Second World War. In these elections, Solidarity won an overwhelming victory. By August of 1989, a coalition government consisting of Solidarity, the communist party, and two smaller opposition parties was being created. It marked the first time that a communist nation had peacefully ceded a share of power to independent political groups.

Walesa was born in Popowo, a town in northern Poland. After graduating from vocational school, he found employment as an electrician at the Lenin Shipyard in the Baltic coastal city of Gdansk. It was there that he began to make a name for himself as a labor spokesman. Spurred by his strong religious beliefs and by nationalistic pride, Walesa's activism was meant to provide the workers of communist Poland with a greater voice in the affairs of their country. In 1970, he participated in a series of "bread riots" protesting the high price of food. In 1976, he played a prominent role in a wave of labor strikes which swept across the country; Walesa's involvement in the protests led to his being fired from the shipyard. For the next four years he traveled the country, working in various factories. Whenever his labor union activism drew criticism from communist party officials, he was fired or jailed. Despite the difficulties of this period, Walesa helped to organize the labor union Solidarity as an independent alternative to the government-run unions.

With the election of a Polish cardinal as Pope John Paul II in 1978, and the pope's subsequent visit to Poland in 1979, Poles gained a renewed sense of hope and possibility. This hope led to increased activity by Solidarity. In 1979, Walesa was one of 65 workers to sign a charter of workers' rights which called for legal strikes and independent unions in Poland. Some 60,000 copies of the document were distributed. The following July, when the government doubled the price of meat, workers at the Lenin Shipyard went on strike in protest. Walesa emerged as their leader. The strike soon spread to other cities, and the demands grew to include recognition of Solidarity as a legal, independent union. Facing economic disaster because of the strike, the government submitted to the demands.

Labor agitation did not end with the legalization of Solidarity. During the course of 1980 Walesa led several strikes to demand such reforms as a five day work week. These continuing actions worried not only the Polish communist government but the Soviet Union as well. By December of 1980 some 55 Soviet army divisions were poised on the Polish border, threatening an invasion should Solidarity prove too powerful a challenge to the Polish government. Over the course of the next two years the tensions continued between the workers and the entrenched party bureaucrats. On March 27, 1981, Solidarity organized the largest strike in Poland's history, involving nearly 13 million workers from all parts of the country. Other strikes protested food shortages and police violence against workers, and called for free elections.

Walesa's efforts to keep pressure on the government without provoking a violent response ended in failure in November of 1982 when Polish leader Wojiech Jaruzelski declared martial law and banned the Solidarity union. Communist tanks and troops took control of the major cities, and Walesa and other union officials were jailed for nearly a year. Upon his release from prison in 1983, Walesa was awarded the Nobel Peace Prize. But because of the official ban on Solidarity, he was forced to curtail his union activities for several years.

When martial law was finally lifted, union organizing began anew, but it was not until January of 1989 that the communist government again agreed to negotiate with Solidarity. In April 1989, the communist party allowed Solidarity to field candidates in Eastern Europe's first scheduled open election since the Second World War. Poland's worsening economy, and Western reluctance to loan money to the financially beleaguered nation, were major factors in the government's decision to allow free elections. With the economic instability, the government simply could not survive a prolonged strike should Solidarity have chosen to call one. In the June elections, Solidarity won an overwhelming victory, capturing 99 of 100 seats in the Polish senate, and all of the 161 contested seats in the main legislative body. As *Newsweek* reported, "Districts where the [communist] party ought to have run well went to the opposition: Army bases, government enclaves, even security-police headquarters." Solidarity even won in districts where communist party candidates ran unopposed, with voters casting write-in votes against the established government. As communist party chief Jaruzelski later admitted, "Our defeat is total. A political solution will have to be found." By August of 1989, a coalition government was being forged which included the communist party, Solidarity, and two minor opposition parties. Although the change in government was tremendously important, at least one observer commented that "many Poles have little faith that any new government, even one led by non-Communists, can reverse the devastating effects of 45 years of misguided central planning and an entrenched system of state monopolies."

Despite the inherited problems the new government faces, Walesa's heroic efforts have peacefully reformed his nation's political system and given a voice to the demands of its people. For millions of his countrymen, he is a symbol of hope and confidence in the future of Poland. Speaking of the historic election victory, Walesa told a crowd of supporters, "This is our greatest achievement. . . . I ask you all to take responsibility for Poland."

Sources

▶ **Books**

Craig, Mary, *Lech Walesa and His Poland*, Continuum, 1986.

Dobbs, Michael and others, *Poland: Solidarity: Walesa*, McGraw-Hill, 1981.

Walesa, Lech, *The Book of Lech Walesa*, Simon & Schuster, 1982.

Walesa, Lech, *A Way of Hope*, Holt, 1987.

▶ **Periodicals**

Detroit News, "Poland's Non-Communist Government Faces Mammoth Challenges," August 21, 1989, p. 6A.

National Review, "Man of the Year," January 23, 1981, pp. 32-37.

Newsweek, "Solidarity's Stunning Win," June 19, 1989, pp. 42-43, "To Join or Not to Join," July 17, 1989, p. 33, "Poland Pays the Price," August 14, 1989, pp. 26-27.

New York Times, "The Workers' Champion," December 14, 1981, p. 20, "Lech Walesa Is Awarded the 1983 Nobel Peace Prize," October 6, 1983, p. 1.

New York Times Magazine, "Lech! Lech! Lech!," October 23, 1988, pp. 36-46.

Alice Walker

"The black woman is one of America's greatest heroes. The cruelty of the black man to his wife and family is one of the great tragedies. It has mutilated the spirit and body of the black family and of most black mothers."

Born February 9, 1944, in Eatonton, Georgia, Walker is a prize-winning writer.

A lthough Walker had written acclaimed poetry, short stories, and novels in the 1960s and 1970s, it was not until the publication of her 1982 novel *The Color Purple* that she became widely regarded as one of America's premier black woman writers. Her works are generally praised for confronting the pain and struggle encountered by black people, especially black women living in the South. Believing that many black women are unsung heros—often suffering cruel treatment by men and enduring bouts of hopelessness—Walker states: "I'm really paying homage to people I love, the people who are thought to be dumb and backward but who were the ones who first taught me to see beauty."

In Georgia, Walker was born the eighth child of Willie Lee, a sharecropper and dairy farmer who earned $300 annually, and Minnie Tallulah, who worked as a maid. Her parents were both storytellers who, recalled Walker, "always spoke with metaphorical richness." Walker began to write down these stories at an early age, also writing poetry. After an accidental BB gun shot in the eye left her partially blind and extremely self-conscious due to disfiguring scar tissue, Walker became introverted and turned more avidly to reading and writing for comfort. Later, though, when the scar tissue was removed, she became quite popular in school and was valedictorian of her high school senior class. In addition, Walker's disability enabled her to obtain a scholarship to attend Atlanta's Spelman College, an all-black women's school.

Once at Spelman in 1961, Walker became involved in the civil rights movement, participating in demonstrations. She soon found Spelman too restrictive an institution, though, and she decided to take a scholarship at Sarah Lawrence College in Bronxville, New York. The following summer, at the age of twenty, Walker traveled to the African nations of Kenya and Uganda, places she found inspirational. She returned to Sarah Lawrence deeply depressed, however, for she was pregnant. Undergoing an abortion, Walker profusely wrote poetry in the week immediately following the operation. The poems—touching on subjects of love, death, Africa, and the civil rights movement—were admired by a teacher, who submitted them to an agent. The poetry was published as *Once* in 1968.

Walker received a bachelor's degree from Sarah Lawrence and went on to work to register voters and to restore welfare rights in the South. Residing in Mississippi on a writing fellowship, Walker met civil rights lawyer Melvyn Leventhal, who is white. The couple moved to New York, where they lived together for a year and married in 1967. Meanwhile, Walker continued to write. "To Hell With Dying," a short story concerning a young girl's love for a dying elderly man, was published in 1967. That year, Walker and Leventhal moved to Jackson,

Mississippi, where they were the first legally married biracial residents. Walker taught at two colleges, and after the publication of her first novel, *The Third Life of Grange Copeland*, she moved to Massachusetts and lectured from 1972 to 1973. Walker's *Revolutionary Petunias and Other Poems* was published in 1973 and nominated for a National Book Award. One year later, she and Leventhal returned to New York, where Walker became a contributing editor for *Ms.* magazine. In addition, she finished her second novel, *Meridian*, which was applauded for its treatment of civil rights issues.

Although her writing received much acclaim, Walker's fiction was also criticized for portraying an overly negative view of black men, while depicting black women characters as sympathetic. The author firmly stands behind her decision to create this type of representation, however, asserting that the black woman "has been oppressed beyond recognition. Her men have actually encouraged this oppression and insisted on it." Walker conveys this point of view in her most noted work, 1982's *The Color Purple*. Epistolary in form, the novel relates the struggle of the poor abused black Celie, oppressed by men but liberated and strengthened by her close relationships with her sister Nettie and the flamboyant Miss Shug.

The Color Purple affirmed Walker's reputation as a leading recorder of the black experience in America. Celebrated for its presentation of black folk speech, as well as its depiction of women's triumph over the oppression of racism and sexism, *The Color Purple* earned Walker the Pulitzer Prize and was adapted into a successful motion picture. According to Peter S. Prescott writing in *Newsweek:* "*The Color Purple* is an American novel of permanent importance, that rare sort of book which (in Norman Mailer's felicitous phrase) amounts to 'a diversion in the fields of dread.'"

Since divorcing Leventhal in 1976 and sharing joint custody of daughter Rebecca, Walker has resided in California, a location she finds conducive to writing. Her works following *The Color Purple* include *In Search of Our Mother's Gardens: Womanist Prose* and *Living by the Word: Selected Writings, 1973-1987*, books that continue to probe the sexism and racism consistently besetting black women. *The Temple of My Familiar*, a spiritual novel exploring the relationships of species, races, and sexes throughout history, was published in 1989.

Although still very much concerned with civil rights issues, Walker is reportedly less arduous in her battle against oppression. "Lately," she stated, "I've come to believe that you have some help when you fight. If a country or person oppresses folks, it or he will pay for it." Walker concluded: "I had to live a lot and it wasn't all painless. Much of it was hurt. But I learned that you can get a lot out of whatever happens to you."

Sources
▶ **Books**

Walker, Alice, *The Color Purple*, Harcourt, 1982.

▶ **Periodicals**

Ms., "Do You Know This Woman?," June, 1982, pp. 35-37, 89-94.

Newsweek, "A Long Road to Liberation," June 21, 1982, pp. 67-68.

Publishers Weekly, August 31, 1970, pp. 195-97.

Elie Wiesel

"*T he only role I sought was that of witness. I believed that, having survived by chance, I was duty-bound to give meaning to my survival, to justify each moment of my life.*"

Born September 30, 1928, in Sighet, Hungary, author and educator Elie Wiesel is an authority on the Holocaust.

Address: c/o Boston University, 745 Commonwealth Avenue, Boston, Massachusetts 02115

E lie Wiesel, recipient of the Nobel Peace Prize in 1986, is a writer, educator, and Holocaust survivor whose nearly two dozen works seek to confront the despair and meaninglessness engendered by the experience of Auschwitz and, by the very act of survival and remembrance, conquer that despair. Steeped in the storytelling tradition of his Hasidic faith, Wiesel's novels, plays, and essays draw on the particularities of the Jewish Holocaust experience and illuminate the plight of the persecuted everywhere.

Eliezer Wiesel was born the only son of four children to Shlomo and Sarah (Feig) Wiesel, Hasidic Jews, and as a child Wiesel studied the great Hebrew tests.

In 1944, when the Nazis ordered the deportation of Sighet's 15,000 Jews, Wiesel and his family were transported to the Auschwitz concentration camp, where thousands of Jews were being exterminated every day. Wiesel's mother and younger sister died in the gas chambers, and he did not discover that his elder sisters had survived until the war was over.

For the next nine months Elie and his father endured the horrors of Auschwitz. "Never shall I forget the little faces of the children," recalled Wiesel, "whose bodies I saw turned into wreaths of smoke beneath a silent blue sky." As Soviet troops approached the camp in January 1945, the inmates were forced to march to another concentration camp at Buchenwald, in Germany, where, weakened by the march, dysentery, and starvation, Shlomo Wiesel died. Three months later, Buchenwald was liberated by U.S. troops and Wiesel was free. He moved to France and lived there the next twelve years.

From 1948 to 1951, Wiesel studied in Paris at the Sorbonne University, where he devoted himself to literature, philosophy, and psychology while earning his living as choir director, summer camp counsellor, and teacher of Hebrew and the Bible. He also worked as a journalist, traveling in 1948 to Israel for the French newspaper *L'Arche,* and again in 1951 to India as correspondent for the Tel Aviv daily *Yedioth Ahronot.* In 1956, on assignment in New York City, Wiesel was struck and seriously injured by a taxi cab. He was confined to a wheelchair for a year, and in the resulting confusion with his French papers, was encouraged to apply for U.S. citizenship. The following year, he became a feature writer for the New York *Jewish Daily Forward,* and he has lived in the United States ever since.

In 1954, at the urging of French writer Francois Mauriac, Wiesel began to write about the Holocaust and his own survival. Two years later, his first book, *Un di Velt Hot Geshvign* ("And the World Remained Silent"), appeared in Yiddish. Attempts to have the 800-page manuscript accepted for publication in France proved unsuccessful, so Wiesel edited it to less than 150 pages and executed the French translation himself. In 1958 it was published in French as the novel *La Nuit* and in 1960 it appeared in the United States as *Night* (after being rejected for publication twenty times).

Since that first novel, Wiesel has published over two dozen semi-autobiographical novels, plays, and essays. Several deal with the testamental prophets and the ancient legends of his youth, and the plight of Jews around the world, particularly in the Soviet Union. The need to remember and to bear witness to the Holocaust, however, has always been his primary motivation as a writer.

In 1985, members of the West German Bundestag recommended Wiesel for the Nobel Peace Prize, which he was awarded the following year. The same year he was also awarded the Congressional Gold Medal of Achievement, one of the highest honors conferred by the United States.

Elie Wiesel continues to write and teach at Boston University. "I have always felt that words mean responsibility," he said recently. "I try to use them not against the human condition but for humankind, never to create anger but to attenuate anger, not to separate people but to bring them together."

Sources

▶ **Books**

Abramowitz, Molly, *Elie Wiesel: A Bibliography*, Scarecrow, 1974.

Brown, Robert McAfee, *Elie Wiesel: Messenger to All Humanity*, University of Notre Dame Press, 1983.

Estess, Ted L., *Elie Wiesel*, Ungar, 1980.

Greenberg, Irving, and Alvin Rosenfeld, editors, *Confronting the Holocaust: The Impact of Elie Wiesel*, Indiana University Press, 1978.

Roth, John K., *A Consuming Fire: Encounters with Elie Wiesel and the Holocaust*, John Knox Press, 1979.

Wiesel, Elie, *The Night Trilogy: Night, Dawn, The Accident*, Farrar, Strauss, 1987.

▶ **Periodicals**

New York Times Book Review, "Why I Write: Making No Become Yes," April 14, 1985. pp. 13-14.

Paris Review, "The Art of Fiction: Interview With Elie Wiesel," spring, 1984, pp. 130-178.

People, "Ronald Reagan Is Tutored on the Holocaust by One Who Survived It, Writer Elie Wiesel," May 6, 1985, pp. 46-47.

Time, "Author, Teacher, Witness: Holocaust Survivor Elie Wiesel Speaks for the Silent," March 18, 1985, pp. 79-82.

Roy Wilkins

"N *othing is more important than a good education."*

Born August 30, 1901, in St. Louis, Missouri, civil rights leader and fighter for Blacks' rights Roy Wilkins died September 8, 1981.

Roy was born into a family that was financially and socially disadvantaged. His mother was Mayfield (Edmondson) and his father William D. Wilkins. Roy was a loner from childhood, liking to work and think for himself.

After his mother died and his father succumbed to alcoholism, Roy was sent to St. Paul, Minnesota, to stay with his uncle Sam Williams and his wife Elizabeth. Roy flourished under the management of these two kindly and gentle people. About his uncle Sam, Roy said: "He was the warmest, kindest man I have ever met. Over the years he taught me that the world was not the universally hostile place my own father had taken it to be; that a man could get along if he had faith in the goodness of other people, kept his eye peeled for their weakness—and believed in himself." About his kind and thoughtful aunt, Roy always remembered that she had taught him: "Nothing is more important than a good education." Roy never forgot this message.

Roy grew up among whites in a St. Paul where color of skin did not matter; the important thing was character. In high school he became president of the Literary Society and editor of the high school paper *The Cogwheel*. After graduation from high school, he attended the University of Minnesota. While there he started working for the Urban League and NAACP, two leading organizations dedicated to the rights and advancement of Blacks. In 1931, because of his success with the NAACP while in college, Roy moved to New York City to become Assistant Secretary of that organization, working under Walter White. This increased involvement drew Roy more and more into the battle for the rights of Blacks. His first arrest in the cause came in 1934 when he tried to picket a U.S. Conference on crime. On May 17, 1954 the U.S. Supreme Court overturned in *Brown* v. *Board of Education* the fifty-eight year old *Plessy-Ferguson* ruling giving separate but equal facilities for whites and blacks. Roy called this decision "one of life's sweetest days," because it gave equal opportunity to all. Roy fought hard for this opportunity. He felt that white people's call to "go slow" on civil rights was really a plea to "go nowhere," and he wanted to move.

Roy became Executive Director of the National Association for the Advancement of Colored People after Walter White died. According to him the NAACP had "become the oldest, wiliest, and best-organized civil rights group in the country," and he determined to keep it moving forward. When Rosa Parks was arrested in Montgomery, Alabama, for refusing to give up her seat on a bus, and when Autherine Lucy was being refused admittance to the University of Alabama, Roy and the NAACP took up the cases, and ultimately won them.

During these years many thoughtful whites, including novelist William

Faulkner and politician Adlai Stevenson, were cautioning Blacks to go slow and thus to give the whites a little relief and breathing space. Roy stormed against the relief. He wanted to keep pressure on because he thought only strength and persistence were effective against opposition. Roy found "keeping faith with the democratic process in light of such constant reversals was difficult," but he tried. He depended upon the courts, and especially the U.S. Supreme Court, to finally find for justice.

Suspicious as he was of politicians, Roy was especially fearful of Lyndon Baines Johnson, thirty-sixth president of the U.S., but he was to be proved wrong. LBJ became the most effective President in righting the wrongs imposed upon Blacks. Speaking before a joint session of the U.S. Congress, LBJ said that the Blacks' cause was everyone's cause: "really it is all of *us* who must overcome the crippling legacy of bigotry and injustice. And we shall overcome." At these words Roy was nearly overcome: "I had waited all my life to hear a President of the United States talk that way. . . . And at that moment, I confess, I loved LBJ."

Through the years Roy and the NAACP were criticized for their stand against using violence and for their belief in the value of the courts. But they opposed the philosophy of such organizations as the Congress of Racial Equality (CORE) and the Student Non-Violent Coordinating Committee (SNCC) because of their opinion that all whites were devils and that the only salvation for Blacks was separating from whites and living alone. Roy objected most to the notion that Blacks should separate from whites altogether.

It is difficult to tell precisely how much the NAACP and Roy Wilkins accomplished through the years. He felt that the "most concrete legacy of the black power movement was to make the term 'Negro' a dirty word." Roy felt that the word "Black" is no better. "There's not a word in the English language that couldn't be considered a white man's word," he declared. On the positive side, he said, "Two of the best words are 'freedom' and 'liberty'. 'Negro' is not the bad word. 'Hatred' is the bad word and 'hatred' and 'enslavement'.

Roy's personal role in the fight for the rights of Blacks was recognized often through the years. He was the recipient of numerous honorary degrees, and received many awards, including the Spingarn Medal from the NAACP, 1964, the Freedom Award, 1967, the Theodore Roosevelt Distinguished Service Medal, 1968, the Presidential Medal of Freedom, 1969, the Zale Award, 1973, and the Joseph Prize for Human Rights, 1975.

Perhaps his greatest statements about his belief in America came at the end of his autobiography, where he spoke with hope and confidence:

"We have believed in our Constitution. We have believed that the Declaration of Independence meant what it said. All my life I have believed these things, and I will die believing them. I share this faith with others—and I know that it will last and guide us long after I am gone."

Sources

▶ **Books**

Wilkins, Roy, *Standing Fast: The Autobiography of Roy Wilkins*, Viking, 1982.

▶ **Periodicals**

Black Enterprise, "In Memory of Roy Wilkins and the Struggle That Goes On," November, 1981, p. 9.

Essence, "Roy Wilkins, the Quiet Warrior (1901-1981)," December, 1981, p. 14.

National Review, "Roy Wilkins, RIP," October 2, 1981, p. 1125.

Newsweek, "Roy Wilkins, 1901-1981," September 21, 1981, p. 52.

New Yorker, "Notes and Comment," September 21, 1981, p. 33.

Time, "He Overcame," September 21, 1981, p. 21.

Frank Lloyd Wright

"*N*ot only do I intend to be the greatest architect who has ever lived, but the greatest who will ever live. Yes, I intend to be the greatest architect of all time.*"*

Born June, 8, 1869, in Richland Center, Wisconsin, American architect Frank Lloyd Wright died on April 9, 1959, in Phoenix, Arizona.

F rank Lloyd Wright is considered by many the greatest architect of the twentieth century. In a career that spanned nearly seven decades, Wright designed and built more than six hundred structures and was responsible for some of the world's most innovative buildings, including the Imperial Hotel in Tokyo and the Guggenheim Museum in New York City. He studied civil engineering at the University of Wisconsin but left before graduation to take a job as a draftsman with famed architect Louis Sullivan. After he split with Sullivan he made a name for himself as an independent architect by de-emphasizing the traditional and conservative building styles prevalent during the 1890s. He became a leading proponent of "organicism" in architecture; his buildings would blend with their natural surroundings and were made of natural materials such as stone and wood rather than artificial materials such as plaster and paint. Hallmarks of Wright's designs came to include homes built close to the ground with broad roofs, spacious rooms, and large stone fireplaces.

The most celebrated architect of his age, Wright never spoke modestly of his achievements and he always offered opinions on more than just architecture. His books generally combined architecture with wit and wisdom on subjects ranging from politics to economics to morality. On the fringe of the architectural establishment for most of his career, he never belonged to the American Institute of Architects (AIA) and he scorned most buildings that he did not design. Fellow architects either worshipped or despised him, but by the 1940s his genius was well established throughout the world. He died in 1959, just before his ninetieth birthday.

Wright's father, William Russell Wright, was a minister, and his mother, Anna, was a schoolteacher who urged her son from an early age to pursue a career in architecture. When Wright was fourteen his father deserted his wife and three children, and young Frank worked on a farm to help support the family. After graduation from high school he enrolled at the University of Wisconsin in Madison, where he studied civil engineering (an architecture program had not yet been established). Wright left after only three years and traveled to Chicago, where he secured a draftsman position with Sullivan, renowned as the first architect to design skyscrapers. Wright married at age twenty-one and by his mid-twenties, to support his five children, he was forced to take architectural designing jobs on the side. His moonlighting soon angered Sullivan, and the two parted ways after six years. Wright opened his own architectural firm in Chicago shortly thereafter.

Wright's architectural designs of the 1900s reflected his philosophy that buildings must be "organic," or that they should blend into the landscape outside and be completely functional inside. The homes designed during this "Prairie" period, reminiscent of Midwestern plains, were built low and with long horizontal sight lines. Wright has also designed and built two noteworthy buildings by 1906, one for the Larkin Company in Buffalo, which was the first American office building to use metal-bound plate-glass doors and windows and air conditioning, and the Unity Temple Church in Oak Park, Illinois, which was the first in which Wright used poured concrete in its construction.

Known in Chicago society as a progressive architect and an unpredictable man, in 1909 Wright left his wife and six children for Mamah Cheney, the wife of a Chicago businessman, but they never married. After a trip to Europe in 1911, Wright built a house near his childhood home in Spring Green, Wisconsin, that he named Taliesin, Welsh for "shining brow." The house was set on the brow of a small hill, just off the bank of the Wisconsin River. In addition to the main house Wright built out-buildings to house students, for he intended to start an architectural school there. Wright initially took on several apprentices, and he lived there with Cheney and her children.

But in 1914, three years after Taliesin was built, tragedy struck. While Wright was in Chicago designing a building, an unstable servant killed Mrs. Cheney, her two children, and four other people. He then set fire to Taliesin. Wright was distraught, and although he rebuilt Taliesin, he was uncertain if he could design again. His spirits were uplifted, however, when he met an unconventional Parisian sculptress named Miriam Noel, whom he eventually married.

From 1915 to 1922, Wright was involved in designing and building the Imperial Hotel in Tokyo, commissioned by the Japanese Government. Employing an innovative technique that he claimed would make the building earthquake-proof, instead of building the structure on solid ground Wright built it on stilts sunk in mud. Other architects scoffed, but Wright was soon vindicated. A severe earthquake struck Tokyo in 1924, and while other buildings crumbled, the Imperial Hotel merely swayed.

Wright's personal life continued to take strange turns during the 1920s. Soon after his marriage to Noel in 1922, Wright sensed that she was losing her grip on reality. Complaining that she felt stifled, she took a six-month vacation in Mexico; at the same time Wright met a woman from Montenegro, Olgivanna Hinzenberg, and quickly fell in love with her. He filed for divorce, but Noel charged Wright with desertion and Hinzenberg with alienation of affection. Wright, Hinzenberg, and even Hinzenberg's daughter were locked in jail several times because of domestic violence (Noel stormed into Wright's house on at least one occasion and destroyed furniture and art). It was two years before

Wright was able to disentangle himself from Noel and marry Hinzenberg, which he did in 1928.

Despite the turmoil of his personal life, Wright continued to operate his apprentice program at Taliesin, where established and aspiring architects alike clamored to be guests. Eventually tiring of the winter weather in Wisconsin, Wright built Taliesin West near Phoenix, Arizona, where he and his apprentices and guests would spend five months a year. Wright's notoriety seemed to be catching up with his professional life, though, and he received almost no offers for design during the late 1920s and the Depression years, despite his recognized status as one of the world's premier architects. In 1935, however, Wright and his students at Taliesin were commissioned to redesign the weekend home of a Pittsburgh businessman in Bear Run, Pennsylvania. The house they designed, called "Falling Water," was built into the site over a waterfall, following Wright's lifelong belief that houses should be organic. "Falling Water" is one of the most famous houses in the world and remains a hallmark of ingenuity.

In 1939, Wright completed another of his outstanding buildings, the Johnson Wax building in Racine, Wisconsin. At the age of seventy Wright not only designed the building but he helped build it. The structure became another architectural masterpiece, featuring a roof supported by thin concrete shafts, unusual interior spaces, and birdcage-like elevators. Other impressive buildings followed, including the Unitarian Church in Madison, the Price Tower in Bartlesville, Oklahoma, and a Greek Byzantine church in Milwaukee. He also designed the campus of Florida Southern College in Lakeland and the Guggenheim Museum in New York City. In all, Wright designed more than six hundred structures, ranging from towering cathedrals to a small bank in Spring Green.

Wright was awarded many major honors for architecture and in 1949 was given the prestigious American Institute of Architects' gold medal. Its accompanying citation called Wright a "titanic force" in architecture, ironic since Wright had spent his entire professional life denouncing most architects and their work and had reserved particularly acerbic criticisms for the AIA. Wright's stature had become so great internationally, however, that the AIA, over many dissenting voices, had voted to honor Wright.

Wright died in Phoenix, Arizona, in 1959, at the age of eighty-nine. His influence on the design of buildings in the United States and abroad is difficult to overestimate. Although his houses themselves are not widely emulated, his use of space and form have had a lasting and profound impact on the architecture we see today. The continuing

appreciation of his designs and his influence on the American architectural scene are testament to his innovative genius.

Sources

▶ **Books**

Farr, Finis, *Frank Lloyd Wright: A Biography*, Scribner, 1961.

Smith, Norris Kelly, *Frank Lloyd Wright: A Study in Architectural Content*, Prentice-Hall, 1966.

Twombly, Robert C., *Frank Lloyd Wright: His Life and His Architecture*, Wiley, 1979.

Willard, Charlotte, *Frank Lloyd Wright: American Architect*, MacMillan, 1972.

Wright, Frank Lloyd, *An Autobiography*, Horizon Press, 1977.

Wright, Olgivanna, *Frank Lloyd Wright: His Life, His Work, His Words*, Pitman, 1970.

▶ **Periodicals**

Life, "Frank Lloyd Wright," August 12, 1946, pp. 84-96, "Guardian of a Great Legacy," June 11, 1971, pp. 44-54.

Newsweek, "Medal for a Titan," March 28, 1949, "The Great Dissenter," April 20, 1959, pp. 98-99, "The Wright Stuff," February 1, 1988, pp. 52-54.

Saturday Evening Post, "Frank Lloyd Wright: Defiant Genius," January 7-February 4, 1961.

Time, "Ahead of His Time," February 9, 1948, pp. 68-69.

Chuck Yeager

"I was born with unusually good eyes and coordination. . . . My nature was to stay cool in tight spots. Is that 'the right stuff'? All I know is I worked my tail off to learn how to fly. . . . And in the end, the one big reason why I was better than average as a pilot was because I flew more than anyone else."

Born February 13, 1923 in Myra, West Virginia, Chuck Yeager is an Air Force fighter pilot and test pilot.

C huck Yeager is today one of America's most respected test pilots, having been canonized in Tom Wolfe's bestselling book *The Right Stuff* as "the most righteous of all possessors of the right stuff." When Yeager joined the Army Air Corps in 1941, however, he had never even seen an airplane. After being decorated as a fighter pilot during World War II, Yeager became a test pilot, and in 1947 became the first person to survive a flight at the speed of sound. During the 1950s, Yeager tested many of the Air Force's experimental planes, and in the 1960s flew over a hundred combat missions in the Vietnam War. Wolfe's book and the 1983 movie of the same name made Yeager a celebrity; he became a much sought-after public speaker and in 1985 wrote an autobiography which became a bestseller. The press has called Yeager "a true American hero, a symbol of the intrepid, curious, enterprising American spirit." Yeager downplays his hero status: "The real reason I was suddenly a hot commodity went beyond all the exposure I was getting. . . . America needed a hero to hug, and I was it."

As a youngster growing up in West Virginia, Yeager was interested in sports, music, and gardening. He was the second of five children. His childhood was spent in small towns of West Virginia; Hamlin, where he lived for some years, seemed like a big city with its population of 400 people. After graduating from Hamlin High School, with war against Nazi Germany raging in Europe, Yeager enlisted in the Army Air Corps.

Yeager's first job in the Air Corps was as an airline mechanic. His father had been an expert mechanic, and Yeager had learned a great deal about engines as a child. Soon, however, ambition led him to apply for a flying position. He later recalled, "Hell, I hadn't even seen an airplane before I joined up." He was accepted as a pilot soon thereafter.

In March 1943, Yeager was commissioned as a reserve flight officer. In November of that year, his fighter group was sent to England to begin flying missions against Nazi Germany. He flew eight missions successfully, shooting down two German planes, before being shot down himself and wounded on his ninth mission. He was fortunate enough to be picked up by the French Underground, and was hidden for a few days at a French farmhouse. He was then led over the Pyrenees into Spain by a group of hardy French Resistance fighters known as the Maquis. After days in the freezing weather of the Pyrenees, he made it to a small town in Spain, where he was promptly thrown into jail by the local police. It was only a half-hearted arrest, however; the police did not even search him. Since Yeager carried a small saw for exactly this type of situation, he used it to cut through the bars of the cell and escaped. He was eventually rescued by the British Royal Air Force and returned to England.

Yeager later returned to action in the war and flew 55 more missions in Europe. In one dogfight he shot down five enemy planes, a rare feat in Air Force history. Following the war, he received several awards and medals, including the Distinguished Flying Cross and the Purple Heart.

In 1946, following the war, Yeager became a flight instructor at Perrin Field, Texas. Several months later, he was reassigned to Wright-Patterson Air Force Base near Dayton, Ohio. In February, 1947, he received a regular Air Force commission as a captain. Later that year, he volunteered as a test pilot to fly the X-1 research plane. Test pilots fly airplanes which are experimental, and therefore run risks which most air travellers do not; test pilots help fix problems which aircraft have so that future pilots and civilian passengers will not have to face unnecessary risks. Yeager was entering a high-risk profession.

The X-1 was a small, stubby-looking plane with four rocket fuel openings in its tail. It had been flown for several years by test pilots up to eight-tenths of the speed of sound (the speed of sound at sea level is about 763 miles per hour; at 40,000 feet in the air, sound travels at about 662 miles per hour). In October of 1947, Yeager travelled to Muroc Air Force Base in the Mojave Desert of southern California. On October 14, the X-1, with Yeager as pilot, was carried to 26,000 feet in the air by an Air Force B-29. The B-29 dropped the X-1, and Yeager fired the plane's first rocket. The X-1 shot away from the B-29 at a tremendous speed. Yeager guided the plane up into space at a forty-five degree angle, firing the other rockets at timed intervals. At a height of 40,000 feet, he reached and surpassed the speed of sound, the first time a human being had travelled at such a speed and survived. Several minutes later, his fuel used up, Yeager guided his powerless X-1 to a safe landing in the desert.

Yeager later described his sensations as he broke the sound barrier: "The faster I got, the smoother the ride was. Suddenly . . . [I was] flying supersonic! It was so smooth that Grandma would be sitting up there sipping lemonade. . . . The guys in the . . . tracking van interrupted to report they heard what sounded like a distant rumble of thunder: my sonic boom! The first one by an airplane ever heard on earth."

It was not until June of 1948 that the news of Yeager's flight was officially released to the American public and the world. Yeager was presented with the Mackay Trophy for the outstanding military aviation feat of the year. He was also awarded the Collier Trophy by President Truman.

Yeager continued his test pilot activities in the early 1950s. In 1953, he piloted an Air Force X-1A rocket plane to a speed of 1650 miles per hour, establishing another speed record and regaining his title as the "World's Fastest Man." It was reported that on that flight, following his record-setting speed at 70,000 feet, his plane went out of control and dropped 50,000 feet before he was able to regain control and land the plane safely.

Yeager would later comment that his fear of death made him extremely thorough in his knowledge of the plane's equipment and in his preparation for flight. Thus, he was always careful to complement his skill as a pilot with careful preparation for the dangers which lay ahead. Nevertheless, Yeager credits a great deal of luck to his having survived numerous dangerous situations.

In 1954, Yeager left his post at Edwards Air Force Base in California to work at the 12th Air Force headquarters in West Germany, where he made test flights with nuclear weapons. In 1962, he returned to Edwards AFB with his new rank of colonel to become Commander of the Aerospace Research Pilot School. He later served in Spain and Pakistan, and flew 127 combat missions during the Vietnam War. He retired from the Air Force in 1975 at the rank of Brigadier General.

Since his retirement from active duty, Yeager has continued to fly planes and receive recognition for his prior achievements. In 1976, the U.S. Mint issued a medal commemorating his flight through the sound barrier. In 1983, the motion picture "The Right Stuff" was made from the book by Tom Wolfe, in which Yeager was portrayed as the man with "the rightest stuff of all." Yeager was suddenly a celebrity again; he had been a hero following his flight breaking the speed of sound, but he was now in greater demand for speaking engagements than ever before. Through the 1980s, Yeager also made a series of television commercials which made his name and face recognizable to nearly ever American.

In his autobiography, Yeager summed up his view of an active life: "There's so much more I want to do; I've never lost my curiosity about things that interest me. I haven't yet done everything, but by the time I've finished, I won't have missed much. If I [die] tomorrow, it won't be with a frown on my face. I've had a ball."

Sources

▶ **Books**

Ayres, Carter M., *Chuck Yeager: Fighter Pilot*, Lerner Publications, 1988.

Cox, Donald W., *America's Explorers of Space*, Hammond, 1967.

Levinson, Nancy S., *Chuck Yeager: The Man Who Broke the Sound Barrier: A Science Biography*, Walker & Co., 1988.

Lundgren, William R., *Across the High Frontier: The Story of a Test Pilot, Major Charles E. Yeager, USAF*, Morrow, 1955.

Taylor, John W. R., *Great Moments in Flying*, Roy, 1956, pp. 119-126.

Yeager, Charles E., and Leon Janos, *Yeager: An Autobiography*, Bantam, 1985.

Yeager, Chuck, and Charles Leerhsen, *Press On!: Further Adventures in the Good Life*, Bantam, 1988.

▶ **Periodicals**

Newsweek, "Fastest Man—and the Men Not Far Behind," February 22, 1954, pp. 31-36, "Right Stuff? Hell, It's Just Luck," July 1, 1985, pp. 56-58.

Saturday Evening Post, "They Fly Our X-Ships," July 1, 1950, pp. 26-27.

Time, "Man in a Hurry," April 18, 1949, pp. 64-71.

U.S. News & World Report, "I Don't See Myself as a Hero," January 13, 1986, pp. 65-66.

Jeana Yeager and
Dick Rutan

"*M*y goal was] to take a step into the future."—
Jeana Yeager

"We support each other very nicely. I would fly around the world with her again."—Dick Rutan

Test pilots Yeager, born about 1952 in Texas, and Rutan, born about 1945, made the first nonstop airplane flight around the world in 1986.

Address: c/o Voyager Aircraft, Inc., Hangar 77, Mojave, California 93501.

J eana Yeager and Dick Rutan set a world record on December 23, 1986, when they flew nonstop around the world in an airplane especially designed by them and Dick's brother, Burt Rutan. Jeana Yeager, who worked at various jobs including horse training and drafting, and enjoyed hobbies such as skydiving and small aircraft flying, met Richard Rutan, a former fighter pilot, at an air show in 1980. He persuaded her to join him in Mojave, where he was a test pilot for the Rutan Aircraft Factory. Dick Rutan and his brother Burt decided to try to break the existing record for a flight with no stops with Jeana as copilot and Dick as pilot.

It took five years to build the *Voyager*, as the plane was appropriately named, and took up all of the trio's time and money. They rented a shed at Mojave Airport for $65 a month, sold souvenirs, accepted donations, and obtained free material and equipment through their connections in the aviation world. The biggest problem in building the craft was to create a light airplane that could carry a very heavy fuel load, enough to take the two pilots around the world. The unique design of the plane was very similar to that used by the Wright brothers, and incorporated an H-shaped design, called the "canard" configuration. The wing span was unusually long at 111 feet. The only metal in the plane was in the engines, fasteners, cables, and fittings. There were two engines, a 110-horsepower engine in the rear, used for high altitudes, and a more powerful engine in front, used for takeoffs and landings, and for special maneuvers. The entire weight of the plane was only 1,860 pounds, and at take-off it contained 9,400 pounds of fuel, thereby carrying five times its own weight.

The cockpit was seven and a half feet long by about three feet wide, so naturally the pilots were concerned about their ability to survive for almost two weeks in such cramped quarters. During the four-and-a-half day test flight, Jeana consumed less than a gallon of water and became dehydrated. She fainted during the news conference which was held after the landing, yet still had positive things to say about the flight. "It was not the mental torment we were told it was going to be. As we got into it, everything fell into place very nicely. It was fairly comfortable."

But the real test was the actual flight, which ran into trouble from the very start, when the wings scraped the runway during takeoff. Dick Rutan was able to take off successfully, but the two later ran into trouble with Typhoon Marge, near the Philippines. Said Yeager, "I was never terrified until after the worst moments were behind us." The two fed on precooked dinners, and exercised, but sleep proved to be difficult and fatigue became a big problem for them both. Over the entire continent of Africa, they had to maneuver around storms, and it was reported that Jeana in particular had become badly tossed about and bruised.

The two pilots had their ups and downs, and on the final day of the flight, Burt Rutan told the press, "One minute they are so high, and the next it's hard for them even to get words out." The crew made a near-perfect landing one day ahead of schedule, however, and seemed to be in very good spirits. The *Voyager* is now on display in the National Air and Space Museum in Washington, D.C.

Jeana Yeager and Dick Rutan live together in a modest home in Mojave, California. Both pilots are extremely private people, and avoid publicity. They have a close comradeship, which proved to be very successful during their long and arduous journey.

Sources
▶ **Periodicals**

Newsweek, "Around the World in 11 Days," September 22, 1986, p. 12.

Time, "Flight of Fancy," December 29, 1986, p. 26.

Photo Credits

Permission to reproduce photographs appearing in *Contemporary Heroes and Heroines* was received from the following sources:

AP/Wide World Photos: pp. 1, 6, 9, 17, 30, 34, 38, 56, 69, 74, 92, 109, 129, 132, 135, 159, 164, 172, 181, 185, 193, 197, 201, 206, 209, 213, 234, 250, 264, 269, 273 (Winnie Mandela), 277, 285, 289, 299, 302, 306, 321, 365, 369, 376, 380, 392, 405; © Gamma-Liaison: p. 14; Courtesy of the office of the President of Costa Rica: p. 22; Courtesy of NASA: pp. 26, 64, 167, 326, 372; UPI/Bettmann Newsphotos: pp.43, 83, 97, 155, 221, 242, 292, 295, 311, 331, 337, 346, 351, 387, 421, 425, 430, 435; Courtesy of the United Nations (31216): p. 48; Courtesy of Women's Action for Nuclear Disarmament: p. 52; Erich Hartmann/Magnum Photos: p. 60; Courtesy of Shirley Chisholm: p. 78; Courtesy of Marva Collins: p. 88; Courtesy of Norman Cousins: p. 102; Courtesy of Francis Crick: p. 105; Courtesy of Vine Deloria, Jr.: p. 115; © The Walt Disney Company: p. 118; Courtesy of the Kansas State Historical Society, Photograph Collection: p. 123; Courtesy of the Digit Fund: p. 139; Courtesy of Betty Fox: p. 143; © 1989, Copyright by Cosmo Press, Geneva and Anne Frank Fonds: p. 147; © Matthew Cobleigh Photography. Courtesy of Betty Friedan: p. 151; Photograph by Russ Busby: p. 177; Courtesy of the United Nations (40308): p. 190; Reuters/Bettmann Newsphotos: pp. 217, 230, 273 (Nelson Mandela), 360, 409; Courtesy of Barbara Jordan: p. 225; Courtesy of John Fitzgerald Kennedy Library: p. 238; Photograph by Bachrach. Courtesy of Henry Kissinger: p. 247; Photograph by Mary Ann Halpern. Courtesy of Candy Lightner: p. 255; The Bettmann Archive, Inc.: pp. 260, 281; Courtesy of the Linus Pauling Institute of Science and Medicine: p. 316; Reproduced by permission of the Franklin D. Roosevelt Library: p. 342; Courtesy of Carl Sagan: p. 356; © 1989 Andrew Tregubov: p. 383; NBC Today Show. Courtesy of Gloria Steinem: p. 397; Courtesy of Margaret Thatcher: p. 402; © Kelly Wise: p. 413; © Jerry Bauer: p. 417.

Index

Personal names, place names, events, institutions, awards, and other subject areas or key words contained in *Contemporary Heroes and Heroines* entries are listed in this index with corresponding page numbers indicating text references. Page numbers are given in bold type for each of the volume's main entries.

Index